FIRST EDITION

THE ROLE OF RELIGION IN ANCIENT CIVILIZATIONS

SELECT READINGS

written and edited by
Kim Woodring

cognella® | ACADEMIC PUBLISHING

Bassim Hamadeh, CEO and Publisher
Kassie Graves, Director of Acquisitions and Sales
Jamie Giganti, Senior Managing Editor
Jess Estrella, Senior Graphic Designer
Angela Schultz, Senior Field Acquisitions Editor
Michelle Piehl, Project Editor
Alexa Lucido, Licensing Coordinator
Abbey Hastings, Associate Production Editor
Joyce Lue, Interior Designer

Cover image copyright © Depositphotos/egal.

Printed in the United States of America

ISBN: 978–1-5165–0061-1 (pbk) / 978–1-5165–0062-8 (br)

CONTENTS

PROLOGUE

How religion is viewed historically varies with the individual historian. Some view religion as an integral part of a civilization, and others reserve a place for religion in history on the proverbial back burner. It is important for a historian to realize that the representation of religion should include the uniqueness of each religion, but it should also present commonalities between them in order to facilitate historical comparison. It is also important to understand that each civilization had distinctive religious traditions but, over thousands of years, these became interconnected and sometimes fused to form a new religion.

I wanted to create this book because, in my years of teaching, I have utilized many texts, but I could never find a textbook that addressed the importance of religion in civilizations. I want my students to understand civilizations as a whole system, which includes not only religion but also political and social characteristics. The articles in this book focus on the civilization as a whole with an emphasis on the religious practices. It is my hope that this book will encourage my students to evaluate civilizations and their cultures critically and historically.

I would like to thank those who have educated and encouraged me on my path in the world of history and archaeology: Dr. Doug Burgess, Dr. Mel Page, and Dr. Jay Franklin; my husband, Mickey Woodring; my children, Matthew and Rebecca; and especially all of my students. I never intended to write what I consider a textbook, even though the books I have used in the past did not quite satisfy my needs in the classroom. The lack of including religion in those textbooks gave rise to the idea for this book. It is my way of extending the historical importance of religion beyond the common one found in textbooks.

Introduction

The following article by Peter N. Stearns is intended as a quick review of world history from 2.5 million years ago. The information in the article should provide a good base to build on for learning world history. The foundational information presented by Stearns provides background support for the building of knowledge of world history and religion in the early civilizations.

A World History Skeleton

By Peter N. Stearns

This chapter is an introductory guide to world history, a summary of a standard framework—a textbook in a few pages. Emphases are threefold: first, most obviously, since history is a time-based discipline, what are the definitions of key time periods and what are the main features of each? Second, within each period (different regions move into different positions depending on timeframe) what are the geographical highlights? And third (some periods feature change in certain topics—providing the main focus—but substantial continuities in others) what are the key subjects in each period? The chapter introduces the more analytical focus explored in later chapters, but it can also be used as a highlights-in-advance approach to any of the large textbooks that will expand on each of the points here in greater detail. It's the woods, for this purpose, in advance of the trees.

Peter N. Stearns, "A World History Skeleton," *World History: The Basics*, pp. 17-35. Copyright © 2011 by Taylor & Francis Group. Reprinted with permission.

THE EARLY STAGES: 2.5 MILLION BCE TO 10,000 BCE

All comprehensive world histories start well before what historians used to call the advent of recorded history, i.e. the arrival of writing. The early human story is also enlivened by all sorts of recent new discoveries, based on fossil finds in Africa and on improved methods of carbon testing for dates and also genetic analysis. From the advent of human-like species to the timing of human migration from Asia to North America, novel findings have pushed back what had been regarded as standard dates and opened some exciting debates about the long period of early human history and about the relationship of human evolution to that of other primates.

For world history purposes, several points are central. First, the human species went through complex and lengthy evolutionary development, from its first appearance two and half million years ago, or perhaps even longer, in East Africa. Various distinct species not only emerged but in some cases migrated to other areas. The arrival of the species to which all contemporary people belong, *Homo sapiens sapiens*, was a late result of this long process. Gradually, through superior adaptability—particularly for changing conditions in hunting animals, where short bursts of speed became a priority; through outright warfare; and through intermarriage, *Homo sapiens sapiens* became the only human species around, upwards of 120,000 years ago. Crucial genetic changes, including the capacity for speech and language, accompanied this final (to date) major evolutionary process.

TECHNOLOGY AND MIGRATION

Early humans also generated at least two other basic achievements. First, as humans operated within a hunting-and-gathering economy, where men hunted and women gathered nuts, seeds and berries, they gradually became increasingly skillful tool-users. Humans are not the only species to find objects in nature that they can use as tools and weapons, but they ultimately gained the ability not only to find but to manufacture tools, shaping bone, wood and stone to serve more precise purposes, particularly for hunting and fishing (including ultimately manufacturing early boats). The advent of the Neolithic, or new Stone Age period about 11,000 years ago, capped this process of tool improvement within the confines of stone-age technology.

The second big news was migration, which several human species had accomplished but which *Homo sapiens sapiens* took up about 70,000 years ago. The reasons for migration were simple: hunting and gathering groups, usually about 70–80 strong, need a lot of space, on average over 2 square miles per person. Any small population increase forces some members of the group to push out into new territory, or there will not be enough food. Most important was the surge of groups from Africa across the Red Sea to the Middle East, from which some bands headed north and west, into the Middle East, Central Asia and Europe, and another stream ultimately reached eastern Asia. From Asia also, groups ultimately ventured to the islands of Southeast Asia and to Australia—at a point at which the Southeast Asian land mass extended much farther southward than is the case today. And, by 25,000 BCE or perhaps earlier (there is debate about this), other Asian groups crossed from Siberia across what was then a land link to present-day Alaska, from which some moved quickly southward, reaching other parts of both North and South America. By 10,000 BCE a small global human population—about 10 million people in all—inhabited virtually all the areas where people now live. This dispersion reflects the adaptability of the human species. It also produced increasing differentiation, though not at the basic genetic level (which means, the different groups of humans could still interbreed) but rather in languages and cultural practices.

In sum: for the long early periods of human history, look for: the main phases of the evolutionary process but particularly the ultimate characteristics of *Homo sapiens sapiens*; grasp the nature and the social implications of the hunting and gathering economy; look for the major phases of tool use and particularly the improvements attained by the time of the Neolithic period. And, perhaps above all, register on the nature, timing and implications of human migration.

MAIN PERIODS IN WORLD HISTORY: ONE SKETCH

ADVENT OF AGRICULTURE

The early periods of human history were transformed by the arrival of agriculture, or what is sometimes called the Neolithic Revolution. This is the first sweeping change in the basic context for human history, and

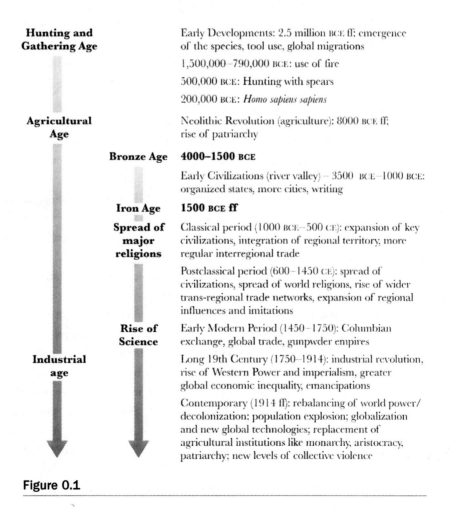

Hunting and Gathering Age	Early Developments: 2.5 million BCE ff; emergence of the species, tool use, global migrations
	1,500,000–790,000 BCE: use of fire
	500,000 BCE: Hunting with spears
	200,000 BCE: *Homo sapiens sapiens*
Agricultural Age	Neolithic Revolution (agriculture): 8000 BCE ff; rise of patriarchy
Bronze Age	**4000–1500 BCE**
	Early Civilizations (river valley) – 3500 BCE–1000 BCE: organized states, more cities, writing
Iron Age	**1500 BCE ff**
Spread of major religions	Classical period (1000 BCE–500 CE): expansion of key civilizations, integration of regional territory, more regular interregional trade
	Postclassical period (600–1450 CE): spread of civilizations, spread of world religions, rise of wider trans-regional trade networks, expansion of regional influences and imitations
Rise of Science	Early Modern Period (1450–1750): Columbian exchange, global trade, gunpwder empires
Industrial age	Long 19th Century (1750–1914): industrial revolution, rise of Western Power and imperialism, greater global economic inequality, emancipations
	Contemporary (1914 ff): rebalancing of world power/decolonization; population explosion; globalization and new global technologies; replacement of agricultural institutions like monarchy, aristocracy, patriarchy; new levels of collective violence

Figure 0.1

world historians usually pay a great deal of attention to it. Responding to improved tool use and, probably, reductions in the big game available for hunting, people (surely inspired by imaginative women, who had been the seed-handlers for the species) began deliberately planting grains. They also domesticated a wider range of animals (the dog had been the first domestication achievement, of obvious assistance in hunting), including cows, horses, sheep and pigs.

The advent of agriculture is both historically tricky, and fundamentally important. The tricky aspects are, first, that agriculture did not arise tidily in all areas at the same time. Furthermore, some regions only adopted agriculture quite recently, long relying on different economic systems which, while less significant than agriculture, also deserve attention. Finally, even when agriculture was established and began to spread, the process of dissemination was surprisingly slow.

DATES AND DISSEMINATION

The first instance of agriculture emerged in the Black Sea region in the northern Middle East, around 9000–8000 BCE, and was based on the cultivation of barley, oats and wheat. From this site, agriculture would gradually spread to other parts of the Middle East, to India, to northern Africa (and possibly all of Africa) and to Europe. But agriculture was separately invented in at least two other places: Southeast Asia, based on rice cultivation, around 7000 BCE; and Central America, based on corn, around 5000 BCE, with dissemination from both of these centers. There may have been other separate inventions, for example in sub-Saharan Africa. We don't know for sure in some cases if the arrival of agriculture reflects dissemination or new discovery.

Even when agriculture was established, it spread only gradually. It took thousands of years for agriculture to reach key parts of Europe, for example. The slowness of diffusion had two causes. First, contacts among peoples were halting, particularly outside individual regions: news of major developments did not travel fast. But second, there were lots of reasons not to appreciate agriculture. Compared to hunting and gathering agriculture required more hours of work (particularly from men); it challenged male hunting prowess; it led to other problems, such as a new incidence of epidemic diseases once groups of people began to settle and concentrate rather than moving around. It was, in sum, a big change, and many groups long resisted even when they knew of the possibility. It is historically and philosophically important to realize that agriculture was not pure gain but, like most major shifts in human history, an interesting mixture of plusses and minuses.

Finally, partly because of climate and soil conditions, a number of regions did not adopt agriculture at all until much more recent times. Huge areas, including much of North America, persisted in hunting and gathering, though this was sometimes spiced by a bit of seasonal agriculture. Other major human groups moved to a nomadic herding economy, rather than agriculture, relying on domesticated animals (horses, cattle, camels) rather than farming. Nomadic groups never developed the population levels of successful agricultural regions. But their control over key regions and their ability to contact agricultural centers through trade, migration and invasion give them great importance in world history until at least 500 years ago. The most important nomadic region was central Asia, but nomadic tribesmen in the Middle East and parts of sub-Saharan Africa also deserve attention; the key herding regions developed in and around a great arid zone that stretches from the Sahara desert in the West to central Asia and western China in the east.

The Neolithic revolution, then, involves a somewhat scattered chronology, a surprisingly slow and uneven spread, and the emergence of important alternatives.

It was, nevertheless, a fundamental development in world history. Even with its drawbacks, like greater vulnerability to contagious disease, it produced larger food supplies than hunting and gathering could, and so permitted expansions in the human population. Agriculture allowed families to have more children and, even with characteristically high infant death rates, more children surviving to adulthood. Its service in expanding the human species was ultimately irresistible to many regions. Human population began to grow, doubling every 1600 years to reach a level, worldwide, of 120 million by 1000 BCE.

NATURE OF AGRICULTURAL SOCIETIES

This means in turn that, several thousand years ago depending on region, a new economic system took shape that would last until about 300 years ago (and that still predominates in many places). It's vital to realize that most of textbook world history coverage involves agricultural societies, usually with a fairly short section on the experience of the human species before agriculture and a longer section on industrial, or post-agricultural, changes. World historians can easily demonstrate that within the framework of agriculture, important changes and important variations would occur. Some agricultural societies, for example, never generated many significant cities, whereas others produced a lively urban economy and culture. So there is every reason to devote substantial attention to the ways different agricultural regions changed and diverged. But still, the fact that they were agricultural commands attention.

For agricultural societies shared several key characteristics, no matter where they cropped up and no matter how much they changed. Most agricultural societies quickly developed more permanent settlements, usually in peasant villages. This allowed communities to clear land; dig wells; and sometimes set up irrigation systems; but also to develop connections that only a settled existence could allow. All agricultural societies focused primary attention on growing food; most generated a bit of surplus, but it was limited. Few agricultural societies could ever free up more than about 20% of the population for nonagricultural pursuits, including urban life, and many kept even more on the land. Limited surplus also helps explain why so many agricultural societies generated a well-defined, but rather small, elite of wealth and power. Agricultural societies also emphasized marked disparities between men and women, in patriarchal systems that gave men preeminent power. Historians have discussed why this occurred, in contrast to hunting and gathering societies where women's economic importance assured them a more prominent role and voice. Because agricultural societies increased the birth rate, more of women's time was taken up in pregnancy and early child care. In most (though not all) cases, men took primary responsibility for bringing in the major crops, assisted by children and, in peak season, by their wives. Women's day-to-day work was also vital, in caring for gardens and animals around the house, but men overmatched them and presumably claimed disproportion power in consequence. Additionally, agriculture redefined childhood, seeing children primarily as a source of family labor. This explains why an increase in birth rate was vital, but also explains why agricultural societies emphasized the importance of obedience and discipline as primary qualities for children.

A final note: all agricultural societies generated some concept of a week (though they differed widely on how many days it had), the only major time unit that is invented entirely by humans, with no relationship to any natural process. Presumably weeks were desirable to provide a leisure day, amid intense work, and to permit time for some trading activities. Often, a period for spiritual activity was designated as part of the weekly cycle, instead of simply leisure time per se.

Despite a common foundation, agricultural societies varied greatly, even in the specific interpretation of features like patriarchalism. But the common features and constraints must be factored in for any comparison, for there were limits to variation as well.

CIVILIZATION

Several thousand years after the arrival of agriculture, some human societies began to change and, in many ways, complicate their organizational structure. The result—the more complex structure—is what many world historians mean when they talk about the advent of civilization. Compared to other kinds of agricultural societies, civilizations had more surplus production, beyond what was needed for subsistence. They could on this basis afford more occupational specialties, from government personnel to skilled craftspeople. They also, typically, displayed more inequality than non-civilizations did. Beyond this, civilizations normally had more elaborate cities, and a clearer urban culture, than non-civilizations did, where if there were cities at all they were usually small and scattered. More cities also meant more need for trade, to provide food and the exchanges necessary for food. Civilizations had formal governments and at least small bureaucracies, rather than the less formal leadership present in simpler societies. They were societies with states, rather than "stateless". Most civilizations, finally, had writing, which helped government bureaucracies; which helped trade, through better and more standard record-keeping; and which encouraged fuller retention of knowledge than purely oral transmission could.

LOCATIONS

The first civilization emerged in the Tigris-Euphrates river valley—the region often called Mesopotamia—around 3500 BCE. It was preceded by some important technological improvements with the agricultural economy, including the wheel, the use of metal (bronze, an alloy of copper and tin) for tools and weapons, and of course the invention of the first writing system. The Sumerian people introduced their cuneiform writing style, and then the first known organized government on the heels of these key developments. Early civilizations emerged in several other centers soon thereafter: in Egypt; in the Indus river valley of present-day Pakistan; and, a bit later, in northern China along the Yellow River. All four of these early civilizations operated around complex irrigation systems along major rivers. Irrigation required particularly elaborate organization and legal arrangements, lest one group take all the water and deprive everyone else; this undoubtedly encouraged the need for more formal government. Irrigation also helped generate particularly productive agriculture, which provided further resources that could be used to help support cities and generate tax revenues for governments. A fifth early civilization case, considerably later, emerged in Central America with the Olmec peoples, but this was not based on irrigation systems primarily.

It is important to note that, for a long time, many agricultural peoples did not generate civilizations. They operated successfully without the civilization apparatus, often with some small cities as trading centers but without writing or formal government. Civilization did tend to spread, partly through conquest, but in some places, like West Africa, "stateless" agricultural economies continued to function until relatively recent centuries. Civilization, in other words, was not a quick or inevitable product of the advent of agriculture.

RIVER VALLEY CIVILIZATIONS

In North Africa and in several parts of Asia, the four early civilization centers operated for many centuries. They developed more formal legal structures; the first known law code, the code of the King Hammurabi, came from a later Mesopotamian regime. The centers developed characteristic monuments, the most famous of which emerged in Egypt with the great pyramids. They produced art and literature, some of which has survived to the present. The first known literary work, almost certainly a written record of what had been an oral story, the *Gilgamesh*, came from Mesopotamia. Some of them generated extensive trade and travel. From Mesopotamia, for example, traders sought sources of tin and also precious material, like the stone *lapis lazuli* found only in Afghanistan.

For world history, the most important achievement of the river valley civilizations was to generate types of social infrastructure that would not have to be reinvented, including writing and formal laws. Early civilizations introduced money, obviously vital for more extensive trade. Several of them invented further technological improvements, for example in the manufacture of pottery. Several also developed new understandings in mathematics and science, revolving around issues of measurement and calculation of the seasons. So: look at the early civilizations to determine what their durable achievements were, that might outlast their own centuries of operation. Urban development, for example, was one common feature: there were about eight cities in the world with over 30,000 inhabitants by 2250 BCE, but sixteen cities that large by 1250 BCE.

At the same time, each of the river valley civilizations had something of its own character, and together they allow the possibility of comparison. It is also true that we know far more about some of the river valley cases than others—the Indus river valley's history is particularly challenging, because scholars have not yet translated the writing system. Egypt and Mesopotamia are most commonly compared, with different religions and cultures, different political systems and social structures, even (though both were patriarchal) different approaches to women.

Comparison of internal characteristics leads to two other topics for the early civilization period: the durability of characteristics and regional outreach. We know that the river valley civilizations introduced specific arrangements from which we continue to benefit—like the Mesopotamian notion of measuring in units of 60, which we still use for calculations of the circumference of circles or minutes in an hour. Did they also generate more profound cultural features that still shape particular societies? Some scholars have argued, for example, that Mesopotamia and Egypt developed ideas about the separation of humans from nature that would later shape major religions like Christianity and Islam, and that also differ from characteristic south or east Asian approaches to the same subject. The fact is that we don't know enough about either early comparisons or later connections to be sure.

We are on firmer ground in noting how the river valley civilizations generated influences that went beyond their initial centers, helping to spread particular civilization systems. Egypt, for example, had trade and cultural influences both on other parts of the eastern Mediterranean, including Greece, and even more important on the upper Nile river valley, where they helped shape important African societies like Kush and, later, Ethiopia. Equally clearly, a series of aggressive Mesopotamian empires gained control over larger parts of the Middle East, bringing a variety of active contacts as a result. It was not surprising, thus, that a Mesopotamian story about a great flood showed up later in Jewish culture and the Bible. The Indus River civilization traded widely. All of this set the stage for later contacts and expansions.

END OF THE EARLY CIVILIZATION PERIOD

The early, or river-valley, civilization period drew to a close around 1000 BCE, though there were no sweeping events to mark the change. The period of big empires ended for a time in the Middle East. This allowed some important smaller societies to emerge, particularly in the eastern Mediterranean. The sea-faring Phoenician peoples were one such, forming cities at various points around the Mediterranean Sea. Of even more lasting importance were the Jewish people, whose first definite historical records date from about 1100 BCE and who began to shape the world's first great monotheistic religion, of importance in its own right and the seedbed of two other later, great religions from that region of the world. Egyptian dynasties continued for a time after 1000 BCE but with declining vitality. The Indus River civilization disappeared entirely—and we don't know exactly why, possibly because of local environmental exhaustion. China, the last of the river valley civilizations, demonstrated greater continuity, with the Zhou dynasty, formed shortly before 1000, continuing, though amid weak organization, for several centuries beyond.

What is clear, particularly outside of China, is that a new series of civilizations, partly co-located with where the early civilizations had been and certainly building on their achievements, was actively in the wings by 1000 BCE or shortly thereafter. These civilizations would assume greater power than the river valley societies had mustered. They would also benefit immensely from the use of iron, rather than bronze, for tools and weapons. Iron use, introduced in southwestern Asia around 1500 BCE, generated a metal far stronger than bronze, the basis both for greater agricultural productivity and for fiercer warfare. Here was a technological underpinning for the next great era in world history.

THE CLASSICAL PERIOD, 1000 BCE TO 600 CE

The most obvious focus of world history during the 1500 or so years after 1000 BCE is on the expansion and development of major societies in China, India, Persia and the Mediterranean. In each of these cases, some combination of government conquests (facilitated by tighter military organization and iron weaponry), new migrations of people, and diffusion of key cultures led to the establishment of civilization zones much larger than what the river valley societies had attained. China thus expanded to embrace more southern territory. Indian culture and social organization fanned out from a new base along the Ganges River, gradually reaching additional portions of the subcontinent. A new Persian Empire arose and for several centuries controlled the Middle East and some territory beyond. Finally, beginning with expansionist Greek city states and ending with the vast Roman Empire, a Mediterranean civilization developed that would ultimately embrace southern Europe, substantial chunks of the Middle East, and North Africa.

These expanded territories had to be linked and integrated in various ways. Governments began to promote new road systems, a vital aspect of developments in China, Persia and Rome. The Persian Empire even established the world's first postal service, along with carefully-spaced inns for travelers. All the classical civilizations worked to promote internal trade, taking advantage of specialty areas within the society. Thus China built north-south canals to facilitate exchanges between rice-growing regions in the south and grain growing areas in the north. Greece and Rome promoted active trade in the Mediterranean, with olives and grapes coming from southern Europe in exchange for grains from places like North Africa. Cultural integration involved efforts to spread belief systems and even languages to provide more common currency within the expanded territory. Thus the Chinese promoted the use of Mandarin for the upper class throughout the country, while in the eastern Mediterranean use of Greek spread well beyond Greece itself. In India, the development of the Hindu religion, but also the spread of Buddhism provided common religious interests through much of the subcontinent. Greek and Roman artistic styles spread widely through the Mediterranean region, establishing monuments that still draw tourists today from Turkey to Tunisia to France and Spain. Finally, all of the expanding civilizations at various points established empires, uniting all or (in India's case) most of the civilization territory under a single government. The establishment of the Chinese Empire, particularly under the Han dynasty, was the most important imperial development, in terms of long-term consequences, but Persia, Rome and the two imperial periods in India (Mauryan and Gupta dynasties) were milestones as well. Many empires tried to solidify their political hold by moving peoples to promote further loyalty and integration: the Chinese moved northern Chinese populations south, to further unity, while both Greek and Roman governments sent out colonies to help tie some of the more distant regions to the homeland.

The classical period is defined, then, above all by expanding large-regional civilizations, with new forms of economic, cultural and political integration creating new ties within the new regional units.

DISTINCTIVE FEATURES

In the process, each of the new civilizations also established a sense of core traditions, which in many cases would outlast the classical period itself. These traditions were cultural above all, but they also included political impulses and social ideas. Each civilization thus developed some defining characteristics that provided at least some degree of unity within the territory—though more clearly among upper than among lower classes—and that could differentiate each major civilization from the other. Civilization here takes on a second meaning: not only a form of human organization, but also a set of identities and identifying features.

Not surprisingly, given this definitional aspect, each set of markers was somewhat distinctive. The Indian tradition was defined by a strong religious impulse, with Hinduism ultimately the most important carrier and with artistic achievements illustrating religious beliefs; but also by the beliefs and practices surrounding the caste system. Political achievements were significant but less central. China, in contrast, came to emphasize the importance of a strong state and a bureaucratic upper class, linked to the importance of Confucian philosophy and social beliefs. The classical Mediterranean tradition, amplified in different though related ways by Greece and then Rome, emphasized the importance of politics and (most commonly) aristocratic rule, but also the characteristic literary and artistic traditions that related to a civic, polytheistic religion.

The Mediterranean also was defined by substantial reliance on slavery, a labor system that was much less important in India and China.

The Persian case is a bit harder to handle. The powerful Persian Empire was matched, on the cultural side, by the development of the distinctive Zoroastrian religion. Persia would be conquered however by Alexander the Great, coming from Greece, and Persian and Greek elements intermingled for a time. Later, after the classical period, Persian culture would be transformed by the arrival of Islam. Still, a Persian tradition (for example, in art) and a separate Persian Empire periodically revived. The contemporary nation of Iran builds on this complex tradition.

Overall, however, the classical period gains significance in world history from the fact that each key regional civilization established a number of lasting features, including central cultural traditions, important elements of which can still be identified today. The classical achievements continue to inspire awe: contemporary Iranians for example cast back to Persia as part of their own sense of identity, just as many Westerners or Russians remain fascinated with Greece and Rome. In key cases, classical traditions continue not just to impress, but to shape ongoing reactions. India grapples with legacies of the caste system, though it was outlawed in 1947. China continues to reflect particular interests in the importance of a strong state and political order. In no case does the classical tradition define contemporary civilizations, for far too much has changed; but the influence is real.

The significance and durability of classical traditions, but also key differences, obviously suggest the importance of comparison in approaching the classical period as a whole. The Roman and Han Chinese Empires form a particularly obvious comparative pairing, but other opportunities are also vital, for societies in general and for individual topics like religion or science. The similarities among the classical experiences must be retained as well as the different features and identities.

COMPLEXITIES IN THE CLASSICAL PERIOD

The formation of extensive regions and some durable traditions constitutes the most obvious structure for the classical period and for comparison, but there are other issues to watch as well:

- First, the classical systems did not emerge fully formed; in each case, they developed over time. Classical China, for example, developed a strong state tradition only after several centuries.
- Second, the classical traditions must not be oversimplified. Each of these large, complex civilizations embraced a variety of currents. Indian religion and religious art deserve note, obviously, but so does the rise of Indian science and mathematics. And there were several major Indian religions at this point.
- Third, analysis of the separate classical civilizations must not prevent identifying some underlying dynamics. For example, the use of iron plus the political and economic innovations in the classical period encouraged population growth. Between 1000 BCE and 1 CE world population doubled, to 250 million people. This was a global development to an extent, reflecting the expansion of agriculture, but it concentrated particularly in the classical civilizations. At their height Rome and China each had populations of about 55 million people.

- Fourth, attention to the separate patterns of the classical civilizations must be balanced by awareness of their interactions, and their related impact on some surrounding regions. Patterns here varied. Greece and Persia, and later Rome and Persia, had many contacts, particularly through war. Exchanges between India and China heated up toward the end of the classical period with the main result the importation of Buddhism in China. More important still were the two major sets of routes that linked the classical civilizations and also drew in other participants, for example with Ethiopia in northwestern Africa. A series of overland connections, from western China through central Asia and into India, Persia and through the Persian road network to the Mediterranean, have been called the "Silk Roads." Interest in Chinese silk spread among the upper classes even as far away as Rome. Most of this trade was through short, several-hundred-miles stages. At most one Roman group went directly to China, and mutual Chinese–Roman knowledge was limited. The trade route, however, did create awareness of the desirability of products from distant points. A second network ran through the Indian Ocean. Romans were sending expeditions to India on a regular basis by the time of the Empire, from ports on the Red Sea, and groups of Romans actually set up export operations in Indian cities with particular interest in pepper.

DECLINE AND FALL

Between 200 and 600 CE the great classical empires fell. The Han dynasty in China was first to go, collapsing in 220 and opening a 350-year period of frequent invasions and small, warring states. The Roman Empire began to decline from about 180 onward, gradually losing territory and suffering less effective government. The imperial government in the West collapsed entirely in the fifth century. A separate Roman government had by that point been set up in Constantinople (formerly Byzantium), and an eastern or Byzantine Empire, focused on present-day Turkey and southeastern Europe, persisted for several centuries. India's Gupta Empire collapsed in the sixth century, after a period of decline.

The end of the classical period reflected important invasions by hunting and gathering or nomadic peoples. Particularly important were incursions from the Huns of central Asia. Different Hun groups attacked China, a bit later Europe, and also the Guptas. A devastating series of epidemic diseases hit the classical world, particularly China and Rome, disrupting the economy and morale alike. New political problems also jeopardized trade, including the Silk Roads, generating new economic constraints on individuals and governments alike.

The accumulation of changes added up to the end of the classical period. For many regions, political and economic stability deteriorated for some time. Political unity in the Mediterranean world ended outright, and has never since recovered. Change in India was less drastic. Though large political units became less common, unless imposed from outside, Indian economic and cultural life continued along familiar patterns. Hinduism and the caste system spread southward in the subcontinent. In China, a long period of disruption yielded, late in the sixth century, to a new dynasty and the revival both of imperial government/ bureaucracy and of Confucianism. The different regional results of the period of classical decline were extremely important in shaping the next period in world history. They also affected ongoing use of the classical heritage, which was much more direct in China, India and Byzantium than around the bulk of the Mediterranean.

THE POST CLASSICAL PERIOD, 500 CE TO 1450 CE

This period is variously named, and is sometimes subdivided. World historians largely agree, however, on several major themes for the centuries involved—themes to which most major societies had to react. The onset of the period was shaped by the turmoil in much of the classical world. Several regions, including Western Europe and India, did not recover the degree of political organization they had developed during the classical period.

During this period, a large number of new regions established the apparatus of civilization, including more important cities and formal government. Japan, Russia, northwestern Europe, additional parts of sub-Saharan Africa (both West Africa and eastern Africa down the Indian Ocean coast), additional sections of central and Andean America were key cases in point.

During the period also, a number of newer areas, in trade contact with more established centers, began a process of deliberate imitation, particularly in technology and culture. Japan thus explicitly copied many features from China, Russia looked to the Byzantine Empire, Western Europe borrowed both from Islamic civilization and from Byzantium, Africa interacted with Islam and so on. Imitations often involved religion or philosophy, artistic forms, as well as agricultural techniques.

The two most important overarching themes in the postclassical period were the spread of major missionary religions and the acceleration of trans-regional trade among societies in Asia, Africa and Europe. Both of these developments permanently altered the framework for world history and the experiences of literally millions of people in different areas.

MISSIONARY RELIGIONS

Buddhism was a well established religion by 500 CE. Christianity had started five centuries before, gaining ground slowly within the Roman Empire (about 10% of the Roman population was Christian by the fourth century), then much more rapidly when the Roman government began to provide support. Islam, the newest world religion, began around 600 CE and would initially enjoy the most rapid spread of all. All three of the expanding religions reflected the political and economic troubles of the late classical period, which prompted more interest in otherworldly goals. They were also strongly supported by vigorous missionary efforts. During the post-classical centuries, hundreds of thousands of people converted, usually from some form of polytheism, to one of the world religions, one of the great cultural shifts in human history.

TRADE CONNECTIONS

The second great change involved intensification of trans-regional trade, backed by important improvements in ships and navigational devices. Arab traders, soon supplemented by Persians and others, established a strong route across the Indian Ocean, linking the Middle East to India, Southeast Asia and the Pacific coast of China. Clusters of Arab traders located in southern Chinese ports. Connecting to this route in turn was an Arab-African network down the African east coast; a trans-Sahara overland connection from West to North Africa; a route from Scandinavia through western Russia to Constantinople, with contacts with Arab trade; a bit more gradually, links from Western Europe to the Mediterranean and hence to Arab merchants,

Japan's regular trade with Korea and China was a final major connection. More regions, exchanging more goods of wider variety, were important components of this whole network. Other interactions were attached: Arabs, for example, learned the Hindu numbering system and then spread it more widely, with the result that Europeans called the numbers Arabic as they began to adopt them. Knowledge of paper, a Chinese invention, spread more widely. Maps and travel accounts both expanded and improved.

Technological advances included new sailing ship design, by the Arabs, and toward the end of the period additional shipping improvements from China. The introduction of the compass, initially from China, was a huge navigational gain, and it spread quickly around the Indian Ocean and thence to Europe.

Contacts facilitated technological exchanges and exchanges of different crops (new strains of wheat, for instance, spread from Africa to Europe) that helped improve agriculture. This in turn began to accelerate world population gains following the declines in the late classical period, with levels reaching almost half a billion by 1350 CE. At the end of the period, the rapid spread of bubonic plague from China through the Middle East and Europe briefly reduced population levels, however.

The postclassical period began to draw to a close when Arab power and political effectiveness started to decline, by the twelfth to thirteenth centuries. New commercial rivals for the Arabs arose, including European (particularly Italian) merchants in the Mediterranean but also Indian and Southeast Asian Muslims in the Indian Ocean. The Arab empire—the caliphate—began to lose significant territories, and it was finally toppled late in the thirteenth century.

IMAGE CREDITS

Fig. 1.0: Copyright © Wikiwatcher2 (CC BY-SA 3.0) at https://commons.wikimedia.org/wiki/File%3AReligion_timeline_graph.jpg.

Fig. 1.1: Copyright © Chamois rouge (CC BY-SA 3.0) at https://commons.wikimedia.org/wiki/File:Centres_of_origin_and_spread_of_agriculture_v2.svg.

Section I
Rise of Civilization and Polytheism

The following chapters include articles that discuss the beginning of civilizations and two of the first successful civilizations, Mesopotamia and Egypt. These chapters bring together a wealth of information about the earliest civilizations and their religions. In Chapter 1, "The Traditional Base: Civilizations and Patriarchy" provides general information about world civilizations, including their agricultural economies, contact with other civilizations, and patriarchal societies. In Chapter 2, "The Mesopotamian Religions" discusses the Mesopotamian religions and their contribution to the religions of other civilizations that came after the Mesopotamian civilization. In Chapter 3, "The Egyptian Religion" presents a synchronized approach to Egyptian religion, which can be complicated and difficult to learn.

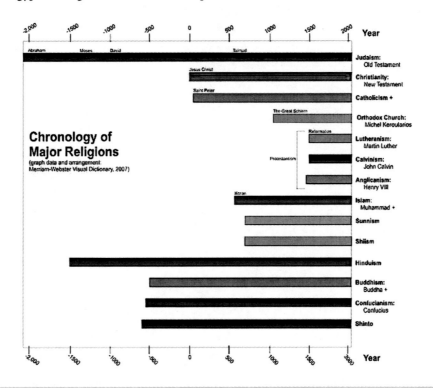

Chronology of Major Religions
(graph data and arrangement: Merriam-Webster Visual Dictionary, 2007)

The Road to Humanity

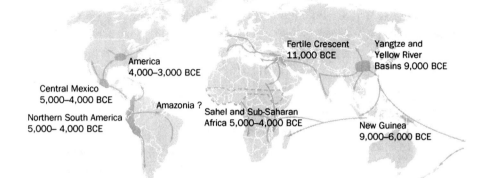

D'après J. Diamond et al. (2003) "Farmers and Their Languages: The First Expansions", Science

OBJECTIVES:

1. Understand changes that led to the emergence of agriculture.
2. Understand and be able to define "civilization."
3. Understand the distinctive features of civilizations.
4. Understand changes that define each period of civilization.

The Traditional Base: Civilizations and Patriarchy

By Peter N. Stearns

B y the fourth millennium BCE, a number of societies were beginning to move toward that phase of organization called "civilization". While contacts among different groups were virtually as old as the existence of the human species, most early civilizations formed somewhat separately. Mesopotamian civilization, arising after 3500 BCE, thus differed from Egyptian civilization, which emerged soon after in North Africa, not too far to the south. By the fourth millennium BCE also, most agricultural societies had developed new forms of inequality between men and women, in a system often termed patriarchal—with husbands and fathers dominant. Civilizations would usually deepen patriarchy, and at the same time they would define its details in distinctive ways that fitted the wider beliefs and institutions of each individual civilization. In this sense, in putting a particular stamp on patriarchy, each civilization linked gender issues to aspects of their cultural and institutional structure. This chapter, setting the stage for the study of the impact of societal contacts on gender systems, takes up these several developments: civilizations, contacts, patriarchy, and particular patriarchies and exceptions.

Human society began on the basis of small groups of people, in bands of hunters and gatherers. With this structure, people had fanned out into most habitable areas of the world by 12,000 BCE. Then, around 10,000 BCE, in the northern Middle East, agriculture was introduced, radically changing the economic framework for human life in those regions that accepted it. As agriculture spread, many societies formed more stable residential patterns, though there were important groups that continued a hunting and gathering existence or relied on the nomadic herding of animals, as in large stretches of Central Asia. Agriculture also allowed the generation of some surplus production over immediate needs. On the strength of surplus, small numbers of people could specialize in non-agricultural activities, such as craft manufacturing, religion or government. Improvements in agricultural production were gradual, but around 4000 BCE, again initially in and around the Middle East, an important series of inventions ushered in further change, of which the introduction of the wheel and the use of metals, particularly bronze, headed the list. Resulting from this in turn, around 3500 BCE, the first civilization formed in Sumeria, in the Tigris–Euphrates valley. This was soon followed by the establishment of other river-valley civilization centers, along the Nile in Africa, the Indus in northwestern India and the Yellow River in China.

Civilizations differed from other kinds of agricultural societies in that they had formal governments, rather than less explicit and distinct leadership. They relied more on cities, though only a minority of people lived there. They encouraged higher levels of trade. Most of them, also, had writing, which facilitated bureaucratic and commercial activities.

There are two important problems in highlighting civilizations as key units in world history. The first involves recognizing that neither agriculture nor civilization captured all major groups of people, even thousands of years after the form was first established. Nomadic herding groups, in regions like Central Asia, provided a key alternative. So did groups, like many Indian tribes in North America, that combined hunting with transitory, slash-and-burn agriculture. Some of these societies avoided the kind of patriarchy that dominated civilizations. While most nomadic groups also played up the inferiority of women—for women's economic functions declined when gathering was displaced by herding—there were exceptions, with some nomadic societies avoiding full patriarchy; and many hunting groups maintained strong economic roles for women. They might emphasize sharp distinctions between men and women—for example, in assuming that men had special responsibilities for warfare or for prowess as horsemen—but they often did not set up the kind of systematic inequality characteristic of major civilizations. The existence of alternatives to full patriarchy obviously created the possibility for a host of complex encounters—when, for example, the gender assumptions of a nomadic or hunting group came into direct contact with those of a patriarchal civilization.

The second problem involves the concept of civilization itself. World historians often debate this term. Civilization as a form of human organization involving cities and organized states, among other things, is hardly superior to other societies in gender terms. Civilizations often extend and formalize inequalities; but they are different from the other forms, and they are important to study because they have embraced the largest concentrations of people since their origins. Different civilizations—Chinese, for example, or

Indian—develop distinctive characteristics. This is the second use of the term. A good bit of the world history of gender involves tracing the particular values and institutions individual civilizations developed, and what happened when they encountered other civilizations. Even here there is some danger of oversimplifying or stereotyping a particular civilization, or of ignoring similarities underneath surface distinctions.

It remains true that leaders of civilizations delighted in claiming special qualities, as part of promoting unity within and separation from the outside world. Almost all civilizations thus developed a pronounced sense of how different they were from "others"—whom the Greeks would call "barbarians". While not all civilizations expanded greatly, there was some expansionist tendency in order to add resources and relieve population pressure. With expansion came an obvious need to identify some common features—whether in language, religion or political style—that would hold the territory and its often diverse populations together. Each civilization developed something of its own flavor. Egypt emphasized a strong monarchy, pronounced concern for the afterlife and a rather cheerful, colorful art. Mesopotamia, more prone both to natural disasters and to political instability, placed less stress on a single, central government; its religion was more pessimistic, looking to punishments in the afterlife. On the other hand, Mesopotamia introduced a more extensive interest in science.

The early civilization period, in the four Afro-Eurasian centers, lasted until about 1000 BCE, by which point several had collapsed or weakened, often in the face of a new set of invasions from nomadic groups, such as the Indo-European tribes, from Central Asia. There followed a classical period in the history of civilizations. In the Mediterranean (involving North Africa, West Asia and southern Europe), in India and in China, larger civilization complexes began to emerge from 800 onward. Classical civilizations expanded their cultural, political and commercial apparatus. Internal trade increased, allowing different regions within the civilization to specialize. More ambitious governments formed empires. China promoted the most durable imperial tradition, but empires were recurrently important in India and in Greece and particularly in Rome as well. Key statements of cultural values—Hinduism and Buddhism in India, Confucianism and Daoism in China, civic religion but also secular philosophy in Greece and Rome—helped provide a cultural cement. These cultures offered some unity, at least in the upper classes, throughout the society: Chinese gentry could speak and write the same language and participate in a common philosophical system. The shared cultures and institutions also helped extend the sense of identity, of separateness from other societies.

As agricultural economies and then civilizations formed, cultural contacts of various sorts continued. Because the human species has so often been migratory, contacts and exchanges were virtually endemic. Through them, well before the classical period, various areas had gained access to new food stuffs, originally not natural to the region, and to new technologies—including agriculture and metalworking. Migrations and periodic nomadic invasions provided one source of contact. Trade was another. Well before the classical period, trade routes extended from China through India and Central Asia to the Middle East and the Mediterranean; collectively, these are sometimes called the Silk Road, for the principal item of exchange. At the same time, the impact of many contacts was fairly limited. Very rich people in the Mediterranean liked Chinese silk—a favorite fabric in the Roman Empire, for example—but they knew almost nothing about China, as there was no direct travel. Trade occurred in stages.

Most developments within a civilization remained internal, just as the bulk of commerce did. Constraints included not only the considerable suspicion of outsiders, but also the fact that long-distance travel was slow and risky, which limited the extent and impact of exchange. The great classical civilizations rarely had immediate contact with each other. Most were buffered by zones inhabited by nomads or less organized agricultural peoples. Contacts extended out, without usually reaching the next major civilization. Thus both the Middle East and Egypt, and then the classical Mediterranean, established links with the developing center along the upper Nile River in sub-Saharan Africa, initially called Kush. China, under the Han dynasty, had some influence in Korea and Vietnam. India, the most active trading society, exchanged with various parts of Southeast Asia including present-day Indonesia.

The most striking example of direct contact between the largest classical civilizations, prior to the final centuries of the classical era after 300 CE, involved Alexander the Great's conquests in the fourth century BCE, through the Middle East and Persia and into northwestern India. A Greek-influenced kingdom, Bactria, was established in this part of South Asia (parts of present-day Pakistan and Afghanistan) for over a century. From this unusual exchange, parts of South Asia for a time imitated Hellenistic artistic styles, with statues of Buddha draped in Mediterranean-style clothing. India also utilized some mathematical concepts developed in Greece. Further, the exchange encouraged later Indian rulers to think about sending Buddhist emissaries to the Middle East. There they won no real converts, but did possibly introduce ethical concepts that would influence philosophical systems like those of the Stoics and, through them, Christianity. This was an important result, but overall the contact, exceptional in the first place, had few durable consequences. Civilizations themselves gained greater coherence from internal exchanges—like the spread of Confucianism from north China to the south or the increasing impact of northern Indian institutions, including Hinduism and the caste system, on south India. But the most characteristic political and cultural forms of each civilization were rather separate: Confucianism was Chinese, Hinduism (except for a bit of outreach to Southeast Asia) was Indian, and so on.

While civilizations developed, amid contacts but also the limitations of exchange, gender systems—relations between men and women, assignment of roles and definitions of the attributes of each sex—had been taking shape as well. Indeed, the biggest change affecting gender—the rise of agriculture—predated civilization itself. Ultimately this evolution would intertwine with that of the civilizations.

The shift from hunting and gathering to agriculture had gradually ended a system of considerable equality between men and women. In hunting and gathering, both sexes, working separately, contributed important economic goods. Birth rates were relatively low, kept that way in part by prolonged lactation. The result facilitated women's work in gathering grains and nuts, for too-frequent childbirth and infant care would have been a burden. Women's work in turn often contributed more caloric value to the society than hunters did—though hunters always claimed greater prestige. Settled agriculture, where it spread, changed this in favor of more pronounced male dominance. While cultural systems, including polytheistic religion, might refer to the importance of goddesses, held to be the generators of creative forces associated with fertility and therefore vital for agriculture, the new economy promoted greater gender hierarchy. Men were now usually responsible for growing grain; women's assistance was vital, but men supplied most of the food. The birth rate went up, partly because food supplies became a bit more reliable, partly because there was more use for children as laborers. This was probably the key reason why men took over most agricultural functions, as motherhood became more time-consuming. This meant that women's lives became defined more in terms of pregnancy and childcare. This was the setting for a new, pervasive patriarchalism.

In patriarchal societies, men were held to be superior creatures. They had legal rights lacking to women (though law codes protected women from some abuse, at least in principle). Thus king Hammurabi's laws in Mesopotamia, from the second millennium BCE, decreed that a woman who has "not been a careful housewife, has gadded about, has neglected her house and has belittled her husband" should be "thrown into the water". There were no equivalent provisions for men, though the code did establish that a wife could leave her husband if he did not furnish her upkeep.

Many agricultural societies prevented women from owning property independently. Many allowed men to take multiple wives (if they could provide for them). Most punished women's sexual offenses—for example, committing adultery—far more severely than they punished men's. Indeed, some historians have argued that a key motive for patriarchy rested in the felt need to make as sure as possible that a wife's children were sired by the husband. Given the importance of property in agricultural societies (in contrast to hunting and gathering), men came to feel an urge to control their heritage to later generations, and that began with regulating wives' sexuality. Other symptoms were equally important. Sons were preferred over daughters. Many families used infanticide to help control their birth rate, and infant daughters were more often put to death. Culturally, the patriarchal systems emphasized women's frailty and inferiority. They urged largely domestic duties, and sometimes restricted women's rights to appear in public. Patriarchy's reach was powerful and extensive. Many women were so intimidated and isolated by the system that protest was unlikely—though it was also true that individual women could achieve some satisfaction by manipulating husbands and sons or by lording it over inferior women in the household.

The advent of civilizations—always initially within the framework of an agricultural economy—served mainly to consolidate patriarchy, not to introduce fundamental innovations. Yet civilization did have two kinds of impact: further inequality and some interesting differentials in style and emphasis.

On the first point, within agricultural civilizations, women's inequality tended to increase over time, as the civilizations became more successful. Jewish law, arising a little later than the Hammurabic Code, was more severe in its treatment of women's sexuality or public roles. In other parts of the Middle East, a custom arose of insisting on veiling women in public, as a sign of their inferiority and the fact that they belonged to their fathers or husbands. Deterioration of women's roles in China, over time, showed in the appearance of the custom of footbinding under the Tang dynasty, after the classical period had ended; small bones in a girl's foot were broken to prevent easy walking, and the resulting shuffling gait was taken as a sign of beauty and respectable modesty. Pressures of this sort bore particularly on upper-class women, where families had enough wealth to bypass women's productive work; they tended to spread, however, and had symbolic impact even more widely. Chinese footbinding ended only in the early twentieth century.

The reasons for the trend of deterioration in established civilizations involved the growing power of male-dominated governments, which tended to reduce some of women's informal political role within families. The key factor, though, was the increase of prosperity, particularly for the upper classes, which permitted the emphasis on women's ornamental rather than practical roles.

The power of patriarchy bore most heavily on women, but obviously it affected definitions of masculinity as well. Men, whatever their private personalities, were supposed to live up to their dominant roles. They should avoid coddling women, especially in public. Often, they were supposed to be ready to assume military or other leadership duties, and of course they were in principle responsible for the economic survival of the family. In many cases, oldest sons were particularly privileged, even among males, for patriarchy could provide a pecking order based on capacities to assume full power within families. Some societies allowed certain categories of men somewhat different definitions, to indulge in more woman-like behavior or attire or to emphasize homosexual orientations. Other groups of men might be singled out: in a number of religions priests were supposed to avoid sex, while men who watched over wives and concubines in a ruler's court (and who sometimes gained considerable political power in part because they could not sire children to rival those of the king or emperor) might be castrated, as eunuchs—a backhanded testimony to the emphasis on male sexuality.

Patriarchy also shaped the development of boys, encouraging complex relationships with mothers and fathers alike. At least in the upper classes, fathers appeared as remote, authoritarian figures in their sons' lives. Emotional ties to mothers, often lifelong, could be intense.

While agriculture and then civilization progressively deepened inequalities between men and women, one final point is crucial, and it was well established during the early civilization period of world history: particular patriarchal systems varied greatly, and the systems were not universal in any event. The same emphasis on distinctive definitions of overall culture or political institutions that civilizations forged in their gestation periods applied also to ideas about men and women and their roles.

It is not always clear why civilizations' gender systems differed—just as it is hard to explain why classical Indian society ended up emphasizing religion more than China did, or why Greece and China differed in their definitions of science. Once the differences were launched, in gender as in other matters, they tended to persist. Comparisons here are subtle: all the river-valley and classical civilizations were patriarchal, even as they enforced distinctive specific roles and cultures. The similarities and the differences could be equally important.

Among the early river-valley civilizations, neighboring Egypt and Mesopotamia clearly illustrated the potential for patriarchal emphases to differ. Whereas Mesopotamia stressed women's inferiority and subjection to male control, Egyptian civilization gave women more credit, at least in the upper classes, and experienced the rule of several powerful queens. The beautiful Nefertiti, as wife of the pharaoh Akhenaton, was influential in religious disputes during his reign. Later, Cleopatra played a powerful though ultimately abortive role as Egyptian queen, struggling to modify the controls of the Roman Empire. Women were also portrayed elaborately in Egyptian art, and provisions for their burial could be elaborate (though never rivaling those for powerful men). Both women and men could become stars on the body of the sky goddess Nut, one way in which afterlife was envisaged. There was no doubt about Egyptian patriarchy. An Egyptian writer, Ptah Hotep, made this clear in around 2000 BCE as he wrote: "If you are a man of note, found for yourself a household, and love your wife at home, as it beseems. Fill her belly, clothe her back.... . But hold her back from getting the mastery." Still, in daily life and in social impact, the Egyptian system was distinctive.

Not all agricultural societies allowed polygamy; India differed here from China and the Middle East. Some societies traced the descent of children from the mother—this was and is true in Jewish law—rather than the father. This did not prevent inequality, but it gave motherhood more cultural and legal importance. Legal codes could vary greatly with regard to women's property rights or their ability to leave an unhappy marriage. Cultural representations varied widely. In some religions, goddesses played a vital, powerful role, while in other cultural systems male principles dominated more fully. China, with less religious emphasis, thus offered less symbolic outlet for women than did India, with its strong interest in goddess figures, or the Mediterranean, with its gender-diverse polytheism.

Variations affected men as well. Societies with strong religions, like India, might give top billing to men as priests and holy figures, in contrast to societies like the classical Mediterranean that tended to stress military and athletic qualities for ideal men. Approaches to homosexuality or bisexuality varied. In Greece and Rome, upper-class men often took boys as protégés and lovers. This was not seen as conflicting with normal family roles or with a strong emphasis on masculine prowess.

The differences possible in patriarchal systems showed clearly in the three main classical civilizations. China instituted the most thoroughgoing patriarchy, as part of the Confucian emphasis on hierarchy and order. Man in the family was in principle like the emperor in society: he ruled. Women were urged to be subservient, proficient in domestic skills. Ban Zhao was an influential woman who, despite her position or perhaps because of it, wrote a classical patriarchal manual for her sex (some time in the first century CE; it became China's most durable women's manual, republished into the nineteenth century). Her advice: "Humility means yielding and acting respectful, putting others first ... enduring insults and bearing with mistreatment ... . Continuing the sacrifices means serving one's husband-master with appropriate demeanor." Industrious pursuit of household duties and conceiving sons rounded out the lives of successful women, according to the Chinese system.

India's system contrasted. Women were held to be inferior; Indian thinkers debated (without agreement) whether a woman would have to be reincarnated as a man in order to advance spiritually if she had led a worthy life, or whether she could proceed directly to a higher realm. Marriages were carefully arranged by parents to assure larger family goals, often when girls and boys were quite young. Women were supposed to serve fathers and then husbands faithfully. In contrast to China, however, Indian culture paid considerable and approving attention to women's cleverness and beauty. Love and affection gained greater credit, which could link women and men informally, despite basic inequality; mothers-to-be were surrounded by solicitude. Emphasis on confining women domestically was also lower in classical India.

Classical civilization in the Mediterranean presented yet a third case. Strong emphasis on rationality in philosophy and science helped launch a tradition of distinguishing between male intellectual traits and the more emotional, inferior mental powers of women. Greek thinkers urged that women be treated well, while stressing their inferiority and their largely domestic roles. Not only public roles, but also athletics were confined to men. Raping a free woman was a crime, but carried a lesser penalty than seducing a wife—for the latter involved winning affections and loyalty away from the husband. But some women held property; their public presence was greater than in China. And conditions improved in the Hellenistic era, at least in the upper classes, as women participated in cultural pursuits and in commerce (though under male guardianship).

Furthermore, in Rome, women's conditions again improved with time—another exception to the general pattern (though there was a subsequent downturn after the first century CE, under the Empire). Early Roman society imposed harsh penalties on women, for example for sexual offenses. "The husband is the judge of the wife. If she commits a fault, he punishes her; if she has drunk wine, he condemns her; if she has been guilty of adultery, he kills her." Later Roman interest in the rule of law, however, plus a desire to encourage stable family life, brought some improvements. The powers of the husband were curbed by the establishment of family courts, composed of members of the wife's as well as the husband's family of origin, in cases of dispute or accusation. Women freely appeared in public and attended major entertainments. While they were punished for adultery through the loss of a third of their property, these provisions were relatively mild compared with other patriarchal civilizations. Finally, Roman literature, like Greek, was filled with stories of active, whimsical goddesses as well as of gods.

In sum: variation coexisted with patriarchy, before and during the classical period, even as some important societies escaped full patriarchy altogether. Differences affected male roles and definitions as well as those for women. Trends over time differed, too.

Here was a fertile context for the complex impact of cultural contacts, when different societies gained some mutual knowledge. Precisely because patriarchy generated tensions in relationships between men and women, with men anxious to preserve dominance but sometimes uncertain about how this should play out in family settings, and with women usually avoiding protest but not necessarily being overjoyed with their lot, knowledge or assumed knowledge about how another society handled gender issues could have powerful results. It would be easy, particularly for men who were most likely to experience the results of exchanges through trade or war, to use contacts to try to confirm the correctness of their own arrangements, and thereby to exaggerate or distort gender patterns in the other society. The importance and solidity of patriarchy might suggest the need for prolonged, unusual contact in order to break through to new patterns. But contacts could unsettle; they could suggest options and alternatives. Patriarchal standards differed enough from one society to the next to make the contact potentially disruptive, and the potential expanded when confrontations between nomadic societies and established civilizations occurred.

Neither the river-valley civilization period nor the more richly evidenced classical period emphasized the importance of contact with differing standards; the focus was on building separate systems, including patriarchal systems, and integrating diverse peoples through this process. Most people were usually unaware that other societies might do things differently, but exchanges among societies, though rare, did exist, including occasional travels beyond the familiar range. Through these exchanges, in turn, we can gain a first glimpse into possible reactions: how would cultures that had struggled to define gender roles as a key component of the social order deal with occasional evidence that other arrangements were possible?

For by the end of the classical period the possibility of interchange was heating up. Troubles with the political system, particularly in Rome and China, opened new possibilities for contacts, both through outside invasions and through religious missions. Various nomadic peoples pressed into the established civilization territories—Huns from Central Asia into China and later India, Germanic tribes into southern Europe. Buddhist and Christian missionaries were poised to seek converts outside their home base, both in other civilizations and among the less politically organized regions such as Central Asia or northern Europe. What had been a periodic experience during the early civilization and classical period, through invasions, wars and limited trade, now became commonplace, as various peoples gained some sense of other ways in which gender standards could be organized.

The Mesopotamian Religions

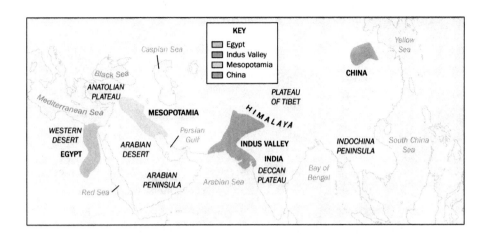

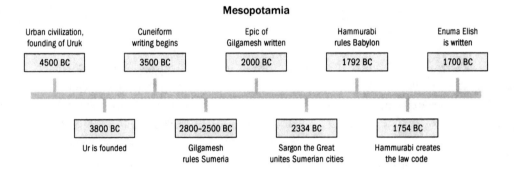

Mesopotamia

Urban civilization, founding of Uruk	Cuneiform writing begins	Epic of Gilgamesh written	Hammurabi rules Babylon	Enuma Elish is written
4500 BC	3500 BC	2000 BC	1792 BC	1700 BC

	3800 BC	2800-2500 BC	2334 BC	1754 BC
	Ur is founded	Gilgamesh rules Sumeria	Sargon the Great unites Sumerian cities	Hammurabi creates the law code

OBJECTIVES:
1. Define polytheism.
2. Identify two aspects of Sumerian and Akkadian religions.
3. Identify correlations between Akkadian creation story and Christian creation story.
4. Define oral tradition and be able to explain the transformation from oral tradition to written tradition.

The Mesopotamian Religions

By Mircea Eliade, translated By Willard R. Trask

HISTORY BEGINS AT SUMER

This is the well-known title of a book by S. N. Kramer. In it, the eminent American Orientalist showed that our earliest information concerning a number of religious institutions, techniques, and conceptions is preserved in Sumerian texts. That is, they represent the earliest *written* documents, whose originals go back to the third millennium. But these documents certainly reflect more archaic religious beliefs.

The origin and early history of Sumerian civilizations are still imperfectly known. It is supposed that a population speaking Sumerian, a language that is not Semitic and cannot be explained by any other known linguistic family, came down from the northern regions and settled in Lower Mesopotamia. Very probably the Sumerians conquered the autochthonous inhabitants, whose ethnic component is still unknown (culturally, they shared in the Obeid civilization). Not long afterward, groups of nomads coming from the Syrian desert and speaking a Semitic language, Akkadian, began entering the territories north of Sumer, at the same time infiltrating the Sumerian cities in successive waves. Toward the middle of the third millennium, under a leader who became legendary, Sargon, the Akkadians imposed their supremacy on the Sumerian cities. Yet, even before the conquest, a Sumero-Akkadian symbiosis developed, which was greatly increased by the unification of the two countries. Thirty or forty years ago scholars referred to a single culture, the Babylonian, the result of the fusion of these two ethnic stocks. It is now generally agreed that the Sumerian and Akkadian contributions should be studied separately, for, despite the fact that the invaders had assimilated the culture of the defeated people, the creative genius of the two was different.

It is especially in the religious domain that these differences are perceptible. From the most remote antiquity, the characteristic emblem of divine beings was a *horned* tiara. At Sumer, then, as everywhere in the Near East, the religious symbolism of the bull, documented from the Neolithic, had been handed down uninterruptedly. In other words, the divine modality was defined by the power and the "transcendence" of *space*, i.e., the stormy sky in which thunder sounds (for thunder was assimilated to the bellowing of bulls). The "transcendent," celestial structure of divine beings is confirmed by the determinative sign that precedes their ideograms and that originally represented a star. According to the vocabularies, the proper meaning of this determinative is "sky." Hence every divinity was imagined as a celestial being; this is why the gods and goddesses radiated a very bright light.

The earliest Sumerian texts reflect the work of classification and systematization accomplished by the priests. First of all is the triad of the great gods, followed by the triad of the planetary gods. We have also been left lengthy lists of divinities of all kinds, concerning whom we very often know nothing but their

Mircea Eliade, "The Mesopotamian Religions," *History of Religious Ideas, Volume 1: From the Stone Age to the Eleusinian Mysteries*, trans. Willard R. Trask, pp. 56-84. Copyright © 1979 by University of Chicago Press. Reprinted with permission.

names. At the dawn of its *history*, the Sumerian religion already proves to be ancient. To be sure, the texts so far discovered are fragmentary and peculiarly difficult to interpret. However, even on the basis of this sparse information, we can understand that certain religious traditions were in the course of losing their original meanings. The process is perceptible even in the triad of the great gods, made up of An, En-lil, and En-ki. As his name shows (*an* = sky), the first is a uranian god. He must have been the supreme sovereign god, the most important in the pantheon; but An already presents the syndrome of a *deus otiosus*. More active and more "actual" are En-lil, god of the atmosphere (also called the "Great Mount"), and En-ki, "Lord of the Earth," god of the "foundations," who has wrongly been taken by modern scholars to be the god of the primordial waters because, in the Sumerian view, the earth was supposed to rest on the ocean.

So far, no cosmogonic text properly speaking has been discovered, but some allusions permit us to reconstruct the decisive moments of creation, as the Sumerians conceived it. The goddess Nammu (whose name is written with the pictograph representing the primordial sea) is presented as "the mother who gave birth to the Sky and the Earth" and the "ancestress who brought forth all the gods." The theme of the primordial waters, imagined as a totality at once cosmic and divine, is quite frequent in archaic cosmogonies. In this case too, the watery mass is identified with the original Mother, who, by parthenogenesis, gave birth to the first couple, the Sky (An) and the Earth (Ki), incarnating the male and female principles. This first couple was united, to the point of merging, in the *hieros gamos*. From their union was born En-lil, the god of the atmosphere. Another fragment informs us that the latter separated his parents: the god An carried the sky upward, and En-lil took his mother, the Earth, with him.[1] The cosmogonic theme of the separation of sky and earth is also widely disseminated. It is found, indeed, at different levels of culture. But probably the version recorded in the Near East and the Mediterranean derive, in the last analysis, from the Sumerian tradition.

Certain texts describe the perfection and bliss of the "beginnings": "the ancient days when each thing was created perfect," etc.[2] However, the true Paradise seems to be Dilmun, a country in which neither illness nor death exists. There "no lion kills, no wolf carries off a lamb … . No man with eye disease repeats: 'My eyes are sick.' … No night watchman walks about his post."[3] Yet, all in all, this perfection was a stagnation. For the god En-ki, the Lord of Dilmun, lay asleep beside his wife, who was still a virgin, as the earth itself was virgin. When he woke, En-ki united with the goddess Nin-gur-sag, then with the daughter whom the latter bore, and finally with the daughter's daughter—for this is a theogony that must be completed in this paradisal land. But an apparently insignificant incident occasions the first divine drama. The god eats certain plants that had just been created; but he was supposed to "determine their destiny," that is, to settle their mode of being and their function. Outraged by this senseless act, Nin-gur-sag declares that she will no longer look on En-ki with the "look of life," and thus he will die. And in fact unknown ills afflict the god, and his increasing weakness presages his speedy death. Finally, it is his wife who cures him.[4]

As it has been possible to reconstruct it, this myth shows instances of rehandling, the purpose of which cannot be determined. The paradisal theme, completed by a theogony, ends in a drama that reveals the crime

---

1   See S. N. Kramer, *From the Tablets of Sumer*, pp. 77 ff., and *The Sumerians*, p. 145.
2   See a new translation of the poem "Gilgamesh, Enkidu, and the Under-world" in Giorgio R. Castellino, *Mitologia sumerico-accadia*, pp. 176–81. On the Egyptian conception of initial perfection, see § 25.
3   After the translation of Maurice Lambert, in *La Naissance du Monde*, p. 106.
4   We follow the interpretation given by R. Jestin, " La religion sumérienne," p. 170.

and punishment of a creator god, followed by an increasing weakness that portends his death. Certainly, a fatal fault is involved, for En-ki *did not behave in accordance with the principle that he incarnated.* This fault came near to compromising the structure of his own creation. Other texts have preserved the lamentations of the gods when they fall victims to fate. And we shall later see the risks run by Inanna in going beyond the frontiers of her sovereignty. What is surprising in the drama of En-ki is not the mortal nature of the gods but the mythological context in which it is proclaimed.

MAN BEFORE HIS GODS

There are at least four Sumerian narratives that explain the origin of man. They are so different that we must assume a plurality of traditions. One myth relates that the first human beings sprouted from the ground like the plants. According to another version, man was fashioned from clay by certain divine artisans; then the goddess Nammu modeled a heart for him, and En-ki gave him life. Other texts name the goddess Aruru as the creator of human beings. Finally, according to the fourth version, man was formed from the blood of two Lăgma gods immolated for the purpose. This last theme will be revived and reinterpreted in the famous Babylonian cosmo gonic poem, *Enuma elish.*

All these motifs, with numerous variants, are documented more or less throughout the world. According to two of the Sumerian versions, the primitive man shared in a way in the divine substance : in En-ki's vital breath or in the blood of the Lăgma gods. This means that there was no impassable distance between the divine mode of being and the human condition. It is true that man was created in order to serve the gods, who, first of all, needed to be fed and clothed.[5] The cult was conceived of as service to the gods. However, if men are the gods' servants, they are not their slaves. The sacrifice consisted primarily in offerings and homage. As for the great collective festivals of the city—celebrated at the New Year or at the building of a temple—they have a cosmological structure.

Raymond Jestin emphasizes the fact that the notion of sin, the expiatory element, and the idea of the scapegoat are not documented in the texts.[6] This implies that men are not only servants of the gods but are also their imitators and hence their collaborators. Since the gods are responsible for the cosmic order, men must obey their commands, for these are based on the norms—the "decrees," *me*—which insure the functioning both of the world and of human society.[7] These decrees establish, that is, *determine,* the destiny of every being, of every form of life, of every divine or human enter prise. The determination of the decrees is accomplished by the act of *nam-tar,* which constitutes, and proclaims, the decision taken. At each New Year the gods fix the destiny of the following twelve months. This, to be sure, is an old idea, found elsewhere

---

5   On the cult, see Kramer, *The Sumerians,* pp. 140 ff.; A. L. Oppenheim, *Ancient Mesopotamia,* pp. 183 ff.

6   Jestin, "La religion sumérienne," p. 184. "'Penitential psalms' appear in the late literature, but the increasing Semitic influence that is discernible in them no longer permits them to be considered genuine expressions of Sumerian consciousness" (ibid.).

7   On the me of the different trades, vocations, and institutions, see Kramer, *From the Tablets,* pp. 89 ff.; *The Sumerians,* pp. 117 ff. The term me has been translated by "being" (Jacobsen) or "divine power" (Landsberger and Falkenstein) and has been interpreted as a "divine immanence in dead and living matter, unchangeable, subsistent, but impersonal, to which only the gods have access" (J. van Dijk).

in the Near East; but the first strictly articulated expression of it is Sumerian and shows the deep work of investigation and systematization performed by the theologians.

The cosmic order is continually troubled, first of all by the Great Serpent, which threatens to reduce the world to chaos, and then by men's crimes, faults, and errors, which must be expiated and purged by the help of various rites. But the world is periodically regenerated, i.e., re-created, by the festival of the New Year. "The Sumerian name of this festival, *à-ki-til,* means 'power making the world live again' (*til* means 'live' and 'live again'; thus a sick man 'lives [again],' that is, is cured); the whole cycle of the law of eternal return is evoked."[8] More or less similar mythico-ritual scenarios of the New Year are documented in countless cultures. We shall have occasion to gauge their importance when we analyze the Babylonian festival *akitu.* The scenario involves the *hieros gamos* between two patron divinities of the city, represented by their statues or by the sovereign (who received the title of husband of the goddess Inanna and incarnated Dumuzi)[9] and a hierodule. This *hieros gamos* actualized the communion between the gods and men—a momentary communion, to be sure, but with considerable consequences. For the divine energy flowed directly upon the city (that is, upon the Earth), sanctified it, and insured its prosperity and happiness for the beginning year.

Still more important than the New Year festival was the one associated with the building of a temple. It was no less a reiteration of the cosmogony, for the temple—the "palace" of the god—represented the most perfect *imago mundi.* The idea is archaic and widely disseminated ... According to the Sumerian tradition, after the creation of man, one of the gods founded the five cities; he built them "in pure places, called their names, apportioned them as cult centers."[10] Since that time the gods have contented themselves with imparting the plans of cities and sanctuaries directly to the sovereigns. In a dream King Gudea sees both the goddess Nidaba showing him a placard on which the beneficent stars are named and a god revealing the plan of the temple to him.[11] The models of the temple and the city are, we might say, "transcendental," for they preexist in the sky. The Babylonian cities had their archetypes in the constellations: Sippar in Cancer, Niniveh in the Great Bear, Assur in Arcturus, etc.[12] This concept is general in the ancient East.

The institution of kingship was similarly "lowered from the sky," together with its emblems, the tiara and the throne.[13] After the flood, it was brought down to earth for the second time. The belief in the preexistence of words and institutions will have considerable importance for archaic ontology and will find its most famous expression in the Platonic doctrine of Ideas. It is attested for the first time in Sumerian documents, but its roots presumably reach down into prehistory. Indeed, the theory of celestial models continues and develops the universally disseminated archaic conception that man's acts are only the repetition (imitation) of acts revealed by divine beings.

---

8 Jestin, "La religion sumérienne," p. 181.
9 See S. N. Kramer, "Le Rite de Mariage sacré Dumuzi-Inanna," p. 129, and his *The Sacred Marriage Rite,* pp. 49 ff.
10 See the text translated by Kramer, *From the Tablets,* p. 177.
11 E. Burrows, "Some Cosmological Patterns in Babylonian Religion," pp. 65 ff.
12 See ibid., pp. 60 ff.
13 See the "Sumerian King List," translated by Kramer, *The Sumerians,* pp. 328 ff.

THE FIRST MYTH OF THE FLOOD

Royalty had to be brought down from the sky again after the flood, for the diluvial catastrophe was equivalent to the end of the world. In fact, only a single human being, named Zisudra in the Sumerian version and Utnapishtim in the Akkadian, was saved. But, unlike Noah, he was not allowed to live on in the new earth that emerged from the waters. More or less divinized, but in any case enjoying immortality, the survivor is transported to the land of Dilmun (Zisudra) or to the "mouth of the rivers" (Utnapishtim). From the few fragments of the Sumerian version that have come down to us we learn that, despite the reluctance or the opposition of some members of the pantheon, the great gods decide to destroy humanity by the flood. Someone mentions the merits of King Zisudra, "humble, obedient, pious." Informed by his protector, Zisudra learns of the decision reached by An and En-lil. The text is here interrupted by a long lacuna. Probably Zisudra received exact instructions for building the ark. After seven days and seven nights the sun comes out again, and Zisudra prostrates himself before the sun god, Utu. In the last fragment that has been preserved, An and En-lil confer on him "the life of a god" and the "eternal breath" of the gods and send him to live in the fabulous land of Dilmun.[14]

The same theme of the Deluge is found in the *Epic of Gilgamesh*. This famous work, which has been fairly well preserved, casts still greater light on the similarities to the biblical narrative. In all probability, we may assume the existence of a common, and quite archaic, source. As has been well known since the compilations made by R. Andree, H. Usener, and J. G. Frazer, the deluge myth is almost universally disseminated; it is documented in all the continents (though very rarely in Africa) and on various cultural levels. A certain number of variants seem to be the result of dissemination, first from Mesopotamia and then from India. It is equally possible that one or several diluvial catastrophes gave rise to fabulous narratives. But it would be risky to explain so widespread a myth by phenomena of which no geological traces have been found. The majority of the flood myths seem in some sense to form part of the cosmic rhythm: the old world, peopled by a fallen humanity, is submerged under the waters, and some time later a new world emerges from the aquatic "chaos."[15]

In a large number of variants, the flood is the result of the sins (or ritual faults) of human beings: sometimes it results simply from the wish of a divine being to put an end to mankind. It is difficult to determine the cause of the flood in the Mesopotamian tradition. Some allusions suggest that the gods reached the decision because of "sinners." According to another, En-lil's anger was aroused by the intolerable "uproar" made by human beings.[16] However, if we examine the myths that, in other cultures, announce the coming flood, we find that the chief causes lie *at once in the sins of men and the decrepitude of the world*. By the mere fact that it exists—that is, that it *lives* and *produces*—the cosmos gradually deteriorates and ends by falling into decay. This is the reason why it has to be re-created. In other words, the flood *realizes*, on the

---

14   See Kramer, *From the Tablets*, pp. 177 ff.; Kramer, *Sumerian Mythology*, pp. 97 ff.; and G. R. Castellino, *Mitologia*, pp. 140–43.

15   On the symbolism implicit in certain flood myths, see Eliade, *Patterns in Comparative Religion*, pp. 210 ff.

16   We shall see (§ 21) that it is always the "noise"—on this occasion, the uproar made by the young gods, preventing him from sleeping—that decides Apsu to exterminate them (see *Enuma elish*, tab. I, lines 21 ff.).

macrocosmic scale, what is symbolically effected during the New Year festival: the "end of the world" and the end of a sinful humanity in order to make a new creation possible.[17]

DESCENT TO THE UNDERWORLD: INANNA AND DUMUZI

The triad of Sumerian planetary gods was made up of Nanna-Suen (the Moor), Utu (the Sun), and Inanna, goddess of the planet Venus and of love. The gods of the Moon and the Sun will have their apogee during the Babylonian period. As for Inanna, homologized with the Akkadian Ishtar and later with Ashtarte, she will enjoy an "actuality" in both cult and mythology never approached by any other goddess of the Near East. At her apogee, Inanna-Ishtar was the goddess at once of love and of war, that is, she governed life and death; to indicate the fullness of her powers, she was called hermaphroditic (*Ishtar barbata*). Her personality was already fully outlined in the Sumerian period, and her central myth constitutes one of the most significant creations of the ancient world. The myth begins with a love story: Inanna, the tutelary goddess of Erech, marries the shepherd Dumuzi,[18] who thus becomes sovereign of the city. Inanna proclaims her passion and her happiness aloud: "I, in joy I walk!… My Lord is seemly for the sacred lap." Yet she has a presentiment of the tragic fate that awaits her husband: "My beloved, my man of the heart … thee, I have brought about an evil for you … you have touched your mouth to mine, you have pressed my lips to your head, that is why you have been decreed an evil fate" (Kramer, "Le rite de mariage sacré," p. 141).

This "evil fate" was decided on the day when the ambitious Inanna determined to go down into the underworld to supplant her "elder sister," Ereshkigal. Sovereign of the Great Above, Inanna aspires also to reign over the World Below. She manages to enter Ereshkigal's palace, but, as she successively passes through the Seven Gates, the gatekeepers strip her of her clothes and ornaments. Inanna arrives stark naked—that is, stripped of all "power"—in her sister's presence. Ereshkigal fixes the "look of death" on her, and "her body became inert." After three days, her devoted friend Ninshubur, obeying the instructions that Inanna had given her before setting out, informs the gods En-lil and Nanna-Sin. But they decline to intervene, because Inanna, they say, by entering a domain—the Land of the Dead—which is governed by inviolable decrees, "sought to meddle with forbidden things." However, En-lil finds a solution: he creates two messengers and sends them to the underworld carrying "the food of life" and "the water of life." By a trick, they succeed in reviving "the corpse, which was hanging from a nail." Inanna was preparing to ascend, when the Seven Judges of the Underworld (the Anunaki) held her back, saying: "Who, having descended into the underworld, has ever ascended from the underworld again unharmed ? If Inanna wishes to ascend out of the underworld, let her furnish a replacement!"[19]

Inanna returns to earth escorted by a troop of demons, the *gallas*; they are to bring her back if she does not furnish them with another divine being. The demons first try to seize Ninshubur, but Inanna stops

---

17   See *Myth and Reality*, pp. 54 ff. According to the version preserved in the *Epic of Atrahasis*, after the flood Ea decided to create seven men and seven women; see Heidel, *The Gilgamesh Epic*, pp. 259–60.

18   According to another version, she first preferred the farmer Enkimdu, but her brother, the sun god Utu, makes her change her mind; see Kramer, *The Sacred Marriage Rite*, pp. 69 ff., and his "Le Rite de Mariage Sacré Dumuzi-Inanna," pp. 124 ff. Except where otherwise specified, we use the translations by Kramer published in the latter article.

19   After the translation by Jean Bottéro, *Annuaire de l'Ecole des Hautes Etudes*, sec. 4 (1971–72), p. 85.

them. Next they all go to the cities of Umma and Bad-Tibira; terrified, their tutelary divinities crawl in the dust at Inanna's feet, and the goddess pities them and decides to search elsewhere. Finally they arrive at Erech. In surprise and indignation, Inanna discovers that, instead of lamenting, Dumuzi was sitting on his throne, richly clad—satisfied, it almost seemed, to be sole sovereign of the city. " She fixed an eye on him: the eye of death! She spoke a word against him: the word of despair! She cried out against him: the cry of damnation! 'This one (she said to the demons), carry him away.'"[20]

Dumuzi implores his brother-in-law, the sun god Utu, to change him into a snake, and flees to the house of his sister, Geshtinanna, then to his sheepfold. There the demons seize him, torture him, and lead him to the underworld. A lacuna in the text prevents us from reading the epilogue. "In all probability, it is Ereshkigal who, softened by Dumuzi's tears, lightens his sad fate by deciding that he should spend only half the year in the netherworld and that his sister, Geshtinanna, should replace him during the other half" (Kramer, "Le rite de mariage sacré," p. 144).

The same myth, but with some significant differences, is narrated in the Akkadian version of the *Descent of Ishtar to the Underworld*. Before the publication and translation of the Sumerian texts, it was possible to believe that the goddess journeyed to the "Land without return" *after* the "death" of Tammuz and precisely in order to bring him back. Certain elements that are absent in the Sumerian version seemed to support this interpretation—in the first place, the disastrous consequences of Ishtar's captivity, which are emphasized in the Akkadian version: human and animal reproduction ended entirely after the goddess's disappearance. This calamity was understandable as following upon the interruption of the *hieros gamos* between the goddess of love and fertility and Tammuz, her beloved husband. The catastrophe was of cosmic proportions, and, in the Akkadian version, it is the great gods who, terrified by the imminent disappearance of life, had to intervene to free Ishtar.

What is surprising in the Sumerian version is the "psychological," that is, human, justification for the condemnation of Dumuzi: everything seems to be explained by Inanna's anger at finding her husband proudly seated on his throne. This romantic explanation appears to overlie a more archaic idea: "death"— ritual and therefore reversible—inevitably follows every act of creation or procreation. The kings of Sumer, like the Akkadian kings later, incarnate Dumuzi in the *hieros gamos* with Inanna.[21] This, to a greater or lesser degree, implies acceptance of the ritual "death" of the king. In this case, we must suppose, behind the story transmitted by the Sumerian text, a "mystery" established by Inanna to insure the cycle of universal fertility. It is possible to perceive an allusion to this "mystery" in Gilgamesh's scornful answer when Ishtar invites him to become her husband : he reminds her that it is she who decreed the yearly lamentations for Tammuz.[22] But these lamentations were ritual: the young god's descent to the underworld was bewailed on the eighteenth of the month of Tammuz (June-July), though everyone knew that he would rise again six months later.

---

20 After the translation by Bottéro, ibid., p. 91. In another version, it is fear that seems to explain Inanna's action. When the demons seized her and were threatening to take her back, "Terrified, she abandons Dumuzi to them! 'This young man' (she says to them), 'chain his feet'" (ibid.).
21 See Kramer, *The Sacred Marriage Rite*, pp. 63 ff., and "Le Rite de Mariage Sacré," pp. 131 ff.
22 Tablet VI, lines 46–47. Bottéro (p. 83) renders: "Tammuz, thy first husband, it is thou who didst establish universal mourning for him."

The cult of Tammuz is disseminated more or less everywhere in the Middle East. In the sixth century, Ezekiel (8:14) cried out against the women who wept for him even at the gates of the Temple. Tammuz ends by taking on the dramatic and elegiac figure of the young gods who die and are resurrected annually. But his Sumerian prototype probably had a more complex structure: the kings who incarnated him, and who therefore shared his fate, annually celebrated the re-creation of the world. But in order to be re-created anew, the world had to be annihilated; the precosmogonic chaos also implied the ritual death of the king, his descent to the under world. In short, the two cosmic modalities—life/death, chaos/cosmos, sterility/fertility—constituted the two moments of a single process. This "mystery," perceived after the discovery of agriculture, becomes the principle of a unified explanation of the world, of life, and of human existence; it transcends the vegetable drama, since it also governs the cosmic rhythms, human destiny, and relations with the gods. The myth relates *the defeat of the goddess of love* and fertility in her attempt to conquer the kingdom of Ereshkigal, that is, *to abolish death*. In consequence, men, as well as certain gods, have to accept the alternation life/death. Dumuzi-Tammuz disappears, to reappear six months later. This alternation—periodical presence and absence of the god—was able to institute "mysteries" concerning the salvation of men, their destiny after death. The role of Dumuzi-Tammuz, ritually incarnated by the Sumero-Akkadian kings, was considerable, for it effected a connection between the divine and human modalities. Eventually, every human being could hope to enjoy this privilege, previously reserved for kings.

THE SUMERO-AKKADIAN SYNTHESIS

The majority of the Sumerian city-temples were united by Lugal-zaggisi, the sovereign of Umma, about 2375 B.C. This is the first manifestation of the imperial idea of which we have any knowledge. A generation later the attempt was repeated, with greater success, by Sargon, king of Akkad. But Sumerian civilization preserved all its structures. The change concerned only the kings of the city-temples: they acknowledged themselves to be tributaries to the Akkadian conqueror. Sargon's empire collapsed after a century, as the result of attacks by the Gutians, barbarians who led a nomadic existence in the region of the Upper Tigris. Thereafter, the history of Mesopotamia seems to repeat itself: the political unity of Sumer and Akkad is destroyed by barbarians from without; in their turn, these are over thrown by internal revolts.

Thus, the domination of the Gutians lasted only a century, and was replaced, for another century (ca. 2050–1950 B.C.), by the kings of the third dynasty of Ur. It is during this period that Sumerian civilization attained its culminating point. But it was also the last manifestation of Sumerian political power. Harassed by the Elamites on the east and, on the west, by the Amorites, who came from the Syro-Arabian desert, the empire fell. For more than two centuries Mesopotamia remained divided into several states. It was not until about 1700 B.C. that Hammurabi, the Amorite sovereign of Babylon, succeeded in imposing unity. He fixed the center of the empire farther north, in the city of which he was the sovereign. The dynasty founded by Hammurabi, which appeared to be all-powerful, reigned for less than a century. Other barbarians, the Kassites, come down from the north and begin to harass the Amorites. Finally, about 1525 B.C., they triumph. They will remain the masters of Mesopotamia for four centuries.

The transformation of the city-temples to city-states and then to the empire represents a phenomenon of considerable importance in the history of the Near East.[23] For our purpose, it is important to cite the fact that the Sumerian language, though it ceased to be spoken about 2000 B.C., retained its function as the liturgical language and, indeed, as the language of knowledge for fifteen more centuries. Other liturgical languages will have a similar destiny: Sanskrit, Hebrew, Latin, Old Slavic. Sumerian religious conservatism is carried on in the Akkadian structures. The supreme triad remained the same: An, En-lil, Ea (= En-ki). The astral triad partly takes over the Semitic names of the respective divinities: the Moon, Sin (which derives from the Sumerian Suen); the Sun, Shamash; the planet Venus, Ishtar (= Inanna). The underworld continued to be governed by Ereshkigal and her husband, Nergal. The few changes, imposed by the needs of the empire—for example, the transfer of religious primacy to Babylon and the replacement of En-lil by Marduk—"took centuries to come about."[24] As for the temple, "nothing essential changed in its general plan ... from the Sumerian phase on, except perhaps the size and number of buildings."[25]

Nevertheless, the contributions of the Semitic religious genius are added to the earlier structures. A first example is that of the two "national" gods—Marduk of Babylon and, later, the Assyrian Assur—who are raised to the rank of universal divinities. Equally significant is the importance assumed in the cult by personal prayers and penitential psalms. One of the most beautiful Babylonian prayers is addressed to all the gods, even to those whom the speaker of the prayer admits that he does not know: " O Lord, ... great are my sins. O god whom I do not know, great are my sins ... . O goddess whom I do not know, great are my sins ... . Man knows nothing; whether he is committing sin or doing good, he does not even know ... . O my Lord, do not cast thy servant down. My transgressions are seven times seven; remove my transgressions."[26] In the penitential psalms the speaker acknowledges his guilt and confesses his sins aloud. The confession is accompanied by precise liturgical gestures: kneeling, prostration, and "flattening the nose."

The great gods—An, En-lil, and Ea—gradually lose their supremacy in the cult. The worshipers address themselves rather to Marduk or to the astral divinities, Ishtar and especially Shamash. In the course of time the latter will become the unrivaled universal divinity. A hymn proclaims that the sun god is revered everywhere, even among foreigners; Shamash defends justice, he punishes the wrongdoer and rewards the just.[27] The numinous character of the gods increases: they inspire a holy fear, especially by their terrifying brightness. Light is considered to be the particular attribute of divinity, and, insofar as the king shares in the divine condition, he himself emanates rays of light.[28]

Another creation of Akkadian religious thought is divination. We also note a multiplication of magical practices and the development of the occult disciplines (especially astrology), which will later become popular throughout the Asiatic and Mediterranean world.

---

23 New institutions (such as the professional army and the bureaucracy) are first documented; in the course of time they will be adopted by other states.

24 Jean Nougayrol, "La religion babylonienne," p. 217.

25 Ibid., p. 236.

26 Translation condensed from F. J. Stevens, in *ANET*, pp. 391–92. The lines cited are 21–26, 51–53, and 59–60.

27 See the translation in *ANET*, pp. 387–89.

28 A. Leo Oppenheim, *Ancient Mesopotamia*, p. 176; E. Cassin, *La splendeur divine*, pp. 26 ff., 65 ff., and passim.

In short, the Semitic contribution is characterized by the importance accorded to the personal element in religious experience and by the exaltation of certain divinities to a supreme rank. Yet this new and grandiose Mesopotamian synthesis presents a tragic view of human existence.

CREATION OF THE WORLD

The cosmogonic poem known as the *Enuma elish* (after its *incipit*: "When on high") constitutes, with the *Epic of Gilgamesh,* the most important creation of the Akkadian religion. Nothing comparable in greatness, in dramatic tension, in its effort to connect the theogony, the cosmogony, and the creation of man, is to be found in Sumerian literature. The *Enuma elish* narrates the origin of the world in order to exalt Marduk. Despite their being reinterpreted, the themes are ancient: first of all, the primordial image of an undifferentiated aquatic totality, in which the first couple, Apsu and Tiamat, can be discerned. (Other sources specify that Tiamat represents the sea, and Apsu the mass of fresh water on which the earth floats.) Like so many other original divinities, Tiamat is conceived of as at once woman and bisexual. From the mixture of fresh and salt waters other divine couples are born. Almost nothing is known about the second couple, Lakhmu and Lakhamu (according to one tradition they were sacrificed in order to create man). As for the third couple, Anshar and Kishar, their names in Sumerian mean "totality of the upper elements" and "totality of the lower elements."

Time passes ("the days stretched out, the years multiplied").[29] From the *hieros gamos* of these two complementary "totalities" is born the god of the sky, Anu, who in his turn engenders Nudimmud (= Ea).[30] By their play and their cries these young gods trouble Apsu's repose. He complains to Tiamat: " Unbearable to me is their behavior. By day, I cannot rest; by night, I cannot sleep. I want to annihilate them, in order to put an end to their doings. And let silence reign for us, at last we can sleep!" (tablet 1, lines 37–39). We can read in these lines the nostalgia of matter (that is, of a mode of being corresponding to the inertia and unconsciousness of substance) for the primordial immobility, the resistance to all movement—the preliminary condition for the cosmogony. Tiamat " began to cry out against her husband. She gave a cry of pain … : 'What! We shall ourselves destroy what we have created! Painful, to be sure, is their behavior, but let us be patient and mild'" (1. 41–46). But Apsu would not be persuaded.

When the young gods learned of their ancestor's decision, "they were left speechless" (58). But the "all-knowing Ea" set to work. With his magical incantations, he makes Apsu sink into a deep sleep, he takes away "his brightness and clothes himself in it," and, after binding him, kills him. Ea thus became the god of the Waters, which he thenceforth named *apsu*. It is in the depths of the *apsu*, "in the chamber of destinies, the sanctuary of archetypes " (79), that his wife, Damkina, gave birth to Marduk. The text exalts the gigantic majesty, the wisdom, and the omnipotence of this last-born of the gods. It is then that Anu resumes the attack on his ancestors. He caused the four winds to rise and "created the waves to trouble Tiamat" (108).

---

29 Tablet I, line 13. Unless otherwise indicated, we follow the translation by Paul Garelli and Marcel Leibovici, "La naissance du monde selon Akkad," pp. 133–45. We have also used the translations by Labat, Heidel, Speiser, and Castellino.

30 Of the divinities of the great Sumerian triad, En-lil is missing; his place was taken by Marduk, son of Ea.

The gods, deprived of rest, turn to their mother: "When they killed Apsu, thy spouse, far from walking at his side, thou didst remain apart without a word" (113–14).

This time, Tiamat decided to react. She formed monsters, snakes, the "great lion," "raging demons," and yet others, "pitiless bearers of arms, unafraid of battle" (144). And "among the gods, her first born, … she exalted Kingu" (147 f.). Tiamat fastened to Kingu's chest the tablet of Destinies and bestowed the supreme power on him (144 ff.). Faced with these preparations, the young gods lose courage. Neither Anu nor Ea dares to confront Kingu. It is only Marduk who accepts the battle, but on condition that he should first be proclaimed supreme god, which the gods hasten to grant. The battle between the two troops is decided by a single combat between Tiamat and Marduk. "When Tiamat opened her maw to swallow him" (4. 97), Marduk hurled the raging winds, which "dilated her body. She was left with her belly swollen and her mouth gaping. He then loosed an arrow, which perforated her belly, tore her entrails, and pierced her heart. Having thus overcome her, he took her life, threw the corpse on the ground, and stood on it" (100–104). Tiamat's partisans tried to escape, but Marduk "bound them and broke their weapons" (111); he then chained Kingu, snatched the tablet of Destinies from him, and fastened it to his own chest (120 ff.). Finally, he returned to Tiamat, split her skull, and cut the corpse in two, "like a dried fish" (137); one half became the vault of the sky, the other half the earth. Marduk set up in the sky a replica of the palace of the *apsu* and fixed the courses of the stars. The fifth tablet reports the organization of the planetary universe, the determination of time, and the configuration of the earth from Tiamat's organs (from her eyes flow the Euphrates and the Tigris, "from a loop of her tail he created the link between sky and earth" [5. 59]; etc.).

Finally, Marduk decides to create man, so that " on him shall rest the service of the gods, for their relief" (6. 8). The conquered and chained gods were still awaiting their punishment. Ea suggests that only one of them shall be sacrificed. Asked who "fomented war, incited Tiamat to revolt, and began the battle" (23–24), all give but one name: Kingu. His veins are cut, and from his blood Ea creates mankind (30).[31] The poem then relates the building of a sanctuary (i.e., his palace) in honor of Marduk.

While using traditional mythological themes, the *Enuma elish* presents a rather somber cosmogony and a pessimistic anthropology. To exalt the young champion, Marduk, the gods of the primordial epoch, and most of all Tiamat, are charged with demonic values. Tiamat is no longer merely the primitive chaotic totality that precedes any cosmogony; she ends by proving to be the producer of countless monsters. Her "creativity" is thus wholly negative. As it is described in the *Enuma elish*, the creative process is very soon endangered by Apsu's wish to annihilate the young gods, that is, in the last analysis, to stop the creation of the universe in the bud. (A certain "world" already existed, since the gods were multiplying and had "dwellings"; but it was a purely formal mode of being.) The killing of Apsu opens the series of "creative murders," for Ea not only takes his place but also begins a first organization in the aquatic mass ("in this place he established his dwelling place… he determined the sanctuaries"). The cosmogony is the result of a conflict between two groups of gods, but Tiamat's troop also includes her monstrous and demonic creatures. In other words, "primordiality" as such is presented as the source of "negative creations." It is from Tiamat's remains that Marduk forms the sky and the earth. This theme, which is also documented in other traditions, can be variously interpreted. The universe, made from the body of an original divinity, shares in its substance. But, after the "demonization" of Tiamat, can one still speak of a substance that is divine?

---

31   We will add that other parallel traditions concerning the cosmology and the creation of man also exist.

Hence the cosmos has a double nature; it consists of an ambivalent, if not frankly demonic, matter and a divine form, for it is the work of Marduk. The celestial vault is formed from one half of Tiamat's body, but the stars and constellations become "dwellings" or images of the gods. The earth itself comprises the other half of Tiamat and her various organs, but it is sanctified by the cities and temples. In the last analysis, the world proves to be the result of a mingling of chaotic and demonic primordiality on the one hand with divine creativity, presence, and wisdom on the other. This is perhaps the most complex cosmogonic formula arrived at by Mesopotamian speculation, for it combines in a daring synthesis all the structures of a divine society, some of which had become incomprehensible or unusable.

As for the creation of man, it continues the Sumerian tradition (man is created to serve the gods), particularly the version that explains his origin from the two sacrificed Lăgma gods. But it adds this aggravating element: Kingu, despite his having been one of the first gods, became the archdemon, the leader of the troop of monsters and demons created by Tiamat. Hence man is made from a demonic substance: the blood of Kingu. The difference from the Sumerian versions is significant. We can speak of a tragic pessimism, for man seems to be already condemned by his own origin. His only hope lies in the fact that it is Ea who fashioned him; hence he possesses a form created by a great god. From this point of view, there is a symmetry between the creation of man and the origin of the world. In both cases, the raw material is constituted by the substance of a fallen primordial divinity, demonized and put to death by the victorious young gods.

SACRALITY OF THE MESOPOTAMIAN SOVEREIGN

At Babylon the *Enuma elish* was recited in the temple on the fourth day of the New Year festival. This festival, named *zagmuk* ("beginning of the year") in Sumerian and *akitu* in Akkadian, took place during the first twelve days of the month of Nisan. It comprised several sequences, of which we will mention the most important: (1) a day of expiation for the king, corresponding to Marduk's "captivity"; (2) the freeing of Marduk; (3) ritual combats and a triumphal procession, led by the king, to the Bit Akitu (the house of the New Year festival), where a banquet was held; (4) the *hieros gamos* of the king with a hierodule personifying the goddess; and (5) the determination of destinies by the gods.

The first sequence of this mythico-ritual scenario—the king's humiliation and Marduk's captivity—indicates the regression of the world to the precosmogonic chaos. In the sanctuary of Marduk the high priest stripped the king of his emblems (scepter, ring, scimitar, and crown) and struck him in the face. Then, on his knees, the king uttered a declaration of innocence: "I have not sinned, O lord of the lands, I have not been negligent regarding thy divinity." The high priest, speaking in Marduk's name, replied: "Do not fear .... Marduk will hear thy prayer. He will increase thy dominion."[32]

During this time the people sought for Marduk, supposed to be "shut up in the mountain" (a formula indicating the "death" of a divinity). As we saw in the case of Inanna-Ishtar, this "death" was not final; yet she had to be redeemed from the lower world. Similarly, Marduk was made to descend "far from the sun

---

32   Texts cited by H. Frankfort, *Kingship and the Gods*, p. 320.

and light."[33] Finally, he was delivered, and the gods assembled (that is, their statues were brought together) to determine the destinies. (This episode corresponds, in the *Enuma elish,* to Marduk's advancement to the rank of supreme god.) The king led the procession to the Bit Akitu, a building situated outside of the city. The procession represented the army of the gods advancing against Tiamat. According to an inscription of Sennacherib, we may suppose that the primordial battle was mimed, the king personifying Assur (the god who had replaced Marduk).[34] The *hieros gamos* took place after the return from the banquet at the Bit Akitu. The last act consisted in the determination of the destinies[35] for each month of the year. By "determining" it, the year was ritually *created,* that is, the good fortune, fertility, and richness of the new world that had just been born were insured.

The *akitu* represents the Mesopotamian version of a quite wide-spread mythico-ritual scenario, specifically of the New Year festival considered as a repetition of the cosmogony.[36] Since the periodic regeneration of the cosmos constitutes the great hope of traditional societies, we shall often refer to New Year festivals. We will mention at this point that various episodes of the *akitu* are found (to confine ourselves to the Near East) in Egypt, among the Hittites, at Ugarit, in Iran, and among the Mandaeans. Thus, for example, "chaos," ritually actualized during the last days of the year, was signified by orgiastic excesses of the Saturnalia type, by the reversal of all social order, by the extinguishing of fires, and by the return of the dead (represented by maskers). Combats between two groups of actors are documented in Egypt, among the Hittites, and at Ugarit. The custom of "fixing the fates" of the twelve months during the twelve intercalary days still persists in the Near East and in eastern Europe.[37]

The role of the king in the *akitu* is inadequately known. His "humiliation" corresponds to the regression of the world to chaos and to Marduk's captivity in the mountain. The king personifies the god in the battle against Tiamat and in the *hieros gamos* with a hierodule. But identification with the god is not always indicated; as we have seen, during his "humiliation" the king addresses Marduk. Nevertheless, the sacrality of the Mesopotamian sovereign is amply documented. We have mentioned the sacred marriage of the Sumerian king, representing Dumuzi, to the goddess Inanna; this *hieros gamos* took place during the New Year festival. For the Sumerians, royalty was held to have descended from the sky; its origin was divine, and this conception remained in force until the disappearance of the Assyro-Babylonian civilization.

The sovereign's sacrality was proclaimed in many ways. He was called "king of the land" (that is, of the world) or "of the four regions of the universe," titles originally appertaining to the gods alone.[38] Just as in the case of the gods, a supernatural light shone from his head.[39] Even before his birth, the gods had predestined him to sovereignty. Though the king recognized his earthly begetting, he was considered a "son of god" (Hammurabi declares that he was begotten by Sin, and Lipitishtar by En-lil). This twofold descent made him supremely the intermediary between gods and men. The sovereign represented the people before the

---

33 The classic authors refer to the "tomb of Bel" (= Marduk) at Babylon. This was in all probability the ziggurat of the Etemenanki temple, considered the god's momentary burial place.

34 Some allusions imply that there were mimed combats between two groups of actors.

35 Just as, in the *Enuma elish,* Marduk had determined the laws governing the universe that he had just created.

36 See Eliade, *Cosmos and History,* pp. 49 ff.; *Myth and Reality,* pp. 41 ff.

37 See *Cosmos and History,* pp. 65 ff.

38 See Frankfort, *Kingship,* pp. 227 ff.

39 This light, named *melammû* in Akkadian, corresponds to the *xvarenah* of the Iranians; see Oppenheim, *Ancient Mesopotamia,* p. 206; Cassin, *La splendeur divine,* pp. 65 ff.

gods, and it was he who expiated the sins of his subjects. Sometimes he had to suffer death for his people's crimes; this is why the Assyrians had a "substitute for the king."[40] The texts proclaim that the king had lived in fellowship with the gods in the fabulous garden that contains the Tree of Life and the Water of Life.[41] (Actually, it is he and his courtiers who eat the food offered daily to the statues of the gods.) The king is the "envoy" of the gods, the "shepherd of the people," named by god to establish justice and peace on earth.[42] "When Anu and En-lil called Lipit-Ishtar to the government of the land in order to establish justice in the land … , then I, Lipit-Ishtar, the humble shepherd of Nippur … , established justice in Sumer and Akkad, in accordance with the word of En-lil."[43]

It could be said that the king shared in the divine modality, but without becoming a god. He *represented* the god, and this, on the archaic levels of culture, also implied that he *was* in a way he whom he personified. In any case, as mediator between the world of men and the world of the gods, the Mesopotamian king effected, in his own person, a ritual union between the two modalities of existence, the divine and the human. It was by virtue of this twofold nature that the king was considered, at least metaphorically, to be the creator of life and fertility. *But he was not a god, a new member of the pantheon* (as the Egyptian pharaoh was). Prayers were not addressed to him; on the contrary, the gods were implored to protect him. For the sovereigns, despite their intimacy with the divine world, despite the *hieros gamos* with certain goddesses, did not reach the point of transmuting the human condition. In the last analysis, they remained mortals. It was never forgotten that even the fabled king of Uruk, Gilgamesh, failed in his attempt to gain immortality.

GILGAMESH IN QUEST OF IMMORTALITY

The *Epic of Gilgamesh* is certainly the best known and most popular of Babylonian creations. Its hero, Gilgamesh, king of Uruk, was already famous in the archaic period, and the Sumerian version of several episodes from his legendary life has been found. Despite these antecedents, however, the *Epic of Gilgamesh* is a product of the Semitic genius. It is in the Akkadian version in which it was composed on the basis of various isolated episodes that we may read one of the most moving tales of the quest for immortality or, more precisely, of the final failure of an undertaking that seemed to have every possibility of succeeding. This saga, which begins with the erotic excesses of a hero who is at the same time a tyrant, reveals, in the last analysis, the inability of purely "heroic" virtues radically to transcend the human condition.

And yet Gilgamesh was two-thirds a divine being, son of the goddess Ninsun and a mortal.[44] At the outset the text praises his omniscience and the grandiose works of construction that he had undertaken. But immediately afterward we are presented with a tyrant who violates women and girls and wears men out in forced labor. The inhabitants pray to the gods, and the gods decide to create a being of gigantic size who

---

40   Labat, *Le caractère religieux de la royauté assyro-babylonienne*, pp. 352 ff. ; Frankfort, *Kingship*, pp. 262 ff.
41   It is the king who, in the role of gardener, took care of the Tree of Life; see Widengren, *The King and the Tree of Life in Ancient Near Eastern Religion*, esp. pp. 22 ff., 59 ff.
42   See the introduction to the "Code of Hammurabi" (I. 50), in *ANET*, p. 164.
43   Prologue to the "Lipit-Ishtar Lawcode," *ANET*, p. 159. See the texts cited and translated by J. Zandee, "Le Messie," pp. 13, 14, 16.
44   A high priest of the city of Uruk, according to Sumerian tradition; see A. Heidel, *The Gilgamesh Epic*, p. 4.

can confront Gilgamesh. This half-savage creature, who receives the name of Enkidu, lives in peace with the wild beasts; they all drink together at the same springs. Gilgamesh obtains knowledge of his existence first in a dream and then from a hunter who had come upon him. He sends a courtesan to bewitch him by her charms and lead him to Uruk. As the gods had foreseen, the two champions compete as soon as they meet each other. Gilgamesh emerges victorious, but he conceives an affection for Enkidu and makes him his companion. In the last analysis, the gods' plan was not foiled; henceforth Gilgamesh will expend his strength on heroic adventures.

Accompanied by Enkidu, he sets out for the distant and fabulous forest of cedars, which is guarded by a monstrous and all-powerful being, Huwawa. After cutting down his sacred cedar, the two heroes kill him. On his way back to Uruk, Ishtar sees Gilgamesh. The goddess invites him to marry her, but he returns an insolent refusal. Humiliated, Ishtar begs her father, Anu, to create the Bull of Heaven to destroy Gilgamesh and his city. Anu at first refuses, but he gives in when Ishtar threatens to bring the dead back from the underworld. The Bull of Heaven charges at Uruk, and its bellowings make the king's men drop dead by hundreds. However, Enkidu succeeds in catching it by the tail, and Gilgamesh thrusts his sword into its neck. Furious, Ishtar mounts the city walls and curses the king. Intoxicated by their victory, Enkidu tears a thigh from the Bull of Heaven and throws it at the goddess's feet, at the same time assailing her with insults. This is the culminating moment in the career of the two heroes, but it is also the prologue to a tragedy. That same night Enkidu dreams that he has been condemned by the gods. The next day he falls ill, and, twelve days later, he dies.

An unexpected change makes Gilgamesh unrecognizable. For seven days and seven nights he mourns for his friend and refuses to let him be buried. He hopes that his laments will finally bring him back to life. It is not until the body shows the first signs of decomposition that Gilgamesh yields, and Enkidu is given a magnificent funeral. The king leaves the city and wanders through the desert, complaining: "Shall not I, too, die like Enkidu?" (tablet 9, column 1, line 4).[45] He is terrified by the thought of death. Heroic exploits do not console him. Henceforth his only purpose is to escape from the human condition, to gain immortality. He knows that the famous Utnapishtim, survivor of the flood, is still alive, and he decides to search for him.

His journey is full of ordeals of the initiatory type. He comes to the mountains of Mashu and finds the gate through which the Sun passes daily. The gate is guarded by a scorpion-man and his wife, "whose glance is death" (9. 2. 7). The invincible hero is paralyzed by fear and prostrates himself humbly. But the scorpion-man and his wife recognize the divine part of Gilgamesh and allow him to enter the tunnel. After walking for twelve hours in darkness, Gilgamesh comes to a marvelous garden on the other side of the mountains. Some distance away, by the seaside, he meets the nymph Siduri and asks her where he can find Utnapishtim. Siduri tries to make him change his mind: "When the gods made men, they saw death for men; they kept life for themselves. Thou, Gilgamesh, fill thy belly and make merry by day and night. On each day make a feast, and dance and play, day and night."[46]

But Gilgamesh holds to his decision, and then Siduri sends him to Urshanabi, Utnapishtim's boatman, who happened to be nearby. They cross the Waters of Death and reach the shore on which Utnapishtim lived. Gilgamesh asks him how he had gained immortality. He thus learns the story of the flood and the

---

45   Except as otherwise indicated, we follow the translation by Contenau, *L'épopée de Gilgamesh*.
46   Tablet X, column III, lines 6–9; after the translation by Jean Nougayrol, *Histoire des religions*, vol. 1, p. 222.

gods' decision to make Utnapishtim and his wife their "kin," establishing them "at the mouths of the rivers." "But," Utnapishtim asks Gilgamesh, "as for thee, which of the gods will unite thee to their assembly, that thou mayest obtain the life that thou seekest?" (11. 198). However, what he goes on to say is unexpected: "Up, try not to sleep for six days and seven nights!" (199). What we have here is, undoubtedly, the most difficult of initiatory ordeals: conquering sleep, remaining "awake," is equivalent to a transmutation of the human condition.[47] Are we to take it that Utnapishtim, knowing that the gods will not grant Gilgamesh immortality, suggests that he conquer it by means of an initiation? The hero has already successfully gone through several ordeals: the journey through the tunnel, the "temptation" by Siduri, crossing the Waters of Death. These were in some sense ordeals of the heroic type. This time, however, the ordeal is " spiritual," for only an unusual power of concentration can enable a human being to remain awake for six days and seven nights. But Gilgamesh at once falls asleep, and Utnapishtim exclaims sarcasti cally: "Look at the strong man who desires immortality: sleep has come over him like a violent wind!" (203–4). He sleeps without a break for six days and seven nights; and, when Utnapishtim wakes him, Gilgamesh reproaches him for waking him when he had only just fallen asleep. However, he has to accept the evidence, and he falls to lamenting again: "What shall I do, Utnapishtim, where shall I go? a demon has taken possession of my body; in the room in which I sleep, death lives, and wherever I go, death is there!" (230–34).

Gilgamesh now makes ready to leave, but at the last moment Utnapishtim, at his wife's suggestion, reveals a "secret of the gods" to him: the place where he can find the plant that brings back youth. Gilgamesh goes down to the bottom of the sea, gathers it,[48] and starts back rejoicing. After traveling for a few days, he sees a spring of fresh water and hurries to bathe. Attracted by the odor of the plant, a snake comes out of the spring, carries off the plant, and sheds its skin.[49] Sobbing, Gilgamesh complains to Urshanabi of his bad fortune. This episode may be read as a failure in another initiatory ordeal: the hero failed to profit from an unexpected gift; in short, he was lacking in wisdom. The text ends abruptly: arrived at Uruk, Gilgamesh invites Urshanabi to go up on the city walls and admire its foundations.[50]

The *Epic of Gilgamesh* has been seen as a dramatized illustration of the human condition, defined by the inevitability of death. Yet this first masterpiece of universal literature can also be understood as illustrating the belief that certain beings are capable, even without help from the gods, of obtaining immortality, on the condition that they successfully pass through a series of initiatory ordeals. Seen from this point of view, the story of Gilgamesh would prove to be the dramatized account of a failed initiation.

DESTINY AND THE GODS

Unfortunately, we do not know the ritual context of Mesopotamian initiation, always supposing that such a thing existed. The initiatory meaning of the quest for immortality can be deciphered in the particular

---

47   See Eliade, *Birth and Rebirth*, pp. 14 if.
48   We may wonder why Gilgamesh did not eat it as soon as he had gathered it, but he was saving it for later; see Heidel, *The Gilgamesh Epic*, p. 62, n. 211.
49   This is a well-known folklore theme: by shedding its old skin, the snake renews its life.
50   Tablet XII, composed in Sumerian, was added later; the incidents narrated in it have no direct relation to the narrative we have summarized.

structure of the ordeals undergone by Gilgamesh. The Arthurian romances present a similar situation; they, too, are filled with initiatory symbols and motifs, but it is impossible to decide whether these belong to a ritual scenario, represent recollections of Celtic mythology or Hermetic gnosticism, or are merely products of the imagination. In the case of the Arthurian romances, we at least know the initiatory traditions that preceded their composition, whereas we know nothing of the protohistory of the initiatory scenario possibly implied in Gilgamesh's adventures.

It has been emphasized, and rightly, that Akkadian religious thought puts the accent on man. In the last analysis, the story of Gilgamesh becomes paradigmatic: it proclaims the precariousness of the human condition, the impossibility—even for a hero—of gaining immortality. Man was created mortal, and he was created solely to serve the gods. This pessimistic anthropology was already formulated in the *Enuma elish*. It is also found in other important religious texts. The "Dialogue between Master and Servant" seems to be the product of nihilism exacerbated by a neurosis: the master does not even know what he wants. He is obsessed by the vanity of all human effort: "Climb the mounds of ancient ruins and walk about: look at these skulls of late and early men; who among them is an evildoer, who a public benefactor?"[51]

Another celebrated text, the "Dialogue about Human Misery," which has been called the "Babylonian Ecclesiastes," is even more despairing. "Does the fierce lion, who eats the best of meat, / Present his dough-and-incense offering to appease his goddess' displeasure? / … [As for me,] have I withheld the meal-oblation? [No], I have prayed to the gods, / I have presented the prescribed sacrifices to the goddess" (lines 50 ff.). From his childhood, this just man has striven to understand the god's thought, he has sought the goddess humbly and piously. Yet "the god brought me scarcity instead of wealth" (lines 71 ff.). On the contrary, it is the scoundrel, the godless, who has acquired wealth (line 236). People "extol the word of a prominent man, expert in murder, / But they abase the humble, who has committed no violence." The evildoer is justified, the righteous man is driven away. It is the bandit who receives gold, while the weak are left to hunger. The wicked man is strengthened, the feeble are cast down (lines 267 ff.).[52]

This despair arises, not from a meditation on the vanity of human existence, but from the experience of general injustice: the wicked triumph, prayers are not answered; the gods seem indifferent to human affairs. From the second millennium, similar spiritual crises will make themselves felt elsewhere (Egypt, Israel, Iran, India, Greece), with various consequences; for the responses to this type of nihilistic experience were made in accordance with the religious genius characteristic of each culture. But in the Mesopotamian wisdom literature the gods do not always prove to be indifferent. One text presents the physical and mental sufferings of an innocent man who has been compared to Job. He is the very pattern of the just man suffering, for no divinity seems to help him. Countless sicknesses have reduced him to being "soaked in his own excrement," and he is already bewailed as dead by his relatives when a series of dreams reveals to him that Marduk will save him. As in an ecstatic trance, he sees the god destroying the demons of sickness and then extracting his pains from his body as one uproots a plant. Finally, his health restored, the just man gives thanks to Marduk by ritually passing through the twelve gates of his temple at Babylon.[53]

---

51 "A Pessimistic Dialogue between Master and Servant," line 84; trans. R. H. Pfeiffer, *ANET*, p. 438.
52 "A Dialogue about Human Misery," trans. Pfeiffer, *ANET*, pp. 439–40.
53 "I Will Praise the Lord of Wisdom," trans. Pfeiffer, *ANET*, pp. 434–37.

In the last analysis, by putting the accent on man, Akkadian religious thought brings out the limits of human possibilities. The distance between men and the gods proves to be impossible to cross. Yet man is not isolated in his own solitude. First of all, he shares in a spiritual element that can be regarded as divine: it is his " spirit," *ilu* (literally, "god").[54] Secondly, through rites and prayers he hopes to obtain the blessing of the gods. Above all, he knows that he forms part of a universe that is unified by homologies: he lives in a city that constitutes an *imago mundi* and whose temples and ziggurats represent "centers of the world" and, in consequence, insure communi cation with heaven and the gods. Babylon was a Bab-il-ani, a " Gate of the Gods," for it is there that the gods came down to earth. A number of cities and sanctuaries were named " Link between Heaven and Earth."[55] In other words, man does not live in a closed world, separated from the gods, completely isolated from the cosmic rhythms. In addition, a complex system of correspondences be tween heaven and earth made it possible for terrestrial realities to be understood and at the same time to be "influenced" by their respective celestial prototypes. An example: Since each planet had its corresponding metal and color, everything colored was under the influence of a planet. But each planet belonged to a god, who, by that fact, was represented by the respective metal.[56] In consequence, one who ritually manipulated a certain metallic object or a semiprecious stone of a particular color felt that he was under the protection of a god.

Finally, numerous techniques of divination, most of them developed during the Akkadian period, made it possible to know the future. So it was believed that certain misadventures could be avoided. The variety of techniques and the large number of written documents that have come down to us prove the high esteem in which the mantic art was held on all levels of society. The most elaborate method was extispicy, that is, examining the entrails of a victim; the least costly, lecanomancy, consisted in pouring a little oil on water, or vice versa, and interpreting the signs that could be read in the shapes produced by the two liquids. Astrology, developed later than the other techni ques, was principally practiced by the royal entourage. As for the interpretation of dreams, it was complemented, from the beginning of the second millennium, by methods of offsetting unfavorable omens.[57]

All the techniques of divination pursued the discovery of "signs," whose hidden meanings were in terpreted in accordance with certain traditional rules. *The world, then, revealed itself to be structured and governed by laws.* If the signs were deciphered, the future could be known; in other words, *time was "mastered,"* for events that were to occur only after a certain interval of time were foreseen. The attention paid to signs led to discoveries of genuine scientific value. Some of these discoveries were later taken over and perfected by the Greeks. But Babylonian science remained a "traditional" science, in the sense that scientific knowledge preserved a totalitarian structure, that is, a structure that involved cosmological, ethical, and existential presuppositions.[58]

---

54   The spirit (*ilu*) is the most important element of a personality. The others are *ištaru* (its destiny), *lamassu* (its individuality; resembles a statue), and *šēdu* (comparable to Lat. *genius*); see A. L. Oppenheimer, *Ancient Mesopotamia*, pp. 198–206.

55   Eliade, *Cosmos and History*, pp. 14 ff.

56   Gold corresponded to En-lil, silver to Anu, bronze to Ea. When Shamash took En-lil's place, he became the "patron" of gold; see B. Meissner, *Babylonien und Assyrien*, vol. 2, pp. 130 ff., 254.

57   J. Nougayrol, "La divination babylonienne," esp. pp. 39 ff.

58   As did, for example, medicine and alchemy in China.

Toward 1500 B.C. the creative period of Mesopotamian thought seems definitely to have ended. During the ten following centuries, intellectual activity appears to spend itself in erudition and compilation. But the influence of Mesopotamian culture, documented from the most ancient times, continues and increases. Ideas, beliefs, and techniques of Mesopotamian origin circulate from the western Mediterranean to the Hindu Kush. It is significant that the Baby lonian discoveries that were destined to become popular imply, whether more or less directly, correspondences between heaven and earth, or macrocosm-microcosm.

Egyptian Religion

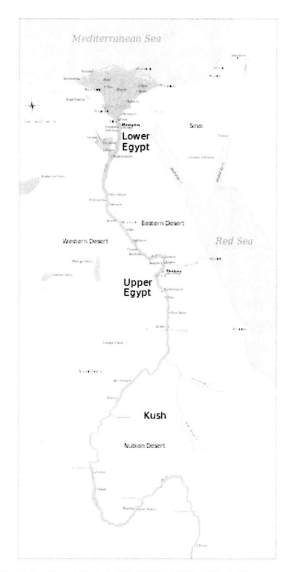

3

Fig. 3.0a: Copyright © Jeff Dahl (CC BY-SA 4.0) at https://commons.wikimedia.org/wiki/File%3AAncient_Egypt_map-en.svg.

Egypt

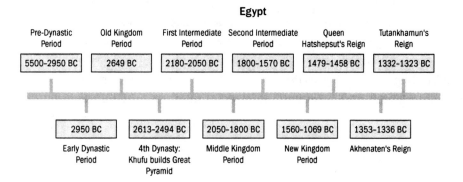

Pre-Dynastic Period	Old Kingdom Period	First Intermediate Period	Second Intermediate Period	Queen Hatshepsut's Reign	Tutankhamun's Reign
5500-2950 BC	2649 BC	2180-2050 BC	1800-1570 BC	1479-1458 BC	1332-1323 BC

2950 BC	2613-2494 BC	2050-1800 BC	1560-1069 BC	1353-1336 BC
Early Dynastic Period	4th Dynasty: Khufu builds Great Pyramid	Middle Kingdom Period	New Kingdom Period	Akhenaten's Reign

The Egyptian Religion

By George Steindorff and Keith C. Steele

He who desires to know the religious notions which prevailed during the golden age of Egypt must follow a backward course and attempt to fathom the cults of that dark primeval age in which the "Two Lands," Upper and Lower Egypt, still existed independently side by side, before there was a unified Egyptian nation. Each city, town, and village possessed its own protective divinity and its sanctuary to which the inhabitants turned for assistance in days of need and danger as they constantly sought the favor of the god by means of prayers and offerings. In his hand lay the weal and woe of the community; he was the lord of the region, the "god of the city," who, like an earthly prince or count, controlled the destiny of his vassals and defended them from their enemies. How closely the god was bound up with his district is very well indicated by the fact that he frequently possessed no name of his own but was simply designated by the name of the site of the cult which belonged to him and in which he was worshiped. Thus the local divinity of the Upper Egyptian city of Ombos was "the Ombite," and the god of Edfu was referred to as "He of Edfu." Of course, each local god usually bore a distinctive name the original meaning of which we are now seldom able to determine. Thus the god of Memphis was called Ptah (Figure 3.1, *a*); the lord of Thebes was named Montu; the ancient tutelary divinity of Herwer was Khnum (Figure 3.1, *b*); in Coptos it was Min, and in Heliopolis it was Atum, who was worshiped. Familiar names among the female divinities are Hathor, the "Lady of Dendera" (Figure 3.1, *c*); Neith, the goddess of Sais (Figure 3.1, *d*); and Sekhmet, the protective goddess of Memphis (Figure 3.3).

The function of these local patron deities was usually limited to their concern for their city, and they possessed no power beyond its limit. There were a few of them, however, who attained a more extensive sphere of influence along with the increase in importance of their native cities. In this manner some of them developed into district or even national gods and acquired dominating positions in the Egyptian pantheon. Thus, when Egypt still consisted of two separate kingdoms, the local gods of the religious capitals—Seth of Ombos and Horus of Behdet—came to be the protective gods of the two states; legend has preserved some memory of the wars which took place between the north and the south. As a pair of divine kings the two gods were supposed to have struggled with each other for a long time in order to determine which

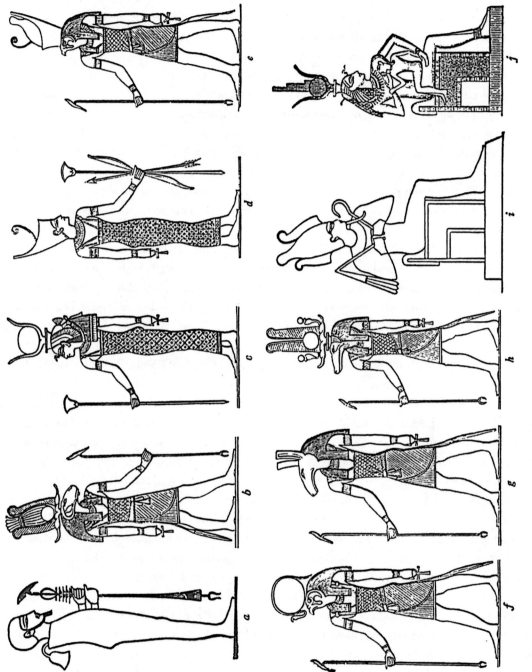

Figure 3.1 A Selection of Egyptian Divinities

(a) Ptah; (b) Khnum; (c) Hathor; (d) Neith; (e) Horus; (f) Re-Harakhti; (g) Seth; (h) Soberk; (i) Osiris; (j) Isis Suckling Her Son Horus

one should have the sovereignty over the Two Lands; but in the end a peaceful settlement was brought about between them under which each of them took as his share a half of the kingdom. When Egypt was later united into a single state, with Upper Egypt victorious over Lower Egypt, Horus became the national god, a position which he maintained through all successive ages (Figure 3.1, *e)*. The king was considered to be the incarnation of his patron lord Horus. Somewhat later, but still in the prehistoric era, when Egypt for the second time split into two independent kingdoms and established new capitals, the local divinities of these two cities—the vulture-goddess of Nekheb (Elkab) and the serpent-goddess of Buto—were elevated to the positions of national divinities, and their worship extended far beyond their original sphere of influence. In a similar manner the cosmic god Amun was transferred from Hermopolis to Karnak in the Eleventh Dynasty so that he eventually became the local god of Thebes and later, through identification with Re (Figure 3.1, *f)*, as "king of the gods," the national god of the New Kingdom.

It happened not uncommonly that the inhabitants of a city emigrated and founded a new home elsewhere. In such an event it is not surprising that they carried with them their patron deity and provided a new cult place for him in the new location. In other cases the people of one district became so impressed by the effectiveness with which some foreign divinity protected his community or the abundance of the blessings and miracles which he showered upon it that they began to make pilgrimages to his shrine or even to supply him with new temples in which, by the presentation of offerings, they also might win the benefits of his powerful favor. In this manner a god was occasionally transferred to a city where he had not originally resided. Sometimes he attracted a circle of worshipers away from the actual patron god of the town or even usurped the native god's position as the tutelary divinity of the city. It was perhaps in some such manner as this that the goddess Neith of Sais acquired her shrine at Esna, or the god Khnum, who was really at home in Hypselis, near Assiut, was accorded worship in Herwer, Esna, and Elephantine.

Already at an early date the concepts of some of the local divinities were extended through emphasis on certain aspects of their character. Some of them in consequence came to preside over certain of the crafts and professions. The falcon-shaped Montu thus became a war-god; Min of Goptos came to be the patron of desert travelers as well as the god of fertility and the harvest. Ptah of Memphis, in whose province the distinctive art of Egypt originated in historic times, was the patron of all artists, metal-workers, and smiths. The powerful Sekhmet of Memphis became a terrible fire-goddess who annihilated her enemies, while Hathor of Dendera was converted into a goddess of love and joy. Horus the falcon became the sun-god who illuminated the world and who as a youthful hero engages in perpetual battle with his adversary Seth the storm-god (Figure 3.1, *g)*. Thoth of Hermopolis (Figure 3.2) was a moon-god who had created the divisions of time and the order of the cosmos; he was also counted the inventor of hieroglyphic writing, the "lord of divine words," and the god of learning. The crocodile-god Sobek (Figure 3.1, *h)* was naturally considered a water-god; he received worship as a patron divinity in towns the special weal and woe of which were peculiarly dependent on water, as was the situation on the islands of Gebelein and Kom Ombo, in the oasis of the Fayyum, or at the town of Kheny at the Nile rapids near modern Silsila. Thus local gods very frequently developed into patron deities of certain professions or into nature gods worshiped throughout the length and breadth of the land.

In addition to these "city gods," there was also a very considerable number of lesser gods, spirits, and demons, who were considered able at times to be of benefit or injury to men and whose favor it was necessary to court, as well as an important class of fairies who rendered assistance to women in travail and who could either hinder or accelerate childbirth. Various protective household gods of grotesque stature were worshiped under

Figure 3.2 Anubis and Thoth Weighing the Heart at the Judgment (British Museum)

the name of Bes. Musicians, dancers, killers of snakes, they also presided over the toilette, the bedchamber, and the pleasures of love. Among the great host of other divinities it is possible to mention here but a few: gods and goddesses of the harvest, spirits who provided healing in times of illness, gods and goddesses of war.

If the inhabitants of a locality lived in peace and carried on friendly intercourse with its neighbors, it was natural that their patron gods should share their friendship. Like the men who worshiped them, they were accustomed to visit one another on certain days, and outside gods were frequently presented with special chapels and their own cults in the temple of a "city god." While the latter thus remained the chief god of his district, he was by no means the only divinity in it to receive the homage of its inhabitants. Instead, an entire circle of other gods and demigods stood beside him as his guests to share the praises and offerings of his worshipers. At a very early time, indeed, the priests undertook to bring various of these gods into some relationship with one another. As a result, it not infrequently happened that a goddess was assigned to the principal god of the city as his wife and a third divinity to the two of them as their son. At Karnak in Thebes, for example, the chief god Amun shared his worship with his wife, the goddess Mut, and their son, the moon-god Khonsu; in Memphis the tutelary god Ptah (Figure 3.1, *a*) was given Sekhmet (Figure 3.3) as a consort and Nefertem as their son; at Abydos, Osiris (Figure 3.1, *i*), his sister-wife Isis (Figure 3.1, *j),* and Horus "the son of Isis" constituted the "triad" or holy family.

Manifold though the Egyptian gods were in name, not less so were the outward manifestations which were attributed to them by their devotees. Most of them were somewhat crude and reminiscent of the fetishism which still holds in its clutches a large proportion of the uncivilized Negro tribes of Africa. The god of Busiris in the Delta was conceived as a pillar with the head and arms of an Egyptian king; the goddess Neith of Sais was a shield to which a pair of crossed arrows had been nailed. The god Ptah of Memphis and the harvest-god Min of Coptos, under whose protection stood the desert road which connected his native city with the Red Sea, were both worshiped as fetishes in semihuman form. However, the divinities were most frequently conceived in purely animal form: Sobek as a crocodile, the god of Mendes as a ram, Thoth of Hermopolis as an ibis, Khnum in the form of a ram; Horus in that of a falcon or sparrow hawk, while his adversary Seth was given the form of some kind of fabulous beast. The protective goddess of Buto was a serpent; that of Nekheb, like the goddess Mut of Thebes, was regarded as a vulture; while Hathor of Dendera was given the form of a cow.

These are all conceptions of the gods which at first thought appear to us not only inherently strange but even as utterly unworthy of a cultured race. The Greeks and Romans reacted in the same manner when they became acquainted with Egypt, and they were free to express their contempt and scorn at finding such primitive religious ideas in a race so admirable for many of its achievements. Nevertheless, similar concepts were widely held by other civilized peoples, including certain of the Semitic tribes and even the earliest Greeks. The Semites found divinity in trees, stones, and animals; from the Greeks likewise we have any number of familiar myths which relate, for example, how Hermes, god of meadow and highway, manifested himself as a heap of stones, Apollo as a wolf, Zeus as a cloud, Artemis as a bear, Hera as a cow, while every student of classical mythology knows that the "sacred animal" of Athena was the owl and that of Zeus was the eagle.

It was customary to house the wooden statue of the divinity in the local temple in its own naos or shrine. On feast days the statue, still in its shrine, was carried in procession on the shoulders of the priests or transported on the river in a sacred bark. In addition, from the very earliest times a specimen of whatever species of animal happened to be sacred to a given temple—the animal in which the local god was accustomed to manifest himself—was kept and carefully tended in the sanctuary. The Greek traveler Strabo, who toured

Figure 3.3

Egypt in the reign of the Roman emperor Augustus, has left a description of the crocodile sacred to the water-god Sobek which was cherished at Arsinoé, the capital of the Fayyum.

> It is fed with the bread, meat, and wine brought by the strangers who come to see it. Our host went with us to the lake, taking along a small meal-cake, some meat, and a small flask of wine. We found the animal lying on the bank; the priests approached and, while some of them opened his jaws, another thrust first the cake into his mouth, then the meat, and finally poured the wine after them. Thereupon the crocodile plunged into the lake and swam to the opposite shore.

In the later period, after the religion had lost more and more of its inner vitality, and the people clung increasingly to outward forms, they carried the animal cults to such extremes that they came to regard each individual of the species in whose form the divinity was believed to reveal himself as sacred and divine. These animals were considered inviolable; to kill one of them in a place dedicated to its species was punishable by the death penalty. In fact, so extreme was the religious zeal of this epoch that it became the custom to embalm each one of the sacred animals at death and to bury it ceremoniously in special cemeteries dedicated to the purpose.

A forward step from crude fetishism was taken already in the prehistoric age when the Egyptian began to represent the divinity in human form. At that time the god appeared with a human face and figure and wore the same type of clothing as the Egyptians themselves. His head, like that of a prince or king, was adorned with a helmet or crown, while the simple skirt was decorated with the tail of an animal attached to the back of the girdle as had been the custom of the rulers of the primeval time. His insignia of authority consisted of baton and scepter, while a goddess regularly carried a papyrus blossom with a long stem. This new interpretation of divinity was bound to react on the more primitive fetishistic beliefs. The crude anthropoid fetish of Ptah developed into a youthful figure "beautiful of face," with shaven head, enveloped in a tightly fitting garment, and standing on a stair or terrace with a scepter grasped in both hands. Those divinities which had formerly been conceived as animals became transformed into human figures surmounted by the heads of the sacred animals from which they were derived. Sobek became a man with the head of a crocodile, Khnum a man with a ram's head (Figure 3.1, *b*); Thoth was represented in human form with the head of an ibis (Figure 3.2), Horus with that of a falcon (Figure 3.1, *e*), while Sekhmet became a woman with the head of a lioness (Figure 3.3).

In addition to the local divinities which were conceived in animal form, still other sacred animals were made peculiar objects of worship. The best known of these is the Mnevis bull, which was honored in Heliopolis, the Buchis bull of Hermonthis (Armant), the "phoenix" (heron) of Heliopolis, and especially the Apis bull of Memphis. According to the late Greek account, the last named was begotten by a ray of sunlight which descended from heaven and impregnated a cow, which would thereafter never be able to give birth a second time. The Apis bull was black with white spots, including a white triangle on the forehead and the figure of a crescent moon on the right side. He usually wore a red cloth on his back. As far back as the Old Kingdom we know that priests were assigned to him, but more extensive information concerning his nature or his cult has not survived. In later times, however, theological speculations sought to create a relationship between this highly esteemed bull and Ptah, the ancient god of Memphis. These eventually resulted in the concept that Apis was the son of Ptah or, by a still more complex dogma, the actual image, "the living reincarnation of Ptah." In the New Kingdom, Amenhotep III caused the deceased bulls to be sumptuously interred in the necropolis of Memphis at Saqqara in mausoleums in the usual style of burial place. In the Nineteenth Dynasty, however, under Ramesses II, a magnificent mortuary gallery was laid out in which the sacred bulls were buried in splendid stone sarcophagi. This subterranean cemetery—a gallery nearly three hundred and fifty feet in length carved out of the solid rock, with a row of niches for the burials of the individual bulls—the so-called Serapeum, was highly venerated as late as the Ptolemaic period, when it attracted great hosts of pious pilgrims.

In general, our knowledge of the most popularly honored divinities is exceedingly limited; we are acquainted with their names and representations, but their nature and character are withheld from our understanding in spite of the multitude of poetic epithets which are applied to them in the hymns and liturgies. It is evident, however, that their gods were not merely the empty, shadowy figures to the Egyptians which they appear to us with our scanty information concerning them. Their ancient worshipers told many a tale of their exploits and marvelous adventures, and these myths will certainly have been elaborated, expanded, and reduced to writing in the bosom of the priesthood where they were principally cherished.

In addition to the local divinities whose activities were confined to a limited sphere on earth, there were other great powers who emerged in nature and embraced the entire world: heaven and earth, sun, moon, and stars, and the Nile. The sky was the "great god"; he was thought of as a falcon which spread his protective wings over the earth or over Egypt. His divine eyes are the sun and moon; when he opens them it is day, when they are closed it is night. The stars are attached to his body, the wind is the breath of his mouth, and the water is his perspiration According to another widely circulated myth, the sky is a goddess, sometimes known by the name of Nut. In primordial times she was closely embraced in the arms of the earth-god Geb, until the god of the atmosphere, Shu, separated them from each other by elevating Nut high above the earth on his uplifted arms and placing himself beneath her. From the union of Geb and Nut sprang a son, Re, the sun-god, and the most popular of the cosmic gods. He travels by day in his bark across the celestial ocean as on the Nile, until at eventide he transfers to another boat in order to descend to the netherworld and there continue his voyage. He was also conceived as a falcon who soared through the sky with bright plumage or as a young hero who carried on a constant struggle with the hostile powers of darkness. As the god of the Upper Egyptian city of Edfu he is depicted as the sun disk with extended wings, a form in which he regularly appeared as a symbol of protection over the doors and elsewhere in the decoration of Egyptian temples.

The nature gods in general never developed a special cult of their own. Gradually, however, an exception was made in the case of Re, and it became customary to present offerings to him under the open sky. The kings of the Fifth Dynasty, who were popularly regarded as children of Re, dedicated to him near the capital of Memphis a unique temple in closure the chief feature of which was a peculiar type of obelisk erected on a huge stone substructure.

The evolution of religious ideas tended in general toward some connection between the local divinities and the celestial powers; the priesthoods of the former obviously sought every opportunity to enhance the reputation of their gods. Thus the falcon-shaped Horus, who by this time had developed into the national god, became identified with the sky-god who, as we have seen, was regarded as a falcon also; he became in consequence the "great god" or "lord of heaven" and received the name Harakhti ("Horus of the Horizon"). In addition, he was identified with Re and henceforth regarded as the sun-god Re-Harakhti. It was but a natural result that Re also should receive the form of Horus, and he is accordingly depicted as a king in human form with the head of a falcon surmounted by the sun disk with pendent uraeus serpent.

In a similar manner other local gods who originally had no connection whatever with the sun and who had never manifested themselves as falcons, as, for example, the crocodile-shaped water-god Sobek, the

Figure 3.4 The Sky-Goddess Nut as a Cow (Biban el-Muluk, Tomb of Sethi I)

ram-shaped gods Khnum and Amun of Karnak, were identified with Re and assigned in consequence the sun disk and the sacred uraeus serpent as designations of rank. The local divinities retained through this development all their old attributes, and the myths which had centered about them were perpetuated by tradition; the inevitable result was a bewildering confusion of tangled and often self-contradictory ideas in the Egyptian religion. Efforts were made in the theology to distinguish at least the various sun-gods from one another; a distinct function was assigned to each one, according to which Khepri—the sun conceived as à scarab—became the morning sun and Atum was worshiped as the evening sun. Nevertheless, it does not appear that the learned priesthood ever succeeded in drawing up a comprehensive system of Egyptian theology.

A similar transformation may be followed among the local female divinities, who tended to become identified with the goddess Nut. So the cow-goddess Hathor developed into a sky-goddess, a fact which led to the logical if rather astonishing conclusion that Nut herself was a cow which was held fast by numerous gods and supported in position by Shu, the god of the atmosphere, while the stars were all attached to her belly, and the sun-god traveled in his bark along her body (Figure 3.4).

Numerous other local gods whose character or appearance was not very sharply differentiated became identified at an early date. Hathor and Isis were thus considered as the same person, while Amun of Karnak, Min of Coptos, and later even Khnum of Elephantine were combined into a single divinity. The tutelary cat-goddess of Bubastis was equated with the goddesses Sekhmet and Pekhet, both of whom were lionesses, and all of them, in turn, were identified with Mut, the mother of the gods and the consort of Amun.

It certainly should not have been too much for a clever brain to have constituted some sort of order out of this mixture of diverse mythological ideas. With some effort to combine the local gods and to conceive them as sun or sky divinities, the Egyptian might well have been drawn naturally to the conclusion that the adoration of ancient patron gods was an obsolete idea and that the worship of a small group of gods or even of one alone was the most reasonable point of view. But who would have possessed the courage to put such a theory into practice and to shelve the ancient cults in order to substitute a new one in their place? Would not the united priesthoods of the entire land have risen up against such an effort in order to defend the rights and individual prerogatives of their gods? Above all, how would the great mass of the people, who clung with deep veneration to the old gods of their homes without the slightest interest in a theological system, have received an announcement that the dominion of their divine protector was at an end and that he had been superseded by another to whom it was now ordered that they must address their prayers and present their offerings? And yet the day was not so far away when just such an attempt was to be ventured—an attempt to overthrow the gods of old and to replace them with a single god in heaven and on earth (see chap. xiv).

The Egyptians failed no less completely to achieve a consistent set of ideas regarding man's destiny in the life after death. Rooted deeply in the hearts of the people was at least the belief that death was really not the end of everything but rather that a man would continue to live on exactly as on earth, provided that the conditions necessary for continued existence were fulfilled. First of all, he must be supplied with food and drink; hence the anxious and constantly reiterated desire of the Egyptians to receive "thousands of loaves, geese, oxen, beer, and all the good things by which a god lives" in the life hereafter. To avoid suffering from hunger and thirst after death, each Egyptian provided his tomb with great jars filled with food and drink or, if he had the means, established endowments the income of which would secure for all time the necessities of life in the netherworld. If he had surviving children or other close relatives, piety demanded that they go forth on the great feast days to the cemetery in order to deposit food and drink offerings at the tomb. Nevertheless, all of these provisions were still insufficient. From the time of the Old Kingdom the walls of the tomb or at least of the coffin were covered with representations of all sorts of objects which by magic could be transformed into the actual products depicted, when they would become available to serve all the physical needs of the dead. The same magical power was believed to be inherent in the relief sculptures or wall paintings in the tombs of the wealthy, where the deceased is shown seated at a richly decked offering-table (Figure 3.5), or where he witnesses the butchering and dressing of the offering-cattle or the rows of peasant girls bringing up products from the mortuary estate.

Beyond all these efforts to provide for the deceased, still another device was employed to achieve the desired end. Again and again one encounters inscriptions in the tombs appealing to each and every visitor or chance passer-by to repeat certain prayers which would conjure up by magic everything required for the enjoyment and nourishment of the deceased. In addition to the articles of food and drink, these objects include various oils, ointments, and cosmetics for the eyes—all of which were frequently provided for funerary use in exquisitely beautiful vases—jewelry, clothing, and even weapons for the protection of the dead against his enemies, as well as numerous other things. In the course of centuries the number and variety of such funerary objects greatly increased; how manifold the tomb equipment of the dead became in the golden age of the pharaonic empire is best illustrated by the treasure from the tomb of Tutankhamun (pp. 228 f.), which contains several thousand objects.

Another important popular belief was combined with these notions of the life after death and the requirements for its support. Each man was believed to possess not only a body but also a soul which survived in the hereafter. This was believed to take the form of a bird or, at a later time, the form of a falcon with the head of the deceased. After death it was thought to depart from the dead body and to fly about freely in the world, though it could at will, especially at night when evil spirits walked abroad, return to the safety of the tomb. However, this could occur only if the body of the deceased was properly preserved and prevented from decomposition. In order thus to enable the soul to recognize the body to which it

Figure 3.5 The Daily Meal within the Tomb (Thebes, Tomb of Djehuti)

belonged, the Egyptians from a very early time devoted the most careful attention to the preservation of the body.

Still another of the favorite Egyptian beliefs concerning the dead was the idea that the departed could assume different shapes and by means of magical formulas transform himself into all sorts of beings, such as a serpent, a falcon, a lily, a ram, or even a crocodile, and in such a form to move about the earth by day. These beliefs later became known to the Greek historians and philosophers, but they were misunderstood and led to the erroneous conclusion that the ancient Egyptians, like the Hindus, had believed in the doctrine of the transmigration of the soul.

The so-called "ka" played an important role in the Egyptian mortuary beliefs. This was a kind of protective spirit or genius which was born simultaneously with the individual and was closely united to him throughout life. In fact, the ka did not share the experience of death but survived the deceased in order to quicken him with its own life-strength and to protect him from his enemies in the hereafter.

The dead, like the living, continued under the protection of their domestic gods, who concerned themselves with the burial and especially with the safety of the departed ones in the grave. There were, however, in many cities special mortuary gods, such as Khenty-Imentiu, "the First of the Westerners" (the dead), who was regularly represented in the form of a jackal. At a very remote time all these divinities receded into the background in favor of Osiris. He was probably a deified king who had once ruled in the Delta city of Busiris and who had met a tragic and untimely death by drowning in the Nile. In the course of time his reputation and then his worship spread throughout Egypt, but the city of Abydos eventually became the chief place in which his cult was celebrated. The saga telling of his life and death became one of the most loved, as it was humanly the most universally comprehensible and appealing of all the stories of the Egyptian gods. Unfortunately, it does not exist in a homogeneous tradition in any native Egyptian text but only in an account recorded by the Greek writer Plutarch. According to his account, Osiris had once ruled as king of Egypt and had showered blessings upon his happy subjects. But he had a wicked brother named Seth, who had designs on his life and the throne. He concocted a conspiracy where by he contrived by trickery in the course of a banquet to have his brother lay himself in an artistically wrought chest. Scarcely had Osiris taken his place in the casket when Seth and his seventy-two confederates sprang upon it, clapped down the lid, and cast it into the Nile, which bore it down to the sea. The waves eventually carried the chest and its contents to the beach near the Phoenician city of Byblos. Meanwhile Isis, the sister and wife of Osiris, wandered throughout the world seeking the body of her husband. After she had located and with some difficulty obtained possession of it, she carried it back to Egypt and mourned the departed Osiris in private. Then she concealed the coffin and departed into the Delta marshes to Buto, where her son Horus was brought up. During her absence Seth, while on a wild-boar hunt, came upon the corpse of his hated brother and, after having in fury divided it into fourteen pieces, scattered the remains throughout the land. The faithful Isis, nevertheless, sought out all the dismembered pieces and buried them wherever she found them, erecting a monument over each one of them. That is the reason why so many different tombs of Osiris were known in Egypt. But after Horus had grown to maturity in the Delta swamps, he came forth to avenge the murder of his father, and a terrible battle ensued in which Horus won the victory. In the end Osiris, through the application of all sorts of magical devices by his pious son, was reawakened to life and henceforth ruled in the west as king of the blessed dead.

The death which according to the legend was suffered by Osiris at the hands of his false brother Seth became the portion of every human being; but, just as Osiris had risen again, so could each man also begin life anew if only the same formulas were spoken and the same ceremonies performed by a faithful son which Osiris' son Horus had once spoken and performed for his father. In this manner the deceased would not only come to Osiris; he was believed actually to become Osiris himself. The entrance to the empire of Osiris depended on magical formulas and spells which must be recited or the knowledge of which must be intrusted to the deceased, in addition to which, however, a virtuous life on earth was likewise regarded as essential to the attainment of eternal life. To that end it was necessary for each individual to appear after death at a judgment in the presence of Osiris and before a court of forty-two judges to declare himself innocent of wrongdoing. Only after this had been accomplished and after the heart of the deceased had been weighed in the balance of righteousness before the god Thoth and found true, was he permitted to enter the world of the hereafter (Figure 3.2).

While the concept of a final judgment reveals at least that the Egyptian possessed lofty ideals of conduct in his daily life, we have but little in formation about the religious thought and practice of the average man. Nevertheless, the meaning of such personal names as Ny-wy-netjer ("I belong to' God"), Mery-Re ("Beloved of Re"), Hor-hotpu ("Horus is merciful"), or Ptah-em-saf ("Ptah is his protection") would indicate that from an early time the Egyptian entertained a sense of intimate contact with his god and believed that the god was not only near to him but interested in his welfare and to some degree like himself. The ancient books of "Teachings for Life" (p. 126) definitely connect the good life as conforming to the will of the god. While the numerous religious hymns are mainly concerned with praise of the god as the lord of heaven and earth, they likewise recognize him as a hearer of prayers who loves and approves of his people. Shortly after 1300 b.c., however, a striking development of personal piety is manifest, and for the first time in Egypt we find the conviction expressed that, even though man is disposed to evil, God is inclined to forgive; while God is bound to punish wrongdoing, his wrath is momentary and his mercy abundant.

Various ideas prevailed concerning the dwelling-place of the blessed dead. For the most part it was thought to be somewhere in the west, in the region of the sunset. It was also believed that the departed were transformed into the shining stars of the sky. Or they lived on in the celestial fields of rushes, where, as formerly on earth, they cultivated the soil, plowed, sowed, and reaped, but where the grain grew to a height of seven cubits (twelve feet). This was truly a wonderful paradise for the Egyptian peasant. But since times changed for the ancient Egyptian also, so that field labor came to be regarded as beneath his dignity, after the Middle Kingdom he caused to be placed in his tomb a series of mummi-form figures provided with farm implements or sacred symbols in order that they might perform his duties for him (Figure 3.6). Upon these ushabtiu was written the name of the deceased together with a magical formula through which they were bought to life and enabled to perform their prescribed duties.

Another doctrine, which originally applied to the king alone, involved an attempt to unify the different conceptions of the hereafter. It was put into writing in the book entitled the "Book of What Is in the Netherworld" and in similar works. According to these texts, there is another earth beneath the familiar earth of men; it is covered by a sky, and through its entire length flows a stream (see p. 65). This netherworld is divided into twelve parts which correspond to the twelve hours of the night and which are separated from one another by great gates. The bark of the sun travels on the stream; in it stands the ram-headed sun-god surrounded like a king by his retinue, as he brings for a brief time light and life to the dark regions through which he fares. This nightly voyage is shared by the deceased, either as the companion of the sun-god or as that god himself, with whom he is thus sometimes identified and with whom he departs from the subterranean world at dawn to continue the journey across the celestial ocean in the bright light of day.

In the earliest times the dead were interred in the natural position of sleep, lying on the left side with knees drawn up against the body and hands before the face. In the Old Kingdom, at first probably in connection with the kings, it became the custom to lay the body in the tomb stretched out at full length. At the same time attempts began to be made to prevent the deterioration of the body by the art of mummification. So successfully was this accomplished that many mummies have preserved in an easily recognizable aspect the features of the deceased (Figure 3.7). In the beginning mummification was, of course, exceedingly simple. The viscera were removed from the body, and the resulting cavity was filled with wads of linen cloth.

Figure 3.6 Ushabtiu (Oriental Institute Museum)

The corpse was then saturated with natron and bound with linen wrappings. At a later period injections of cedar oil were also applied. In the course of time the technique of embalming underwent considerable development. It became the practice to remove the brain from the skull by the use of an iron hook, while resinous pastes were applied to preserve as fully as possible all the contours of the body. As far back as the Old Kingdom the viscera were interred in four vases; these were under the protection of four divinities who were responsible for guarding the deceased against hunger and thirst. In richer burials these vases were placed in chests constructed in the form of a chapel and adorned with appropriate representations of gods and with religious inscriptions (Figure 3.8). The process of mummification lasted no less than seventy days,

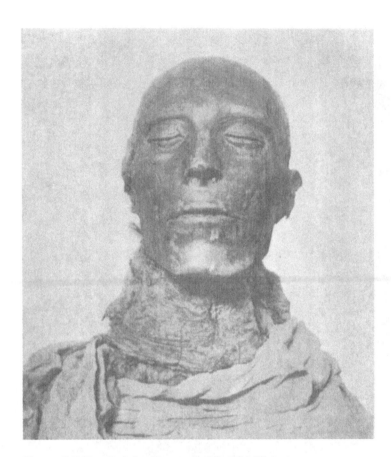

Figure 3.7 Head of the Mummy of Sethi I (Cairo)

after which, all the proper burial ceremonies having been completed, it was laid in the coffin and removed to the tomb (Figure 3.9).

The form of the coffin was altered during the course of the ages. In the Old Kingdom it consisted of a simple rectangular chest of stone or wood. It was a favorite practice to give to it the form of a house with doors in order to symbolize the concept that the coffin was the house of the dead. During the Eighteenth Dynasty it was considered very desirable to construct the coffin in the form of a man or woman arrayed in the costume of the time or in mummiform (Figure 3.10) and to decorate it with all sorts of religious pictures and inscriptions. A single coffin, however, was quite insufficient for wealthy people; they insisted on being buried within the innermost of a nest of three mummiform coffins, all of which were in turn placed within an outermost house like construction, so that the mummy was incased in no less than four different coverings.

Even for the nobles and the most wealthy people the grave in which the body was laid to rest was originally a simple trench excavated into the desert floor at sufficient height to be inaccessible to the water of the Nile inundation. A low mound of earth was heaped over it, before which a small court was laid out to serve as a cult place where offerings might be deposited for the benefit of the dead. It was from this type of grave that the mastaba, as the type of grave employed by the Old Kingdom officials is known to science, was developed. The mastaba consists of a rectangular superstructure built of sun-dried brick

Figure 3.8 Canopic Chest of Tutankhamun (Cairo Museum)

Figure 3.9 Final Rites before the Tomb Door (Thebes, Tomb of Nebamun and Ipuky)

Figure 3.10 Gold Coffin of Tutankhamun (Cairo Museum)

or limestone blocks; in addition, there is a vertical shaft or a stairway leading down to the under-ground burial chamber in which the body is deposited. The cult place lies on the east side of the superstructure; it is a court with a shallow niche, usually in the form of a door, marking the place which was believed to be at the same time the entrance to the tomb and that into the netherworld. A chapel was frequently erected in front of the niche; otherwise a proper cult chamber was constructed in the masonry of the mastaba in such a manner that the "false door" mentioned above was situated in its west wall. As time passed, the inner rooms increased in number as subsidiary chambers were added to the original one. The resulting development was a regular dwelling for the deceased, the walls of which were adorned with inscriptions and richly painted bas-reliefs. The deceased and the members of his family who were buried with him were represented by numerous statues placed in one or more rooms specially provided for the purpose, while figures of male and female servants made of stone or wood were included to care for the recurring needs of their master.

The tomb of the king was in the early period simply an especially large mud-brick mastaba of the type described, but a series of chambers was provided beneath it in order to accommodate his body and those of his retainers, together with all the necessary funerary supplies and equipment. This mastaba eventually developed into the step pyramid and thence into the true pyramid (Figure 4), which from the beginning of the Old Kingdom to the end of the Second Intermediate Period remained the characteristic form of royal tomb.

Section II

Eastern Religions and Enduring Philosophies

The following chapters include articles that discuss Eastern religions and some of the most fascinating philosophies the world has ever seen. In Chapter 4, "Early Civilizations of the Northwest" provides a short overview of the first Indus Valley civilizations; this is limited to information found through archaeological study of the two main cities of the Indus Valley. In Chapter 5, "Goddesses in Vedic Literature" discusses the beginning of Hinduism but specifically addresses the goddesses and their importance in that religion. In Chapter 6, "The Religions of Ancient China" provides a detailed look at Chinese culture and religion. It also discusses matrilineal descent and the symbolism of polarity, which are two important concepts in the history of China. In Chapter 7, "Shinto Religion" presents the Shinto religion, including the concept of Kami and the differences between Confucian and Shinto ideals.

Religion of India

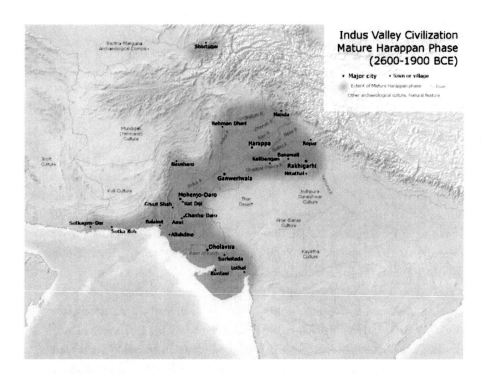

Fig. 4.0a: Copyright © Avantiputra7 (CC BY-SA 3.0) at https://commons.wikimedia.org/wiki/
File%3AIndus_Valley_Civilization%2C_Mature_Phase_(2600-1900_BCE).png

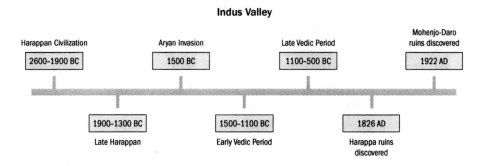

OBJECTIVES:

1. Understand the progression of religion in India, from the Indus Valley civilizations to Hinduism.
2. List other early cities of the Indus Valley discovered after 1958.
3. Explain the evolution of the Indus civilization.
4. Explain what conclusions can be derived about the Indus civilization from evidence found in the great cities.

Early Civilisations of the Northwest

By Hermann Kulke and Dietmar Rothermund

PREHISTORY AND THE INDUS CIVILISATION

When the great cities of Harappa and Mohenjo-Daro were discovered in the 1920s the history of the Indian subcontinent attained a new dimension. The discovery of these centres of the early Indus civilisation was a major achievement of archaeology. Before these centres were known, the Indo-Aryans were regarded as the creators of the first early culture of the subcontinent. They were supposed to have come down to the Indian plains in the second millennium BC. But the great cities of the Indus civilisation proved to be much older, reaching back into the third and fourth millennia. After ancient Egypt and Mesopotamia, this Indus civilisation emerged as the third major early civilisation of mankind.

Harappa and Mohenjo-Daro show a surprising similarity although they were separated by about 350 miles. In each city the archaeologists found an acropolis and a lower city, each fortified separately. The acropolis, situated to the west of each city and raised on an artificial mound made of bricks, contained large assembly halls and edifices which were obviously constructed for religious cults. In Mohenjo-Daro there was a 'Great Bath' (39 by 23 feet, with a depth of 8 feet) at the centre of the acropolis which may have been used for ritual purposes. This bath was connected to an elaborate water supply system and sewers. To the east of this bath there was a big building (about 230 by 78 feet) which is thought to have been a palace either of a king or of a high priest.

A special feature of each of these cities were large platforms which have been interpreted by the excavators as the foundations of granaries. In Mohenjo-Daro it was situated in the acropolis; in Harappa it was immediately adjacent to it. In Mohenjo-Daro this architectural complex, constructed next to the Great Bath, is still particularly impressive. Its foundation, running east to west, was 150 feet long and 75 feet wide. On this foundation were 27 compartments in three rows. The 15-foot walls of these are still extant. These compartments were very well ventilated and, in case they were used as granaries, they could have been filled from outside the acropolis. At Harappa there were some small houses, assumed to be those of workers or slaves, and a large open space between the acropolis and these buildings.

The big lower cities were divided into rectangular areas. In Mohenjo-Daro there were nine such areas, each about 1,200 by 800 feet. Broad main streets, about 30 feet wide, separated these parts of the city from each other. All the houses were connected directly to the excellent sewage system which ran through all the numerous small alleys. Many houses had a spacious interior courtyard and private wells. All houses were built with standardised bricks. The width of each brick was twice as much as its height and its length twice as large as its width.

Figure 4.1 Mohenjo Daro, the so-called 'Priest King', late third millennium BC

(Courtesy of Georg Helmes, Aachen)

But it was not only this excellent city planning which impressed the archaeologists, they also found some interesting sculptures and thousands of well-carved seals made of steatite. These seals show many figures and symbols of the religious life of the people of this early culture. There are tree deities among them and there is the famous so-called 'Proto-Shiva' who is seated in the typical pose of a meditating man. He has three heads, an erect phallus, and is surrounded by animals which were also worshipped by the Hindus of a later age. These seals also show evidence of a script which has not yet been deciphered.

Both cities shared a uniform system of weights and measures based on binary numbers and the decimal system. Articles made of copper and ornaments with precious stones show that there was a flourishing international trade. More evidence for this international trade emerged when seals of the Indus culture were found in Mesopotamia and other seals which could be traced to Mesopotamia were discovered in the cities on the Indus.

Before indigenous sites of earlier stages of the Indus civilisation were excavated it was believed that Harappa and Mohenjo-Daro were merely outposts of the Mesopotamian civilisation, either constructed by migrants or at least designed according to their specifications. These speculations were strengthened by the mention in Mesopotamian sources of countries such as Dilmun, Magan and Meluhha. Dilmun has been identified as Bahrein and Magan seems to be identical with present Oman. Meluhha may have referred to the Indus valley from where Mesopotamia obtained wood, copper, gold, silver, carnelian and cotton.

In analogy to the Mesopotamian precedent, the Indus culture was thought to be based on a theocratic state whose twin capitals Harappa and Mohenjo-Daro obviously showed the traces of a highly centralised

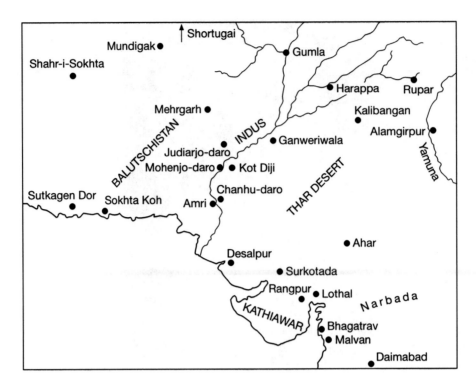

Figure 4.2 Indus civilisation

organisation. Scholars were also fairly sure of the reasons for the sudden decline of these cities since scattered skeletons which showed traces of violent death were found in the uppermost strata of Mohenjo-Daro. It appeared that men, women and children had been exterminated by conquerors in a 'last massacre'. The conquerors were assumed to be the Aryans who invaded India around the middle of the second millennium BC. Their warrior god, Indra, was, after all, praised as a breaker of forts in many Vedic hymns.

However, after the Second World War, intensive archaeological research in Afghanistan, Pakistan and India greatly enhanced our knowledge of the historical evolution and the spatial extension of the Indus civilisation (see Figure 4.2). Earlier assessments of the rise and fall of this civilisation had to be revised. The new excavations showed that this civilisation, at its height early in the late third millennium BC, had encompassed an area larger than western Europe.

In the Indus valley, other important cities of this civilisation, such as Kot Diji to the east of Mohenjo-Daro and Amri in the Dadu District on the lower Indus, were discovered in the years after 1958. In Kathiawar and on the coast of Gujarat similar centres were traced. Thus in 1954 Lothal was excavated south of Ahmadabad. It is claimed that Lothal was a major port of this period. Another 100 miles further south Malwan was also identified in 1967 as a site of the Indus civilisation. It is located close to Surat and so far marks, together with Daimabad in the Ahmadnagar District of Maharashtra, the southernmost extension of this culture. The spread of the Indus civilisation to the east was documented by the 1961 excavations at Kalibangan in Rajasthan about 200 miles west of Delhi. However, Alamgirpur, in Meerut District in the centre of the Ganga–Yamuna Doab, is considered to mark the farthest extension to the east of this culture. In the north, Rupar in the foothills of the Himalayas is the farthest outpost which is known in India. In the west, traces of this civilisation were found in Baluchistan close to the border of present Iran at Sutkagen Dor. This was probably a trading centre on the route connecting the Indus valley with Mesopotamia. Afghanistan also has its share of Indus civilisation sites. This country was known for its lapis lazuli which was coveted everywhere even in those early times. At Mundigak near Kandahar a palace was excavated which has an impressive façade decorated with pillars. This site, probably one of the earliest settlements in the entire region, is thought to be an outpost of the Indus civilisation. Another one was found more recently further to the north at Shortugai on the Amu Darya.

This amazing extension of our knowledge about the spatial spread of the Indus civilisation was accompanied by an equally successful exploration of its history. Earlier strata of Mohenjo-Daro and Harappa as well as of Kalibangan, Amri and Kot Diji were excavated in a second round of archaeological research. In this way continuous sequence of strata, showing the gradual development to the high standard of the full-fledged Indus civilisation, was established. These strata have been named Pre-Harappan, Early Harappan, Mature Harappan and Late Harappan. The most important result of this research is the clear proof of the long-term indigenous evolution of this civilisation which obviously began on the periphery of the Indus valley in the hills of eastern Baluchistan and then extended into the plains. There were certainly connections with Mesopotamia, but the earlier hypothesis that the Indus civilisation was merely an extension of Mesopotamian civilisation had to be rejected.

THE ANATOMY OF FOUR SITES

The various stages of the indigenous evolution of the Indus civilisation can be documented by an analysis of four sites which have been excavated in more recent years: Mehrgarh, Amri, Kalibangan, Lothal. These four sites reflect the sequence of the four important phases in the protohistory of the northwestern region of the Indian subcontinent. The sequence begins with the transition of nomadic herdsmen to settled agriculturists in eastern Baluchistan, continues with the growth of large villages in the Indus valley and the rise of towns, leads to the emergence of the great cities and, finally, ends with their decline. The first stage is exemplified by Mehrgarh in Baluchistan, the second by Amri in the southern Indus valley and the third and fourth by Kalibangan in Rajasthan and by Lothal in Gujarat.

Hindu Religion

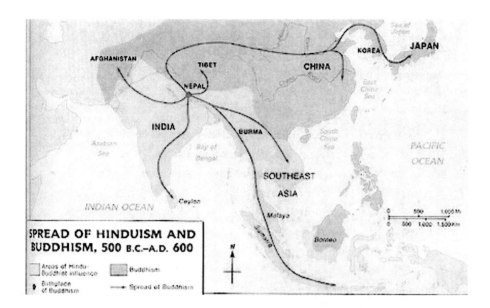

Fig. 5.0: Copyright © (CC BY-SA 3.0) at https://apworldhistorywiki.wikispaces.com/Cross+Cultural+Exchanges+and+the+Silk+Road+2.

OBJECTIVES:

1. Identify the source of Hinduism.
2. Identify four deities and their functions in Hindu religion.

Goddesses in Vedic Literature

By David Kinsley

The Hindu tradition affirms Vedic literature as the foundation, the sacred source, of Hinduism. This body of literature, which is exceedingly vast and varied, is held to be eternal and alone is classed as *śruti,* "that which is heard," or revelation.[1] It is therefore important to survey this literature even though goddesses do not play a central role in the religion that is central to these texts. Another important reason for looking at Vedic literature is that some scholars have argued that the great goddesses of later Hinduism are in fact the same beings mentioned in the *Vedas,* only with new names.[2]

The *Ṛg-veda,* the oldest and most important Vedic text for a study of goddesses, is a collection of mantras, or hymns, celebrating deities, divine presences, or powers. The hymns were sung by *ṛṣis,* great sages who the Hindu tradition affirms did not compose the hymns but heard them directly and then transmitted them, probably in a cultic, sacrificial context. The beings who are celebrated in the hymns of the *ṛṣis* are numerous and diverse. The Ṛg-vedic pantheon, moreover, seems highly unstructured, and it is difficult to reconstruct a coherent Indo-Aryan mythology on the basis of the *Ṛg-veda,* which is primarily interested not in describing the mythological deeds of the deities but in praising the gods in a ritual context—a ritual context that unfortunately is also difficult to deduce in any detail.

It is clear nevertheless, that a few deities dominated Ṛg-vedic religion. Agni, Soma, and Indra, all male deities, are praised repeatedly throughout the *Ṛg-veda* and are the most important gods if frequency of occurrence in the hymns is any measure of their significance. Such gods as Varuna, Mitra, Surya, Bṛhaspati, Viśvakarman, and Tvaṣṭṛ are also fairly significant male powers. Although many goddesses are mentioned in the *Ṛg-veda,* none is as central to the Ṛg-vedic vision of reality as Agni, Soma, or Indra, and only Uṣas among the goddesses could be considered on a par with the male deities of the second rank. We should therefore keep in mind while studying the goddesses in the *Ṛg-veda* that although there are many female deities they do not, either individually or collectively, represent the "center" of Ṛg-vedic religion. In most cases they are mentioned infrequently and must have played minor roles compared to the great male gods of the *Ṛg-veda.*

---

1   Sometimes the idea of *śruti* is narrowed to mean primarily the *Upaniṣads.* The idea of *śruti* often also includes the *Bhāgavad-gītā,* which is much later than most Vedic literature.
2   For example, Sukumari Bhattacharji, *The Indian Theogony* (Cambridge: Cambridge University Press, 1970), pp. 160–161; Stella Kramrisch, "The Indian Great Goddess," *History of Religions* 14, no. 4 (May 1975): 235–265.

USAS

In the *Ṛg-veda* the goddess Uṣas is consistently associated with and often identified with the dawn. She reveals herself in the daily coming of light to the world. A young maiden, drawn in a hundred chariots (1.48), she brings forth light and is followed by the sun (Surya), who urges her onward (3.61). She is praised for driving away, or is petitioned to drive away, the oppressive darkness (7.78; 6.64; 10.172). She is asked to chase away evil demons, to send them far away (8.47.13). As the dawn, she is said to rouse all life, to set all things in motion, and to send people off to do their duties (1.48, 92). She sets the curled-up sleepers on their way to offer their sacrifices and thus renders service to the other gods (1.113). Uṣas gives strength and fame (1.44). She is that which impels life and is associated with the breath and life of all living creatures (1.48). She is associated with or moves with *ṛta,* cosmic, social, and moral order (3.61; 7.75). As the regularly recurring dawn she reveals and participates in cosmic order and is the foe of chaotic forces that threaten the world (1.113.12).

Uṣas is generally an auspicious goddess associated with light (6.64) and wealth. She is often likened to a cow. In *Ṛg-veda* 1.92 she is called the mother of cows and, like a cow that yields its udder for the benefit of people, so Uṣas bares her breasts to bring light for the benefit of human kind (3.58; 4.5). Although Uṣas is usually described as a young and beautiful maiden, she is also called the mother of the gods (1.113.12) and the Aśvins (3.39.3), a mother by her petitioners (7.81), she who tends all things like a good matron (1.48), and goddess of the hearth (6.64).

Uṣas observes all that people do, especially as she is associated with the light that uncovers everything from darkness and with *ṛta,* moral as well as cosmic order. She is said to be the eye of the gods (7.75). She is known as she who sees all, but she is rarely invoked to forgive human transgressions. It is more typical to invoke her to drive away or punish one's enemies. Finally, Uṣas is known as the goddess, reality, or presence that wears away youth (7.75). She is described as a skilled huntress who wastes away the lives of people (1.92). In accordance with the ways of *ṛta,* she wakes all living things but does not disturb the person who sleeps in death. As the recurring dawn, Uṣas is not only celebrated for bringing light from darkness. She is also petitioned to grant long life, as she is a constant reminder of people's limited time on earth (7.77). She is the mistress or marker of time.

PṚTHIVĪ

The goddess Pṛthivī is nearly always associated with the earth, the terrestrial sphere where human beings live. In the *Ṛg-veda,* furthermore, she is almost always coupled with Dyaus, the male deity associated with the sky. So interdependent are these two deities in the *Ṛg-veda* that Pṛthivī is rarely addressed alone but almost always as part of the dual compound *dyāvāpṛthivī,* sky-earth. Together they are said to kiss the center of the world (1.185.5). They sanctify each other in their complementary relationship (4.56.6). Together they are said to be the universal parents who created the world (1.159) and the gods (1.185). As might be expected, Dyaus is often called father and Pṛthivī mother. There is the implication that once upon a time the two were closely joined but were subsequently parted at Varuna's decree (6.70). They come together again when Dyaus fertilizes the earth (Pṛthivī) with rain, although in some cases it is said that together they provide abundant rain (4.56); it is not clear to what extent Pṛthivī should be exclusively associated with the earth alone and not the sky as well.

In addition to her maternal, productive characteristics Pṛthivī (usually along with Dyaus in the *Ṛg-veda*) is praised for her supportive nature. She is frequently called firm, she who upholds and supports all things (1.185). She encompasses all things (6.70), is broad and wide (1.185), and is motionless (1.185), although elsewhere she is said to move freely (5.84). Pṛthivī, with Dyaus, is often petitioned for wealth, riches, and power (6.70), and the waters they produce together are described as fat, full, nourishing, and fertile (1.22). They are also petitioned to protect people from danger, to expiate sin (1.185), and to bring happiness (10.63). Together they represent a wide, firm realm of abundance and safety, a realm pervaded by order (*ṛta*), which they strengthen and nourish (1.159). They are unwasting, inexhaustible, and rich in germs (6.70). In a funeral hymn the dead one is asked to go now to the lap of his mother earth, Pṛthivī, who is described as gracious and kind. She is asked not to press down too heavily upon the dead person but to cover him gently, as a mother covers her child with her skirt (10.18.10–12).

The most extended hymn in praise of Pṛthivī in Vedic literature is found in the *Atharva-veda* (12.1). The hymn is dedicated to Pṛthivī alone, and no mention is made of Dyaus. The mighty god Indra is her consort (1.6) and protects her from all danger (12.1.11, 18). Visnu strides over her (12.1.10), and Parjanya, Prajāpati, and Viśvakarma all either protect her, provide for her, or are her consort. Agni is said to pervade her (12.1.19). Despite these associations with male deities, however, the hymn makes clear that Pṛthivī is a great deity in her own right. The hymn repeatedly emphasizes Pṛthivī's fertility. She is the source of all plants, especially crops, and also nourishes all creatures that live upon her. She is described as patient and strong (12.1.29), supporting the wicked and the good, the demons and the gods. She is frequently addressed as mother and is asked to pour forth milk as a mother does for a son. She is called a nurse to all living things (12.1.4), and her breasts are full of nectar. The singer of the hymn asks Pṛthivī to produce her breasts to him so that he might enjoy a long life. Pṛthivī is also said to manifest herself in the scent of women and men, to be the luck and light in men, and to be the splendid energy of maids (12.1.25).

In sum, Pṛthivī is a stable, fertile, benign presence in Vedic literature. She is addressed as a mother, and it is clear that those who praise her see her as a warm, nursing goddess who provides sustenance to all those who move upon her firm, broad expanse. The *Ṛg-veda* nearly always links her with the male god Dyaus, but in the *Atharva-veda* and later Vedic literature she emerges as an independent being.

ADITI

Although the goddess Aditi is mentioned nearly eighty times in the *Ṛg-veda*, it is difficult to gain a clear picture of her nature. She is usually mentioned along with other gods or goddesses, there is no one hymn addressed exclusively to her, and unlike many other Vedic deities she is not obviously associated with some natural phenomenon. Compared to Uṣas and Pṛthivī, her character seems ill defined. She is virtually featureless physically.

Perhaps the most outstanding attribute of Aditi is her motherhood. She is preeminently the mother of the Ādityas, a group of seven or eight gods which includes Mitra, Aryaman, Bhaga, Varuna, Dakṣa, and Aṁśa (2.27.1). Aditi is also said to be the mother of the great god Indra, the mother of kings (2.27), and the mother of the gods (1.113.19). Unlike Prthivī, however, whose motherhood is also central to her nature, Aditi does not have a male consort in the *Rg-veda.*

As a mothering presence, Aditi is often asked to guard the one who petitions her (1.106.7; 8.18.6) or to provide him or her with wealth, safety, and abundance (10.100; 1.94.15). Appropriate to her role as a mother, Aditi is sometimes associated with or identified as a cow. As a cow she provides nourishment, and as the cosmic cow her milk is identified with the redemptive, invigorating drink *soma* (1.153.3).

The name Aditi is derived from the root *dā* (to bind or fetter) and suggests another aspect of her character. As *a-diti,* she is the *un*bound, free one, and it is evident in the hymns to her that she is often called upon to free the petitioner from different hindrances, especially sin and sickness (2.27.14). In one hymn she is asked to free a petitioner who is tied up like a thief (8.67.14). In this role as the one who binds and loosens Aditi is similar in function to Varuna, who in fact is one of her sons. Aditi thus plays the role of guardian of *rta,* the cosmic-moral order. As such she is called a supporter of creatures (1.136). She supports creatures by providing or enforcing *rta,* those ordinances or rhythms that delineate order from chaos.

Aditi is also called widely expanded (5.46.6) and extensive, the mistress of wide stalls (8.67.12), and in this respect one is reminded of Prthivī. In fact, Aditi and Prthivī become virtually identified in the *Brāhmaṇas.*[3]

SARASVATĪ

The close association between natural phenomena and such Vedic goddesses as Uṣas and Prthivī is also seen in the goddess Sarasvatī, who is associated with a particular river. Although scholars have debated precisely which river she was identified with in Vedic times (the Sarasvatī River of that period has since disappeared), in the *Rg-veda* her most important characteristics are those of a particular mighty river. Indeed, at times it is not clear whether a goddess or a river is being praised; many references hail the Sarasvatī River as a mighty goddess.

Sarasvatī is called mighty and powerful. Her waves are said to break down mountains, and her flood waters are described as roaring (6.61.2, 8). She is said to surpass all waters in greatness, to be ever active, and to be great among the great. She is said to be inexhaustible, having her source in the celestial ocean (7.95.1-2; 5.43.11). She is clearly no mere river but a heaven-sent stream that blesses the earth. Indeed, she is said to pervade the triple creation of earth, atmosphere, and the celestial regions (6.61.11–12).

She is praised for the fertility she brings the earth. She is praised or petitioned for wealth, vitality, children, nourishment, and immortality, and as such she is called *subhaga* (bountiful). As a fecund, bountiful presence, she is called mother, the best of mothers (2.41.16). As a nourishing, maternal goddess, she is described in terms similar to Prthivī: she quickens life, is the source of vigor and strength, and provides good luck and material well-being to those whom she blesses. In one particular hymn she is called upon by unmarried men who yearn for sons. They ask to enjoy her breast that is swollen with streams and to receive from her food and progeny (7.96.4-6; 1.164.49). She is sometimes petitioned for protection and in this aspect is called a sheltering tree (7.95.5) and an iron fort (7.95.1), neither image being particularly fluvial.

---

3   For example, *Śatapatha-brāhmaṇa* 2.2.1.19; 3.2.3.6, 19; 4.5.1.2; *Aitareya-brāhmaṇa* 1.8.

Sarasvatī is also closely related to Vedic cult, both as a participant in or witness of the cult and as a guardian of the cult. She is invoked with and associated with the sacrificial goddesses Idā and Bhāratī and with the goddesses Mahī and Hotrā, who are associated with prayer (7.37.11; 10.65.13). She is said to destroy those who revile the gods and to be a slayer of Vṛtra, a demon of chaos.

Sarasvatī is described particularly as a purifying presence (1.3.10). Her waters cleanse poison from men (6.61.3). Along with rivers and floods in general, she cleanses her petitioners with holy oil and bears away defilements (10.17.10)

Anticipating her later nature as a goddess of inspiration, eloquence, and learning, the hymns of the *Ṛg-veda* also describe Sarasvatī as the in citer of all pleasant songs, all gracious thought, and every pious thought (1.3.10–12). In this vein she is similar to the Vedic goddess Vāc (speech), with whom she is consistently identified in the *Brāhmaṇas.*[4]

VĀC

Although the significance of sound and speech as the primordial stuff of creation is primarily a post-Ṛg-vedic concept, it is apparent even in the *Ṛg-veda* that sound, and especially ritual speech, is powerful, creative, and a mainstay of cosmic-ritual order. The goddess Vāc, whose name means "speech," reveals herself through speech and is typically characterized by the various attributes and uses of speech. She is speech, and the mysteries and miracles of speech express her peculiar, numinous nature. She is the presence that inspires the *ṛsis* and that makes a person a Brahman (10.125). She is truth, and she inspires truth by sustaining Soma, the personification of the exhilarating drink of vision and immortality (10.125). She is the mysterious presence that enables one to hear, see, grasp, and then express in words the true nature of things. She is the prompter of and the vehicle of expression for visionary perception, and as such she is intimately associated with the *ṛsis* and the rituals that express or capture the truths of their visions. In an important sense she is an essential part of the religious-poetic visionary experience of the *ṛsis* and of the sacrificial rituals that appropriate those visions.

Perhaps reflecting her role as the bestower of vision, Vāc is called a heavenly queen, the queen of the gods (8.89), she who streams with sweetness (5.73.3) and bestows vital powers (3.53.15). She is described as a courtly, elegant woman, bright and adorned with gold (1.167.3). She is, like most other Vedic goddesses, a benign, bounteous being. She not only bestows on people the special riches of language, she is praised in general terms for giving light and strength; one hymn says that she alone provides people with food. She is, then, more than a kind of artificial construct, a personified abstract. She is a pervasive, nourishing deity who stimulates organic growth as well as providing the blessings of language and vision. She is often invoked as a heavenly cow (4.1.16; 8.89) that gives sustenance to the gods and men. She is also called mother, as it is she who has given birth to things through naming them. Her benign nature is also celebrated for enabling people to see and recognize friends. Bearing her mark of intelligible, familiar speech, one friend may recognize and commune with another (10.71). Thus Vāc is a bounteous cow who provides, first, the

---

4 For example, *Śatapatha-brāhmaṇa* 14.2.1.12; *Aitareya-brāmaṇa* 6.7; *Kauṣitaki-brāhmaṇa* 5.1; 10.6; 12.2, 8; 14.5.

lofty, discerning vision of the *ṛsi;* second, the ritual formulas of the priest; and third, the everyday language of people which enables them to establish themselves as a community of friends.

Vāc's character is richly developed in the *Brāhmaṇas* in a series of myths and images that associate her with creation and ritual. Vāc's indispensability in ritual and cult (in which spoken or chanted mantras are essential) is emphasized in myths that tell of how the gods stole her or seduced her away from the demons after the creation of the world and, having obtained her, instituted sacrificial rituals that sustain the creation and produce bounty, life, and immortality for the gods.[5] Without her the divine rituals would not have been possible. In her role as creator, Vāc is said to create the three *Vedas,*[6] and the three *Vedas* are in turn equated with the earth (*Ṛg-veda*), the air (*Yajur-veda*), and the sky (*Sama-veda*).[7] At another place she is said to have entered into the sap of plants and trees, thus pervading and enlivening all vegetation.[8] Prajāpati, the central deity in the *Brāhmaṇas,* is described as initiating creation by impregnating himself by comingling his mind and his speech.[9] Elsewhere it is said that Vāc, having been created by Prajāpati's mind, wished to become manifest, to multiply herself, to extend herself, and so it was that creation proceeded, impelled by Vāc's urge to create.[10]

Vāc plays a significant role in Vedic literature, not only in terms of being mentioned often but also from a theoretical point of view. Theologically it is suggested that she is coeternal with Prajāpati. Although the *Brāhmaṇas* are not consistent, sometimes stating that Vāc is created by Prajāpati, she does seem to have a theologically exalted position in these texts. There are also hints that it is through Vāc, or in pairing with her, that Prajāpati creates. This is different from the role of *śakti* in later Hindu philosophic schools, in which the male counterpart of *śakti* tends to be inactive. Prajāpati toils and desires the creation. Nevertheless, her role in the *Brāhmaṇas* is suggestive of the nature of *śakti* in later Hinduism. Her role vis-à-vis Prajāpati is also suggestive of the theory of *śabda-brahman* (the absolute in the form of sound) and the *sphoṭa* theory of creation (in which the world is created through sound).

NIRṚTI

The Vedic goddesses we have looked at so far are generally benign, protective deities to whom the hymnist typically appeals for wealth, strength, and general well-being. The goddess Nirṛti has no such benign qualities. She is not mentioned very often in the *Ṛg-veda,* but when she is, the concern of the hymn is to seek protection from her or to ask that she be driven away. The scattered references to her seem to equate her with death, ill luck, and destruction. There is just one hymn in the *Ṛg-veda,* 10.59, in which she is mentioned several times, but that hymn sums up very well Nirṛti's nature. After four verses in which renewed life, wealth, food, glorious deeds, youth, and continued long life are requested from the gods, the following refrain is invoked: "Let Nirṛti depart to distant places." Decay, need, anger, cowardice, old age, and death:

5 *Śatapatha-brāhmaṇa* 3.2.1.18–3.2.3.30.
6 Ibid. 5.5.5.12.
7 Ibid. 4.6.7.1–3.
8 Ibid. 4.6.9.16.
9 Ibid. 6.1.2.5–11.
10 Ibid. 10.5.3.4–12.

these are the ways in which Nirṛti manifests herself. She thus represents a dark side to the Vedic vision of the divine feminine.

Later Vedic literature describes Nirṛti in far more detail and mentions her more frequently than does the Ṛg-veda. Appropriately, she is said to be dark, to dress in dark clothes, and to receive dark husks for her share of the sacrifice,[11] although once she is said to have golden locks.[12] She lives in the South, the direction of the kingdom of the dead,[13] is associated with pain,[14] and is repeatedly given offerings with the specific intention of keeping her away from the sacrificial rituals and from the affairs of people in general.

RĀTRĪ

The goddess Rātrī is almost always associated with the night. Indeed, she is the night, and as such she is the presence or power that is petitioned by people for comfort and security in the dark hours before the triumphant return of the dawn. Her physical appearance is rarely mentioned, although she is sometimes described as a beautiful maiden along with her sister, Uṣas, the dawn. She is called glorious and immortal and is praised for providing light in the darkness, bedecked as she is with countless stars. Generally she is pictured as a benign being. She is lauded for giving rest to all creatures.[15] She is praised for bestowing life-sustaining dew[16] and with Uṣas is said to provide and strengthen vital powers.[17] She is especially invoked to protect people from dangers peculiar to the night. Thus, she is petitioned to keep wolves away, to protect against thieves,[18] and to protect people from any creature that might do them harm in the night.[19]

Despite Rātrī's usually benign nature, some texts refer to her in negative terms or associate her with things inimical to people, in the Ṛg-veda she is chased away by Agni, the god of fire (10.3.1), and also by Uṣas (1.92.11). Rātrī is called barren (1.122.2) and gloomy (10.172.4) in comparison with her bright and bounteous sister, Uṣas. Occasionally she is associated with the very creatures or dangers of the night from which she is elsewhere asked to protect people.[20] Rātrī, then, is not only the guardian of the night, the protectress of people during the dark hours of their rest, but the night itself and those things, both benign and hostile, which inhabit the night.

The majority of references to Rātrī in the Ṛg-veda link her with Uṣas, who is said to be her sister. Usually they are said to be two lovely maidens, sometimes twins. Together they are called powerful mothers (1.142.7) and strengtheners of vital power (5.5.6). They are also called weavers of time and mothers of eternal law. In their alternating, cyclical, and endless appearances, they represent the stable, rhythmic patterns of the cosmos in which light and dark inevitably follow each other in an orderly, predictable manner. Together

---

11 *Taittirīya-brāhmaṇa* 1.6.1.4.
12 *Atharva-veda* 5.7.9.
13 *Śatapatha-brāhmaṇa* 5.2.3.3.
14 Ibid. 9.1.2.9.
15 *Ṛg-veda* 1.34.1; *Atharva-veda* 19.47.2.
16 *Atharva-veda* 19.48.6.
17 *Ṛg-veda* 5.5.6.
18 Ibid. 10.127.6.
19 *Atharva-veda* 19.48.3.
20 Ibid. 19.49.4

they illustrate the coherence of the created order: the ordered alternations of vigor and rest, light and dark, and the regular flow of time.

MINOR VEDIC GODDESSES

Several goddesses known to the Ṛg-veda are mentioned so infrequently that it is difficult to perceive what their distinctive natures might have been. Some of these minor goddesses seem to be synonymous with abundance. Puraṁdhi, Pārendi, Rākā, and Dhiṣaṇā, none of whom is mentioned more than about a dozen times in the Ṛg-veda, are all associated with bounty and riches. As is the case with most Vedic goddesses, their natures appear to be benign and their presences revealed through material well-being. Sinivālī is also a benign goddess but is specifically associated with progeny. She is described as mistress of the family, broad-hipped, and prolific. When she is invoked it is to grant the petitioner offspring (2.32; 10.184).

Another group of minor goddesses seems to be associated primarily with the sacrificial cult of the Ṛg-veda. When Ila, Bhāratī, Mahī, and Hotrā are mentioned, they are almost always being summoned to take their place on the sacrificial grass prior to a ritual. They are also almost invariably grouped with Sarasvatī. Iḷa (Iḍa in the *Brāhmaṇas)* seems to be associated with the sacrificial offering itself, specifically the cow from which many sacrificial objects were taken. She is called butter-handed and butter-footed, which is reminiscent of Agni's description as the presence or deity who actually takes the sacrifice and transmits it to the other gods. While it may be the case that these goddesses are some type of personification of certain aspects of the sacrificial ritual, they are mentioned so seldom, and almost always along with a list of many other deities, that such a conclusion seems only a guess, with the possible exception of Iḷa (Iḍa). Why these goddesses happen to be invoked with Sarasvatī is also not clear. There is no indication that they are associated with rivers, and Sarasvatī is not a particularly important goddess in the sacrificial ritual itself.

The most interesting references in the Ṛg-veda to the goddess Sūryā, the daughter of the sun god Surya (sometimes Savitṛ), concern her wedding. All the gods desire her, but her father wishes to give her to Soma; however, it is settled that the first to reach the sun will wed her. The twin gods, the Aśvins, win the race and the bride, and although Sūryā is said to be given to the god Pusan (6.58.4) and to be wooed by Soma (10.85.9), the other references to her in the Ṛg-veda almost always describe her as riding in the chariot of her twin husbands, the Aśvins, who after winning her are said to have attained all that they desired (8.8.10). Although it may be implied that Sūryā is fair and desirable, there is actually little description of her beyond the rather obscure picture of her in the Ṛg-veda (10.85) in which she seems to be likened to the sacrifice and is said to pervade the cosmos. Her husband in this hymn is Soma; the hymn may be describing the interdependence of Soma and the sacrifice (personified as Sūryā) in the metaphor of a marriage. The Aśvins in this hymn are the groomsmen of her father, which is unusual.

References to Dānu, Saraṇyū, and Sarama are so infrequent and so lacking in description that it is difficult to even speculate on what their distinctive natures might have been. Dānu is identified as the mother of the cosmic demon Vṛtra, who is defeated by the god Indra. She is compared to a cow (1.32.9), although her son, who is described as without hands and feet, is more reptilian in appearance. The word *dānu* is used elsewhere in reference to the waters of heaven; it may be that Dānu was associated with the formless, primordial waters that existed prior to creation, the waters in which Vṛtra hid and which he withheld from creation until they were freed by Indra's mighty deed.

Saraṇyū is the daughter of Tvaṣṭṛ and the sister of Viśvarūpa. She is said to marry the god Vivasvat (10.17.1) and to give birth to twins, Yama and Yamī (the progenitors of the human race). It has been suggested that her nature is essentially impetuous, for her name means "quick, speedy, nimble,"[21] but there are no references to this aspect of her nature in the *Ṛg-veda*. Saramā, whose name has a similar meaning, "the fleet one," is in later literature known as the mother of dogs, a heavenly bitch. But there is no indication of this aspect in the *Ṛg-veda*. In the *Ṛg-veda* her only significant action is to seek out the thieving Paṇis, who have stolen cows, and to act as Indra's messenger to the Paṇis in negotiating the return of the cows. Perhaps her ability to track and cross rivers hints at her later canine nature.

One hymn of the *Ṛg-veda* (10.146) refers to a goddess of the forest, Araṇyānī. From this one hymn we get a rather clear picture of the goddess. She is an elusive figure who vanishes from sight and avoids villages. She is more often heard than seen. She speaks through the sounds of the forest, or one may even hear her tinkling bells. She seems to make her presence known especially at evening, and those who spend the night in the forest sometimes think they hear her scream. She never kills unless provoked by some murderous enemy. She is sweetly scented, is mother of all forest things, and provides plenty of food without tilling.

This goddess is interesting for two reasons. First, she hints at an archaic type of goddess known as the mistress of animals, although there is no specific reference to her guarding animals or providing them for human hunters. Second, she sounds very much like the Yakṣīs of the later Indian tradition, those female beings who dwell in the forest, are worshiped away from the village, and who have, despite their generally benign qualities, certain uncanny characteristics. This late hymn of the *Ṛg-veda* may well be an early literary reference to a Yakṣī or to a goddess modeled on those indigenous creatures of the Indian forests.

Several important Vedic gods are said to have wives or consorts. None of these goddesses is mentioned very often in Vedic literature, but it is important to note their existence in light of subsequent Hindu mythology, in which many of the most important goddesses are consorts of well-known Hindu gods, and also in light of the later Hindu concept of *śakti*. The names of these early goddesses are usually formed simply by the addition of a feminine suffix to the god's name: for example, Indrāṇī, Varunāṇī, Agnāyī, and in later Vedic literature Rudrāṇī (the wife of Rudra). With the exception of Indrāṇī, these goddesses have no independent character of their own. They are mentioned so infrequently and are so lacking in descriptive detail that they appear to be mere minor appendages to their husbands, who are powerful beings in the Vedic pantheon. Indrāṇī is mentioned far more often than any other goddess of this type, but even so it is clear that she is greatly over shadowed by her husband, Indra. She is described as beautiful, and one hymn of the *Ṛg-veda* pictures her as jealous of rivals (10.86). She is also called by the name Śacī, which denotes power and suggests the later idea of *śakti,* the feminine, personified might of the gods of later Hindu mythology. Indeed, in another hymn (10.159) Indrāṇī-Śacī boasts of having won her husband by conquering him and brags that he is sub missive to her will. In the same hymn, however, she goes on to petition the gods to rid her of rivals for Indra's favor, and elsewhere she is said to stay at home (3.53.6). Despite suggestions of the later *śakti* idea, then, Indrāṇī is actually a minor goddess of little power, despite her boasts to the contrary.

---

21 Kramrisch, "The Indian Great Goddess," pp. 236–239.

CONCLUSION

Several conclusions concerning goddesses in Vedic literature are clear. First, none of them rivals the great male gods in these texts. Indeed, Uṣas, the most popular goddess (in terms of the number of times she is mentioned and the number of hymns addressed specifically to her), is only a deity of the third rank. In short, male deities dominate the Vedic vision of the divine.

Second, there is evidence that some of the Vedic goddesses survive in the later Hindu tradition. Pṛthivī persists in later Hinduism and becomes associated with the god Viṣṇu. She is often called Bhūdevī (the goddess of the earth) and appears in myths primarily in the role of supplicant to the gods because of the burden of having to sustain a notoriously evil demon. Sarasvatī also continues to be known in the later tradition and becomes popular primarily as a goddess of learning, wisdom, and culture. Although the goddess Vāc disappears, in later Hinduism Sarasvatī might be said to express Vāc's primary meaning as inspired speech, and the idea of the creation of the world through sound probably finds inspiration in the ideas about Vāc in Vedic literature. Similarly, the idea of *śakti*, though it is not developed in Vedic literature, is suggested in the various consorts of the male deities, especially in Śacī (Indrāṇī). Many of the Vedic goddesses, however, simply disappear in the later Hindu tradition. Uṣas and Aditi, for example, are rarely found in later texts.

Third, many of the most important goddesses of the later tradition are not found at all in Vedic literature or are simply mentioned by name in passing. Such important goddesses as Pārvatī, Durgā, Kālī, Rādhā, and Sītā are unknown in early Vedic literature. Śrī, though she appears in later Vedic literature, is not fully developed and does not occupy the central role that she does in the later tradition. Furthermore, none of the Vedic goddesses is clearly associated with battle or blood sacrifice, both of which are important associations in the myths and cults of several later Hindu goddesses.

Fourth, there is no one great goddess in the Vedic literature. Although some scholars have affirmed her existence in this literature,[22] she quite simply is nowhere mentioned. There is no evidence that the authors of the Vedic texts supposed that all the individual goddesses are manifestations of one great goddess. Since the Vedic texts do not assume a great god who manifests himself in individual gods, I fail to under stand why such an assumption should be made for the female deities. It is as if the sexual identification of the goddesses is so overwhelmingly significant that one is justified in lumping them all together. But clearly the goddesses vary greatly and are as distinct from one another as the male gods are from one another.[23] The Mahādevī (great goddess) does not appear until the medieval period in Hinduism, and she is the product of a carefully articulated theology. Although some goddesses *are* conflated with one another at certain times and places and in certain texts, even in Vedic literature,[24] this does not justify imposing on such examples a much later, systematic *śākta* theology.

---

22 J. Przyluski, "The Great Goddess of India and Iran," *Indian Historical Quarterly* 10 (1934): 405–430; Kramrisch, "The Indian Great Goddess," pp. 235–265.

23 In Vedic literature some gods are frequently identified or associated with each other. We have noted above, for example, that Pṛthivī and Dyaus, Vāc and Sarasvatī, and Pṛthivī and Aditi are often identified or associated with each other. These identifications, however, are selective and consistent and should not lead us to suppose that the authors of Vedic literature presupposed that all deities were manifestations of one great god or one great goddess. While a very strong and articulate monistic position arises in Upaniṣadic literature, there are only hints of this position in earlier Vedic texts.

24 In the *Brāhmaṇas* Pṛthivī is identified with Aditi, and Sarasvatī is some-times identified with Vāc.

Chinese Religion and Confucianism

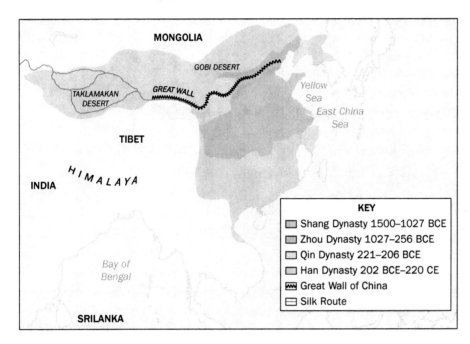

OBJECTIVES:

1. Identify the earliest Chinese culture.
2. Identify the three ideas/beliefs found in the religious documents of the Yang Shao culture.
3. Define matrilineal descent.
4. Identify the characteristics of the Shang period in China.
5. Explain the symbolism of polarity.

The Religions of Ancient China

By Mircea Eliade, translated By Willard R. Trask

RELIGIOUS BELIEFS IN THE NEOLITHIC PERIOD

For the historian of culture as well as for the historian of religions, China represents an unusually advantageous field of research. The earliest Chinese archeological documents, for example, go back to the sixth and fifth millenniums, and in at least some cases it is possible to follow the continuity of the different prehistoric cultures and even to define their contribution to the forming of classical Chinese civilization. For, just as the Chinese people arises from many and various ethnic combinations, its culture constitutes a complex and original synthesis in which the contributions of several sources can nevertheless be discovered.

The earliest Neolithic culture is that of Yang Shao, so termed from the name of the village in which vessels of painted clay were discovered in 1921. A second Neolithic culture, characterized by a black pottery, was discovered near Lung Shan in 1928. But it was not until after 1950 that, as a result of the numerous excavations made during the preceding thirty years, it became possible to classify all the phases and the general outlines of the Chinese Neolithic cultures. By the help of radiocarbon dating, the chronology was substantially modified. At Pan Po (in Shensi Province) the earliest site belonging to the Yang Shao culture was brought to light; radiocarbon dating indicates ca. 4115 or ca. 4365. In the fifth millennium the site was occupied for 600 years. But Pan Po does not represent the earliest stage of the Yang Shao culture.[1] According to Ping-ti Ho, the author of the latest syn thetic study of Chinese prehistory, the agriculture practiced in the sixth millennium was a local discovery, as were the domestication of certain animals, ceramics, and the metallurgy of bronze.[2] Yet, only recently, the development of the Chinese Neolithic cultures and Bronze Age was explained by a dissemination of agriculture and metallurgy from several centers in the ancient Near East. It is not our part to take sides in this controversy. It seems indubitable that certain techniques were invented or radically modified in China. It is no less probable that protohistorical China received numerous cultural elements of Western origin, disseminated across Siberia and the Central Asian steppes.

The archeological documents can give us information about certain religious beliefs, but it would be wrong to conclude that those beliefs represent all the religious beliefs of the prehistorical populations. Their mythology and theology, the structure and morphology of their rituals, can scarcely be made out solely on the basis of the archeological finds. Thus, for example, the religious documents revealed by the discovery of the Neolithic Yang Shao culture refer almost entirely to ideas and beliefs connected with sacred space, fertility, and death. In the villages the communal building is placed at the center of the site, surrounded by

---

1   Ping-ti Ho, *The Cradle of the East*, pp. 16 ff.
2   Ibid., pp. 43 ff., 91 ff., 121 ff., 177 ff.

small houses half underground. Not only the orientation of the village but the structure of the house, with its central mud pit and its smokehole, indicates a cosmology shared by many Neolithic and traditional societies (cf. §12). Belief in the survival of the soul is illustrated by the utensils and foodstuffs placed in the graves. Children were buried, close to the houses, in large urns having an opening at the top to permit the soul to go out and return.[3] In other words, the funerary urn was the dead person's "house," an idea that found ample expression in the cult of ancestors in the Bronze Age (the Shang period).

Certain clay vessels, painted red and decorated with the so-called death pattern, are especially interesting.[4] Three iconographic motifs—triangle, chessboard, and cowrie—are found only on funerary vessels. But these motifs are bound up with a rather complex symbolism that associates the ideas of sexual union, birth, regeneration, and rebirth. It may be supposed that this decoration indicates the hope of survival and of a rebirth in the other world.

A design figuring two fishes and two anthropomorphic figures probably represents a supernatural being or a "specialist in the sacred," a sorcerer or priest.[5] But its interpretation is still doubtful. The fishes certainly have a symbolism that is at once sexual and connected with the calendar (the fishing season corresponds to a particular period of the yearly cycle). The distribution of the four figures may suggest a cosmological image.

According to Ping-ti Ho (pp. 275 ff.), the societies of the Yang Shao period obeyed the laws of matrilineal descent. In contrast, the following period, that of Lung Shan, indicates passage to a patrilineal society, characterized by the predominance of the ancestor cult. Following other scholars, Ho interprets certain stone objects and their reproductions on painted vases as phallic symbols. Like Karlgren, who saw the derivation of the pictogram *tsu*, designating the ancestor, from the drawing of a phallus, Ho sees in the multiplication of phallic emblems the importance attained by the ancestor cult.[6] The "death pattern," as we have seen, certainly involves a sexual symbolism. But Carl Hentze explains the various "phallic" objects and designs as representing a "house of the soul"; certain ceramics from Yang Shao represent models of little huts—which are at the same time funerary urns—comparable to the similar documents from European prehistory and to the Mongol hut. These "little houses of the soul," abundantly attested to in the prehistory of China, are the forerunners of the "ancestor tablets" of historical times.[7]

In short, the Yang Shao and Lung Shan cultures reveal the beliefs that are typical of other Neolithic civilizations: solidarity among life, fertility, death, and the afterlife and hence the conception of the cosmic cycle, illustrated by the calendar and actualized in the rites; the importance of the ancestors, a source of magico-religious power; and the "mystery" of the conjunction of contraries (also proven by the "death pattern"), a belief that in a way anticipated the idea of the unity/totality of cosmic life, which will be the dominating idea in later periods. It is important to add that a great part of the Neolithic heritage was until recent times preserved, with the inevitable changes, in the religious traditions and practices of the Chinese villages.

---

3   Ibid., pp. 279 ff. Similar beliefs and practices are found in certain prehistoric cultures of the Near East and of eastern Europe.

4   See J. G. Anderson, *Children of the Yellow Earth*, p. 315; Kwang-Chih Chang, *The Archaeology of Ancient China*, p. 103; cf. Hanna Rydh, "Symbolism in Mortuary Ceramics," passim.

5   There is a good reproduction in Ho, *Cradle of the East*, p. 154, Figure 9.

6   Ibid., p. 282; cf. B. Karlgren, "Some Fecundity Symbols in Ancient China," pp. 18 ff.

7   See Carl Hentze, *Bronzegerät, Kultbauten, Religion im ältesten China der Shangzeit*, pp. 49 ff., 88 ff., and his *Das Haus als Weltort der Seele*, pp. 23 ff. and figs. 10–12. These two works supply a large number of parallels chosen from cultures historically or morphologically related to the archaic civilization of China.

RELIGION IN THE BRONZE AGE: THE GOD OF HEAVEN AND THE ANCESTORS

We are decidedly better informed about Chinese history from the time of the Shang dynasty (ca. 1751–1028). The Shang period corresponds in general to the protohistory and the beginning of the ancient history of China. It is characterized by the metallurgy of bronze, the appearance of urban centers and capital cities, the presence of a military aristocracy, the institution of royalty, and the beginnings of writing. As for the religious life of the period, the documentation is comparatively full. First of all we have a rich iconography, best exemplified by the magnificent bronze ritual vessels. In addition, the royal tombs provide information concerning certain religious practices. But it is especially the countless oracular inscriptions, incised on animal bones or tor toise shells, that are a precious source.[8] Finally, some later works (for example, *The Book of Odes*), which Karlgren calls "free Chou texts,"[9] contain much ancient material. We should add, however, that these sources give us information concerning the beliefs and rituals of the royal clan; as in the Neolithic period, the mythology and theology remain for the most part unknown.

The interpretation of these iconographic documents is not always certain. Scholars agree in recognizing a certain analogy with the motifs documented on the painted pottery of Yang Shao[10] and, in addition, with the religious symbolism of the following periods. Hentze (*Bronzegerät*, pp. 215 ff.) interprets the con junction of polar symbols as illustrating religious ideas related to the renewal of Time and to spiritual regeneration. No less important is the symbolism of the cicada and of the *t'ao-t'ieh* mask, which suggests the cycle of births and rebirths, of light and life emerging from darkness and death. No less remarkable is the union of antagonistic images (feathered snake, snake and eagle, etc.), in other words the dialectic of contraries and the *coincidentia oppositorum*, a central theme for the Taoist philosophers and mystics. The bronze vessels represent urn-houses.[11] Their form is derived either from ceramics or from prototypes in wood.[12] The admirable animal art revealed by the bronze vessels probably originated in wood engravings.[13]

The oracular inscriptions inform us of a religious conception that was absent (or imperceptible?) in the Neolithic documents, namely, the preeminence of a supreme celestial god, Ti (Lord) or Shang Ti (The Lord on High). Ti commands the cosmic rhythms and natural phenomena (rain, wind, drought, etc.); he grants the king victory and insures the abundance of crops or, on the contrary, brings on disasters and sends sicknesses and death. He is offered two kinds of sacrifices: in the sanctuary of the ancestors and in the open fields. But, as is the case with other archaic celestial gods (see our *A History of Religious Ideas*, vol. 1, §§14 ff.), his cult shows a certain diminution of religious primacy. Ti is found to be distant and less active than

---

8   These exemplify a method of divination that was quite widely practiced in northern Asia: the question was asked, the bones or shells were heated, and the diviners interpreted the shapes of the resulting cracks. Then the question and answer were inscribed beside the cracks.

9   Bernhard Karlgren, "Legends and Cults in Ancient China," p. 344.

10   The salamander, the tiger, the dragon, etc., still in use in the iconography of Chinese popular art, are cosmological symbols that are already documented at the end of the Neolithic. See Hentze, *Bronzegerät ... der Shangzeit*, pp. 40 ff., 55 ff., 132 ff., 165 ff.

11   Hentze, *Das Haus als Weltort der Seele*, pp. 14 ff. and passim.

12   Li Chi, *The Beginnings of Chinese Civilization*, p. 32.

13   Ibid., p. 35.

the ances tors of the royal lineage, and he is offered fewer sacrifices. But he alone is invoked in matters of fecundity (rain) and of war, the sovereign's two chief preoccupations.

In any case, Ti's position remains supreme. All the other gods, as well as the royal ancestors, are subordinate to him. Only the king's ancestors are able to intercede with Ti; on the other hand, only the king can communicate with his ancestors, for the king is the "one man."[14] The sovereign strengthens his authority with the help of his ancestors; belief in their magico-religious power legitimized the domination of the Shang dynasty. In their turn the ancestors depend on the offerings of cereals, blood, and flesh that are brought to them.[15] It is futile to suppose, as certain scholars do,[16] that, since the ancestor cult was so important for the reigning aristocracy, it was gradually adopted by the other social strata. The cult was already thoroughly implanted, and very popular, in the Neolithic period. As we have just seen (pp. 5 ff.), it formed an essential part of the religious system (structured around the anthropocosmic cycle) of the earliest cultivators. It is the preeminence of the king, whose first ancestor was supposed to descend from Ti, that gave this immemorial cult a political function.

The king offers two series of sacrifices: to the ancestors and to Ti and the other gods. Sometimes the ritual service is extended over 300 or 600 days. The word "sacrifice" designates the "year," since the annual cycle is conceived as a complete service. This confirms the importance of the calendar, which guarantees the normal return of the seasons. In the great royal tombs near Anyang, exploration has revealed, in addition to animal skeletons, numerous human victims, presumably immolated in order to accompany the sovereign into the other world. The choice of victims (companions and servants, dogs, horses) emphasizes the considerable importance of the hunt (ritual hunt?) for the military aristocracy and royal clan.[17] A number of questions preserved by the oracular inscriptions are concerned with the advisability and the chances for success of the king's expeditions.

The tombs had the same cosmological symbolism and performed the same function as the urn-houses: they were the houses of the dead. A similar belief could explain human sacrifice offered at the time when buildings were newly begun, especially temples and palaces. The victims' souls insured the durability of the construction; it could be said that the building that was raised served as a "new body" for the victim's soul.[18] But human sacrifice was also practiced for other purposes, about which our information is scanty; it can be supposed that the end sought was the renewal of time or the regeneration of the dynasty.

Despite the gaps, we can make out the principal lines of religion in the Shang period. The importance of the celestial god and the ancestor cult is beyond doubt. The complexity of the sacrificial system (bound up with a religious calendar) and of techniques of divination presupposes the existence of a class of "specialists in the sacred"—diviners, priests, or shamans. Finally, the iconography shows us the articulations of a

---

14 The expression "I, the one man" (or perhaps, "I, the first man") is documented in the oracular inscriptions; see David N. Keightley, "Shang Theology and the Genesis of Chinese Political Culture," p. 213, n. 6.

15 As Keightley remarks (ibid., pp. 214 ff.), the cult of ancestors emphasized the royal lineage's aspect as the source of religious and political authority. The doctrine of the "Mandate of Heaven," usually considered to be an invention of the Chou dynasty, has deep roots in the theology of the Shang.

16 For example, Ho, *Cradle of the East*, p. 320.

17 Li Chi, *The Beginnings of Chinese Civilization*, pp. 21 ff. The author draws attention to the animal motifs (tiger, stag) in the decorations of bronze vessels (p. 33). We may add that these are emblematic animals, carrying a quite complex cosmological and initiatory symbolism.

18 See Eliade, *Zalmoxis, the Vanishing God*, pp. 182 ff.

symbolism, at once cosmological and soteriological, that is still inadequately understood but that seems to anticipate the chief religious conceptions of classical China.

Japanese Religion

> ## OBJECTIVES:
>
> 1. Define Kami and list the different types.
> 2. Understand the difference between Confucian ideals and Shinto ideals.
> 3. Know who the yamabushi were and their functions in Shinto.
> 4. What movement solidified the Shinto restoration?

Shintō Tradition

By Victoria Kennick Urubshurow

The indigenous religion of Japan is known as **Shintō**. The Japanese archipelago comprises four main islands: Hokkaidō, Honshū, Shikoku, and Kyūshū. Early migration patterns to and from these islands are not well understood. The distant ancestors of the Japanese people are Mongols from Korea, Malayo-Polynesians from China and the South Pacific, and the Caucasian-like "hairy" **Ainu** peoples who seem to have been the first inhabitants of the islands. By the time the Japanese were first recorded in history in the 200s CE the immigrant groups were already an ethnically unified people—except for pockets of Ainu who today are found far to the north on Hokkaidō. Although the physical distance between the Japanese islands and the mainland is not great, until modern times travel proved to be difficult and the political will to engage with Korea and China varied with the times. In general there was no continuous contact between Japan and the mainland until the mid-1800s.

Early Shintō was fundamentally an expressive religion that focused on purification and communion with the **kami**. Over time Shintō went through several key changes—particularly as it interfaced with Buddhist and Confucian traditions from China. The various Shintō

TIMELINE

	BCE	
Jimmu Tennō	660 (traditional)	Yayoi (Bronze-Iron) period
	250 BCE–250 CE	
	CE	
Pimiku	?201–?269	
Shōtoku Taishi	574–622	
	712	*Kojiki* complete
	720	*Nihongi* complete
	710	Nara established as capital
	794	Heian established as capital
	618–907	Tang dynasty in China
	960–1279	Song dynasty in China
Murasaki Shikibu	b. 978?	15 shōguns rule
	1192–1867	Kamakura era
	1192–1333	Tokugawa era
	1603–1867	Christianity banned
	1614	First Thanksgiving pilgrimage to Ise (others 1705, 1771, 1830)
	1650	
Motoori Norinaga	1730–1801	
Nakayama Miki	1798–1887	
	28 March 1868	Official separation of Buddhism from Shintō
	1870–1945	
		State Shintō
Emperor Hirohito	1901–1989	
	1945–1952	Japan under Allied forces
	1 January 1946	Emperor Hirohito declares his humanity
Emperor Akihito	b. 1933 (r. 1990–present)	
	1996	2000th anniversary of Ise

traditions include folk elements, Shintō-Buddhist variations, and Shintō as an imperial cult. Yet through the transformations Shintō kept its expressive character with a focus on ritual. The earliest Shintō writings existing today are two extensive chronicles: the *Kojiki* (Record of Ancient Matters) and the *Nihongi* (History of Japan), both issued in the eighth century CE. They begin with creation stories and continue into what amounts to a fairly reliable history of events that occurred after 400 CE. The main character in the stories is **Amaterasu**, who is the divine energy of the sun. She is said to be the ancestor of Japan's imperial family whose line continues unbroken from the first human emperor Jimmu until today. Historians place Jimmu's reign somewhere between 550 and 800 CE, while Shintō tradition situates him in the seventh century BCE.

The Japanese people have often practiced Shintō along with other traditions. This remains true today in Japan where the **Kami Way** permeates Japanese culture regardless of other religious influences.

PART 1
SHINTŌ PLAYERS

THE ULTIMATE PRINCIPLE

Mysterious—nature—life—creative energy

Kami are vast myriads of mysterious entities that form the focal point of indigenous Japanese religion. Some modern Japanese interpreters translate the term "kami" (which is used in both singular and plural) as "high," "above," and "lifted up." Kami as an ultimate principle may be thought of as life energy and may be described as mysterious. Japanese people have felt the mysterious kami presence in powerful and unusual objects or situations including storms, sprouting rice, animals, ancestors, heroic humans, work, trees, minerals, rocks, heavenly bodies, and more. In general, kami are associated with mysterious life-giving energies. Sometimes kami are specifically linked to dynamic powers involving growth and reproduction. For example, the sprouting of rice first signals that creative (*musubi*) kami are at work.

Kami have been distinguished in terms of the way natural objects express themselves. With their subtle aesthetic sense the Japanese have perceived many fine aspects of nature. For example, Shintō tradition speaks of a "soft and fast sun," "long, soft continuous breezes such as those which rustle the leaves of trees," winds that "disperse the morning mists," and so forth (Herbert 1967: 465, 490). It may not be too far-fetched to call the Mysterious Creative Life Energy of Nature the ultimate principle of Shintō.

> Since every feature of Nature is either a child of the greatest Kami or at least under the special care of a Kami who is their child, it is not surprising to find that every beauty and power of Nature is the object of a respect which may amount to worship. This is true of practically every one of them, from celestial bodies to the very herbs and stones, from rivers and mountains to wind and thunder.
>
> (Herbert 1967: 465)

Kami are not solidly associated with the mere physicality of objects. Kami are an energetic life presence that manifests here and there. Not all trees, for example, would be automatically recognized as kami. Rather, kami energy might be recognized in an unusual tree with a triple-trunk or a tree with branches all bending in the same direction.

IMAGINAL PLAYERS

The mysterious life current that is Shintō's ultimate principle manifests in innumerable ways. General categories into which kami might be divided to understand their many workings are: (1) nature kami and (2) mythic kami.

Nature kami

- **Trees.** Trees seem to have been among the earliest kamis to be revered by the Japanese people. Among trees the *sakaki* (Cleyera japonica; pine) is most precious. The sakaki is found around many Shintō shrines and its branches are used in Shintō rituals.
- **Food.** Kami of growth come down from the mountains into the rice fields. Key Shintō agricultural rites are addressed to the creative kami of growth and food. Among the most popular kamis is Inari who is associated with the harvest, food, and fertility.
- **Animals.** Some wild animals have been recognized as kami, such as the wolf, tiger, hare, wild white boar, white deer, and snake. The fox is thought to be a kami messenger and came to be associated with Inari whose shrines have many fox statues, big and small.
- **Mountains.** Mountains were among the earliest natural objects to be perceived as kami by the Japanese people. Visiting mountain shrines is a common form of Shintō pilgrimage. Mountains are revered especially by hunters, woodcutters, and charcoal-makers whose livelihood depends upon them.
- **Geological entities.** Shintō includes recognition of various kami associated with the earth and cosmos. Some of these are clay, stones, lightning, metals, minerals, gemstones, stars, sun, and moon. Many forms of water are also recognized to have a kami presence, including springs, wells, rivers, the ocean, rain, and storms.
- **Human constructions.** Crossroads and houses are among the human constructions that are protected by kami. Many of these kami are deeply embedded in age-old Japanese folk traditions and remain unnamed. Often flowers are offered with reverence to the many household kami who protect the gate, kitchen, cooking stove, lavatory, well, and so forth.

Mythic kami

Many kami of nature came to be associated with Shintō stories relating how they came into existence or their role in various events of sacred history. Two Japanese chronicles (the **Kojiki** and **Nihongi** compiled in the eighth century CE) tell stories about several nature kami, including the kami of the sun, storms, and the moon.

Amaterasu

Amaterasu, the sun kami, became especially important to the Japanese identity. Her magnificence becomes apparent in this passage where she prepares herself for a confrontation with her brother:

> And she forthwith, unbinding her august hair, twisted it into august bunches; and both into the left and into the right august bunch, as likewise into her august head-dress and likewise on to her left and her right august arm, she twisted an augustly complete [string] of curved

jewels eight feet [long] of five hundred jewels; and slinging on her back a quiver holding a thousand [arrows], and adding [thereto] a quiver holding five hundred [arrows], she likewise took and slung at her side a mighty and high [-sounding] elbow pad and brandished and stuck her bow upright so that the top shook; and she stamped her feet into the hard ground up to her opposing thighs, kicking away [the earth] like rotten snow and stood valiantly like unto a mighty man.

(deBary *et al.* 2001: 22, adapted from Chamberlain, *Ko-ji-ki*, pp. 45–59)

Clan kami

Some mythic kami are revered as *uji-gami* (tutelary clan deities). The social status of a clan was reflected in the authority and power of its kami protector. The Imperial Clan claimed unique and superior status among all humans due to their exclusive descent from Amaterasu through Jimmu Tennō, the first emperor manifesting as a human. Of lesser status were members of Divine Clans, whose members claimed descent from mythic kami through Jimmu Tennō's companions or through noble families who ruled Japan prior to Jimmu Tennō's reign. Uji-gami shrines distributed throughout Japan served as a political bond. Eventually Shintōists used the tutelary clan kami system to protect not only families but also their extended alliances in villages and districts.

Guild kami

Many Japanese professions are linked to tutelary kami named in the *Kojiki* and *Nihongi*. Traditional guilds traced their tutelary kami back to episodes involving Amaterasu. For example: (1) mirror makers revere the kami who made the mirror that enticed Amaterasu to come out from hiding in a cave, (2) jewelers revere the kami who made the eight-foot-long string of 500 jewels worn by the sun kami, and (3) dancers and **geisha** have as their tutelary kami Ame-no-uzume who danced to entertain Amaterasu. There is a sense that these tutelary guild kami not only protect, but also enable (*yosasu*) human beings to act in this world on their behalf.

EXCEPTIONAL PLAYERS

From time to time Shintōists regard a human being as a living kami. This is always the case with the Japanese emperors, and occasionally true of heroic or uncommonly powerful people such as shamans. Thus in the Shintō context, the most exceptional players in the drama of religions are the emperors and the charismatic people mentioned above.

Emperors

Japan's emperors all belong to the Yamoto clan, which traces back to Amaterasu. She sent her grand-son Ninigi down from the High Plain of Heaven to the Luxuriant-reed-plain land-of-fresh-rice-ears (i.e., Japan). The sun kami presented Ninigi with a troupe of entertainment kami, and three objects that would serve as imperial regalia: (1) a mirror, (2) a jewel, and (3) a sword. Ninigi ruled and passed

Figure 7.1

"Japan—a straw culture." Japan has been called a straw culture (*wara no bunka*) linked to 2,000 years of rice cultivation. Villagers store rice straw on poles or slim trees creating a tent-like effect (seen here in a refined and stylized form). Japanese folk culture introduced numerous items made of rice straw, such as sandals, hats, coats, mats, utensils, ropes, masks, and even tree protectors—shown in this picture as they appeared in winter at Nijo Castle in Kyōto. Would one be wrong to detect a kami presence here?

the imperial regalia down the line. Jimmu, his great-grandson, became the first emperor to gain control over the region of Yamoto. Thus the Yamoto clan traced its imperial line from Emperor (Tennō) Jimmu who was the first ruler in Amaterasu's line to serve in the form of a human being. Modern historians place Jimmu Tennō's reign somewhere in the Asuka and Nara periods (552–794 CE), while the traditional date for his accession to the throne is given as 660 BCE, based on symbolic calculations from the Chinese calendar. All members of the Imperial Clan family are high-born, but only the one who becomes emperor is associated with the quality of kami.

Charismatic humans

Shintō tradition demarcates no hard and fast division between humans and kami. Thus ritual specialists or individual charismatic individuals who commune with the kami are occasionally identified as kami themselves. Here are some examples of human beings who keep close contact with the kami:

- *Miko.* Ritual specialists known as miko (female shamans) typically entered a state of kami possession to seek protection for the community, fruitful harvests, and communication with the dead.

- *Shrine priestesses.* For generations, young women of the Yamoto ruling families served as shrine priestesses (*saiō*) in Amaterasu's shrine at Ise. There they could commune with the kami.
- *Spirits of the dead.* War heroes or people with unusual faith and commitment who served the emperor (hence Japan) have occasionally been recognized as kami. Sometimes restless spirits of people who die by accident or in some other unfortunate way are also placated.

HISTORICAL PLAYERS

Shintō tradition shifted its focus several times in the course of Japanese history—often in response to key changes in Japan's political-cultural environment. The following six players represent these turning points:

- *The Yayoi cultural period*: Queen Pimiku (?201– ?269 CE) lived when the Japanese people practiced early Shintō.
- *About 300 years later*: Crown-prince Shōtoku (574–622) was born when Japan adopted the Buddhist tradition and centralized power under the emperor on a Confucian model.
- *About 400 years later*: Murasaki Shikibu (b. ?978 CE) was born when Japanese culture was distinguishing itself in the midst of Chinese influences.
- *About 200 years later*: The first shōgun was appointed by the emperor as general of the army (in 1192), which ushered in a feudal style of rule in the midst of new Chinese influences.
- *About 700 years later*: The Imperial House of Japan restored its absolute power through the Meiji regime that began with the defeat of the fifteenth shōgun in 1867 and the establishment of Shintō, the official state cult.
- *About 100 years later*: The **Tenrikyō** sect started by Nakayama Miki (1798–1887) blossomed into one of the most successful "newly arisen religions" after the fall of the Meiji government in World War II.

Queen Pimiku (?201–?269 CE)

The Japanese people made a great economic transition after many generations of fishing, hunting, and gathering. During the Yayoi period (250 BCE–250 CE) they adopted the technology of wet rice agriculture from Korea and China. Around the same time they developed metalworking skills in bronze, copper, and iron. The new rice-growers revered kami who descended from the mountains for their planting festivals (*matsuri*) and returned to the mountains after grateful farmers offered first fruits to them. Late in this Bronze-Iron period there lived a woman called Pimiku (?201–?269 CE). According to Chinese historians of the third century CE, Pimiku ruled a region of Japan known as Yamatai (possibly on Kyushu, but this location is disputed by present-day scholars). It appears that Pimiku was a miko (female shaman), for their *Record of Wei* said of this unmarried woman, "She occupied herself with magic and sorcery, bewitching the people" (Tsunoda 1951: 13). The chronicle goes on to say that following some political turmoil after Pimiku passed away, order was restored when Iyo (a 13-year-old female relative of Pimiku) became ruler. Subsequently it appears that leaders coming from the Yamoto plain began to rule the queen's land. This was the Imperial Family who traced their descent from Amaterasu. The Chinese historians fill out the picture of life on the queen's land by describing a number of practices that seem to represent early Shintō customs:

> Men, great and small, all tattoo their faces and decorate their bodies with designs … . The Wa [i.e., Japanese], who are fond of diving into the water to get fish and shells, also decorated their bodies in order to keep away large fish and waterfowl. Later, however, the designs became merely ornamental. Designs on the body differ in the various countries—their position and size vary according to the rank of the individual … .
>
> When death occurs, mourning is observed for more than ten days, during which period they do not eat meat. The head mourners wail and lament, while friends sing, dance, and drink liquor. When the funeral is over, all members of the whole family go into the water to cleanse themselves in a bath of purification.

When they go on voyages across the sea to visit China, they always select a man who does not arrange his hair, does not rid himself of fleas, lets his clothing [get as] dirty as it will, does not eat meat, and does not approach women. This man behaves like a mourner and is known as the fortune keeper... .

Whenever they undertake an enterprise and discussion arises, they bake bones and divine in order to tell whether fortune will be good or bad. First they announce the object of divination, using the same manner of speech as in tortoise shell divination; then they examine the cracks made by the fire and tell what is to come to pass.

In their meetings and in their deportment, there is no distinction between father and son or between men and women. They are fond of liquor. In their worship, men of importance simply clap their hands instead of kneeling or bowing.

(Tsunoda 1951: 10–13)

This *Record of Wei* points out religious customs of the early Japanese people that persist today in Shintō. Remnants of Pimiku's political system and reverence for miko are found today in Okinawa. Moreover, the *kami no michi* makes use of water purification, divination, *sake* as a sacred drink, shamanism, and simple reverential handclaps. Meanwhile, tattoos lost relevance for the Japanese. In the early days of Shintō there seem to have been no fixed shrines. Kami were thought to dwell only for a short time in the human world—but in natural surroundings far from human habitation. The kami manifested spontaneously and rites were performed where the kami presence had been felt. This was likely to have been around a special tree, grove, forest, rock, cave, mountain, river, seashore, or similar. Before conducing a rite, a temporary square space (*himorogi*) was set up. This might have a sacred pine tree with a shoulder-high rope around it. The kami was invoked and thought to leave afterwards. Gradually more permanent shrines were set up where the kami were thought to dwell on a semi-permanent basis—or at least be closely associated with a **goshintai** (symbolic body) that was ceremoniously placed in the inner sanctum of the shrine to represent them or embody their mysterious presence.

Crown-prince Shōtoku Taishi (574–622 CE)

Shōtoku Taishi was born just when China was on the verge of entering its highly creative Tang era (618–906 CE) in which Buddhist, Confucian, and Daoist traditions had ongoing productive literary and artistic encounters. Empress Suiko (r. 592–628) appointed Shōtoku as regent, giving him virtually complete authority to govern. Soon after the Japanese received their first Buddhist teachings through Korea (traditionally in either 538 or 552 CE), they made a prolonged and intensive effort to import nearly every available aspect of Chinese culture. In this connection Shōtoku was a key influence in promoting the Buddhist tradition in Japan. He also paved the way for the Japanese to adopt Tang-era fine arts, orchestral court music and dance, literature, technology (weaving, metal working, lacquer ware), social ethics, law codes, a landholding and tax system, architecture, town planning, philosophy, and a system of political governance.

Shōtoku strengthened Japan's cultural link to China. He sent a large embassy of monks and scholars to China in 607 CE. When they returned (some after his death) they patterned the Yamoto court after the Tang Chinese model. This was accomplished by a group of Chinese-educated Japanese in the Taika Reform

(645–646). Following Shōtoku's lead, embassies to China continued for the next two and a half centuries, spanning the whole Tang era in China. Shōtoku is credited with first calling the Japanese ruler *Tennō* (emperor, heavenly sovereign) instead of *daio* (great king). This ideologically presented the Japanese ruler according to a Chinese model, whereby government was justified according to Heaven's mandate. Calling the first emperor Jimmu Tennō gave assurance that the heavenly sovereign was not mortal, but a living kami. In connection with the title Tennō, Japanese emperors were called Aketsu-mikami (manifestation of kami) or Arahito-gami (kami appearing as human). This added a Shintō religious value to the Chinese concept.

Shōtoku introduced seventeen moral guidelines to the Yamoto court in 604 CE. His "constitution" included a mixture of practical matters and religious counsel that reflected Confucian and Buddhist influences. It calls for officials to do things such as: revere the Three Jewels (of Buddhist tradition); avoid class prejudice, gluttony, covetousness, and anger; engage in the consultative process; and (perhaps most significant) recognize a single sovereign of the entire country. Contemporary historian George B. Sansom noted that the "interest [of the seventeen articles] lies in the fact that they represent not a new system of administration but a turning point in the ideals of government, inspired by the new learning, both religious and secular, from abroad" (Sansom 1962: 72). And though he personally seemed to have become a Buddhist, Shōtoku maintained all Shintō imperial rites, agricultural festivals, and so forth.

Just under a century after Shōtoku passed away, the Imperial Family built their capital in 710 CE at Nara on the Yamoto plain. Nara was built (on a smaller scale) according to the Chinese model of the Chinese Tang capital. Buddhist monasteries grew so quickly around Nara that after less than a century a new ruler thought it prudent to extract the imperial palace from its surroundings. An attempt to move the capital nearby to Nagaoka (near Heian) proved troublesome due to internal intrigue, violence, and what were perceived as resultant illnesses and deaths. Thus the new capital (also built on the Chinese model) was finally constructed not far away at Heian in 794 CE. The city is part of today's Kyōto. In the year 838 CE the last great embassy left Japan for China. It returned the following year. After that Japan shifted its focus. The years between 900 and 1200 marked a transformative time during which the Japanese defined their newly enriched culture. Many centuries later the Tokugawa-era scholar Motoori Norinaga (1730–1801) reflected back upon this time of cultural redefinition. He noted that the native Japanese sentiment at times was obscured in the process of assimilating so many elements of Chinese civilization. But Motoori remarked on one woman whose extraordinary work of Japanese literature managed to sustain and capture the quintessential Japanese sensibility toward life—its pathos. The woman was Murasaki Shikibu (b. ?978 CE), a lady-in-waiting to the Heian Empress Akito at the Heian court.

Murasaki Shikibu (b. ?978 CE)

Murasaki Shikibu was among the ladies of the Heian court who wrote in Japanese because they were not educated in Chinese. They learned the new *kana* syllabary that was developed out of Chinese characters for use in recording the Japanese tongue. And with enthusiasm women of the Heian court developed a whole new form of literature. The contemporary historian Edwin O. Reischauer explained the phenomenon this way:

> For the most part, educated men, much like their counterparts in medieval Europe, scorned the use of their own tongue for any serious literary purpose and continued to write histories, essays, and official documents in Chinese; but the women of the imperial court, who usually

had insufficient education to write in Chinese, had no medium for literary expression other than their own language. As a result, while the men of the period were pompously writing bad Chinese, their ladies consoled themselves for their lack of education by writing good Japanese, and created, incidentally, Japan's first great prose literature.

(Reischauer 1970: 34–35)

Thus the Japanese women's intuitive writing became what later nativists like Motoori Norinaga recognized as the genuine feature of the Japanese mindset. Around the year 1000 CE Sei Shōnagon wrote the Pillow Book (*Makura no Sōshi*) and Murasaki Shikibu wrote the ***Tale of Genji*** (*Genji Monogatari*). Together they provide a picture of court life among Heian nobles of the day.

Murasaki lived right in the middle part of the Heian era (794–1185) at the height of the power and influence of the famous Fujiwara family. In fact, she married a Fujiwara lieutenant who was in the Imperial Guard. The Heian government amounted to a Fujiwara oligarchy and the rise of a court aristocracy. In Murasaki's day the nobles

BOX 7.1 CULTURE CONTRAST: THE JAPANESE SHINTŌ IDENTITY

In spite of the massive adoption of cultural elements from China, it is important to bear in mind that the Chinese never invaded Japan. The Japanese tended to modify what did not suit them and maintained their cultural identity. The persistence of a Japanese worldview and culture may be seen in the following examples:

Adoption. Contrary to Confucian ideals, the Japanese continued to maintain hereditary government posts, as inheritance was deeply embedded in their aristocratic society. The automatic nature of inheritance was somewhat tempered by the long-standing Japanese custom of adoption, which allowed a man to choose his successor. When there was no male heir the Japanese adopted the husband of a daughter, a young relative, or even someone who was not related by blood.

Bushidō. The Japanese rejected the Chinese-style draft army, as they did not need a large army. Beyond that they maintained the military as an aristocratic profession. In medieval Japan the Shintō military tradition developed the **Bushidō** (way of the warrior-knight) code. These eight attitudes that characterize a warrior were: (1) loyalty, (2) gratitude, (3) courage, (4) justice, (5) truthfulness, (6) politeness, (7) reserve, and (8) honor. There is the flavor of the Confucian tradition running through these, as well as the Zen Buddhist focus of mind and fearlessness. Yet the product was something with a native Japanese flavor that seems to have continued to the present day.

Japanese language. The Japanese initially adopted Chinese characters for writing and chose Chinese as their literary language. Yet they continued to speak Japanese, which was quite a distinctive language. Moreover, during the 800s CE they adapted the Chinese ideograms to the Japanese language with two syllabaries (known as *kana*) that used simplified characters to phonetically represent Japanese syllables. For example, they wrote the "Collection of Myriad Leaves" (*Manyōshū*) whose 4,516 native poems were copied syllable by syllable in Chinese characters used in a phonetic manner to represent the Japanese words.

generally regarded country people as uncivilized. The gentlepersons of the court developed the Japanese language of politeness, and a culture of luxury with its ceremony, elegant pastimes, cosmetics for men and women, attention to penmanship, and so forth. Perhaps the most distinctive cultural development of the Heian era was in the realm of Japanese literature. Neglecting the thirty-one-syllable poem that was popular at the court, Murasaki wrote what is counted as the world's first novel. It records court life centered on the figure of Prince Genji and his family circle. The book shows psychological sensitivity, but also records elements of the emerging Japanese culture. Murasaki observed this scene, for example:

> A number of grey-haired old ladies were cutting out and stitching, while the young girls were busy hanging out quilts and winter cloaks over lacquered clothes-frames. They had just beaten and pulled a very handsome dark-red under-robe, a garment of magnificent colour, certainly unsurpassed as an example of modern dyeing—and were spreading it out to air.

> (Murasaki 1993: 624)

The very object of a Heian book was counted as part of its artistry—as the paper and perfume conveyed a particularly Japanese sense of aesthetics. But while the upper crust of Heian society were busy developing their highly refined blend of Chinese and Japanese influences, some religious specialists living in the mountains were blending foreign and native influences as well. These were the **yamabushi** (mountain priests or hermits). They can be distinguished from miko (female shamans) and Shintō priests (*onshi* or *oshi*) by their particular functions, which combine Buddhist practice with folk Shintō elements.

The yamabushi were ascetics with uncut hair who lived in the mountains conducting physical and spiritual practices to acquire power over spirits of the dead. The order of yamabushi that survives today is the Shugen-dō, founded by a priest of the En family in the mid-600s CE. For a while their numbers declined, but the sect was revitalized and reorganized by a Shingon Buddhist monk named Shōbō (832–909). The yamabushi worked as a team with miko as assistants. (Sometimes they also married these miko.) The yamabushi used special techniques to help the miko go into a trance to find out for a client what grudge a spirit of the dead was holding. After interpreting the miko's announcement the yamabushi would remedy the problem. Thus the miko diagnosed and the yamabushi exorcised. The yamabushi would go from one mountain to another and from one village to another. Some were ballad singers or musicians as well. And though Shugen-dō was affiliated with the Tendai and Shingon Buddhist traditions, it shows considerable Shintō influence in its connection with sacred mountains, the service of the miko, and so forth. Some yamabushi even became Shintō priests. Nowadays the yamabushi still exist in Japan, meeting villagers to pray for good harvests, exorcise negative spirits from houses, conduct healings, and so forth. They seem to resemble the characters noted by the third-century CE Chinese historians who observed that on voyages across the sea to China the Japanese always have a man with them "who does not arrange his hair."

Fifteen shōguns (1192–1867)

Culturally, with the decline of the Heian court, **samurai** warriors replaced the Fujiwara courtiers. This was due to economic changes as the military leaders gained more local influence in the countryside. The rise of a samurai class represented the militarization of Japanese society. The emperor still maintained the position as ruler seated in Heian. But from a practical point of view the leaders of various semi-independent estates came to control Japanese political life. Finally in 1192 these estates came under a single leader's control. This was Minamoto Yorimoto—the first man appointed by the emperor as shōgun ("generalissimo"). This meant that he was given command of the emperor's army. Thus began the Kamakura era (1192–1333). The shōgunate settled in Kamakura, some 300 miles from Heian (Kyōto), and kept their political liaison intact.

The downfall of the Tang dynasty in China had come after a major persecution of Buddhism in 845 CE. In response to the chaotic atmosphere on the mainland, Japan had discontinued its envoys to China and went through 300 years of isolation. Now, with the emergence of the first shōgun, that isolation was about to end (only to be imposed again in 1600 for about 300 years by the Tokugawa regime!). Medieval Japanese history can be measured between the moment the first shōgun took power in 1192 and the moment the fifteenth and final shōgun was deposed in 1867. The fifteen military chiefs stand like bookends encompassing a whole new orientation toward life flowing from a second period of intensive contact with China. But what the Japanese encountered in 1200 was not a China of the Tang dynasty with its flowering of three traditions—Buddhist, Daoist, and Confucian. Rather the Japanese encountered the Song dynasty (960–1279) in China. There, Pure Land and Chan Buddhist traditions percolated in the midst of a growing neo-Confucian Chinese cultural pride. Japanese Buddhist teachers of the Kamakura era who were disillusioned with the state of Buddhism in their country enthusiastically embraced the Buddhist traditions that Song China had to offer. Hōnen, Shinran, and Nichiren promoted Pure Land, True Pure Land, and Nichiren Buddhist practices that began filtering through all levels of Japanese society. Eisai and Dōgen promoted Rinzai and Sōtō Zen (Chan) Buddhist practices that appealed to the samurai.

Throughout this medieval period the Japanese people distinguished Buddhist and Shintō traditions as the Buddha Way (butsu-dō) and the Kami Way (kami no michi or shen-dao). Shintō shrines (jinja) were distinguished from Buddhist temples (tera) but both were contained in religious complexes to serve complementary functions. A tera would be built within the precinct of a jinja so that the Buddhist priest could perform rituals propitiating the kami. The reverse was also done, whereby kami were enshrined in Buddhist temples. Sometimes the kami were thought of as buddhas or bodhisattvas. As in the community, so both Shintō and Buddhist religious practices were observed in Japanese homes. Some people maintained both **kamidanas** (Shintō altars) and **butsudans** (Buddhist altars) for their households.

In time the Kamakura power base weakened. After several more generations of decline in the effectiveness of the Japanese feudal system, a talented member of the Tokugawa family was poised to take a firm grip on Japan. In the interest of creating unity in Japan Tokugawa Ieyasu (1542–1616) became shōgun in 1603. He instituted a far-reaching bureaucracy that lasted until 1867 with the fall of the Tokugawa regime. Under Tokugawa rule there was no class mobility, no intermarriage, and each family was required to register at the local Buddhist temple. Temple officials kept census records, while Zen Buddhist monasteries became centers for the arts and neo-Confucian studies. The presence of the kami no michi is felt strongly in medieval Japan through the arts. And though the arts of tea, the sword, flower arranging, and so forth are often called Zen arts, a Shintō influence thoroughly pervades them (see Box 7.3).

The Tokugawa regime instituted a new government based on neo-Confucian ideas and political practices derived from interpretations of Confucian literature by Zhu Xi (1130–1200). The neo-Confucian ideology was well suited to monarchic rule because it gave a strong sense that everything under heaven is governed by a single principle (li), which is embodied in the ruler. Hayashi Razan (1583–1657), the first official Japanese neo-Confucian, promoted the Chinese doctrine of five social relationships in these terms:

Heaven is august, Earth is ignoble. Heaven is high, Earth is low. Just as there is a distinction of high and low between Heaven and Earth, in the society of men, a prince is noble while the subject is common. Proper decorum calls for a hierarchy between the noble and the common, the elder and the younger persons … . Unless the distinction between the prince who is noble and the subject who is common is maintained, the land cannot be governed … . If the Way that distinguishes the prince as the subject, and the father and the son is followed, and the principle of distinguishing the high and the low, the exalted and the vulgar is upheld, the Way of Heaven will prevail above, and human relationships will be clear below.

(quoted in Hane 1972: 165)

The Tokugawa rulers maintained a strict isolationist policy, and closed Japan in reaction to a century of Christian influences. Christianity first came with the Portuguese traders in 1542. At first Christianity was welcomed along with Portuguese guns. But Christians experienced a backlash when Tokugawa Ieyasu realized that their loyalty to God's authority was greater than their loyalty to the state. In 1614 the shōgun gave all foreign priests one month to leave Japan. Two years later he ordered all Japanese Christians to renounce their religion and become Buddhist on pain of death. At this point the Japanese Christians (some of whom were already second and third generation) were either martyred, recanted, or began to practice secretly. By 1640 most traces of the **Kirishitan** religion were gone. Throughout the Tokugawa era, people had to undergo a yearly ritual of "treading pictures" (*fumi-e*) at the Buddhist monasteries. This involved stepping on images of Jesus Christ or the Virgin Mary to prove their rejection of the Christian tradition.

The Imperial House of Japan

Crown-prince Shōtoku's Japan with its three complementary traditions transformed in the course of 1,300 years into a society apparently dominated by Buddhist and Confucian traditions. By the late Tokugawa era, some nationalistic activists became adamant about removing foreign elements from Shintō and restoring it to the center of Japanese life. They bemoaned the fact that the emperor had become little more than a figurehead through 600-plus years of powerful military rule under the fifteen shōguns from the year 1192. The Japanese effort toward a Shintō restoration was crystallized by two nativist Japanese movements that emerged in the late 1700s and continued to grow in influence until Japan was defeated by the Allies in World War II: (1) **kokugaku** (nativism or national learning) sought to define, restore, and nurture the native Japanese mindset; (2) **kokutai** (national essence or national spirit) aimed to wrest power from the Tokugawa shōgun and restore full authority to the Imperial House of Japan, which traced back through Jimmu Tennō to Amaterasu. The nationalistic ideology of kokutai was fed by the literary and philological work of kokugaku (see Box 7. 2).

BOX 7.2 INTERPRETATIONS: THE KOKUGAKU WAY TO READ

Motoori Norinaga (1730–1801) was a Japanese literary scholar of kokugaku (nativism, national learning). As a nativist he wanted to discover the core spirituality-mentality of the Japanese people. Motoori felt that in ancient times when words were conveyed through the mouths of people and heard by the ears of people (i.e., through oral transmission) there was an accord between meaning (*kokoro*), an event (*koto*), and a word (*kotoba*). To get a better sense of the oral tradition, Motoori wrote in the antique style and favored words in contemporary Japanese usage that hearkened back to the Nara period (710–794) when the Japanese still used much of their antique language. He noticed that old words are not necessarily strange sounding. Yet he found that word choice and word order were significant cultural markers. Thus Motoori taught nativist readers to adjust Chinese phrases that were alien to the Japanese people (e.g., illegitimate elder brother, legitimate wife, national polity). He also noted that the Chinese expressions "day and night" and "mountains and sea" should be corrected to the Japanese wording of "night and day" and "sea and mountains." Motoori felt that authentic Shintō values were reflected in the ancient songs preserved in the *Kojiki* and the *Nihongi* where "one will find that things are not stated to excess, and that the ways of the world and the inner thoughts of people are known by intuition" (Motoori 1997: 146–147).

Motoori further identified *mono no aware* (the pathos of things, the sorrow of human existence) as a characteristic feature of a Japanese understanding of the world. He identified Murasaki Shikibu's *Tale of Genji* (ca. 1000 CE) as a prime example of such pathos. Motoori saw in her novel an emotional truth steeped in the melancholy of the human condition. He observed that Murasaki's work was not riddled with Buddhist and Confucian morality that would judge Genji's adultery. Rather, with true Japanese sensibility she wrote a work that was:

> simply a tale of human life that leaves aside and does not profess to take up at all the question of good and bad and that dwells only on the goodness of those who are aware of the sorrow of human existence (*mono no aware*).... [The] illicit love affairs described in the tale [are] there not for the purpose of being admired but for the purpose of nurturing the flower of the awareness of the sorrow of human existence (*mono no aware*).

(deBary *et al.* 2005: 485)

According to his Shintō intuitive belief (based particularly on the *Kojiki*) Motoori said the world was created by kami, and the Japanese people were descended from Amaterasu. He felt that a debt of gratitude is owed to the sun kami whose radiance continues to sustain the world. He claimed that the proper way to live was the ancient way in accord with how the kami established life on earth. With a universalistic outlook Motoori said that the Way of the Sun Goddess was "the true Way that permeates all nations within the four seas" (deBary *et al.* 2005: 500).

In 1868 the Meiji government replaced the Tokugawa regime and restored full authority to the Imperial House of Japan. The Meiji government replaced the Tokugawa state sponsorship of Buddhism with state sponsorship of Shintō and identified thirteen groups as non-Shintō religions officially designating them as Sect Shintō. These sects were considered as separate religions and their places of worship were called churches (*kyokai*) as opposed to shrines (*jinja*). During this time the Meiji government supervised Buddhists, Christians, and **New Religions** (Shinkō Shūkyō, literally "newly arisen religions") and other sects. They all dedicated themselves to the Imperial House. In 1882 a Bureau of Shrines was established and a legal distinction between Shrine Shintō (*jinga Shintō*) and Sect Shintō (*kyoha Shintō*) was made. This did not involve the construction of new shrines. Rather it awarded a new status to shrines that qualified as Shintō shrines, as opposed to those whose affiliations were regarded as other. In the midst of this reform, the hereditary Shintō priesthood was abolished and priests became government appointees. Beneath the government officials were priests of the Shintō shrines appointed by the government who maintained the state rituals. The people themselves continued to worship kami at their local shrines.

The Meiji government undertook an imperial campaign on the mainland. Victories in the Sino-Japanese war (1894–1895) and Russo-Japanese war (1904–1905) were part of a Japanese strategy to become a world stage player instead of capitulating to the forces of European colonialism. Japan focused on strengthening Japan against Western powers. During these Japanese wars of aggression parents often traveled to Shintō shrines (on what was known as the 100-shrine pilgrimage, for example) to appeal to the kami to protect their sons doing military duty. Japan's

Figure 7.2

"Long-legs and Long-arms watch the sunrise." Living on the seashore of north China facing Japan are two mythical beings: Ashinaga (Long-legs) and Tanaga (Long-arms). They like to go fishing together. Ashinaga carries Tanaga far from shore—and there in the deep water Tanaga scoops up fish. Shibata Zeshin (1807–1891) painted this scene with the symbol of his native Japan (the sun) on the horizon. What religious or political meaning might the artist have intended in doing so?

emperors of the twentieth century rode white horses and donned military uniforms. Imitating the ancient style of government, they served in both a political and religious capacity. Thus the emperors performed Shintō rituals at the Grand Shrines of Ise to commune with Amaterasu. After 1890 education of Japanese students was permeated with nationalistic ideas, with an ethic of filial piety toward the emperor who was to be viewed as a father figure. Japanese schools had shrines with a picture of the emperor and upon hearing the emperor's name they jumped to attention. History was taught beginning with the divine ancestry of the emperor and the Japanese people. Obedience to one's superior was required and self-sacrifice came to be regarded as a key virtue. This nationalistic education came to a halt suddenly when on 1 January 1946 Emperor Hirohito (1901–1989) was forced to declare that he was not divine. Japan lost to the Allies in World War II and was obliged to forgo having an army. The existence of Shintō as a state institution had lasted for about seventy years in all.

Nakayama Miki (1798–1887)

A popular theistic movement led by individual charismatic teachers sprouted up in the late Tokugawa era (mid-1800s) in the midst of depressed social and economic conditions. The Meiji government later designated these various groups by the term New Religions. At the start, the New Religions attracted followings mainly among poor farmers and urban laborers. Their leaders obtained their authority through personal experience of the divine, based on the traditional Shintō notion that kami manifest themselves through exceptional people. Most of these groups "derived their inspiration from occult practices prevalent among the mountaineer priests [yamabushi]" (Anesaki 1930: 310). Some New Religions sprang from Buddhist roots and some had undertones of Kirishitan (i.e., Christian) belief. However, most of the New Religions were grounded in Shintō and recognized the traditional kami of the *Kojiki* and *Nihongi*, such as Amaterasu, Izanagi, and Izanami (see Table 7.1).

Characteristic features of the New Religions include: (1) charismatic, shamanic leadership, (2) an emphasis on spiritual healing and purification, (3) reverence for ancestors, and (4) an expectation of happiness and success in this world (see Picken 1994: 260–263). In general, women tend to play a more prominent role in the New Religions than in traditional Shintō or Buddhist communities, and participation is geared toward the lay community.

The earliest Shintō-derived New Religion is Tenrikyō (Religion of Divine Wisdom) founded by Nakayama Miki (1798–1887). She was a peasant from Yamoto who practiced the Pure Land Buddhist tradition that focused gratitude toward Amida (Amitabha) Buddha for his universal compassion. One day Nakayama's son became ill and she hired a healer. Because the healer's assistant could not attend the consultation, he asked Nakayama to serve as a channel of healing energy. In doing so, she became possessed by a kami—and continued to have experiences of kami possession from that day forward. A kami called Tenri Ō no Mikoto (Lord of Divine Wisdom) spoke through Nakayama. The kami presented itself also as Oyagama (God the Parent) and began working healing miracles through her. The kami asked that Nakayama's family dedicate all their belongings to the poor, and she took this message to heart. Nakayama's daughter had faith in the mission and together they spread teachings that urged people to recover their original nature of sincere piety (*makoto-shinjitsu*) by cleansing themselves of eight dusts: grudge, covetousness, hatred, selfish love, enmity, fury, greed, and arrogance. Nakayama's fame spread. Disciples regarded her as the Kami no

Table 7.1 Japanese New Religions: a sample

Sect name/Founder[1]	Social status of parents	Conversion experience[2]
KUROZUMI Kurozumi Munetada (M)	Shintō priest	(35) Union with Amaterasu Ōmikami, the Sun Kami
TENRIKYŌ Nakayama Miki (F)	Ruined landowner	(41) Possession by 10 kami, organized by Tenri Ō no mikoto (Supreme Kami of Divine Wisdom)
KONKŌ Kawate Bunjirō(M)	Poor farmer	(45) Inspired, possessed by Konjin or Konkō-Daijin (Great Kami of Gold)
ŌMOTO Deguchi Nao (F) Deguchi Onisaburō(M)	Poor carpenter; poor peasant	(56) Chosen, possessed by Konjin (Great Kami of Gold); (27) Entranced, called by Ko-matsu-no-mikoto (Kami of a Small Pine Tree)
HITONO-MICHI Kaneda Tokumitsu (M) Miki Tokuchika (M)	Small-scale merchants	52) Inspired by the Rising Sun and came to the view that kami is one, not many
REIYŌ-KAI Kotani Kimi (F)	Poor peasant	(25) Chosen, possessed by kami and spirits; Related to Nichiren Buddhist tradition
RISSHŌ-KŌSEI-KAI Naganuma Myōko (F)	Poor laborer	(50) Chosen, possessed by spirit of Nichiren and other Buddhist figures
SŌKA-GAKKAI Makiguchi Tsunaburō (M) Toda Jōsei (M)	Farmer; fisherman	(59) Preach monotheistic theology based on Nichiren's teachings. (Toda Jōsei organized the Sōka-Gakkai sect.)

Notes [1] Male (M) or female (F).
[2] Age when converted is in parenthesis.
Source: Adapted from Hori (1968: 230–231).

Yashiro (living shrine of the kami) whose message of healing and charity was a prescription for realization of God's kingdom as harmonious life on earth.

Nakayama was imprisoned on several occasions, but managed to write down messages from Oyagama that came through her in two books, the *Mikagurauta* and the *Ofudesaki*. Among her revelations were songs of thirty-one syllables and deliberate physical movements. The shaman's poetic utterances and dance steps became the basis for Tenrikyō liturgy whose central rite is the Kagura Zutome (salvation dance service). In a revelation Nakayama identified a site (the *jiba*) as the sacred place from where human beings originally came. At that spot she later passed away in the midst of a liturgical performance. Nakayama's disciples worked with profound enthusiasm to build a great temple at the jiba, which they called "Terrace of Nectar" (*Kanrodai*). Tenrikyō adherents believe that the founder never died, but continues to exist as a powerful spiritual presence in the temple sanctuary from where she helps do away with social ills and prepare for the *kanrodai sekai* (perfect divine kingdom)—a new world order in which human beings will live joyous and blissful lives. Along with Sōka Gakkai (of Buddhist derivation) Tenrikyō has proved to be the most popular and successful among the Japanese New Religions. More than 200 churches are spread throughout the world, mostly for the sake of Japanese emigrants.

In modern times Shintō has gone through two major upheavals. During the Meiji era the institution of hereditary Shintō priesthood became defunct as the rulers officially appointed priests. In the early 1900s Japan had some 200,000 shrines that were nationalized by the Meiji government. In 1945 the Allies abolished the Imperial Cult after their victory that ended World War II. Shintō shrines suddenly lost all state sponsorship. Stranded with no funding and no organization, priests became ordinary citizens and many did not continue to practice their Shintō vocation. After Shintō shrines were made private their numbers diminished to around 80,000. The New Religions finally gained complete freedom of organization and practice in 1945. In 1946 the Association of Shintō Shrines was formed as an affiliation of local shrines. Priests and committees drawn from among worshipers managed these shrines. Ownership of the land and buildings was privatized and fundraising became a key aspect of support. In the face of this regrouping Japanese New Religions have become very popular, especially these two: (1) Sōka Gakkai, a Buddhist offshoot of Nichiren teaching from Kamakura era, and (2) Tenrikyō, a Shintō offshoot from the Tokugawa era (1603–1867). At the same time the number of Shintōists seems to be dropping annually (see Table 7.1). Nowadays there are over 2,000 New Religions whose membership ranges from a mere one hundred all the way to Sōka Gakkai's estimated sixteen million (on Tenrikyō and other religions that emerged on the world stage in this era see Box 7.4).

PART 2
SHINTŌ TEXTURE

FOUNDATIONAL TEXTURE

The Record of Ancient Matters (*Kojiki*) and the History of Japan (*Nihongi* or *Nihon-Shoki*) are the earliest Shintō writings still in existence (dating from 712 CE and 720 CE). They gave names to several of the myriad kami. Among those named, Amaterasu became the most famous due to her standing as ancestor of the Yamato clan. The Emperor Temmu (r. 673–686) was interested in having a record of Japan's history. Thus the scribes began to record stories that had been transmitted orally over generations by a guild of *kataribe* who may have been kami-possessed. The books contain myths, poems, and historical statements. These formed the foundation for Shintō rituals. They also provided the classic references on various tutelary kami of the clans and guilds. The two texts contain material from what may have been independent mythic cycles. For instance, different versions of creation are told in each book.

- The *Kojiki* tells of steaming mud and water out of which grew a plant with seven branches. Each branch held two kami who were brother and sister. These seven pairs of twins were dispersed throughout the cosmos and after an undetermined span of time a brother–sister team was born. They were called Izanagi (He-Who-Invites) and Izanami (She-Who-Invites).
- The *Nihongi* begins with a Chinese-style myth of creation in which the cosmos was formed from an egg-like mass that separated into a male (yang) heavenly portion and a female (yin) earthly portion.

Regardless of such differences, the content of the two texts overlaps considerably. Both contributed to Shintō lore about the kami and Japan's sacred history.

Stories in the *Kojiki* and *Nihongi*

The Record of Ancient Matters and History of Japan both describe the creation of the islands of Japan as follows: Izanagi and Izanami stood on a cloud bridge that spanned the sky. Izanagi stirred the muddy water with jeweled spears given to them by the other kami. Islands formed where the mud splashed. Izanagi and Izanami descended to the new land and engaged in a primordial union that made them husband and wife.

Thereafter, Izanagi and Izanami created waters, winds, fire, fields, substances that could be eaten, mountains, and other things. Izanami made fire but was badly burnt in the process. She turned her skull and ribs into caves and other bones to rocks. After she perished Izanagi sought her in Yomi (= darkness), the underworld. There he saw Izanami putrefying with maggots. Izanagi escaped from his underworld pursuers and purified himself in a stream.

Izanagi needed to be purified after escaping from Yomi due to his contact with death. Thus he purified himself. This became the prototype for the Great Purification of Shintō tradition. To become free from pollution Izanagi washed three parts of his body, and from each a kami child was born: (1) from his left eye was born the sun, (2) from his nose, the storms and thunder, and (3) from his right eye, the moon. The sun was Amaterasu, the Heaven-Shining-Great-August-Deity, who came to rule the High Plain of Heaven. The storm was her elder brother Susano-o, His-Swift-Impetuous-Male-Augustness. He came to rule the earth. The moon was Takamagahara, the sun's younger brother who became her consort and helped her rule.

The *Nihongi* says that Izanagi and Izanami together as a couple created the three children. After making the land, they consulted, saying, "We have now produced the great-eight-island country, with the mountains, rivers, herbs, and trees. Why should we not produce someone who shall be lord of the universe?" (deBary *et al.* 2001: 21; adapted from Aston, *Nihongi*, I:18–20). They then produced Amaterasu. After that came the moon kami, a "leech child which even at the age of three years could not stand upright" whom they therefore abandoned to the winds, and then Susano-o. This last kami would figure largely in the cultural memory of the Japanese people. The *Nihongi* describes Susano-o as follows:

> This god has a fierce temper and was given to cruel acts. Moreover he made a practice of continually weeping and wailing. So he brought many of the people of the land to an untimely end. Again he caused green mountains to become withered. Therefore the two gods, his parents, addressed Susa-no-o no Mikoto, saying, "Thou art exceedingly wicked, and it is not meet that thou shouldst reign over the world. Certainly thou must depart far away to the Nether-land." So they at length expelled him.

> (deBary *et al.* 2001: 21; adapted from Aston, *Nihongi*, I:18–20)

Susano-o committed several polluting acts for which he was fined and banished from the High Plain of Heaven, including: (1) damaging Amaterasu's rice fields, (2) defiling her house by voiding excrement in her New Palace at the time of celebrating the Feast of First Fruits, and (3) intending to go to see his mother in the polluted place of Yomi. After his banishment Susano-o carried out several deeds that helped restore him to the good graces of the other kami. He slew a serpent that had eight heads and eight tails. In one tail of the serpent Susano-o came upon a great sword that was to become one of the three imperial regalia. Eventually he came back into the good graces of all the kami.

On one occasion Susano-o startled his sister as she was weaving. The *Nihongi* says:

> Then Amaterasu started with alarm and wounded herself with the shuttle. Indignant of this, she straightway [*sic*] entered the Rock-cave of Heaven and, having fastened the Rock-door, dwelt there in seclusion. Therefore constant darkness prevailed on all sides, and the alternation of night and day was unknown.
>
> (deBary *et al.* 2001: 24; adapted from Aston, *Nihongi*, I:40–45)

The series of acts performed by various kami to persuade the Heavenly Shining One to come out again have lived for centuries in Shintō ritual. After this disaster, eighty myriad kami met at the Tranquil River of Heaven. They made a plan to persuade the sun to come out. They brought roosters to call each other outside the cave, and replanted a 500-branched *sakaki* tree taken from Mount Kagu in Yamoto. They decorated the upper branches with strings of jewels and an eight-hand mirror, and the lower branches with blue and white offerings. Some recited a liturgy. A troupe of kami danced and made music while kami Ame-no-uzume, the Terrible Female of Heaven, displayed herself with elegant gestures.

> [She] took in her hand a spear wreathed with Eulalia grass and, standing before the door of the Rock-cave of Heaven, skillfully performed a mimic dance. She took, moreover, the true Sakaki tree of the Heavenly Mount Kagu and made of it a headdress; she took club-moss and made of it braces; she kindled fires; she placed a tub bottom upwards and gave forth a divinely inspired utterance.
>
> (deBary *et al.* 2001: 25; adapted from Aston, *Nihongi*, I:40–45)

This inspired utterance piqued Amaterasu's curiosity. The Heavenly Shining One asked herself, "Since I have shut myself up in the Rock-cave, there ought surely to be continual night in the Central land of fertile reed-plains. How then can Ame no Uzume no Mikoto be so jolly?" (deBary *et al.* 2001: 25; adapted from Aston, *Nihongi*, I:40–45). Attracted by the music, roosters, glimpses of light glancing off the jewels, and the sacred speech, Amaterasu peeked out of the Rock cave, and then emerged from hiding. To prevent the world from again suffering in darkness the kami placed a **shimenawa** (a huge rope) across the cave's mouth.

Myth, history, and ritual

Shintō tradition says that Susano-o went to Korea and then to Izumo on the western coast of the Japanese island of Honshū. There his descendant Ōkuni-nushi (Great Land Master) ruled the earth for some time. Eventually Amaterasu noticed the unruly conduct under the governance of his descendants, and decided to send her grandson to rule. Shintōists revere Susano-o as a protector. He is enshrined at the Yasaka Jinja in Kyōto, among other places. From a historical point of view it appears that stories about Susano-o derive from a cult centered at Izumo that historically was filtered into the Yamoto cult, which derived from Amaterasu's grandson Ninigi (Ruddy-Plenty). Amaterasu's clan set up their government on the Yamoto plain across the mountains from Izumo on the eastern side of Honshū. Amaterasu's shrine was set up at Ise, near the east coast of the island. Amaterasu is enshrined at other locations but the Ise shrine contains the sacred mirror as her goshintai (symbolic body) and continues to be her main dwelling place. In the Edo period (1615–1868) Amaterasu become a popular object of worship as a few million Shintō pilgrims visited the Grand Shrines of Ise.

SUPPORTIVE TEXTURE

Modern Shintō theology

Until modern times, Japanese thinkers tended not to establish any Shintō doctrines. The social ethics and philosophical views of Confucian and Buddhist traditions seem to have occupied them instead. Yet with an interest in defining the Shintō contribution to Japanese thought, some philosophers are working to clarify the principles of Shintō ethics. Hiraï Naofusa identified the "life-attitude of **makoto**" as the "source" of Shintō ethics:

> *Makoto* is a sincere approach to life with all one's heart, an approach in which nothing is shunned or treated with neglect. It stems from an awareness of the Divine. It is the humble, single-minded reaction which wells up within us when we touch directly or indirectly upon the workings of the Kami, know that they exist, and have the assurance of their close presence with us.
>
> While on the one hand we sense keenly our baseness and imperfection in the presence of the Kami, on the other hand, we will be overwhelmed with ineffable joy and gratitude at the privilege of living within the harmony of nature.

> (Quoted in Herbert 1967: 71–72)

Other Shintō ethical values related to makoto are said to be: righteousness, individual and community harmony, cheerfulness of heart, thankfulness to nation, society, and family, effort to be a good citizen and member of society and family, devotion to the common interest, tolerant generosity that involves a "mental search for variety," benevolence, propriety and reverence, filial piety, industriousness, exercise of a strong will, and consciousness of shame. Many of these Shintō values are reminiscent of basic Confucian ethics (see Herbert 1967: 72ff.). Yet Shintō thinkers feel that the overriding value of makoto (as sincerity, cleanliness, honesty, and conscientious) gives Shintō ethics a Japanese quality. The Shintō sensibility also includes a subtle and personal feeling for nature, coupled with a sense of the pathos of things (*mono no aware*).

Some conservative Shintōists object to philosophizing, which amounts to an apologetic response to modern Western attitudes that fault religions with no explicit moral rules. They say that an authentic Shintō ethic is spontaneous and intuitive. This alternative view of Shintō ethics holds that human beings need freedom and become paralyzed by needless rules. Jean Herbert, a modern interpreter of Shintō, reported the gist of such a conservative viewpoint:

From a purely practical angle, if a man follows the pattern of life which has been bequeathed to him by his ancestors the Gods, what need is there to codify rules of conduct for various arbitrary groups of occasions? It is only when the man should fall so low as to be divorced from the life which children of the gods should live that he must resort to principles of morality—which otherwise would have a paralyzing effect and infringe upon the freedom which is his heirloom and which he needs.

(Herbert 1967: 69)

They believe that as children of Amaterasu the Japanese have an innate capacity to act properly when guided by the principles of purity demonstrated by the kami. They recognize that rules are created in times of alienation from the way of the kami, and find a solution in reconnecting with the kami no michi. One approach of going back to traditional Shintō principles is through *misogi* (purification). The process of purification starts with the outer cleansing and culminates in an understanding that the deepest level is "pacifying the soul" (*chin-kōn*).

CROSS-OVER TEXTURE

Japanese poetry

Many early Japanese poets wrote in the Chinese language, in the Chinese style—and even took on Chinese pen-names. But poetry is one aspect of culture that the Japanese soon made to suit themselves. The radical differences between the Chinese and Japanese languages motivated new explorations into the possibilities of poetic expression. The development of pivot words (*kake-kotoba*) and the later **haiku** form seems to have captured the Japanese sentimentality.

Pivot words

In the Japanese language each syllable generally has one consonant followed by one vowel. Many words contain other words within them. There are also many homonyms. These are words that sound the same but have different meanings embedded within other words which makes for rich possibilities of layers of expression. Thus in Japanese poetry the feature of word association is called the "pivot word" around which several meanings are linked. In his study of Japanese literature Donald Keene said, "The function of the 'pivot-word' is to link two different images by shifting in its own meaning" (Keene 1955: 4–5). Keene provided the following double translation of this poem by Shin Kokinshū (dated 1205 CE) based on his understanding of the pivot words and alternate meanings of the sounds:

> *Kie wabinu, utsurou hito no, aki no iro ni, mi wo kogarashi no, mori no shita tsuyu.*
> (1) Sadly I long for death. My heart tormented to see how he, the inconstant one, is weary of me, I am weak as the forest dew.
> (2) See how it melts away, that dew in the wind-swept forest, where the autumn colors are changing!

(Keene 1955: 6)

BOX 7.3 SYMBOLS: THE PRESENCE OF KAMI IN JAPANESE LIFE

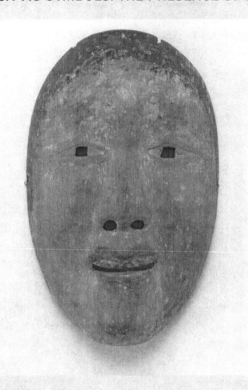

Figure 7.3

"Shintō mask: a young woman's face." Through the history of Shintō performance many styles of mask evolved to carry a rich array of symbolic meanings. One convention used the shape of eye openings to indicate the age of female characters portrayed by the mask: square openings for young women and half circles for older women. Note the eyes of this mask worn during the 1500s or 1600s. Masks are used in many types of Shintō performances including dance and processions, as well as court and religious rituals.

The stories of Izanagi, Izanami, Amaterasu, Susano-o, and other kami impacted the development of Japanese culture through many centuries, and give meaning to the life of Japanese people to this day. Here are some examples of stories that expressed themselves through ritual, art, and politics.

The three imperial regalia. Amaterasu bestowed three objects upon her grandson Ninigi before sending him down to Japan from the High Plain of Heaven: mirror, jewel, and sword. According to archeological evidence, the Japanese had used spears, swords, and mirrors made of bronze at least 500 years before the sacred stories about the imperial regalia were written down. They became imperial regalia that were passed down through generations of emperors. An enthronement transmission with these three imperial regalia was televised in 1989 with the accession of Emperor Akihito (Heisei).

The shimenawa rope. The shimenawa is a specially braided straw rope that demarcates the sacred space of Shintō shrines in memory of the time Amaterasu retreated to the Rock-cave after being shown disrespect by her brother Susano-o.

The troupe of kami. The dance and music created by the kami to entertain Amaterasu became the seed of Japanese theater. During the late 1300s and 1400s in the courts of the shōgun traditional Japanese dance was used in Nō drama. Nō performance involved a handful of actors who portrayed Shintō myths (such as Amaterasu being coaxed out of the cave by kami) and historical episodes through chant and dance movements. Ame-no-uzume, whose elegant gestures made Amaterasu joyful, is popular in the geisha tradition.

The sun. Amaterasu as the sun appears on a white background at the center of the Japanese flag. The connection between the ruler and the sun kami may indicate the early presence of a solar cult in Japan. The Yamoto ancestor cult used beads, mirrors, and items related to the horse. Scholars interpret the custom of keeping white imperial horses as another indication of connections between the ruling family and a solar cult.

Ninigi. The ancestral connection between Amaterasu's grandson Ninigi and his descendant Jimmu was taken to mean that every Japanese emperor was a living kami. Prior to World War II no ordinary person could even look at the emperor and no one could look down at him from above. These taboos pertained to the notion that the emperor was semi-divine.

Tanka

A twenty-volume collection of Japanese poems called the *Manyōshū* (Collection of Myriad Leaves) dates from the eighth century CE. Many of its 4,516 poems are *tanka* or "short poems" with a 5-7-5-7-7 syllable structure. The tradition ordinarily calls for a natural scene to be expressed in the first three lines, with their five, seven, and five syllables. The last two lines bring a wave of emotion that reveals a parallel between nature and the human condition. Here is an example:

Haru tateba	When spring comes
kiyuru koori no	the melting ice
nokori naku;	leaves no trace;
Kimi ga kokoro mo	Would that your heart too
ware ni tokenan.	melted thus toward me.

(Reischauer and Craig 1978: 27)

Haiku

Haiku is a Japanese art form of three poetic lines in a 5-7-5 format that was based on the older tanka form. Here subtle connections between nature and aspects of life are compressed into a mere seventeen syllables. Among the most famous haiku artists was Matsuo Bashō (1644–1694) who was born as a low-ranking samurai. He gave up that social position in 1672 and moved to the city of Edo, whose population was approaching one million. He began to concentrate on writing poetry, and focused on the lowly side of city life. Although Bashō became accomplished as a professional poet in the city, he turned to a life of lonely wandering during the ten years before he passed away. Consider these translations of Bashō's haiku by James H. Foard:

Yuku haru ya	Spring departs –
Tori naki uo no	Birds cry; fishes' eyes
Me wa namida.	Fill with tears.
Toshi toshi ya	Years and years –
Saru ni kisetaru	The monkey keeps wearing
Saru no men.	A monkey's mask.

Samidare ya   Constant rain –
Kaiko wasurau   The silkworms are sick
Kuwa no hata   In the mulberry fields.
                  (Foard 1976: 381, 385, 384, 379)

Bashō and other great haiku poets captured the double sense of Japanese aesthetics as they expressed both **wabi** (loneliness) and **sabi** (poverty). Wabi is reflected in the sense of the person as but a small, humble part of the vast mysteriousness of nature. Sabi is reflected in the simplicity of haiku whose three lines are lean and minimal.

BOX 7.4 A SPIRITUAL PATH: JAPANESE AESTHETICS

Wabi-sabi. Wabi and sabi are two notions central to Japanese aesthetics. Wabi is an experience characterized by longing, tearfulness, nostalgia, aesthetics appreciation, loneliness, and sincerity. Sabi refers to things that are weathered, rustic, stark, or imperfect—which convey a sense of poverty, leanness, chilliness, or simplicity. Often an encounter with something sabi brings up a feeling of wabi.

Wabi and sabi intermingle in the purity of living apart from society in the heart of nature where one lives purified by nature (wabi) without pretense (wabi) in a simple way (sabi) in poverty (sabi). Wabi and sabi also intermingle in the Japanese arts, including: (1) martial arts (archery, self-defense, the sword), (2) literary arts (poetry, calligraphy), and (3) arts of sacred spaces (flower arrangement, tea). The way of tea (cha-do) shows how even drinking a cup of tea can serve as a kind of spiritual path that leads to deeper awareness of reality.

The way of tea. Tea seeds were brought to Japan from China by the Zen Buddhist Eisai (1141–1215) during the Kamakura period. It was the age of the samurai who increasingly went to study the arts in Zen monasteries and drink tea. The way of tea developed into a Japanese art form that reflects Shintō sensibilities to nature and the Buddhist contemplative attitude and awareness of interdependence. The tea ceremony takes place in silence in a small thatched tea hut, ideally placed in a beautiful natural setting. Powdered green tea is spooned into boiling water in a pot situated low in the floor of the tea hut where a fire burns. Scrolls with single-line poems hang on the walls. Each tea bowl is unique with its own flaw. Tea-drinkers listen to the sounds of nature outside the hut and hear them reflected in the tea preparation. The sound of the boiling water echoes the sound of the wind flowing through the pine trees outside the tea hut. The whisking of tea mimics the rustling of leaves outdoors. In the midst of the loneliness of wabi and the simplicity of sabi those practicing the way of tea gain a deep sense of the mysterious presence of kami—perhaps in the wind, in the trees, in the boiling water, and in the tea itself. Ultimately, tea is no-tea. Zen master Seisetsu (1746–1820) said that whoever enters into the realm of no-tea realizes: No-tea is no other than the Great Way (*ta-tao*) itself (Suzuki 1970: 310).

PART 3
SHINTŌ PERFORMANCE

PURITY AND COMMUNION IN SHINTO RITUAL

Shintō rituals from archaic times until today have been concerned with two things: (1) removing impurities, and (2) maintaining communion with the kami. **Tsumi** is impurity or pollution. It is associated with disasters, sickness, and errors. Impurities that happen to human beings include injury, death, immodest behavior, contagious disease, wounds, and other ill things. Tsumi is not considered necessarily within the control of a human being, but all states of pollution must be purified. Sometimes whole groups of people must be purified. A person cannot exist in the right relationship with the kami in a polluted condition. Therefore at the very least all those who approach the Shintō shrine wash their mouth and hands at the "water purification place" (ablution pavilion). There are three basic Shintō means of removing impurities: (1) *harai* (purification through rites), (2) *misogi* (purification with water), and (3) *imi* (avoidance of the sources of pollution). Beyond the ritual ways of removing pollution are three means of maintaining a close relationship with the kami to develop the proper attitude toward life: (1) keeping a kamidana in the home, (2) visiting local shrines and making pilgrimages to Ise or other prominent shrines, and (3) participating in festivals.

Harai (purification through rites)

Shintōists call priests to ritually purify situations in which pollution has become or may become a problem. People may go to festivals, visit shrines, or call priests to travel to a site to perform a harai (ritual purification). Shintōists generally seek to be purified through rites performed by a priest at times of: (1) groundbreaking, (2) misfortune, (3) travel, (4) home cleaning, (5) marriage, and (6) communal purification. A few examples should suffice to give a sense of these rites: (1) On the occasion of groundbreaking a priest is called in to pacify kami in the area where a new building is to be erected. (2) Japanese tradition considers special times in people's lives when they are more likely to encounter misfortune than usual, such as in a woman's thirty-third year and a man's forty-second year. On these years purification is sought. (3) Someone who is going on a trip will seek safe travel and request protection from the kami through ritual purification. (4) On many occasions a Shintōist will want a house or business establishment freed from pollution, such as for home cleaning at New Year, after a death, at the start of an election campaign, and upon opening a new business. (5) A Shintō wedding ceremony is called a Shinzen Kekkon. It involves purification of the couple and their families, and concludes with a drink of sake to commune with the kami. (6) At times an entire community wants to be rid of pollution and seeks purification.

Misogi (purification with water)

Misogi involves water purification done by pouring water over oneself by hand, by buckets or ladles, crouching in a river or ocean, or standing beneath a waterfall. Misogi Shuhō or waterfall purification is among the key Shintō rituals. People are led through the ritual by a priest who performs ritual movements that include esoteric mudras (hand gestures) for purification. The leader directs some physical exercises, pours sake into the waterfall and throws salt both into the falls and on to the participants. Entering the waterfall first, the leader then directs each person to follow and informs him or her of the proper time to exit the falls. Men wear a loincloth and headband, while women wear a headband and usually a white *kimono*, a formal divided skirt, and wide-sleeved outer robe that reaches the knees. They allow the rushing sacred mountain water to fall on the backs of their necks and shoulders, saying, "Harae tamae kiyome tamae rokonshōjo," ("I beg for removal of impurity. I beg for cleansing. Make pristine all six elements"). Misogi Shuhō usually takes place late at night or at the crack of dawn. Some people undertake the ritual often.

Imi (avoidance of pollution)

Imi is the avoidance of pollution incurred by using taboo words (such as saying the word for "cut" at weddings) or doing taboo acts (like getting married on "Buddha's death" day). Imi is required of people who have been polluted by contact with a corpse, snakebite, incest, leprosy, tumors, and so forth. Anyone who is ritually unclean may be cursed as he or she approaches a Shintō shrine. Thus Shintōists practice imi to avoid pollution whenever possible.

Keeping a kamidana (home altar)

Each morning offerings of food (e.g., cooked rice) and drink (e.g., water) are set on the altars. The kamidana has representations of local and national kami, and homage is paid to the kami morning and evening. Many Japanese make an annual pilgrimage to a major shrine. From those sites (especially Ise, which is Amaterasu's shrine) they bring back sacred objects (which may simply be blessed paper) to place on their home shelves (kamidana) or attach to doors, put in stables, and so forth. Kami are also asked to bless people's homes during construction. Ritual specialists invoke them when the threshold, central pillar, kitchen, and bathroom are built. By contrast, the butsudan has representations of Buddhas, ancestor tablets, and ashes of the deceased. Tablets are inscribed with a new Buddhist name, and are generally kept for thirty-three or fifty years. On the Buddhist altar are ancestors of the main family of the oldest son in the father's line. Special offerings are made in conjunction with Buddhist memorial masses and particularly during forty-nine days of mourning.

Visiting a Shintō shrine

Common Shintō practitioners (not priests) go to the Shintō shrine and walk on foot beyond the point where the **torii** stands as a gateway. This walk has a purifying effect. Someone with an illness, open wound, flowing blood, or who is in mourning should not approach the shrine (though this practice may be somewhat relaxed in the present day). It is appropriate to remove hats, scarves, and coats. Ritual actions include several instances of bowing, handclapping, bell ringing, and kneeling to make an offering. It is common for people to go to Shintō shrines on important occasions of their personal lives such as: (1) when new business is conducted, (2) when a soldier goes to war, or (3) when children are born, start school, get married, and so forth.

Participating in shrine festivals (matsuri)

Festivals are an aspect of Shintō that goes back to the earliest days of planting and harvesting rice, and today matsuri is the heart of all Shintō activities. The shrine festivals follow a four-part sequence: (1) invoking the kami, (2) making offerings to the kami, (3) entering into communion with the kami, and (4) sending the kami back. A Shintō priest, having undergone a personal purification ritual, makes a ritual invocation that calls the kami to the shrine and opens the doors of the shrine's inner sanctum. Offerings such as rice, salt, water, sake, rice cakes, fish, seaweed, vegetables, grain, and fruit are present for the kami. In village festivals the Shintō participants carry a portable shrine (*mikoshi*) and march in procession. Young men dressed in festive clothing shout and act in ways reminiscent of ecstatic kami-possession and sometimes rush through the streets. The ceremony involves dancing, drumming, and singing in addition to contests. Performances may include ritual Japanese dances by shrine maidens (called miko), a lion dance, a Nō performance, or a Sumo wrestling contest. All performances are meant as entertainment for the kami, and the contests serve as forms of divination. For example, the outcome of tug-of-war, Sumo wrestling, horse-racing, archery, and swordsmanship competitions indicates the kami's will. The heart of a festival is entering into communion with the kami. For this a feast is prepared. Wooden casks of sake are broken open and consumed as a means of communing with the kami. The feast may end with silent meditation. Finally the kami formally are sent back and the doors of the inner sanctum are closed.

KEY POINTS

- Kami are the mysterious presences revered in Shintō tradition. They are mainly understood either as aspects of nature or as divine figures from the *Kojiki* and *Nihongi*. Various kami function as tutelary (guardian) kami for clans, guilds, and locations.
- Shamanism has been a long-standing aspect of Shintō. According to Chinese historians of the third century CE, a Japanese ruler called Pimiku was a shaman. Japanese women shamans are called miko, and they sometimes work together with yamabushi to contact spirits of the dead.
- Throughout China's Tang era (618–907 CE) the Japanese deliberately imported elements of Chinese civilization, forming (among other things) their basic model for imperial rule. Late in the Chinese Song era (960–1279) the Japanese were deeply impacted by neo-Confucian ideology as well as Pure Land and Chan (Zen) Buddhist traditions.
- One of the most striking ways that the Japanese culturally distinguished themselves was through literature. Nativist interpreters such as Motoori Norinaga (eighteenth century CE) claim that the authentic Japanese sentiment is the "pathos of life," which can be felt clearly in Murasaki Shikibu's *Tale of Genji*.
- The Tokugawa shōgunate unified Japan and oversaw a period of nearly 300 years of peace. This was achieved through a strict isolationist policy and government based on a neo-Confucian ideology of a highly stratified society, and a widespread network of Buddhist monasteries to which families officially were attached.
- The Shintō tradition continued to impact daily life throughout various political and cultural transformations in Japan. A strong sense of nationalism developed among the Japanese people as they were affected by State Shintō from 1868 until 1945 when Japan was defeated by the Allies in World War II.
- Since the end of World War II the New Religions in Japan have gained tremendous popularity—especially Sōka Gakkai (derived from the Nichiren Buddhist tradition) and Tenrikyō (based in part on the Shintō belief in kami-possession).

STUDY QUESTIONS

1. Define the term "kami" and name two types of kami recognized in the Japanese Shintō tradition. Review stories about the kami given in the *Kojiki* and *Nihongi*.
2. Describe the religious life of the early Japanese people and reflect on connections between early forms of worship and religious practice today.
3. What impact did the import of Chinese civilization (sometimes through Korea) have on Japanese religious and political life? When were the periods of most intensive contact between Japan and China?
4. Name two Japanese contributions to world literature, and identify a couple of great authors. (Hint: Think of the novel and haiku.)
5. Define kokutai and kokugaku. What was their impact on life and thought in Japan in the century or so prior to World War II?
6. Describe the rise of the New Religions in Japan, with specific reference to the origins and beliefs of Tenrikyō.
7. Describe Shintō ethics and practices today in terms of: (1) the importance of makoto, (2) removal of impurities, and (3) maintaining communion with the kami.

GLOSSARY

Ainu Early Caucasian-like people living in Japan with a distinctive culture.

Amaterasu The kami of the sun, from whom all Japanese emperors are said to be descended according to Shintō belief.

Bushidō Way of the warrior-knight; code of conduct for samurai that appeared earlier but was formalized around 1600 in the Tokugawa era.

butsudan Household Buddhist altar in Japan.

geisha A professional group of women entertainers in Japan, trained from childhood in singing, dancing, and the art of conversation.

goshintai A sacred object used in a Shintō shrine to represent or embody a kami presence.

haiku Seventeen-syllable poem in three lines of 5-7-5 format that developed in Japan.

kami (singular or plural) (literally, high, above, lifted up) Mysterious creative life energies that form the focus of Shintō worship.

Kami Way (Japanese: kami no michi) Another name for Shintō.

kamidana (literally, kami shelf) Shintō home altar for use in kami worship.

Kirishitan A Japanese Christian.

Kojiki (Record of Ancient Matters) Earliest surviving Shintō book (completed in 712 CE).

kokugaku Nativism or national learning; a literary-philological cultural movement from the Tokugawa era (1603–1867) dedicated to understanding and restoring the kokutai (national essence) of Japan.

kokutai (literally, national essence or national polity) Ideology promoted during the Meiji era (1868–1912) in Japan to justify the establishment of State Shintō.

makoto The life-attitude of sincerity that is the core value of Shintō tradition.

New Religions (Japanese: Shinkō Shūkyō) The "newly arisen religions" that developed in Japan starting in the late Tokugawa era, including Tenrikyō and Sōka Gakkai. *Nihongi* (***Nihon-Shoki***) (History of Japan) Second oldest Shintō book (completed in 720 CE).

sabi (Japanese) Principle in Japanese art indicating an objective simplicity (poverty). See wabi.

samurai (literally, men who serve) Members of the military class in medieval Japan.

shimenawa (literally, enclosing rope) Ceremonial rope braided with rice straw displayed in Shintō sacred places.

Shintō Japan's indigenous religion; Shintō is the Chinese pronunciation of the Japanese term *kami no michi*, Kami Way; it comprises the Chinese characters for *shen* (spirit) and *dao* (way).

Tale of Genji (*Genji Monogatari*) First novel in world literature, written by Murasaki Shikibu around 1000 CE about life in the Heian court.

Tenrikyō (literally, Religion of Divine Wisdom) A Japanese New Religion founded by Nakayama Miki (1798–1887) after being possessed by a kami.

torii (literally "bird-perch") Gateway to a Shintō shrine; also symbols marking places associated with kami.

tsumi Pollution in Shintō. Harai is purification. Thus a Shintōist removes sumi by means of harai.

uji-gami A tutelary clan kami in the Shintō tradition.

wabi (Japanese) Principle in Japanese art indicating a subjective loneliness. See sabi.

yamabushi Mountain ascetics who combine elements of Shintō and Buddhist traditions in their practices of healing and exorcism.

KEY READING

deBary, W. Theodore, Keene, Donald, Tanabe, George, and Varley, Paul (2001) *Sources of Japanese Tradition*, 2nd edn, vol. 1, New York: Columbia University Press.

deBary, W. Theodore, Gluck, Carol, and Tiedemann, Arthur E. (2005) *Sources of Japanese Tradition*, 2nd edn, vol. 2, New York: Columbia University Press.

Herbert, Jean (1967) *Shintō: At the Fountain-head of Japan*, New York: Stein & Day.

Hori, Ichiro (1968) *Folk Religion in Japan: Continuity and Change*, ed. Joseph Kitagawa and Alan Miller, Chicago, IL: University of Chicago Press.

Kitagawa, Joseph M. ([1966] 1990) *Religion in Japanese History*, New York: Columbia University Press.

Picken, Stuart D. B. (1994) *Essentials of Shintō: An Analytical Guide to Principal Teachings*, Westport, CT: Greenwood Press.

Sansom, George B. (1962) *Japan: A Short Cultural History*, revised edn, New York: Appleton-Century-Crofts (first published in 1943).

Section III
Religion of Nature, Provinces, and Empires

The following chapters include articles that discuss the religions of Greece and Rome and the province of Roman Britain. They also contain information on the nature-centered religions of Africa and Mesoamerica. In Chapter 8, "The Ancient Sources for Early Roman History" provides information on primary sources relating to Roman history, and "Religion and Burial" offers a lengthy discussion on religion and burial in Roman Britain. In Chapter 9, "Greek and Roman Insights into the Nature of Religion: Socrates, Plato, Aristotle, Cicero, Seneca" presents thoughts about religion from some of the prominent writers of the ancient world like Socrates and Cicero. In Chapter 10, "African Traditional Religion, Nature, and Belief Systems" discusses the prominence of nature in African religion. In Chapter 11, "From Teotihuacan to Tenochtitlan: Their Great Temples" contains information about the great religious temples of the Mesoamerican cultures.

Roman Britain Religion

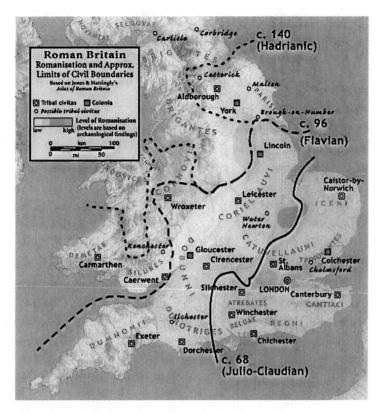

Fig. 8.0a: Copyright © Notuncurious (CC BY-SA 3.0) at https://commons.wikimedia.
org/wiki/File%3ARoman.Britain.Romanisation.jpg.

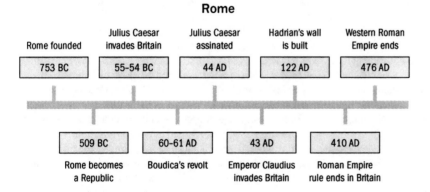

OBJECTIVES:

1. Understand what made Roman Britain religion unique.
2. Define syncretization.
3. Define Romanization.
4. Understand why Roman Britain culture was unlike that of any other
   Roman province.

The Ancient Sources for Early Roman History

By Gary Forsythe

T he history of Rome's regal period and early republic is highly problematic due to the fact that ancient accounts were written during the second and first centuries B.C., long after the events that they described.[1] Consequently, modern historians often disagree substantially in their interpretations and reconstructions, depending upon their presuppositions concerning the reliability of the ancient sources and the criteria by which ancient traditions should be considered accurate. Thus a serious study of early Roman history cannot be undertaken without a clear understanding and continual examination of the nature and veracity of the ancient sources that purport to record the history of Rome's distant past. The two most important ancient accounts of early Rome that have survived from antiquity are the first ten books of Livy's *History of Rome* and the *Roman Antiquities* of Dionysius of Halicarnassus, both of which were composed during the closing decades of the first century B.C. But since these two narratives came at the end of nearly two hundred years of a long and varied historiographical tradition, and were the authors' own synthesized redactions of earlier histories which are now lost except in fragments,[2] a survey of the ancient sources for early Roman history may properly begin with an overview of Livy's and Dionysius's predecessors.[3]

---

1   For other treatments of this subject, see Raaflaub and Cornell in Raaflaub 1986, 47–65; Ogilvie and Drummond in *CAH* VII.2 1989, 1–29; Cornell 1995, 1–30; and Oakley 1997, 3–108.

2   The term "fragment" is used by modern scholars of ancient history to refer to a portion of a lost ancient historical account that now survives in another surviving ancient literary text. A fragment can be either a verbatim quotation from a lost work or a paraphrase of a portion of its content. See Brunt 1980. In some instances (e.g., Cincius Alimentus, Postumius Albinus, and C. Acilius), we possess only a few fragments from a lost work and are therefore almost entirely ignorant of the work's nature and content, but in other cases (e.g., Cato, Calpurnius Piso, Claudius Quadrigarius, and Valerius Antias), the fragments are sufficiently numerous to give us a fairly clear picture of the work's structure, overall reliability, and historical methodology. The fragments of the lost histories of Roman republican authors are set out in their Greek and Latin texts in Peter 1914. It should be noted, however, that Peter ignored as fictitious the numerous citations of republican writers in the *Origo Gentis Romanae*, a short Latin treatise of late antiquity concerned with Roman mythology from primordial times down to the city's foundation by Romulus. For the rehabilitation of this work's citations see Momigliano 1958. The Latin text of this treatise is published in Pichlmayr 1970. In recent years, other editions of the lost histories of republican Rome have been produced, usually accompanied with a detailed introduction, notes, commentary, and/or translation into a modern language: Chassignet 1996 for Q. Fabius Pictor, L. Cincius Alimentus, A. Postumius Albinus, C. Acilius, and the *Annales Maximi*; Chassignet 1986 for Cato; Santini 1995 for Cassius Hemina; Forsythe 1994 for Calpurnius Piso; and Walt 1997 for Licinius Macer.

3   For other surveys of some or all of these writers, see Badian 1966; Gabba in *Origines de la République Romaine* 1967, 135–69; Gentili 1975; Rawson 1976; Forsythe 1994, 25–73; and Forsythe 2000.

THE ANNALISTIC TRADITION

As they did in many aspects of culture and literature, the Romans adopted the practice of historical writing from the Greeks, but the Greeks themselves did not begin to pay serious attention to Rome in their historical accounts until the Pyrrhic War (280–275 B.C.), when Rome was completing its subjugation of Italy and was involved in a war with the Greek city of Tarentum. Timaeus, a native of the Sicilian Greek town of Tauromenium, in his detailed history of the western Greeks from earliest times down to the eve of the First Punic War between Rome and Carthage (i.e., 264 B.C.), not only narrated the events of the Pyrrhic War but also treated Rome's mythical origin and early history in some detail. He visited Lavinium in Latium and made inquiries concerning the nature of the Penates worshipped by the Latins. He was somewhat familiar with the Roman yearly sacrifice of the October Horse, which he explained with reference to the Romans' descent from the Trojans. He dated the foundations of Rome and Carthage to the same year (814/3 B.C.); and he ascribed the invention of Roman bronze money to King Servius Tullius.[4] Another Sicilian Greek, Philinus of Acragas, wrote a contemporary historical account of the First Punic War (264–241 B.C.), but it was the momentous nature of the Second Punic or Hannibalic War (218–201 B.C.) that apparently prompted two Roman senators, Q. Fabius Pictor and L. Cincius Alimentus, to write the first native histories of Rome.[5] Their works were written in Greek, the literary language of the Hellenistic world, and they did not simply narrate the history of the Second Punic War but also recounted Roman affairs from mythical times down to their own day. Fabius Pictor's surviving fragments suggest that the traditions of the regal period were already well developed and in large measure resembled what we find in Livy's first book. Yet Dionysius (1.6.2) indicates that although the histories of Pictor and Alimentus were relatively detailed concerning Rome's foundation and the period of the Punic Wars, they passed over the intervening time span in a summary fashion.

Two other Roman senators, A. Postumius Albinus and C. Acilius, composed similarly all-encompassing histories of Rome, but since we possess very few fragments from these works, their scale and nature are unknown.[6] The first Latin narrative of Roman history was written by the poet Q. Ennius (239–169 B.C.), who composed his *Annals* in dactylic hexameter verse (see Skutsch 1985). This national epic—heroic, moralizing, and patriotic in nature—was a staple for educating Roman schoolboys and thus shaped the Romans' view of their past until its account of Rome's Trojan origin was supplanted by Vergil's *Aeneid* during the Augustan principate. The poem treated the Trojan connection and the regal period in the first three books, the early republic in the next two, and Roman affairs from the Pyrrhic War onwards in the remaining thirteen. The first Roman history composed in Latin prose was written by Cato the Elder (234–149 B.C.), and after that, with few exceptions, the Romans wrote their histories in Latin. Cornelius Nepos in his brief biography of Cato (3.3–4) describes the work as follows:

---

4   For Timaeus in general see T.S. Brown 1958, Momigliano 1977, and Pearson 1987. Concerning the Penates, October Horse, foundation date, and Servius Tullius, see Dion. Hal. 1.67.4; Polyb. 12.4 b 1; Dion. Hal. 1.74.1; and Pliny *NH* 34.43. All Timaeus's fragments are collected in Jacoby 1950, no. 566.

5   In addition to the modern works cited above nn.2–3, see Timpe 1972 and Verbrugghe 1979 for two contrasting treatments of Fabius Pictor, and see Verbrugghe 1982 for Cincius Alimentus.

6   Since Fabius Pictor, Cincius Alimentus, Postumius Albinus, and C. Acilius wrote their Roman histories in Greek, their fragments were collected in Jacoby 1958 as historians nos. 809–10 and 812–13.

He set about writing history in his old age. It consists of seven books. The first book contains the deeds of the kings of the Roman people, whereas the second and third books describe the origin of each Italian community, and for this reason it seems, all the books were called *Origines*. The First Punic War is in the fourth book, and the Second Punic War is in the fifth book. All these matters are described in a summary fashion. He narrated the remaining wars in the same manner down to the praetorship of Servius Galba [150 B.C.], who plundered the Lusitanians. He did not mention the commanders of these wars by name, but he recorded affairs without names. In these books he set forth the events of Italy and the two Spains as well as what seemed marvelous in these areas. He expended much energy and care upon these books but no learning.

The numerous fragments from this work bear out Nepos' description. The second and third books seem to have resembled the kind of Greek ethnographic history found in Herodotus and the fragments of Timaeus. The fragments from the last four books are largely concerned with the military affairs of the middle republic, and the fragments from the first book treat the regal period. Thus there is a strong possibility that Cato ignored the traditions of the early republic altogether, or at least treated them in a very cursory fashion.[7]

Following Cato, L. Cassius Hemina wrote a history probably comprising no more than five books, the first of which seems to have resembled the second and third books of Cato's *Origines* in recounting the mythical origins of the towns and peoples of central Italy. The work's second book covered both the regal period and the early republic. The surviving fragments suggest that Hemina had relatively little interest in military affairs but was keenly interested in religion and cultural history.[8] L. Calpurnius Piso Frugi composed a historical account in seven or eight books, which he probably published after his censorship of 120 B.C. Like Livy and Cato, Piso treated the regal period in his first book, while the events of the early republic were narrated in his second and third books. The latter, probably the most detailed account of the early republic written thus far, described events by using an annalistic framework and may have been the very first Roman historical account to employ this kind of structured narrative to depict the early republic (Forsythe 1994).

All histories of Rome written thus far by Romans had been composed by senators and were relatively brief accounts of names, dates, and major events. By the close of the second century B.C., however, detailed Greek histories such as that of Polybius, comprising thirty-nine books to describe in great detail Rome's conquest of the Mediterranean during the period 264–146 B.C., inspired Romans to write much lengthier works and to experiment with writing historical monographs on individual wars. Moreover, the writing of history was no longer a preserve of the Roman senator experienced in public affairs. It now became the occupation of men who possessed great literary skills, but who often lacked a practical knowledge of politics, diplomacy, and warfare. Thus, for example, Coelius Antipater (c. 100 B.C.), using earlier detailed histories written by Greeks, wrote a history of the Hannibalic War in seven books; and Sempronius Asellio,

---

7 On this matter see Forsythe 1994, 46–48; 2000, 4. For a general discussion of Cato's *Origines,* see Astin 1978, 211–39 with Kierdorf 1980.

8 For Hemina see Rawson 1976, 690–702; Scholz 1989; Forsythe 1990; and Santini 1995.

patterning his work after Polybius, devoted fifteen books to the period c. 150–90 B.C. Conversely, from this point onward other authors wrote greatly expanded histories of Rome from its foundation down to their own day. The first such was Cn. Gellius, whose work comprised at least ninety-seven books. His first book seems to have been patterned after the second and third books of Cato's *Origines* and the first book of Cassius Hemina in describing the mythical origins of the various peoples and communities of Italy. Romulus's reign was treated at the end of his second book and the beginning of his third. The expansive scale of Gellius's history is apparent from the fact that he described events of the year 389 B.C. in his fifteenth book, whereas Livy treated the same matters in his sixth. This literary expansion was largely achieved through the inclusion of lengthy speeches and battle narratives, which—for early Rome—were entirely invented and were intended to enliven his work and make it more entertaining for his readers. Although Livy did not make direct use of Gellius's history, Gellius was a major source for Licinius Macer and for Dionysius, who was apparently attracted to his rhetorical incontinence and meticulous attention to fictitious details.[9]

During the 80s and 70s B.C., Q. Claudius Quadrigarius, probably in reaction against the fictional character of Gellius's treatment of early Rome, compiled a history whose starting point was not Rome's mythical origin but the Gallic capture of Rome in 390 B.C. Quadrigarius chose to begin his narrative at this point because he believed that during the Gauls' occupation of the city all written records had been destroyed, and all historical traditions concerning events prior to 390 could therefore be regarded as untrustworthy (see Plutarch's *Numa* 1.2). Livy paraphrased this sentiment at the beginning of his sixth book and used Quadrigarius as a source throughout his second pentad. The fragments suggest that Quadrigarius was almost exclusively interested in military affairs.

During the last generation of the Roman republic, major histories were written by C. Licinius Macer, Valerius Antias, and Q. Aelius Tubero, all of whom Livy and Dionysius used as sources for their own works (see Ogilvie 1965, 7–17). As tribune of the plebs in 73 B.C., Macer was a staunch proponent of the populist politics of the day, which sought to restore full, traditional powers to the plebeian tribunate by overturning the restrictions placed upon the office in the recent constitutional reforms of the dictator Sulla.[10] Macer's fragments clearly display his keen interest in the struggle of the orders during the early republic. In fact, three fragments (Livy 7.9.3, 9.46.3, and 10.9.7–13 with 10.11.9) demonstrate that Macer was not averse to outright fabrication in order to enliven his narrative with spurious conflicts between patrician and plebeian officials. But perhaps the most sensational and shameless fabricator of the Roman annalists was Valerius Antias, who probably composed his history, consisting of at least seventy-five books, during the period c. 65–45 B.C. His work is frequently cited by Livy, who complains of his unreliability and indicates that he enjoyed inventing both major occurrences and minor details.[11] Thus by the time that Livy and Dionysius came to write history, Roman historiography had a complex development

---

9   For Gellius see Rawson 1976, 713–17 and Forsythe 1994, 163–64 and 229–32. For the practice of literary embellishment in ancient historiography see Wiseman 1979a, 3–40.
10   For Sallust's rendition of Macer's fiery political oratory during his tribunate, see Sallust *Historiae* III.48.1–28 = pp. 420–31 of the Loeb Classical Library edition of Sallust. For a detailed analysis of this speech see Walt 1997, 11–28.
11   For example, see Livy 3.5.12–13. For Antias and Livy in general, see Howard 1906, and for a discussion of Antias' influence upon the late annalistic tradition in his glorification of members of the Valerian family during the regal period and the early years of the republic, see Wiseman 1998, 75–89.

of nearly two hundred years behind it, and there were numerous sources at hand from which they could fashion their own works.

THE ANTIQUARIAN TRADITION

In addition to this rich and varied historiographical tradition, antiquarian scholarship, a similar but separate literary tradition, likewise arose and flourished during the last two centuries B.C., and the results of its research often provide modern scholars with valuable information about early Rome. Like the ancient historical accounts just surveyed, however, the antiquarian literature of the Roman republic survives almost entirely through its use by later extant authors. Roman antiquarians were not directly concerned with reconstructing and narrating the political and military history of the Roman state. They were interested in the history of the Latin language, including the original meaning and history of words. Nonetheless, since much of their research involved investigating the language, meaning, and terminology of religious and legal documents surviving from earlier times, their writings often devoted considerable attention to the history of Roman social, political, military, religious, and legal institutions and practices. The Roman antiquarian tradition can perhaps be said to begin with the publication of a treatise on the Roman religious calendar, written by M. Fulvius Nobilior, consul in 189 B.C. and a patron of the poet Ennius.

Several significant antiquarian writers flourished during the second half of the second century B.C. Besides writing histories of Rome, Fabius Maximus Servilianus (consul 142 B.C.) and Numerius Fabius Pictor (a descendant of Rome's first native historian) both wrote treatises on pontifical law. Junius Gracchanus, who received his surname from having been a close friend of the revolutionary politician C. Sempronius Gracchus (died 121 B.C.), wrote a work entitled *De Potestatibus,* which concerned the history of Roman customs and institutions and the powers of the various magistrates.[12] L. Aelius Stilo (c. 150–80 B.C.) published works on the archaic language of the hymn of the Salian priests and on the Law of the Twelve Tables. Atticus (110–32 B.C.), intimate friend of Rome's greatest orator, Cicero, not only shared his antiquarian learning with the latter (whose voluminous extant writings were thus enriched), but his Book of Chronology (*Liber Annalis*) outlined the whole of Roman history in a single volume and set forth its chronology in such a definitive and convincing manner that the scheme was adopted by Varro, and from the Augustan age onward this so-called "Varronian" chronology was the official chronology of the Roman state (see the Appendix).[13]

The greatest Roman antiquarian of all was M. Terentius Varro (116–27 B.C.), who throughout his long life wrote at least fifty-five treatises on a wide range of subjects.[14] According to one ancient source, Varro had completed the writing of 490 volumes by his seventy-eighth year. Unfortunately, the only one of his works that has survived to us intact is a treatise on agriculture (*De Re Rustica*), but substantial portions of his twenty-book examination of the Latin language (*De Lingua Latina*) have come down to us and contain much valuable information on early Roman institutions. In addition, a considerable amount of his scholarship, especially in the area of religion, has been preserved for us indirectly in the writings of later ancient

---

12   For the fragments see Bremer 1896 I. 37–40.
13   For Atticus's life and scholarly activity, see Münzer 1905 and Perlwitz 1992.
14   For an evaluation of Varro see Baier 1997.

authors such as Pliny the Elder, Aulus Gellius, Servius, Macrobius, and the Christian writers Tertullian, Lactantius, Arnobius, and Augustine.

The last major Roman antiquarian important for the study of early Rome is Verrius Flaccus, who flourished during the Augustan age and was therefore a contemporary of Livy and Dionysius. A significant portion of his scholarship, like Varro's, has been preserved indirectly in the writings of later surviving authors. One of his most important treatises, *De Significatu Verborum*, was a kind of antiquarian dictionary, in which archaic Latin words and phrases were arranged in alphabetical order, and their meanings were discussed and explained. Although this work has not survived, we possess a later abridgement of it by Sex. Pompeius Festus (c. 200 A.D.). A substantial portion of Festus's text (A-L) has been lost, but this loss is partially remedied by the survival of an eighth-century A.D. summary of the work by Paulus Diaconus. Despite the unfortunate state of its preservation, Festus's text contains much valuable information for the modern student of early Rome.[15]

LIVY AND DIONYSIUS OF HALICARNASSUS

Livy (59 B.C.–A.D. 17) was born at Patavium (modern Padova or Padua) in northeastern Italy, not far from Venice. He does not appear to have held any public office or to have performed any military service, but allusions to him in the works of Seneca the Elder and Quintilian indicate that he was a rhetorician by training and profession.[16] In his later years, after he had gained a reputation as a writer of Roman history, he is said to have encouraged the literary endeavors of Augustus's grandnephew Claudius (later emperor 41–54 A.D.), who wrote two histories: one of Carthage, and another of the Etruscans. Livy seems to have begun writing his history of Rome around 30 B.C. and might have still been writing right up to his death. The history comprised 142 books, beginning with Rome's foundation and ending with the year 9 B.C. The books of the history were clearly organized into groups of five (pentads) or of ten (decades) and were probably published in installments of five or ten books (Stadter 1972). Of the 142 books, only 1–10 and 21–45 have survived. The first ten books cover Roman affairs down to 293 B.C. and constitute our single most important source on early Roman history. This first decade may have been published around 20 B.C. (Luce 1965). Books 21–45 narrate Roman history for the years 218–167 B.C. Livy's history was so successful that it was soon acknowledged as the standard account of the Roman republic and eventually supplanted all earlier histories. Nevertheless, the work's huge size proved a hindrance to its complete preservation. In later centuries abridged versions abounded. Consequently, although only about one-third of the entire work has survived intact, we possess brief summaries of all the books, as well as later ancient condensations and adaptations of the history.

Livy did not possess the keen analytical intellect of a Thucydides, nor was he a shameless fabricator like Valerius Antias. Livy's real talent lay in his ability to arrange his material skillfully and economically, to construct an artistically pleasing narrative, and to depict individual episodes with great dramatic effect. Since most events covered in his history long preceded his own time, Livy did not engage in any original

---

15   Modern scholars normally cite Festus according to the pagination of the Teubner text edited by W. M. Lindsay; and in order to signify the fact that this text, rather than some other earlier edition, is being used, *L* is placed after the relevant page number.

16   Seneca *Controv.* 9.1.14; 9.2.26; 10. praef. 2; Quintilian 1.5.56; 1.7.24; 2.5.20; 8.1.3; 8.2.18; 10.1.39; and 10.1.101.

research into official documents, but was content to compare and synthesize the different accounts of earlier historians. Generally speaking, he adopted an agnostic attitude toward the received traditions of early Rome, and he did little more than try to reconcile discrepancies in his sources by using arguments from probability, a mainstay of ancient rhetorical training. Thus Livy was not particularly concerned with ascertaining detailed points of historical fact. Rather, he was much more interested in larger moral and patriotic themes. Like many other ancients, he believed that the value of history lay in providing people with good and bad models of conduct to be emulated and to be avoided respectively. His history has a decidedly moral and patriotic tone.[17]

Dionysius of Halicarnassus was an exact contemporary of Livy.[18] He came to Rome in 30 B.C. and began teaching Greek rhetoric to members of the Roman upper class. In addition to having written critical treatises on famous Greek orators, Dionysius wrote a stylistic critique of the Greek historian Thucydides, which he dedicated to the Roman historian and jurist Q. Aelius Tubero (Pritchett 1975). A century earlier, Polybius had published his detailed history in Greek of Rome's conquest of the Mediterranean during the period 264–146 B.C., but since all other historical accounts written in Greek had failed to treat early Roman history in as much detail as the Latin annalists of the late republic, Dionysius undertook to write such an account for his fellow Greeks. The product was his *Roman Antiquities,* comprising twenty books and covering Roman affairs from earliest times down to 264 B.C. The work was completed by 7 B.C. and was Dionysius's own synthetic redaction of the histories of Cn. Gellius, Licinius Macer, Valerius Antias, Aelius Tubero, and other native Roman writers. Only the first eleven books of this work, treating events down to 449 B.C., have survived. Portions of the remaining nine books have come down to us in excerpts made by later Byzantine writers. The work is far more lavish and rhetorical than Livy's first decade. This often makes for tedious reading. Even the most casual comparison of Dionysius's history with Livy's first ten books reveals the latter's judiciousness and discriminating restraint and the former's unbridled verbosity. Nevertheless, since Dionysius was writing for a Greek audience whom he assumed to be not particularly well informed concerning Roman customs and institutions, his narrative is oftentimes more informative than Livy's, because the latter tends to omit many details with which his Roman readers were familiar. Furthermore, even though Livy and Dionysius generally drew upon the same earlier historical accounts for compiling their narratives, their treatments of individual events often diverge markedly, thus providing modern scholars with important glimpses into the heterogeneity of the Roman annalistic tradition.

---

17 Walsh 1963 and 1974 are two excellent surveys of Livy and his work. Dorey 1971 and Schuller 1993 are collections of essays written by different authors on various aspects of Livian scholarship. Ogilvie 1965 is a detailed commentary on the first pentad. Oakley 1997 is a thorough introduction to the second pentad and exhaustive commentary on Book VI. Oakley 1998 is a similarly detailed commentary on Books VII-VIII. A third volume soon to be published by the same author will treat Books IX-X. Phillips 1982 is a detailed bibliographical essay concerning modern scholarship on Livy's first ten books. Luce 1977, 139–297 is an excellent treatment of Livy's methods in writing his history by synthesizing earlier historical accounts. Forsythe 1999 discusses Livy's historical methods and judgment throughout the first decade. Gutberlet 1985 attempts to detect the influence of the political violence of the late republic in Livy's first ten books. Ridley's study in Eder 1990, 103–38 is the single best essay on Livy's attitude toward the struggle of the orders.

18 For a relatively recent treatment of Dionysius and his *Roman Antiquities* in the broader context of Augustan Rome and Greek society, see Gabba 1991. For an examination of his ideas on historical writing, see Sacks 1983. For his ideology in portraying the regal period, see Fox 1996, 49–95.

CICERO AND DIODORUS SICULUS

Two other ancient writers important for early Roman history and therefore deserving comment are Cicero and Diodorus. M. Tullius Cicero (106–43 B.C.) was Rome's greatest orator, whose numerous speeches and nearly one thousand letters make the years 65–43 B.C. the best documented period of classical antiquity. Besides speeches and letters, Cicero wrote a large number of philosophical and rhetorical essays that contain valuable allusions to events in earlier Roman history. Two essays of particular interest to the modern scholar of early Rome are *De Re Publica* and *De Legibus,* which were roughly patterned after Plato's two famous works, *The Republic* and *The Laws.* Book 2 of *De Re Publica* traces the political and constitutional history of the Roman state as an ideal model for the evolution of the mixed constitution. Unfortunately, the text is not complete and contains many gaps, but it is still an important narrative for the tradition of the regal period and of the early republic down to 449 B.C. Books 2–3 of *De Legibus* discuss the laws that an ideal state should possess; and since these laws are largely those of the Roman state, the treatise is a valuable source of information concerning Roman institutions.

Diodorus Siculus was a Sicilian Greek, who wrote a universal history of the ancient world in forty books, beginning with the mythical past and coming down to the year 60 B.C. He seems to have written during the 50s, 40s, and 30s B.C. Only Books 1–5 and 11–20 have been fully preserved, and the latter narrate the events of the fifth and fourth centuries B.C.; but since Diodorus for this period is almost entirely interested in recording the events of mainland Greece, the Persian Empire, and the western Greeks, he describes Roman affairs very briefly and usually only when there is some truly momentous event to relate, such as the decemviral legislation, the Gallic capture of Rome, or major events of the Second Samnite War. Otherwise, he is content merely to record the names of Rome's eponymous magistrates for each year along with the name of the eponymous archon of Athens. Consequently, his narrative is an additional source for the early list of Roman magistrates, even though the lists, especially of the colleges of military tribunes with consular power, often contain omissions and errors due to his carelessness or that of later copyists (Drummond 1980). Nevertheless, Diodorus's list of Roman magistrates contains a few major differences from those of Livy, Dionysius, and the *Fasti Capitolini* which are of historiographical interest (Drachmann 1912). Since some of his detailed Roman material differs from Livy's account, there has been much modern scholarly speculation concerning the nature and identity of his Roman source or sources (Perl 1957 and Cassola 1982, 724–58). Since Mommsen (1879) advanced the view that Diodorus's source for Roman affairs was Fabius Pictor, modern scholars have sometimes given his account of events preference to others, but Mommsen's hypothesis has now been generally discredited (Beloch 1926, 107–32 and Klotz 1937), and the oddities of Diodorus's Roman material can usually be attributed to the author's own carelessness and general indifference to the details of the annalistic tradition.

ANCIENT DOCUMENTARY SOURCES

Now that Rome's annalistic and antiquarian traditions have been briefly sketched, it may be reasonably asked upon what kind and quality of information these ancient historical and antiquarian works were ultimately based. One possible source of information that has figured prominently in modern scholarly treatments of early Roman history is the Pontifical Chronicle or *Annales Maximi,* whose genesis Cicero (*De Oratore* 2.52–53) describes as follows:

From the beginning of Roman affairs to the chief pontificate of P. Mucius [130–115 B.C.], the chief pontiff [= pontifex maximus] used to write down all matters year by year, publicized (or recorded) them on a whitened board (*album*), and placed the tablet (*tabulam*) in front of his house, so that the people could learn from it. Even now they are called the Chief Annals (*Annales Maximi*). This form of writing has been followed by many who have left behind unembellished records of mere dates, persons, places, and deeds.

Servius Auctus, commenting in late antiquity on Vergil's *Aeneid* 1.373, gives the following description of the chronicle's content:

Every year the pontifex maximus had a whitened tablet (*tabulam dealbatam*), upon which he first wrote the names of the consuls and of other magistrates. He then used to jot down day by day the events at home and abroad, both on land and sea, worthy of record. The ancients filled eighty books with these yearly commentaries of the pontiff's diligence, and they called them the Chief Annals (*Annales Maximi*) from the chief pontiffs by whom they were composed.

The nature and history of Roman pontifical record keeping has been much discussed, and many different theories have been advanced.[19] The most likely explanation, supported by ancient Babylonian astronomical diaries and medieval monastic Easter calendars, is that the whitened board of the chief pontiff was calendrical in nature.[20] Other ancient sources indicate that during republican times, at the beginning of each month the rex sacrorum announced to the assembled Roman people the festivals to be observed that month. This announcement probably included the month's legal calendar as well (Varro *Ling. Lat.* 6.27, Servius Auctus *ad Aen.* 8.654, and Macrobius *Saturnalia* 1.15.9–13). A whitened notice board must have been employed to supplement and reinforce these monthly oral proclamations, and in the course of time the chief pontiff, who was in charge of the custom, used the board to record events bearing upon his supervision of the public religion. The early Romans believed that the individual days of the year were either auspicious or inauspicious; and the pontiffs, who were responsible for regulating the calendar, were probably interested in recording the dates of major public events in order to determine empirically the favorable or unfavorable nature of each day of the year. Moreover, at the end of each year any pertinent data must have been copied from the whitened board into a more permanent and less bulky record, such as a linen scroll or wooden codex, and a new notice board was used for the next year. According to Cicero, the custom of this notice board went far back into the past and was not discontinued until P. Mucius Scaevola was chief pontiff.

Many modern scholars have concluded that while Scaevola was chief pontiff, all accumulated pontifical data were compiled into the eighty books of the *Annales Maximi*, but Frier (1979, 27–48 and 192–200) has argued that Scaevola simply discontinued the custom of posting a notice board, and that the eighty-book edition mentioned by Servius Auctus was not compiled until early imperial times. This view, however, has been refuted in detail (Forsythe 1994, 53–71 and 2000, 7–8). Among other things, the contemporaneous

19   For an overview of modern scholarly opinions, see Frier 1979 10–20, 162–72, and 179–80. See also Crake 1940; Bauman 1983, 290–98; Drews 1988a; Forsythe 1994, 53–71; Bucher 1995; and Forsythe 2000, 6–8.
20   For analogous ancient Babylonian record keeping, see Sachs 1948. For a discussion of the origin and nature of medieval monastic chronicles, see Thompson 1942, 158 ff.

works on pontifical law by N. Fabius Pictor and Fabius Maximus Servilianus constitute very strong circumstantial evidence that interest in such matters was characteristic of the late second century B.C. In fact, Pictor's and Servilianus's works were probably reworkings of the recently consolidated *Annales Maximi,* whose content they helped to disseminate and to incorporate into the developing Roman annalistic tradition. More recently, Bucher (1995) has argued that the *Annales Maximi* took the form of a series of inscribed bronze tablets nailed up on the outer wall of the Regia, but his thesis rests upon a flawed interpretation of Cicero's *De Oratore* 2.52 quoted above (Forsythe 2000, 8–25). He regards *album* and *tabulam* as referring to two different objects, a whitened notice board and a bronze tablet; but the variation is more plausibly taken as Cicero's use of two different words to describe the same thing so as to avoid verbal repetition in two adjacent phrases. Note that Servius Auctus combines *tabula* with an adjectival form of *album* to describe the pontiff's wooden notice board. Even if we were to factor in pontifical material relevant to the civil law, which in fact was most likely preserved in its own separate archive, there never could have been enough pontifical material to fill eighty papyrus scrolls of the average size used for books of literary prose. To judge from the nature of our surviving sources, by Scaevola's day the amount of authentic pontifical material preceding the middle of the fourth century B.C. must have been quite modest. Frier's down-dating of the eighty-book edition to the early empire only shifts this embarrassing problem from one chronological context to another. On the other hand, when supplemented with other religious material and traditions already recorded in published histories, the pontifical material accumulated during the early and middle republic might have easily filled eighty wooden codices: for a bulky codex, even one of numerous thin wooden leaves, could not hold as many columns of writing as a papyrus scroll. Thus, eighty wooden codices comprising the *Annales Maximi,* suspended by hooks from rafters in a public building like other Roman official records, might have contained the equivalent of only fifteen to twenty average-sized books written on papyrus.[21]

The historical accounts of Livy and Dionysius contain certain kinds of information that modern scholars have generally supposed to derive ultimately from the Pontifical Chronicle: the list of annually elected consuls (*fasti consulares*), major military defeats and the celebration of triumphs, the deaths of priests, the dedications of new temples and the institution of new religious celebrations, plagues, food shortages, and the occurrence of unusual phenomena that the Romans regarded as divine prodigies requiring expiation (e.g., eclipses, monstrous births, and damage or death caused by lightning).[22] Such material forms a very small portion of Livy's and Dionysius's narratives. At most the historical data preserved in the *Annales Maximi* would have provided their accounts with a skeletal chronological framework of major events, whose narrative had to be fleshed out by other means. The surviving fragments from the works on pontifical law written by N. Fabius Pictor and Fabius Maximus Servilianus, whose content probably resembled that of the *Annales Maximi,* largely contain detailed contemporary religious regulations and verbal formulae used in ceremonies (Peter 1914, 114–16 and 118). This suggests that the eighty books of the *Annales Maximi* comprised a relatively small amount of truly historically relevant data. It seems likely that histories such as that of Calpurnius Piso, written about the time of the compilation of the *Annales Maximi,* were the

---

21   For the history of the ancient book form, see Kenyon 1951, and for a survey of Roman archival practices, see Posner 1972, 160–223.

22   For a skeptical view concerning the Pontifical Chronicle as the source of Roman prodigy lists, see Rawson 1971a, but for counterarguments see Ruoff-Väänänen 1972. On the names of priests preserved in Livy, see Rüpke 1993.

first works to incorporate systematically the relevant historical data gleaned from the Pontifical Chronicle, including an annalistic framework, and that subsequent historians did not need to consult the work directly but simply took the material over indirectly from other accounts.

Another important source of documentary information for later ancient writers is thought to have been the texts of treaties and laws inscribed on durable materials such as stone or bronze, so that they still existed in historical times and were thus available to those interested in examining them. According to Dionysius (4.58.4), an ox-hide shield bearing the text of a treaty between Rome and Gabii, concluded during the reign of Tarquinius Superbus, was preserved in the temple of Dius Fidius on the Quirinal. Cicero (*Pro Balbo* 53) indicates that the Cassian Treaty with the Latins, dating to the year 493 B.C., was still to be seen during his own day engraved on a bronze column behind the Rostra in the Forum. Polybius (3.22–26) succeeded in locating the texts of three early treaties between Rome and Carthage, and used their contents to reconstruct the early diplomatic history between the two states. There can be no doubt that if such texts were properly dated and their main provisions accurately related, treaties could serve as important landmarks in charting Rome's growing sphere of interest and influence in international affairs over the course of time. But the surviving ancient evidence suggests that Polybius's translation and detailed explication of the early treaties between Rome and Carthage rarely, if ever, had parallels in other ancient accounts of early Rome.

Dionysius (4.26) states that the sacred law attributed to King Servius Tullius, prescribing sacrificial procedures for the cult of Aventine Diana, could still be seen in his day, carved in archaic letters on a bronze tablet; and inscriptions of the early principate indicate that this so-called Aventine Canon was still serving as a model for Roman religious ceremonies.[23] Dionysius (10.32.4) also says that a law passed in 456 B.C., which regulated private settlement on the Aventine Hill, was inscribed on a bronze tablet and placed in Diana's temple. According to Livy (3.55.13), the plebeian aediles from the middle of the fifth century B.C. onwards were responsible for preserving the texts of senatorial decrees in the temple of Ceres on the Aventine. Thus it appears that at least some original documents of the early republic still existed in later historical times. The chances of a document's survival must have been enhanced if it had been engraved on bronze or a durable type of stone, if it happened to be deposited in a temple where it might be left undisturbed as a religious dedication, and if its provisions did not become obsolete but continued to be somehow relevant. Only documents of particular importance, however, were likely to be engraved on stone or bronze, and many of the inscribed bronze tablets from early times were probably eventually melted down so that the metal could be reused. The great majority of laws and other official documents must have been written on much more perishable materials such as wood, parchment, and linen.

Apart from the question of preservation, we may wonder how accurately ancient historians and antiquarians could read and interpret archaic Latin texts. Polybius (3.22.3) states that the language of the oldest treaty between Rome and Carthage was so archaic that even the most learned Romans of his day had difficulty in understanding it. As a general rule, legislative language tends to be convoluted and cryptic, and the actual content of laws is frequently complex, so that the brief summaries of supposed landmark statutes which we encounter in Livy and Dionysius, reported at second hand from earlier accounts at best,

---

23   Inscriptions of the early empire from Narbo in Gaul, Salonae in Dalmatia, and Ariminum in northern Italy refer to this canon as forming the basis of cultic charters. See respectively *ILS* 112, 4907, and *CIL* XI: 361.

may not be very reliable. Furthermore, even if the text of a law survived into later times and was readily comprehensible, the document would have contained no information regarding the political and historical circumstances surrounding its passage. This could only be supplied by oral tradition or by the researcher's own imagination, both of which might be quite unreliable.

It just so happens that the chance discovery of an archaic Latin inscription furnishes us with one clear instance in which we can see how ancient historians and antiquarians dealt with such material. In 1899, the Italian archaeologist Giacomo Boni unearthed an inscribed stone from beneath a black marble pavement in the Forum near the Comitium and Rostra. The stone is oblong, measuring about two feet in length with four lateral faces; since one end is thicker than the other, it has the shape of an obelisk. It is therefore likely that before it was buried beneath the ancient pavement of the Forum in imperial times, it stood upright on its thicker end. Along the length of the four lateral faces have been inscribed sixteen lines of very early Latin, whose meaning is rendered even more problematic by the fact that a portion of the stone's upper end was broken off, so that the text is incomplete (see Gordon 1983, #4). On the basis of the shapes of the inscribed letters, modern scholars generally agree in dating the inscription to about 500 B.C., making it one of the oldest surviving Latin texts. Although the precise meaning of the document is uncertain,[24] four words are beyond dispute: (1) *sakros* = classical Latin *sacer*, masculine nominative singular, meaning "sacred" or more likely "accursed," thus alluding to the imposition of a religious sanction upon an offender of this law; (2) *recei* = classical Latin *regi*, indirect object in the dative case of *rex*, meaning "king," thus referring either to the Roman king or to the rex sacrorum of the fledgling republic; (3) *kalatorem* = classical Latin *calatorem*, direct object in the accusative case, meaning "herald" or "crier," referring to a minor official who was a kind of usher, possibly for the *rex*, whose duty was to clear a path for the king in public; (4) *iouxmenta* = classical Latin *iumenta*, nominative or accusative neuter plural, meaning "beasts of burden" and hence also "wagons," "carriages," "vehicles."

Since this so-called *cippus* of the *lapis niger* was not taken down and solemnly buried until imperial times, it must have stood near the Rostra throughout the republic and was therefore on permanent display for inspection by anyone interested in it. Ancient Roman historians and antiquarians, who probably had the benefit of examining the text in an undamaged state, thought that this inscribed stone was a tombstone, one thing which it certainly is not. At least three different views were offered concerning the identity of the alleged grave's occupant. One was that it was the tomb of Faustulus, the herdsman who had rescued and raised Romulus and Remus, and who had been killed at this site in the Forum when the followers of Rome's twin founders fell to quarreling over the auspices for naming the city. A second view was that it was the tombstone of Hostus Hostilius, the grandfather of King Tullus Hostilius, who had been killed during the fighting in the Forum Valley between the Romans under Romulus and the Sabines under T. Tatius, following the rape of the Sabine women. A third view was that it was the grave of Romulus himself.[25] All three of these conjectures associate the inscribed stone with the reign of Romulus, thereby dating it to the second half of the eighth century B.C.

---

24 For two differing interpretations, see R.E.A. Palmer 1969 (a sacred law protecting a grove from pollution) and Dumézil 1979 259–93 (a sacred law regulating the procession of the rex sacrorum along the Sacra Via). Cf. Vine 1993, 31–64. Coarelli (1983, 161–99) has cogently argued that the stone belonged to the Volcanal, a precinct sacred to Vulcan, which contained an archaic altar and column.

25 See Dion. Hal. 1.87.2; 3.1.2; and Festus 184L s.v. *niger lapis*.

ROMAN ORAL TRADITION AND GREEK MYTH

If we liken the use of the ancient literary tradition of early Roman history to modern paleontologists' hypothetical reconstruction of a long-extinct, large, magnificent creature, the documentary data of the Pontifical Chronicle and the texts of laws, treaties, and religious dedications correspond to bones retrieved from an incomplete fossil record, whereas native oral tradition, Greek literary models, and the creative imagination of Roman writers are like the reconstructed flesh, organs, and skin. In this model we may suppose that ancient Roman writers did not possess a complete skeletal framework of early Roman history, that the skeletal remains might even have derived from more than one creature, and that their assemblage of this basic structure might not have been free of errors. B.G. Niebuhr, a German scholar of the early nineteenth century, postulated that much of the content of the later literary tradition concerning the regal period ultimately derived from Roman bardic poems, sung at banquets during the early and middle republic. According to this "ballad theory," the historical deeds of the kings were preserved, albeit distorted, in mythicizing heroic songs, whose content was taken over by ancient historians. An important component of Niebuhr's thesis is Cicero's citation of Cato's *Origines* for the assertion that in earlier times banqueters were accustomed to sing the praises of famous men to the accompaniment of a flute.[26] Although Niebuhr's ballad theory has generally been dismissed by modern scholars,[27] Zorzetti (1990, 289–95) has plausibly explained Cicero's remarks as evidence that early Roman society adopted Greek sympotic culture, including the singing or recitation of lyric verse as a popular form of entertainment. Consequently, while Niebuhr's notion of a fully developed bardic tradition in early Rome is to be rejected, aristocratic banquets could have provided a setting in which the singing of songs contributed in some degree to the formation of a national historical tradition. Yet as modern critics of Niebuhr have pointed out, Cicero's words indicate that this tradition no longer existed in Cato's day.

From the middle of the third century onward, at major annual festivals, Roman playwrights produced for the public stage *fabulae praetextae* (tales in Roman formal dress) that dramatized both major contemporary events and episodes from the received historical tradition (Flower 1995 and Wiseman 1998, 1–16 and 153–64). In recent years, T.P. Wiseman has revived and further refined the notion that performances on the Roman stage were important in the development of Roman historical traditions. His basic working hypothesis is that, in a society in which literacy was not widespread, public spectacles at annual festivals or accompanying triumphs, temple dedications, and aristocratic funerals constituted an important medium for creating, adapting, and propagating popular traditions, which in many instances became part of the later literary historical tradition of the Roman state. Wiseman (1994, 1–22) argues that Roman society was open to Greek and Etruscan influences from very early times, and he uses archaeological finds to suggest that Greek myths and related stories were in circulation in central

---

26   Cic. *Brutus* 75: "Would that there existed those poems which, as Cato has written in his *Origines,* used to be sung many generations before his age at banquets by individual diners concerning the praises of famous men!"

    Cic. *Tusc. Disp.* 1.3: "It is written in the *Origines* that diners at banquets were accustomed to sing of the virtues of famous persons to the accompaniment of a flute player."

    Cic. *Tusc. Disp.* 4.3: "Cato, a very weighty authority, has stated in his *Origines* that among our ancestors there had been a custom at banquets for those who reclined on couches to take turns singing the praises and virtues of famous men to the accompaniment of a flute."

27   For a detailed discussion of Niebuhr's thesis and its history in modern scholarship, see Bridenthal 1972. Cf. Momigliano 1957 and Fraccaro 1957.

Italy during the archaic period. He further surmises that despite the silence of our all-too-faulty sources, public performances of some sort existed at Rome much earlier than is generally supposed; and he conjectures that the stage was the place where the Roman community in large measure created and shaped its collective identity. As will be discussed in chapters 4 and 10 , Wiseman (1995, 126–43) has used this drama hypothesis to explain the evolution of Rome's foundation story. Even though many of his ideas are unavoidably speculative due to the scanty nature of our sources, Wiseman's drama hypothesis offers modern scholars of ancient Rome a new paradigm with which to reexamine old and familiar issues from a fresh perspective.

A less controversial source of early traditions was the well-established practice of delivering a funeral eulogy for a deceased aristocrat, an oration in which not only his own but his ancestors' deeds, virtues, and public offices were enumerated. Polybius (6.53 with Flower 1996, 91–127) gives us a detailed description of this custom for the middle of the second century B.C., but the tradition was obviously much older. Ancient writers even indicate that written copies of such funeral orations were sometimes kept in family archives. Thus aristocratic family traditions, either written or oral, could have been incorporated into later historical accounts. For example, Livy's narration in 8.30 of military operations in Samnium conducted by Q. Fabius Maximus Rullianus in 324 B.C. may derive ultimately from Fabian family tradition through Fabius Pictor. Nevertheless, both Cicero and Livy regarded such family traditions as a principal means by which early Roman history was contaminated with exaggerated or falsified claims. Cicero (*Brutus* 61–62) concluded that by his own day the early history of Roman oratory could not be documented with written texts any earlier than Cato (234–149 B.C.); and he comments on family funeral orations in the following words:

> We regard Cato as quite ancient. He died in the consulship of L. Marcius and M'. Manilius, eighty-six years before my consulship. Nor in fact do I think that there is anyone more ancient whose writings I think should be adduced for sure, unless perchance someone likes this same speech of Ap. Caecus concerning Pyrrhus and some funeral eulogies. By Hercules, they do indeed exist. The families themselves preserved them as their own trophies and records, to be used when someone in the family died, for remembering the praises of their house and for demonstrating their noble lineage, despite the fact that our country's history has been made less accurate by these eulogies. Written in them are many things which did not occur: false triumphs, too many consulships, even forged genealogies, and transitions to the plebs in which people of lower station have been inserted into a clan of the same name, as if I should claim to be descended from the patrician M'. Tullius who was consul with Ser. Sulpicius in the tenth year after the expulsion of the kings.

Livy (8.40.3–5) writes in similar disparaging terms at the very end of his eighth book, assessing conflicting accounts of Roman military operations against the Samnites in 322 B.C.:

> It is not easy to prefer one thing over the other or one author over another. I think that the tradition has been contaminated by funeral eulogies and by false inscriptions on busts, since various families have fraudulently arrogated to themselves the repute of deeds and offices. As a

result, both individuals' deeds and the public records of events have certainly been thrown into confusion. Nor is there any writer contemporary with those times who could serve as a reliable standard.[28]

As already noted, the surviving fragments of Fabius Pictor indicate that his account of the regal period was already well developed: Aeneas's arrival from Troy, the Alban king list, the birth and exposure of Romulus and Remus, the rape of the Sabine women, the treachery of Tarpeia, Servius Tullius's institution of the census and tribal organization, the construction of the Capitoline temple by the Tarquins, and the rape of Lucretia. This suffices to demonstrate that, from Fabius Pictor onwards, Roman historical accounts were a complex mixture of Roman traditions and adaptations of Greek tales and historical episodes.[29] For example, the story of how the infant twins Romulus and Remus were exposed to die but survived is a Roman version of a popular ancient legend told in reference to numerous figures of the Near East and Greece. The tale of Tarpeia is a Roman adaptation of a common Greek folktale in which a maiden of a besieged town falls in love with the commander of the enemy army, betrays her country to her beloved, but is punished with death for her treachery. The rape of Lucretia appears to be a Roman adaptation of the popular story of the homosexual love affair which contributed to the downfall of the Peisistratid tyranny and paved the way for the Cleisthenic democracy at Athens in 510 B.C. This having been said, however, whenever we identify a story in early Roman history as having been patterned after something from Greek literature or history, the question still must be asked whether the Roman account is a mere invention, or whether it is a genuine bit of tradition that has been fleshed out and given greater vividness by the use of a Greek model. In many instances modern scholars have arrived and will continue to arrive at different conclusions, and it is this kind of discretionary interpretive process that makes the modern study of early Roman history such a problematic but exciting endeavor.

---

28 For an excellent discussion of how aristocratic family traditions have muddied the historical waters of the fifth and fourth centuries B.C., see Ridley 1983.

29 For detailed treatment of this subject, see the excellent essays of Ungern-Sternberg and Timpe in Ungern-Sternberg and Reinau 1988, 237–86.

Religion and Burial

By Kim Woodring

"ROMAN DOMINATION, CELTIC ACCEPTANCE, OR MUTUAL UNDERSTANDING"

During the reign of Emperor Claudius in AD 43, the moment the Romans invaded Britain, it was the end for the native Celtic religion. Or was it? When Rome invaded, it established dominance in every aspect of the culture. Generally, Roman invasion meant that the native culture was wiped away and Roman culture adopted by the native people. The reasoning behind this attitude is that the cultures of the conquered people seemed very different to the Romans, so there was no room for compromise in the eyes of the Romans. Historians and archaeologists accepted this idea for years simply because the evidence did not exist to support another scenario. This scholarship persisted up through the turn of the twentieth century, when archaeology began opening doors to a new way of looking at the past. These authors and their views form the foundation of the research for a larger topic in which the practices, including religion and burial, of the Celtic and Roman cultures will be examined to see if they changed after the invasion.

Archaeologists and anthropologists have been studying the use of burial practices since the 1800s. Some anthropologists argue, like E. B. Tylor did in 1871, that belief in spiritual beings existed in dream context, that the disposal of the dead was related to primitive religion, and that those beliefs were the reason behind mortuary practices in society. In 1886, James Frazer maintained that mortuary ritual was motivated by fear of the deceased soul or ghost and that those practices were an attempt by the living to control the ghosts of the dead.[30] These anthropologists were at the beginning of the scholarship on mortuary practices, but the use of burial practices to differentiate cultures is still not used by many anthropologists, archaeologists, and historians. Burial customs have not been considered by many scholars, but some have used them as some type of indicator in their research since the early 1900s.

Statements by British antiquaries like Stuart Piggott suggest that it was strongly considered an important factor. Piggott wrote to E. J. Rudsdale at the Colchester Museum in the summer of 1928, discussing a site called Knighton Hill. This site produced fragments of a burial and pottery and was initially assigned to the Hallstatt period. Piggott did not agree and suggested, "Although I do not for a moment think that all of a sudden there was a terrific invasion of Hallstatt people, all bringing new methods of pottery making, burial, etc., yet I do think that towards the end of the Bronze Age in England there was a steady trickle of new ideas and possible new inhabitants from the continent, bringing with them new cultures. The change from barrow burial to burial in flat urnfields, or as multiple secondaries in earlier barrows, the introduction of the leaf-shaped sword, which has clearly a foreign ancestry, points to a new lot of people."[31] Antiquaries like Piggott obviously considered evidence found in burials an important piece of information. The use of

---

30 Lewis Binford, "Mortuary Practices: Their Study and Their Practice," *Memoirs of the Society for American Archaeology* 25 (1971): 7.
31 Philip Laver, manuscript letter from Stuart Piggott to E. J. Rudsdale, July 2, 1928, Laver Family Collection, reference codeD/Du 888/11, Essex Record Office, Chelmsford, UK.

this type of information has continued until the present, where it is being included in research by not only archaeologists but also by historians to support their ideas on cultural changes.

One of the first historians to take archaeology and incorporate it into his writing about the invasion was R. G. Collingwood. In his work *Roman Britain and the English Settlements*, Collingwood proposes that although the Romans considered Celtic art incompatible, they viewed the Celtic religion in a different light. Both religions were polytheistic, which made for an easy adoption or transition on both sides.[32]

Collingwood believed the reason the Romans tolerated the Celtic religion is because they did not perceive a threat to the state policy. The only threat they viewed was Druidism, and since Claudius abolished this part of the religion in Gaul, a threat thus did not exist. Rome did not require the Celtic people to worship Roman gods; this opened the door for any practice of religion. According to Collingwood, the Romans and the Celts accepted the fact that their religions were similar and eventually melded them together as one religion, with the Celtic religion being the dominant one.[33]

As one example of many about the syncretizing of both religions, Collingwood notes that the god Mars was a duality god for the Romans and the Celts. The Roman soldiers made small altars to Mars in their camps because he was the god of war. The Celts identified Mars with several Celtic gods like Belatucadrus and Camulus. Collingwood uses Mars as the support for his idea that the mixing of the religions was smooth and did not cause any problems between the Romans and the Celts.

Additionally, Collingwood uses archaeology to support his thesis by giving examples of local Celtic cults that made inscriptions in Latin that "testify to the easy relations that existed between Celt and Roman in the matter of worship."[34] He also suggests that the Celtic gods were the prevailing deities in most of the Roman Britain religious practices. Archaeological discoveries support this belief by using the discovered temples in Britain, which the Celts and Romans constructed at the time Christianity became a popular religion. Collingwood's perspective is unique for its time for two reasons. He challenged the idea that Rome came in and took over without a thought for the native people, and he also tried take his vantage point from the Celtic side—not from the Roman side—which most of his colleagues did in the past. His innovative idea stood in the eyes of his contemporaries until the early and mid-1960s.

The 1960s brought another change in how historians viewed the religious relationship between the Celts and Romans. The first of two historians to discuss this aspect of religion in Roman Britain was Peter Blair, in *Roman Britain and Early England 55 b.c.–a.d. 871*. In this work, Blair approaches a new view on how the Celts reacted to Roman religion. He believes the burden of the cost for the temples and the festivals of the Roman religion overwhelmed the native Celts, and this is what spurred the Iceni revolt in AD 60 led by Queen Boudicca.[35]

If this rebellion was against the state religion, then Blair's theory not only contradicts the original theories of the ancient historians, but it also displaces Collingwood's theory of peaceful mixing of religions. He also describes another theory: when the Romans pulled out of Britain, they essentially took their religion

32 R. G. Collingwood and J. N. L. Myres, *Roman Britain and the English Settlements* (London: Oxford University Press, 1937), 261.
33 Collingwood and Myres, 261.
34 Collingwood and Myres, 266.
35 Peter Hunter Blair, *Roman Britain and Early England 55 b.c.–a.d. 871* (Edinburgh: Thomas Nelson and Sons Ltd., 1963), 136.

with them and left no traces in Britain. This theory also goes against Collingwood because his whole theory is centered in the idea of the mixing of the religions. If the mixing occurred, when the Romans retreated, it would be difficult to separate the religious practices.

Blair acknowledges that a comparison of the Roman and Celtic religions reveals that some of the gods are similar, but he never discloses a solid opinion on the mixing theory. The second historian who shares Blair's view is Anne Ross. In her work *Pagan Celtic Britain: Studies in Iconography and Tradition*, she supports Blair's view that in the early days of the Roman occupation, the native people opposed the practicing of the Roman religion, especially the Imperial Cult. Ross moves forward and poses the idea that after the military operations had calmed down against the Celts, they began to mix their representations of Roman gods like Mars.[36]

Ross's theory agrees with Blair's in relation to opposition, although eventually it does agree with the postconflict melding theory as well. But by doing so, Ross's theory conflicts with the ancient historian's theory of complete domination. Ross also believes there was not a disagreement between the Romans and the Celts on artistic representation. She proposes a slow learning curve for the Celtic artists, especially in the transition from wood to stone.

In Ross's view, the Romans were tolerant of Celtic art and allowed artists to learn how to produce art in the Roman style. Ross also incorporates archaeology into her work as a way to support the mixing theory. She does this by using what is termed iconography, or the representation of the gods, in sculpture and art found by archaeologists. Ross takes into consideration that the Romans naturally introduced foreign deities into the Celtic religion, but she believes that "it is oversimplifying the problem to suppose that the coming of Rome meant a sharp severing of the beliefs and attitudes of the natives."[37]

This view agrees with Collingwood's theory because he supported a gradual change over time. The artifacts found represent the deities of the Roman religion, but Ross proposes that by examining these artifacts closely with the native traditions in mind, one can extract the native beliefs from the Roman "stereotyped exterior"[38] of the artifact. Ross's use of archaeology to support the mixing theory and the iconography theory is an excellent example of how, through the years, scholars continue to use archaeology as an intricate part of their research and as a tool to produce a "more balanced attitude toward the interest in the Celtic population"[39] of Roman Britain.

The late 1960s brought some fresh looks at how the religion of Roman Britain may have changed or become a melting pot of Roman and Celtic religion. Two authors in particular present information on this subject. The first author is the previously discussed Anne Ross. The work *Everyday Life of the Pagan Celts* reveals a more in-depth study of the Celtic people and touches on religion by including it as part of the everyday cycle. However, in this work, Ross changes how she views the expression of Celtic religion. Originally, in *Pagan Celtic Britain: Studies in Iconography and Tradition*, she supports the mixing theory, but in this work, she is more supportive of the idea that there was a rise in the Roman religion, then the mixing, and finally a rise in the native religions. Her support for this change in theory is related to the new discoveries in archaeology during the late 1960s.

---

36   Anne Ross, *Pagan Celtic Britain: Studies in Iconography and Tradition* (London: Routledge & Kegan Paul, 1967), 200.

37   Ross, 383.

38   Ross, 383.

39   Ross, 2.

The next author, who wrote during the late 1960s, was Sheppard Frere. His work *Britannia: A History of Roman Britain* proposes a fresh new idea of how religion functioned during the Roman occupation of Britain. Frere suggests that there was a mixing of religions, but it was on an individual scale. He said the individuals chose how much or how little of a variation existed in their worship. The reason for this individualism is because the Roman Empire was "very tolerant of religious variety."[40] Observance of the state religion was the only demand the empire made of its subjects; according to Frere, the Celts were free to "worship what they chose."[41] The only change to this policy was if Rome believed that the religion was a threat to the state—for example, Druidism. If this occurred, the Roman Empire outlawed the religion.

This observance supports Collingwood's original theory previously mentioned. Along with individualism, Frere stresses the localization of deities as being more common than scholars had previously thought. Accordi ng to archaeological artifacts, worship of deities occurred in small amounts and occasionally only existed in one area of Britain. This evidence supports Frere's individualism theory on a local scale because the localization of the deity proves the worship centered on a single tribe or community. Frere does continue in his work to support the melding theory by recognizing that "there is no doubt that religious practice tends to be conservative, and in Roman Britain many primitive Celtic cults and customs continued to be observed side by side with the newer modes of worship."[42]

The next change in scholarship concerning religion in Roman Britain did not occur until over a decade after Frere wrote *Britannia: A History of Roman Britain*. H. H. Scullard's theory in *Roman Britain: Outpost of the Empire* contains some of the same opinions of the past but with two differences. The first difference Scullard contributes is his belief that after the invasion, there was a division of where the change occurred according to the location. He proposes that very little change occurred in the distant districts of Britain, but in more settled areas, the melding began more quickly. This theory holds to parts of all the previous scholarship except to that of Collingwood.

Scullard not only argues against Collingwood's initial theory, but he also strongly disagrees with his theory on the art of Roman Britain. Scullard suggests that there were "two very different streams of artistic tradition that were represented—the native Celtic and imperial Roman."[43] He takes a very strong stand on Collingwood's theory of art and even calls it an "extreme view."[44] He disagrees with the view that portrays the Romans as suppressors of the Celtic art. He expresses disbelief in both this argument and the argument that Celtic art suddenly returned after Rome left Britain.

Scullard believes that there was a mixing of the art styles and that the style presented was predominantly Roman but contained some Celtic representation. However, Scullard's summary of religion in Roman Britain is, in the end, the same as the other theories in that, at some point, the Roman and Celtic gods were "worshipped side by side"[45] by the natives and the Romans. The only change that occurred, according to Scullard, was the name of the deity.

---

40 Sheppard Frere, *Britannia: A History of Roman Britain* (London: Routledge & Kegan Paul, 1967), 361.
41 Frere, 361.
42 Frere, 369.
43 H. H. Scullard, *Roman Britain: Outpost of the Empire* (London: Thames & Hudson Ltd., 1979), 150.
44 Scullard, 150.
45 Scullard, 157.

The next significant literature about Roman Britain religion arrives only five years after Scullard's work. Martin Henig's *Religion in Roman Britain* is one of the most thorough works on Roman Britain religion since Collingwood's *Roman Britain and the English Settlements*. Henig gives a complete survey of the religion in Roman Britain and agrees on some points with the previous theories, but he adds his own innovative ideas to the work. He also relies heavily on archaeology to support the previous theories as well as his own. He agrees that the Romans were very relaxed in their acceptance of other religions that came into the empire but intolerant of any religion like Christianity, which threatened the function of the state.

Henig also has high regard for the work of Anne Ross's theory of iconography as proof that the worship of the Celtic gods continued separate from the Romans. He also produces an idea that the Celts and Romans not only combined deities but their religion also shared the "deep sympathy felt with the natural world."[46] This idea recognizes the mixing of the religions, which is in agreement with the previous authors. However, Henig takes it a step further and supports a common thread between both religions in the form of nature. The previously mentioned authors obviously support the theory of the mixing of religions, but they support the idea that the Celts did not have a choice. Henig also supports this theory, but he believes that during the time the Celts and Romans spent together, the "compromise was not sought; it happened largely by chance."[47] This theory adds a new lens through which to look at the invasion and subsequent "Romanization" period in Britain. Henig suggests the mixing was spurred by the Romans. He also makes his final relation to the previous scholarship by agreeing the religion became localized and evolved accordingly.

It is after this that Henig discusses his final theory on religion in Roman Britain. He believes not only that the religion demonstrated localization but also that class was a factor in how it changed. Henig takes inscriptions found by archaeologists and examines them by using the forms of the inscriptions, such as the formation of names of gods. He says the inscriptions that are not complete in name form are because people did not know how to write the names in proper Latin.[48] Therefore, literacy affected the expression of the religion and is the reason Henig believes that "we would like to know more about these cults which may have remained more primitive and less affected by Roman ways than others, but for that very reason their worshippers lacked the means of communicating theology or ritual to future ages."[49]

Henig takes this idea of class even further by saying that the classes controlled religion. Literacy affected how the people expressed their religion, but it was not the only way that the classes controlled religion in Roman Britain. The fact that Romanization happened became inevitable, but the assertion that "governing classes from the time of Augustus decided that religion was a useful basis for demonstration of loyalty to the Roman State"[50] is a remarkable and new theory for the field. The Celts demonstrated their loyalty to the Roman State through the Imperial Cult.

The aforementioned authors also discuss the Imperial Cult, but they do not connect the cult with the classes in control of the religion in Roman Britain. Henig expresses a new way of looking at the control the Romans had over the Celtic people pertaining to religion. Boudicca, the Celtic queen, revolted due to the forced worship of the Imperial Cult, and although this is mentioned by the previous authors as well

---

46 Martin Henig, *Religion in Roman Britain* (New York: St. Martin's Press, 1984), 20.
47 Henig, 36.
48 Henig, 62.
49 Henig, 63.
50 Henig, 67.

as Henig, it is never fully developed into discussion by them. Henig's additional views on the religion in Roman Britain look skewed to the side of the Romans, but the next author shifts and looks at all three periods.

Two years after Henig published *Celtic Religion in Roman Britain*, Graham Webster produced *Celtic Religion in Roman Britain*. Webster's first opinion expresses disagreement with the ancient historians, just like his colleagues that have been previously mentioned. Webster goes further to explain that this view "completely neglects the timescale of six centuries or eighteen generations, from the first contact with Rome through Julius Caesar, to the moment when the five provinces of Britannia became independent."[51] He also relies heavily on archaeology for support of his theories, but instead of incorporating just one type of artifact—for example, wood—Webster examines artifacts of stone, ceramic, wood, and metal. As stated before, Webster's work incorporates a view from both the Romans' and the Celts' vantage points by looking at them before and after the invasion, but in the end he advocates that the Roman practices may have influenced the Celtic practices.

Webster also agrees with Frere's concept of individualism, but he adds a new twist to the theory. Even though the Celts still celebrated their seasonal festivals to the gods, they began to see how the Romans prospered through trade. When this occurred, according to Webster, they also began to notice how the Romans approached their gods in a personal fashion by making personal vows at a sacred place. This was the beginning of profitability for the Celtic people. Webster believes that when the Celts realized religion could be profitable, the age of temple building began in Roman Britain.[52]

Celtic landowners could "exploit the sanctity of places and the potency of resident spirits" by building temples on their land, which would bring them profit.[53] Webster also believes that this trend did not affect the whole culture. He believes that the Celts involved in this change were the ones located close to or in the Roman settlements. Celtic people engaged in trade were only a small number compared to the rural population, which continued its religious practices in the traditional range.

Webster also contends that since these changes did not affect the Celtic belief of the "unseen world," the process was just natural.[54] Webster concedes that although all these new experiences may have changed certain aspects of the Celtic life, the Celts still celebrated their festivals and continued to worship their own gods as well as the Roman gods. This notion supports the mixing theory of the previous scholarship.

The final scholarship discussed here comes five years after Graham Webster's work. Ronald Hutton's *The Pagan Religions of the Ancient British Isles* takes a chronological look at ancient Britain's religions and how they changed over time. Hutton briefly examines the aspect of personal or group individualism in the Roman Britain culture. He agrees with the previously mentioned authors on individualism and contends that they all "employed the pattern which seemed to work best for them."[55] He also supports the previous authors in the theory that as long as the Celtic people made their sacrifice to the Imperial Cult, the Romans

---

51   Graham Webster, *Celtic Religion in Roman Britain* (New Jersey: Barnes & Noble Books, 1987), 13.
52   Webster, 110.
53   Webster, 110.
54   Webster, 111.
55   Ronald Hutton, *The Pagan Religions of the Ancient British Isles* (Oxford, UK: Blackwell Publishers, 1991), 204.

allowed them to practice their own religions. The one exception was human sacrifice, which the Romans outlawed in all of the Roman Empire.[56]

Although Hutton agrees that the mixing of religious practices occurred, he is uncertain about how much Romanization occurred and how much generalization should pertain to that concept. *The Pagan Religions of the Ancient British Isles* also contains the theory—which addresses the fact that the Roman cults were not the only religions that impinged on the Celtic religious practices—that there were other influences coming into Britain from places like Gaul, Germany, and Italy. Hutton also supports the localization theory but says it is very hard to get a clear and concise understanding about it, especially in the area around Hadrian's Wall.[57]

What some of the previous scholarship sees as distinction, Hutton sees as too much mixing to determine what went into the mix and where it originated. But as such, Hutton goes on to remark that all of the gods, whether they were native or acquired from other locations, were of equal importance to the Celtic and Roman people living in Britain. He then adds that there "were marked local traditions, and a distinction in emphasis between the military and civilian parts of the province and between those places with Roman settlers and those without them, though there seems to have been little difference in the favorite deities of town and countryside."[58]

Hutton's idea that no difference occurred between the town and countryside worship of deities is in contrast with Scullard's view, which proposes that there was a marked difference in the change. Through his little use of archaeological support, Hutton's conclusion on the ancient religions of Britain is that we don't really know enough to support solid scholarship and that what we do know supports the mixing theory, but he also points to the fact that the people of Roman Britain were more "fascinating and baffling" than scholars ever imagined.[59]

Since the improvement of archaeological study in the early twentieth century, there has been a steady stream of new theories about Roman Britain. The scholars mentioned in this discussion agree on some theories about religion in Roman Britain and others totally disagree, but one thing is certain: change occurred in both the Celtic and Roman cultural religious practices. These changes, supported by archaeology, will be the basis for further research on aspects of both cultures, including their burial and religious practices. How we as historians view these changes will influence how future scholars will view them as well, just like Tacitus and Gibbon influenced people like Martin Henig and Anne Ross. However, by continuing the study of the past through archaeology, we will always be opening new and fascinating doors to the past. In the coming years, research will continue, and future scholars will build on the past ideas and form new ones that will change the field of history.

Religion is a very powerful influence on any culture, and the Celtic people of Britain were no different in that respect from any other culture. The evidence on their religion has been assembled from a small number of ancient sources, literary sources, and archaeology. These sources provide information on some of their gods and the Celts' beliefs on life and death. There is a limited amount of information on the Celtic religion, but what is known can be described by modern scholars as pagan or polytheistic. This description

56 Hutton, 205.
57 Hutton, 217.
58 Hutton, 223.
59 Hutton, 341.

is derived through sources that were already in the firm grip of Christianity, which necessitates a cautionary attitude when accepting the information. As such, the information indicates the Celtic religion was varied and complex. The variation and complexity are due in part to the basic nature of polytheism. The Celtic pantheon, just like others, included a god for every aspect of life. Miranda Green, in *The Celtic World*, relates this variation to the Celts' use of animism, which "appears to have underpinned Celtic religion, the belief that every part of the natural world, every feature of the landscape, was numinous, possessed of spirit."[60]

Their belief in this type of the spiritual world made them closer to nature itself. They believed their world and the spiritual world existed in a realm together and that this combination of worlds existed everywhere: "there was no separation between man and the spirits, all living together side by side, here, there and everywhere."[61] The Celtic nature worship had its greater and lesser gods, just as in every polytheistic religion. The greater spirits resided in celestial bodies like the sun, moon, and stars. The lesser spirits existed in things like the grass, flowers, and trees, which connected to the greater spirits in nature.

SACRED PLACES

The Celts believed all of nature contained spirits but that certain places were more sacred than others in the natural world. Greco-Roman writers are the only link to the Celtic belief of sacred groves being used for worship and sacrifice to the gods. Along with Strabo, Lucan's *Pharsalia* produces a classical view on Celtic usage of groves that were "untouched by men's hands from ancient times, whose interlacing boughs enclosed a space of darkness and cold shade."[62] Lucan also describes what the Romans thought to be a barbaric practice of human sacrifice in which the altars and the trees were covered with the flesh and blood of the sacrificial victim.[63] Trees specifically, singly or in groves, seemed to be important to the Celts in their religious practice. A tree symbolized a connection between the world in which the Celts lived and the underworld. The branches of the tree were in their reality; they opened up to the sky, and the roots of the tree led beneath their reality to the underworld. The tree was also a symbol of long life, wisdom, and fertility to the Celtic people.[64] The oak tree was especially important: according to Pliny, "They esteem nothing more sacred than the mistletoe and the tree on which it grows. But apart from this they choose oak-woods for their sacred groves, and perform no sacred rite without using oak branches."[65]

Water was also important to Celtic religious practice. Springs, lakes, and bogs are the most-documented water sources. Evidence for the usage of springs is sparse before the Roman conquest. They were thought to be used for healing purposes by Celts and were associated with powerful healing cults. These Celtic cults and gods continued up through the Roman period by combining the native gods with the Roman gods, as evidenced by places like Bath.[66] Bath is one of the best-known examples of the use of springs as religious sites. Although no evidence exists of Celtic worship at the springs, there are several clues left by the Romans

60 Miranda J. Green, *The Celtic World* (London: Routledge, 1995), 465.
61 Graham Webster, *The British Celts and Their Gods Under Rome* (London: B. T. Batsford Ltd., 1986), 23.
62 Barry Cunliffe, *The Ancient Celts* (London: Penguin Books, 1997), 198.
63 Cunliffe, 198.
64 Miranda Green, *Celtic Myths* (London: British Museum Press, 1993), 50.
65 J. A. MacCulloch, *The Religion of the Celts* (London: Studio Editions, 1992), 198.
66 Anne Ross, *Pagan Celtic Britain* (London: Routledge & Kegan Paul, 1967), 30.

that tell us the Celts also used the sites for religious purposes. Sculptured stones, found at Bath in 1790 and obviously done in classical style by the Romans, also exhibited Celtic influence. The temple pediment consisted of a shield surrounded by wreaths of oak leaves with the depiction of a Gorgon, which is "normally a female in classical mythology, here in Bath he is shown in the guise of a male with the wedge-shaped nose, the lentoid eyes, moustaches and beetling brow of a Celtic god" and "was a perfect example of the conflation between a Roman and native deity."[67] There are also inscriptions dedicated to the goddess Sulis Minerva, a combination of the Celtic and Roman goddesses of healing. These hot springs clearly played an important role in the Celtic religious practice before and after the Romans came to Britain.

Lakes and bogs were also venerated by the Celts, especially for deposition of swords, other battle supplies, and votive objects. Several lakes in Britain have produced objects considered to be offerings to the gods. Both Llyn Cerrig Bach and Llyn Fawr have revealed a large amount of ritual deposition, including weapons, iron tools, chariots, and cauldrons.[68] These deposits are extensive and show a long period of time in which the Celtic people used the lakes. The act of submerging items into the lake may well have represented an offering to the god of the lake, or it also might have symbolized a simple wish of good luck, similar to our wishing wells today. Bogs also served as places to deposit metalwork, but they were possibly additionally used as locations for human sacrifice. The Lindow bog body found in Cheshire suggests that bogs might have been used for ritual sacrifice. The Lindow man showed signs of ax blows, strangling, and throat cutting.[69] Although Anne Ross, in *Lindow Man: The Body in the Bog*, suggests these acts were part of a ritual death, it has not been proven that the bog bodies found in Britain were actually human sacrifices.

SACRIFICE

Sacrifice—human or otherwise—played an important role in Celtic religion. This practice was so important that "when a private person or a tribe disobeys their ruling [the Druids] they ban them from attending at sacrifices. This is their harshest penalty. Men placed under this ban are treated as impious wretches; all avoid them, fleeing their company and conversation, lest their contact bring misfortune upon them."[70] Caesar and Lucan are among the ancient writers who discuss what the Romans considered to be the most "barbaric" part of the Celtic culture. They comment on the sacrifice of animals after a victory. Caesar mentions the practice of human sacrifice but notes that "criminals were preferred as being more pleasing to the gods but that, failing them, others were chosen."[71] The Celts appeared to practice four forms of human sacrifice: hanging, cremation, drowning, and live burial. All of these forms seemed to correlate with the four primary elements of earth, fire, wind, and water. These types of sacrifices corresponded to some festivals, especially the feast of Samhain. The human sacrifices were supposedly used by the Druids,

---

67   Barry Cunliffe, *Roman Bath Discovered* (Charleston: Arcadia Publishing Inc., 2000), 26, 41.
68   Miranda J. Green, *Dictionary of Celtic Myth and Legend* (London: Thames & Hudson, 1992), 130.
69   Miranda J. Green, *The Celtic World* (London: Routledge, 1995), 450.
70   Caesar, *Gallic War*. VI, 13: quoted in Tierney, J. J., "The Celtic Ethnography of Posidonius." Proceedings of the Royal Irish Academy 60 (1959/1960): 271.
71   Myles Dillon and Nora Chadwick, *The Celtic Realms* (Edison: Castle Books, 2003), 15.

the priestly overseers of the Celtic religion, for some type of divination, both of which will be discussed later in the chapter.[72]

The Celts also practiced animal sacrifice. The animal sacrifices also related to Celtic festivals and are thought to be the majority of the sacrifices made to the gods. A variety of animals was used for sacrifice, including bulls, horses, dogs, and pigs. Usually, as in other cultures that used sacrifice, the head and other extremities like hooves were removed, and the meat provided food for the festival feast. The hides of the animals performed a function in rituals as well, such as to protect or induce some type of trance for seers of the cults.[73]

DRUIDS AND DIVINATION

According to the ancient commentaries, the Celtic elite class was divided into three orders: Druids, Vates, and Bards. The Druids controlled the religious aspects such as sacrifice, but they also functioned as philosophers, magicians, doctors, teachers, and historians.[74] This elite class was the main focus of the ancient writers, including Cicero, who supposedly acquainted himself with a Druid named Diviciacus. Cicero said that Diviciacus claimed the Druid "discipline was first instituted in Britain, and from thence transferred to Gaul, for even at this day those who desire to be perfect adepts of their art make a voyage thither to learn it."[75] The most commonly discussed Celtic religious practice was sacrifice. This practice seems totally disgusting and barbarous to observers like Strabo and Caesar. Both writers comment on a ritual sacrifice now known as the Wicker Man. This ritual consisted of filling a large wicker container, often shaped in the form a man, with animals and human beings. Then the Wicker Man was set ablaze, constituting a fire sacrifice to the gods.[76]

The Druids were a central part of all Celtic religion, but especially for both the performance of the sacrificial gift to the gods and for divination. Prediction of the future and knowing the will of the gods formed an integral part of most ancient religions. The Celtic divination practice used animal sacrifices and augury (divination from auspices or omens observed from animal behavior such as birds in flight) to see the future, but they also used human sacrifice. This use of human sacrifice is once again what made the Celts and their religion seem strange and barbarous to other cultures, especially Rome's. Although some of the practices of the Druids were outlawed by Rome, some of them lasted up through the second and third centuries.[77] Sacred places, sacrifices, and divination, as we have seen, were all a part of the Celtic religious experience and controlled by the Druids.

---

72   Caitlin Matthews, *The Celtic Tradition* (Great Britain: Element Books Limited, 1995), 43.
73   Green, *Celtic World*, 439.
74   Green, *Celtic World*, 426.
75   Lewis Spence, *The Mysteries of Britain* (New York: Samuel Weiser, Inc., 1970), 19.
76   Miranda J. Green, *The World of the Druids* (London: Thames & Hudson, 1997), 75.
77   Green, *World of Druids*, 88.

GODS AND GODDESSES

If the Druid priestly class of the Celts—a class comprised of the elite, the educated, and those well trained in their art—survived for so long, then what kinds of gods did they worship? The Celts had many gods; most are unknown, and only around two hundred have been documented. Of those documented, the gods discussed for this purpose will fit into three categories. The first will be those represented in iconography found in Britain; second, those found in inscriptions only; and third, those who clearly show a religious syncretism during the Roman period.

Before the Celts produced images of the gods we recognize from the Roman period, they created representations of sacred animals such as the divine bull and boar found in tumuli like the ones at Lexden Tumulus, which predates the Romans. They provide some of the only evidence for pre–Roman Celtic worship in Britain. The zoomorphic images of the bull and boar represented "strength, ferocity, and invincibility in a war-oriented, heroic society such as that of the Celts" and are even seen frequently on Celtic coinage.[78] The boar symbolized war, hunting, hospitality, and feasting for the Celtic people.[79] The bull embodied strength, power, and ferocity.[80] Both of these animals are depicted in art forms of the Celtic culture. Many other animals, like the stag, dog, and horse, are seen in the Celtic iconography. Along with these animals, there are some "hybrid" animals that appear prominently in Celtic worship. These animals are a mixture of two sacred animals; this mixture, according to the Celtic belief, increased the potential power of the hybrid animal. One example is the ram-headed serpent, which appears early in Celtic contexts and survives in religious representations up through the Roman period. The ram-headed serpent is depicted with three other gods in the Roman period, including the Roman gods Mercury and Mars and the Celtic god Cernunnos.[81]

The Celtic religious transition moves from nonrepresentation of gods to the existence of iconography that represents some of the gods like Cernunnos. The Celts considered this god, whose name means "horned" or "peaked one," to be very powerful.[82] In most of his representations, he is in human form, with the exception of the stag antlers that extend from his head. The most widely recognized depiction of Cernunnos is on the Gundestrup Cauldron from Denmark. Cernunnos is sitting cross-legged, as if mimicking the Buddha.[83] He also is shown with several torques, a Celtic neck ring, and a large purse or sack. The position in which Cernunnos is sitting alludes to the possibility that his worship existed in the pre-Roman period and is therefore not part of the "aniconic deities of the Celts who first found artistic visualization under the impact of Roman civilization."[84] Images of him existed in Cirencester on a stone relief with the ram-horned snakes used to represent his legs. In Hampshire, he appears on a silver coin with a solar wheel between his antlers.[85] Cernunnos represented nature, fertility, and prosperity. He is seen in varied forms with mixtures of symbolism across Europe in all of the Celtic territory.

---

78 Miranda J. Green, *The Gods of Roman Britain* (UK: Shire Archaeology, 2003), 8.
79 Green, *Dictionary*, 44.
80 Green, *Dictionary*, 51.
81 Ross, 430.
82 Green, *Dictionary*, 59.
83 Graham Webster, *Celtic Religion in Roman Britain*. (New Jersey: Barnes & Noble Books, 1986), 55.
84 Phyllis Fray Bober, "Cernunnos: Origin and Transformation of a Celtic Divinity," *American Journal of Archaeology* 55, no. 1 (Jan. 1951): 14.
85 Green, *Dictionary*, 59.

Cernunnos may have existed earlier in the Celtic religion, but he was not the only powerful god with roots in early Celtic religion. Taranis also existed in Celtic worship before the arrival of Rome. He was the Celtic sky/thunder god and one of the three gods mentioned by Lucan in his *Pharsalia*. Lucan said that the worship of and sacrifice to this god were "more cruel than that of Scythian Diana" because of the use of human sacrifice. Lucan even describes how the victims were to be offered according to the preference of the god. Taranis preferred his sacrifices to be made by fire.[86] The fire sacrifice could be a link to his longevity, since Taranis existed before the coming of Rome in Celtic religion. He seems to be a natural occurrence, such as lightning that was transformed into human form when the Romans came to Britain. His name means "thunder" and implies that the act of nature he represented was thunder, lightning, or even a storm.[87]

The second of Lucan's references is to Teutates, the Celtic tribal god. Teutates's role consisted of tribal protection, but he also was related to warfare. Additionally, he is represented on the Gundestrup Cauldron holding a sacrificial human above a bucket and then drowning the victim. The preferred way to sacrifice victims for Teutates was drowning.[88] Although Lucan's writings referred to the Celts of Gaul, these gods were also represented in Britain by inscriptions and iconography, so it is possible that the same sacrificial rituals were performed in Britain.

The goddess Rosmerta is another deity shared with Celtic Gaul. Her name means the "Great Provider" because most of her images include a cornucopia, a *patera*, and mixing buckets. These objects were used to symbolize prosperity and good fortune. She is often shown partnered with a god in Britain to form a divine couple. The Roman god Mercury was most often depicted as her companion on reliefs. This pairing of a goddess and a god may "imply divine marriage and therefore consequential fertility."[89] The large number of reliefs and inscriptions pertaining to Rosmerta alone and with Mercury suggests that she was a very popular goddess with the natives and the Romans. The divine couples are prominent in Britain and provide a very important clue to the effect of Romanization in Britain, which I will discuss in a subsequent chapter.

The Suleviae are also deities shared with other Celtic areas and are most commonly seen as a triad in Britain. They are also referred to as the "Triple Mothers" or "Triple Goddesses" and are connected with healing and sun worship. But their representations clearly show that they were also worshipped by the Celts to seek an ample supply of fertility and general prosperity.[90] The Suleviae seemed to be used in a more personal worship style because they have been found in burial context. Evidence also exists that they were a part of the Roman military devotion in the area around Hadrian's Wall. Representation varies and includes them being depicted with things like *paterae* for prosperity, but most often they are seen suckling infants.

Another important sun deity in Celtic religion is Sulis. She was a healing goddess and was worshipped at the hot springs of Bath. The location was important to the Celts as a natural place of worship and healing.[91]

Triplism and military reverence are both seen with Coventina. A Celtic water goddess, she was worshipped in the Carrawburgh area of Hadrian's Wall. This area is located around a spring that was used to supply a cistern. The cistern and pool eventually became places for people to worship Coventina. The

---

86   Cunliffe, *Ancient Celts*, 191.
87   Green, *Dictionary*, 206.
88   Cunliffe, *Ancient Celts*, 191.
89   Miranda Green, *The Gods of the Celts* (UK: Sutton Publishing, 1986), 95.
90   Green, *Gods*, 82.
91   Green, *Dictionary*, 200.

visitors would throw things like coins (as we do today with a wishing well), jewelry, and figurines into the well. These offerings were given with the hope of healing or possibly a wish for a prosperous rain for the crops. She was very popular and therefore well represented in reliefs, inscriptions, and altars. It has also been suggested that many of the gifts were from women who were pregnant and hoping for a healthy, safe pregnancy and childbirth.[92] The Roman soldiers at the wall probably made dedications to Coventina in thanks for the supply of water or for a safe military tour or battle.

The goddess Epona was another Celtic deity who became popular with the Roman soldiers, but her origin is in Gaul and other continental Celtic areas. Her worship originated in the tribal areas of Aedui and Lingones in Burgundy, which are known for the propagation of fine horses. On the continent as well as in Britain, she was linked to fertility and Earth's bounty. Epona is often represented riding a horse sidesaddle and carrying fruit in a *patera* or a cornucopia.[93] In *The Gods of the Celts*, Miranda Green discusses K. Linduff's suggestion that Epona's representation in the rural areas is more prominent because the Celts used mares to do the farming work, and farming was the work of the women. Green also explains that the popularity of Epona with the soldiers was because it was a "personal, beneficent nature which imposed no restrictions and offered protection both for the cavalryman himself and his horse."[94] Epona's horse also represented fruitfulness and a symbol of life for the Celts; this explains the finding of many horse burials on the continent and in Britain.[95]

The last martial and civilian Celtic gods were the Genius Cucullatus. Images of these gods are centered in the area of Cirencester for the civilian portion and Hadrian's Wall for the military. These gods are depicted as three small male deities, each of whom was always dressed in a cloak, or *cucullus*.[96] They are also seen accompanying the mother goddess, who would connect them to fertility. Also, they are seen holding eggs that link them to fertility, death, and regeneration. In continental Europe, including Gaul, they are seen in singular form, but they are exclusively portrayed with triplism in Britain. Since they are constantly cloaked, they are thought to have a connection to the Otherworld.[97]

DEATH AND THE OTHERWORLD

The belief in life in another realm after death is present in many ancient cultures and religions, including that of the Celts. They believed that the Otherworld was a transitional stage in life and death. The Druids taught that the soul transmigrated at the point of death. Transmigration of the soul is simply transference of the soul from the dying body into another body. The Celts believed the switch did not occur immediately but that the soul became indistinct and displaced for a period of time. Diodorus Siculus suggests that the Celts are not afraid of death because "the belief of Pythagoras prevails among them, that the souls of men are immortal and that after a prescribed number of years they commence upon a new life, the soul entering

92 Green, *Dictionary*, 67.
93 Green, *Dictionary*, 91.
94 Green, *Gods*, 94.
95 Graham Webster, *Celtic Religion in Roman Britain* (New Jersey: Barnes & Noble Books, 1986), 71.
96 Webster, 66.
97 Green, *Gods*, 91.

into another body."[98] Immediately after death, they existed in a void, and if the deceased was not cared for properly at the time of burial, the soul would be lost forever in this void. If they succeeded in having an appropriate burial, then the soul passed into the Otherworld and awaited the time of the rebirth in another body.[99]

The Otherworld existed in Celtic religion as a special, almost joyful place where they feasted and celebrated. If the living traveled to the Otherworld, they would not age while there, but upon returning, they aged the exact amount of time they existed in the Otherworld. This made the Otherworld a dangerous place for the living to go to, since it was considered such a wonderful place that the living might get caught up in the celebrating and not want to return or would lose track of time. Anne Ross believes the revealing of the Otherworld "inspired warriors to bravery and to hold their lives in small regard" and caused the Celtic people to be so warlike.[100]

CELTIC BURIAL

Societal beliefs affect the way in which a society deals with things like birth, marriage, and, especially, death. The Celtic culture was a tribal-based culture that practiced polytheism. The tribal component imposed a societal hierarchy that was visible in the Celtic burial practice along with the religious beliefs in an Otherworld and reincarnation. Although evidence for Celtic burial is scant and complex in Britain, it does exist and can provide some valuable information about the Celts. The burial practices of the ancient Britons during the Bronze Age, before they became known as the Celts, were in mounds or barrows. Mounds or barrows are earthen structures that are round or elongated and that have been formed over one or more burials.[101] Llewellynn Jewitt suggested in *Grave-Mounds and Their Contents* that "barrows were not infrequently surrounded by a circle of stones, set upright in the ground. These circles, in many instances, remain to the present day in different parts of the kingdom, and, the barrow itself having disappeared, are commonly called by the general appellation of Druidical circles."[102]

The barrows were considered community monuments. The dead were either inhumed or cremated, with the burnt remains being placed in urns. Placement of the deceased and the inclusion of grave goods were determined by the status of the individual in the community.[103] Jewitt provides many examples of barrow burials, including those at Roundway Hill, Wiltshire, and Hitter Hill, Derbyshire. At the end of the Bronze Age in Britain, archaeological evidence of burial practices declines to the point of invisibility.

Some scholars suggest that the absence of archaeological evidence for burial before the Early and Middle Iron Ages in Britain could be a result of excarnation. Excarnation is exposure of the body so it can be defleshed—as opposed to inhumation, where the body is buried, or cremation, where the body is burned.[104] Rebecca Redfern, curator of Human Osteology at the Museum of London, suggests that the

---

98   Diodorus Siculus, *Diodorus of Sicily*, trans. C. H. Oldfather (Cambridge, MA: Harvard University Press, 1939), 171.
99   Green, *Celtic World*, 495.
100 Ross, 80.
101 Warwick Bray, "Barrow," in *A Dictionary of Archaeology*.
102 Llewellynn Jewitt, *Grave-Mounds and Their Contents* (London: Groombridge and Sons, 1870), 10.
103 John C. Barrett, "The Monumentality of Death: The Character of Early Bronze Age Mortuary Mounds in Southern Britain," *World Archaeology* 22, no. 2 (October 1990): 183.
104 Warwick Bray, "Cremation," "Inhumation," in *A Dictionary of Archaeology*.

existence of four-post structures and pits containing disarticulated human remains advocates that Celtic people practiced excarnation. She also proposes a timeline, which begins from the Early Iron Age (700 to 450 BC), when excarnation was the primary burial practice of the Celts. In the Middle Iron Age (450–150 BC), they continued to practice excarnation but also began to practice inhumation. Finally, during the Late Iron Age (150 BC–AD 43), they continued the practice of inhumation even after the arrival of the Romans.[105] When this chronology is compared to the archaeological evidence for this time period, it clearly shows the transitions of burial types for the Celtic people in Britain.

Exposure of the body by the ancient Celts is thought to be the first step in a complex funerary ritual. The next step involves the dismemberment of the body, with the long bones and the cranial bones being the most important. According to Redfern's research at Gussage All Saints and Maiden Castle, these disarticulated parts of the bodies are used in secondary burial rituals, which include placement in structured deposits composed of animal bones, pottery, and other cultural objects located at various locations like hillforts. These secondary burials are also thought to be performed for rituals relating to the farming cycle and fertility.[106]

The secondary burials are the beginning of the transition from complete excarnation to inhumation. Inhumations occur in various forms in Britain, but the remains are usually crouched or extended. A crouched or extended inhumation refers to the position in which the body was placed at the time of burial. The body is in the crouched position when the hip and knee joints are bent more than ninety degrees, sometimes referred to as the fetal position.[107] Commonly, the bodies are placed on the left side, with the head situated between the north and southeast positions.[108] The aforementioned Roundway Hill and Hitter Hill barrow burials discovered by Jewitt in 1862 are examples of crouched burials.

An extended inhumation is when the spine and leg bones are in a straight line. The body can be lying on its back, on its face, or, occasionally, on its side.[109] Inhumation continued to be practiced in Britain even after the Roman invasion; it was "deeply rooted" in the area controlled by the Celtic Durotrigian tribe.[110] A shift in burial practices back to cremation is not seen until around 50 BC before the Roman invasion, and it is only prominent in the southeast area of Britain. Cremations are hard to identify archaeologically and are usually found by the identification of the pyre site. Fragments of burnt bone, charcoal, and occasionally some ironwork/metal artifacts survive and become incorporated into the deposits.[111]

There is one tradition that is not necessarily typical of the Celts in Britain as a whole but is worthy of discussion. This rite was practiced in the area of Kent, at that time the territory belonging to the Celtic tribe known as the Cantiaci. This particular burial type has been named the Aylesford-Swarling, after the two cemeteries in which these burials are found. Scholars generally break it up into two phases. The earlier phase is the Welwyn phase, which dates to 50–40 BC. The later Lexden phase dates to 15–10 BC. The body is usually cremated at a site different from the actual burial site. Then the remains are collected and put in a

---

105   Rebecca Redfern, "New Evidence for Iron Age Secondary Burial Practice and Bone Modification from Gussage All Saints and Maiden Castle, Dorset England." *Oxford Journal of Archaeology* 27, no. 3 (2008): 281.
106   Redfern, 282.
107   Warwick Bray, "Inhumation," in *A Dictionary of Archaeology*.
108   Green, *Celtic World*, 492.
109   Warwick Bray, "Inhumation," in *A Dictionary of Archaeology*.
110   Barry Cunliffe, *Iron Age Communities in Britain* (London: Routledge & Kegan Paul, 1974), 294.
111   Mike P. Pearson, *The Archaeology of Death and Burial* (College Station: Texas A & M University Press, 2000), 7.

Figure 8.1 Replication of Welwyn burial in the British Museum.

[Photo by Kim Woodring.]

ceramic pot, a bucket with metal bands, or in a pit. The container is then buried, frequently with other grave goods. Some of the later Lexden phase included up to five pots, metal-banded buckets, and brooches of the La Tène style. The more extravagant burials of this type also included bronze or silver drinking and eating containers and imported amphorae (Figure 8.1).[112]

The location of burials in Britain during the Iron Age ranged from mounds/long barrows (discussed earlier in this chapter) to organized cemeteries. A majority of the burials were located outside of the settlement areas. This change in burial locations shows the progression of civilization within the tribal systems of Britain during the Iron Age even before the arrival of the Romans. This progression and the previous material reveal a question about Celtic burial practices: Did the Celtic people have a typical burial/funerary practice by which they dealt with their dead? Mounds and barrows containing either inhumations or cremations seem to be the typical practice for the Iron Age Celtic people. This type of burial continued from the Neolithic period up until the first century AD, when cemeteries became the normal type of disposal in Britain.

Although the typical burial could be considered mounds, there are also regional variations on this type of burial. In some areas, we see burials like the ones previously discussed, but there are also areas like East Yorkshire, which contain the Arras culture burials. These burials were also barrow burials, but they had some unique attributes. The first unique characteristic is that the mounds in this tradition were surrounded by a square ditch and were arranged together to form large cemeteries. The other is the inclusion of a two-wheeled vehicle and numerous grave goods with the body.

These burials are very similar to the La Tène burials in Europe but lack the inclusion of fine pottery. Archaeologist Barry Cunliffe suggests that the Arras culture "owed its origins to the arrival of high-status newcomers from northern France or Belgium," but it could also be the adoption of these practices by the native Celtic population to distinguish themselves from the other tribes.[113]

Another deviation from the normalcy of mound burial is the "pit burials" at the Celtic hillforts like Danebury in Hampshire. These burials consist of the body, either complete or partial, being put in

---

112   Green, *Celtic World*, 497.
113   Barry Cunliffe, *Book of Iron Age Britain* (London: B. T. Batsford, 1995), 47–48.

grain-storage pits. Miranda Green suggests these pit burials are the "remains of abnormal, outcast members of Celtic society." Since these individuals were "denied the normal mortuary rite," they would be prevented from crossing over to the Otherworld and therefore "maintaining the purity of a society's Otherworld."[114]

This suggestion of abnormal burial leads to another question about Celtic burial and their religious rituals. What about the Celtic religion influenced their burial practices? The previous discussion on Celtic religion supports the fact that they had a strong belief in the Otherworld. Thus, the preparation for the crossing of the spirit into this place can be revealed in the way in which they buried their dead, especially in the Late Iron Age. The Celts were a tribal warrior society that believed in supplying the deceased with everything they might need in the Otherworld. This belief transferred to the burial with the inclusion of things like swords, amphorae, mirrors, and buckets. These objects were included in the burial so they could serve the individuals in the Otherworld, as they did in the living world. Grave goods of this type are most often seen in the Welwyn, Arras, or Aylesford types of burials of the Late Iron Age.

Some swords and other goods were ritually broken to symbolize the death of the object in relation to its owner. This action was believed to release the spirit of the object so it could follow the spirit of the deceased to the Otherworld.[115] Other grave goods include ceramic vessels, joints of meat, and, occasionally, personal jewelry such as brooches or bracelets.[116] The inclusion of grave goods increases after the arrival of the Romans, especially dealing with the religious iconography. The Romans played a large role in how the Celts learned to express their religion and give identity to their gods. The Celtic religion, including its burial customs, is a complicated issue and can be difficult to understand. What we know of Celtic culture and religion is provided by a small but important collaboration of sources. These sources offer a small insight into the Celtic religion before the Roman invasion, and they continue to provide more information about the mixture of the Celt and Roman cultures known as the Romano-British culture. Celtic religious practice must have been appealing to the Romans because it influenced them enough to not only merge their gods but to also change their burial customs.

Just as with any culture, past or present, religion played a large role in the everyday life of the Romans. The amount of information on the Romans and their culture, including religion, is vast. There are many ancient sources, including writings by Caesar, Lucian, and Livy, that pertain to how they viewed and practiced religion. There are also centuries of work, up to and including our time, that exist about the Romans and their culture. The religion of Rome, like many ancient religions, was influenced by other cultures such as those of the Etruscans and Greeks. The Greek influence can be seen in the mythology of the religion with things like the gods and places such as the underworld. But the Romans organized and practiced their religion in a very strict fashion. Romans conducted prayers and rituals in a specific manner because they believed if one word was misspoken, the plea to the god would not be sufficient and could possibly anger the god. The Romans believed in piety and believed themselves to be the most pious. Piety to the Romans meant they needed to be faithful in their practice of rituals because "the life of the individual, as well as the community as a whole, was permeated by these divine powers."[117] Therefore, if the Romans were pious and

---

114   Green, *Celtic World*, 495.

115   Leslie V. Grinsell, *Barrow, Pyramid, and Tomb* (Boulder: Westview Press, 1975), 60.

116   Green, *Celtic World*, 493.

117   Helmut Koester, *Introduction to the New Testament, Volume 1: History, Culture, and Religion of the Hellenistic Age* (New York: Walter de Gruyter & Co., 1982), 363.

followed every step of religious rituals, the gods would favor them and prosperity would reach the whole of Rome.

Roman religion began much like any other primitive religion. The people had a belief system that encompassed gods with no real visual form of representation.[118] The primitive Roman believed that gods were in everything. In *The Roman Spirit*, Albert Grenier says, "On every side primitive man feels himself surrounded by mysterious powers, intangible and invisible."[119] But through the years, and with the influence of the Greeks and Etruscans, the Romans began to develop a history of existence and beliefs for the gods. Romulus, the founder and first king of Rome, sought approval from the gods for the foundation of the city. The layout of the city consisted of a sacred boundary, or *pomerium*. In this boundary, Romulus built the city's first temple to Jupiter. But it was the city's second king, Numa, who is credited for the basic foundation of the Roman religious system. He started the priesthoods of Jupiter, Mars, and Quirinus, the college of the *pontifices*, the Vestal Virgins, the Salii, and the ritual calendar.[120] The end result of this small start was the organized state religion that we are familiar with today.

STATE RELIGION

The religion that Numa founded grew into a religious system that consisted of colleges of priests. The first college was the *collegium pontificum*, the most important in Rome. The *pontifices* had complete control of the state religion. In the time of Numa through the end of the monarchy, these priests were the religious council for the king. During the republic, they were responsible for the organization of the state religion. The office of *pontifex maximus*, the supreme power in the college of pontiffs, was held by the emperors until 381, when Gratian decided to drop the title. The *collegium pontificum* also decided when festivals would be celebrated and kept records of yearly events.[121] The *augures* were members of the second college of priests, and they performed the auspices. The auspices were the signs from the gods interpreted through the observation of things like the flight of birds or lightning.[122] This action was used to determine if a suggested plan of action had divine approval. There were strict rules for the performance of auspices, and the *augures* held lifetime appointments.[123] *Haruspices*, members of the third college, were specialists in the art of divination, particularly interpretation of prodigies. Prodigies were defined by the Romans as "unnatural" events like horrific births or strange natural occurrences.[124] The fourth college consisted of the *fetiales*, who were chosen from the nobility. Their responsibilities involved dealing with foreign nations and performing the rituals when declaring war and making treaties.[125] There are other organizations of the Roman religion, but for this purpose, these four colleges give an overview and provide a basis for the continuing discussion on the Roman religion.

---

118   Albert Grenier, *The Roman Spirit* (New York: Cooper Square Publishers, 1970), 86.
119   Grenier, 85.
120   Mary Beard et al., *Religions of Rome Volume 1: A History* (Cambridge, UK: Cambridge University Press, 1998), 1.
121   Lesley Adkins and Roy A. Adkins, *Handbook to Life in Ancient Rome* (New York: Oxford University Press, 1994), 254.
122   Lesley Adkins and Roy A. Adkins, *Dictionary of Roman Religion* (New York: Facts on File, Inc., 1996), 23.
123   Adkins and Adkins, *Handbook*, 254.
124   Beard, 19.
125   Adkins and Adkins, *Handbook*, 255.

GODS AND GODDESSES

The Romans, just like the Celts, worshipped many gods and goddesses. The ones discussed here will also fit into three categories in relation to the Celts and Roman Britain. The gods or goddesses will first be the equivalent of a Celtic representation; second, those represented in iconography or inscriptions found in Roman Britain; and third, those who clearly show a religious syncretism with the Celtic deities. In contrast to the Celtic religion, the Romans do not show as much transition history from animism to the human representations recognized today. Long before their arrival in Britain, the Romans were worshipping Mars as the god of war and agriculture. Mars was one of the most popular gods of Rome. Early in the religion of Rome, he was equated with spring, nature, and fertility, and he was seen as the protector of cattle. He is depicted as a warrior holding a spear and shield.[126] He can be seen either fully clothed in battle armor or, as in Britain, almost nude, except for his plumed helmet. He can also be represented with his sacred animals, the wolf and the woodpecker. Mars was one of three gods to whom the Romans would sacrifice a bull.[127]

Mercury was identified as the messenger of the gods and the god of trade, abundance, and commercial success. He was sometimes portrayed in Britain with three faces or with phallic symbols for fertility.[128] Mercury is depicted as wearing a hat and shoes with wings, carrying a staff with two entwined serpents (called a caduceus) and a purse full of money. The sacred animals that accompanied Mercury were most often the cockerel, ram, goat, or tortoise. He was also thought to be a trickster deity because of the myth of his theft of Apollo's cattle.[129] Mercury's father, Jupiter, was the supreme god in the Roman pantheon. He is considered to be the father of many gods, goddesses, and demigods like Hercules. Jupiter was a sky god who controlled weather, especially lightning and rain. The Romans believed that any area struck by lightning was a sacred place to Jupiter. He was later referred to as Jupiter Optimus Maximus—the one highest god.[130]

Minerva, another child of Jupiter, was the goddess of wisdom, arts, and war. She was also related to women's domestic activities like spinning and weaving. Minerva originated as an Etruscan goddess, as did many other Roman deities. Several altars dedicated to the have been found were found with channels running from them into the ground. This suggests that Minerva was also an earth goddess. Some sanctuaries with miniatures of body organs have been found, suggesting that she was associated with healing, which would support her appearance at the ruins of Roman Bath in Britain. She is usually shown with a plumed helmet, round shield, and wearing an aegis that has a Gorgon head in the center.[131] Some other deities prominent in Rome and Britain are the Matres, or Dae Matres. The Matres were mother goddesses who were worshipped in a triad. They were usually pictured seated, wearing robes and holding various objects like cereal, bread, or fruit. The Matres were associated with the earth and plentiful harvests as well as healing and medicine. Since they were healing goddesses, they were often found in hot spring areas.[132] Originally a fertility goddess, Fortuna later became associated with fate and luck. She is normally depicted with a wheel or standing on a wheel, which implies stability. But she can also be seen with a cornucopia and a rudder,

---

126   M. F. Lindemans, "Roman Pantheon" (1995), accessed December 19, 2012, http://www.pantheon.org.
127   Adkins and Adkins, *Dictionary*, 141.
128   Adkins and Adkins, *Dictionary*, 152.
129   *Gods, Goddesses, and Mythology*, ed. C. Scott Littleton (London: Cavendish Square Publishing, 2005), s.v. "Mercury."
130   Adkins and Adkins, *Dictionary*, 119.
131   Littleton, 883.
132   Adkins and Adkins, *Handbook*, 266.

symbolizing that she steers destiny.[133] The final god of Rome who warrants mention is Dis Pater, or Pluto. He was the god of the dead and the underworld. He ruled the underworld with his wife, Proserpina, and could only be reached by using oaths or curses.

The Romans had several ways to contact or honor their gods. They said prayers, but not in the form in which modern Christians pray. The Roman prayer consisted of the worshippers saying they would do something for the god or giving to the god, and in return, the god would provide what was asked for.[134] Invoking a god by stating their name was a central part of the prayer because if the god's name was spoken, then they would listen. The pontifices assembled an intricate list of invocations called *Indigitamenta* because it was very important that the prayer addressed the correct god in the proper way in order to make the prayer successful. The other way to ensure that the precise god was summoned was that one could complete the prayer with "whatever name you wish to be called."[135]

Catullus ensures that the goddess Diana will hear him because he begins with:

Dianae sumus in fide　　　　　*Tu Lucina dolentibus*
Puellae et pueri integri;　　　　*Iuno dicta puerperis,*
Dianam pueri integri　　　　　*Tu potens Triuia et notho es*
Puellaeque canamus.　　　　　*Dicta lumine Luna*
O Latonia, maximi　　　　　　*Tu Cursu, dea, menstruo*
Magna progenies Iouis,　　　　*Metiens iter annuum*
Quam mater prope Deliam　　　*Rustica agricolae bonis*
Deposiuit oliuam,　　　　　　*Tecta frugibus exples.*
Montium domina ut fores　　　*Sis quocumque tibi placet*
Siluarumque uirentium　　　　*Sancta nomine, Romulique,*
Saltuumque reconditorum;　　　*Antique ut solita es, bona*
Amniumque sonantum;　　　　*Sospites ope gentem.*

He not only calls Diana by her name, but he includes "by whatever name," and therefore, according to Roman belief, Diana is bound to listen to his request.[136] The Romans believed that, along with using the proper name, there were other rules for saying a prayer in order for the gods to listen and, hopefully, grant the request. The name of the god was not the only requirement for having a successful prayer—they also had to approach the god at the proper location. They had to know where the god was residing at the time of the prayer. If they addressed the gods and goddesses at Mount Olympus and the deities were off visiting another location, then the gods and goddesses would not hear the prayer. The way to solve this problem was to list, in the prayer, all the places the gods and goddesses might possibly be located. When they had appropriately named the gods, located them, and attracted their attention, they had to "convince the god that the request was a reasonable one and within his/her competence to fulfill."[137]

133　Adkins and Adkins, *Dictionary*, 83.
134　Adkins and Adkins, *Handbook*, 276.
135　R. M. Ogilvie, *The Romans and Their Gods: In the Age of Augustus* (London: Chatto & Windus Ltd., 1969), 24.
136　Gaius Valerius Catullus, *Catullus*, ed. and trans. Elmer Truesdell Merrill (Boston: Ginn and Company, 1893), 60.
137　Ogilvie, 29.

The wording of the Roman prayer was like a legal document, including all of the repeated phrases and details. Another method of contacting gods and goddesses was to make a vow. When Romans made a vow, they offered the deities something in return for fulfilling their request. The difference between a prayer and a vow lies in the gift. Gods and goddesses always received a gift when a prayer was made to them. But with a vow, the gift is only given after the suppliant's request has been fulfilled. A curse was considered to be a vow.[138] These ways of contacting the gods were sufficient at times, but the most commonly used means of communication was sacrifice. Sacrifice was the worshipper's way of providing support or revitalizing the god, and in return, the god would supply them with their request.

The difference between giving a gift and a sacrifice is that a sacrifice has to contain life. This is why animals were used for most sacrifices, except those in family cults. The family cults would use a type of cereal cake. The process of a sacrifice made the animal holy and therefore acceptable to offer to the gods. Animals were considered the most potent of sacrifices because they were full of life and they also contained parts like the heart, which held the spark of life. The choice of victim for a sacrifice had specific rules according to each god and the temple in which the sacrifice was to take place. Most temples had a list of appropriate sacrifices, formulated by the priests and posted in the temple. Specifics included things like the gender of the sacrifice matching the gender of the deity as well as the color: white for air deities like Juno and Jupiter and black for underworld deities.[139]

The Romans also believed that the will of the gods could be determined and that the gods sent signs to the people. Divination was a fundamental part of the Roman religion. The priests or magistrates would read signs from things like *auspicia* (the observation of birds) or the interpretation of natural occurrences such as lightning. The Romans also watched for omens that randomly occurred and could be taken as good or bad.[140] Seeking oracles was also a form of divination that was borrowed from the Greek religion. The Sibylline books were a collection of oracles' sayings that were consulted when there was a crisis or a threat to Rome.[141]

The Romans also worshipped another set of deities with whom they were more personally associated than those of the state religion. These existed under the label of spirits and possessed every place and object. The Romans would choose certain spirits because they suited their personal or household needs. The genii were the spirits who guarded the man and enabled him to have children. These spirits were worshipped on the birthday of the *paterfamilias*, or the head of the household. The Lares and the Di Penates were the household spirits who watched over the pantry and garden. The Fates were the controllers of destiny and were often associated with things like full-term births. The Furies were female spirits assigned to carry out vengeance of the gods. The Manes and the Lemures were the spirits of the dead and were worshipped during festivals such as Feralia, Lemuria, and Parentalia. The Romans held many festivals, and these events were celebrated for the gods, the seasons, and even death.[142]

---

138 Adkins and Adkins, *Handbook*, 276.
139 Ogilvie, 41.
140 Ogilvie, 58.
141 Adkins and Adkins, *Handbook*, 280.
142 Adkins and Adkins, *Handbook*, 274.

DEATH, AFTERLIFE, AND BURIAL

The traditions and rituals of the Romans suggest they believed in an afterlife, especially the existence of spirits. The Romans believed that after death, the spirit continues to exist and occupy the tomb. They believed the spirits required sacrifices to survive and remain at peace. The satisfied spirits were the Manes. If they were not appeased by the living, the spirits became the Lemures.[143] It is clear that the dead were not to be ignored but honored.

The Romans would supply libations (sacrifices of liquids) for the dead at the tomb by piercing the tomb or grave with a pipe. This pipe provided the living a way to share food or drink at any time, but especially during a funerary meal. The spirits "get their nourishment, naturally, from the libations that are poured in our world and the burnt offerings at the tomb; so that if anyone has not left a friend or kinsman behind him on earth, he goes about his business there as an unfed corpse, in a state of famine."[144] Although Lucian does not refer to the Manes and Lemures by name, this is a clear example of how strongly the Romans believed in the spirits and the afterlife. The belief in the afterlife can also be seen in the kinds of burial rites the Romans performed, including the types of burial and grave goods.

The Roman belief in the importance of burial can be traced to the earliest Greek influences on Rome. Homer's idea of the underworld is seen in Virgil's *Aeneid*, written during the time of Augustus. In this epic work, Virgil tells the story of Aeneas, the Trojan who travels to Italy and whose descendants eventually found Rome. In Book VI, Aeneas, seeking help to visit his father in Hades, meets Apollo's prophetess. Aeneas performs the sacrifices and prayers required by Apollo to approach the Sibyl. The Sibyl and Aeneas enter Avernus, the cave to the underworld. They approach the River Styx. Aeneas sees all the souls waiting to cross the river and questions the Sibyl as to why they are there and not progressing across the river. The Sibyl replies: "*Haec omnis, quam cernis, inops inhumataque turba est; portitor ille Charon; hi, quos vehit unda, sepulti; nec ripas datur horrendas et rauca fluenta transportare priusquam sedibus ossa quierunt. Centum errant annos volitantque haec litora circum; tum demum admissi stagna exoptata revisunt.*"[145] The Sibyl's reply informs Aeneas that the souls he sees on the shore who are not being transported are the dead who have not been given proper burial; they will remain on the shore until their bones have been put to rest. This quote from the Aeneid is an example of how important burial was in the lives and religion of the Romans; they believed that without a proper burial, you would be lost in the underworld for eternity. Burial was so important to the Romans that they formed burial clubs. These clubs, unlike others in Rome, were tolerated and were allowed to meet once a month to collect contributions. The funds were then used for funeral expenses for any member who had contributed to the club.[146] Some of the burial clubs collected enough money to build *columbaria*, which will be discussed later in this chapter.

For the Romans, burial was a religious obligation performed by family members. When the moment of death arrived, the body was placed on the ground and the last breath was caught by the closest family member, preferably the eldest son. The purpose for these actions was religious in nature. The Romans thought the "body should be returned to the earth from which it came, while the breath was thought of

---

143 Grenier, 95.
144 Lucian, *Lucian in Eight Volumes*, trans. A. M. Harmon (Cambridge, MA: Harvard University Press, 1925), 119.
145 Charles E. Bennett, *Virgil's Aeneid Books I–VI* (Boston: Allyn and Bacon, 1904), 135.
146 J. M. C. Toynbee, *Death and Burial in the Roman World* (Baltimore and London: Johns Hopkins University Press, 1971), 55.

as the soul, which should be caught by a kiss to prevent it's wandering about."[147] Along with the last kiss, the family of the deceased would close their eyes and call out the name (*conclamatio*) of the deceased to confirm the death. Then the family would wash the body with warm water and place a garland of flowers around the neck and a coin in the mouth to give to the underworld ferryman Charon. They clothed the bodies in appropriate robes and bound their jaws. These actions were traditionally done by the women, but they could also hire male *pollinctores* to do the preparations. This is the time when they would make a death mask (if this had not already been done), which would be used later for portraits. Most upper-class families would have already had this done, but for the lower classes, this was done at the time of death, if at all.[148] The body was then placed on a funeral couch (*lectus funebris*) with the feet toward the door and covered with an income-appropriate coverlet, leaving only the face uncovered; this was called lying in state. A branch of cypress or spruce was placed on the door of the house to warn others that the house had been polluted by death.[149] This process, as stated previously, existed only for the upper class. The lower class would proceed with the funeral process quickly in order to rid the house of the prolonged pollution.

The Romans strictly regulated death—especially burial—because of the possibility of pollution. The Twelve Tables outline the requirements and regulations on burial.

Table 8.1: Sacred Law Includes These Rules for Burial:

> *A dead man shall not be buried or burned within the city.*
>
> *One must not do more than this (at funerals); one must not smooth the pyre with an axe.*
>
> *When a man is dead one must not gather his bones in order to make a second funeral. An exception (in the case of) death in war or in a foreign land …*
>
> *When a man wins a crown himself or through a chattel or by dint of valor, the crown bestowed on him … (may be laid in the grave) with impunity (on the man who won it) or on his father.*
>
> *To make more than one funeral for one man and to make spread more than one bier for him … this should not occur … and a person must not add gold.*
>
> *But him whose teeth shall have been fastened together with gold, if a person shall bury or burn him along with that gold, it shall be with impunity.*
>
> *No new pyre or personal burning-mound must be erected nearer than sixty feet to another person's buildings without consent of the owner … the entrance chamber (of a tomb) and burning place cannot be acquired by usucapio.*[150]

Romans living in the country did not have the same concerns about burial as their city counterparts. The "rich and poor alike could be laid to rest in more or less isolated graves ranging in character from the simplest types" to "elaborately carved architecturally impressive monuments."[151] But according to the

---

147   John L. Heller, "Burial Customs of the Romans," *Classical Weekly* 25, no. 24 (May 1932): 194.

148   Valerie M. Hope, *Roman Death: The Dying and the Dead in Ancient Rome* (London: Continuum, 2009), 71.

149   Heller, 194.

150   Naphtali Lewis and Meyer Reinhold, *Roman Civilization Sourcebook I: The Republic* (New York: Harper & Row, 1966), 108.

151   Toynbee, 73.

Twelve Tables, no burial could take place within the city, so most of the burials took place immediately outside the city gates. The monuments usually lined both sides of the road and were of different types and sizes with space between them. The Via Appia Antica has burials that run for miles from the Porta Appia in Rome. The Romans, like the Etruscans, also reserved large plots where "networks of regular streets along which continuous rows of tumuli or blocks of chamber tombs were aligned."[152]

TYPES OF BURIAL

Inhumation was the most common type of burial for Romans. They believed it had been practiced from the beginning, and according to Cicero in *De Legibus*, they "believe that the most ancient form of burial was that which, according to Xenophon, was decreed by Cyrus for himself. The corpse is consigned to the earth, placed and laid out as if it were covered by its mother's blanket. We are told that our own King Numa was buried in the same fashion in the grave which is not far from the altar of Fons; and we know that the Cornelian clan has employed this type of burial up to our own time."[153] The practice of cremation began about 400 BC, but Lucius Cornelius Sulla (138 BC–78 BC) was the first of the Gens Cornelia to practice the rite of cremation. But even during this time, the Romans continued to bury some part of the deceased: a finger, for example. Lucretius suggests cremation (*ignibus imostum calidis torrescere flammis*), inhumation (*urgerive superne obtritum pondere terrae*), and embalmment (*aut in melle situm suffocari*) were the three types of burial practiced during the late republic.[154] Cremation practices existed in parallel with inhumation but became much more popular after Sulla's time and lasted until about AD 130, during Hadrian's reign. Toynbee suggests this decline occurred because of the increase in the popularity of sarcophagus carving. She also proposes that the Romans thought inhumation was a "respectful" way of disposal but that the "change of rite would seem to reflect a significant strengthening of emphasis on the individual's enjoyment of a blissful hereafter."[155]

LOCATION OF BURIAL

When the funeral was over, the Romans took their dead outside the city gate and placed them in tombs for inhumation burial. The body had been prepared for burial and ready to go to its final resting place. The tomb had been previously created, either for another family member or for the current individual. The tomb contained the sarcophagus in which the body would be placed and finally sealed for eternity. The tombs were usually elaborately carved with representations of the deceased, gods, feasts, dedications, and prayers. The combinations of carvings that could be found on the tomb and sarcophagi are infinite. The first century AD shows a transition from cremation back to inhumation with the appearance of funerary couches with effigies of the deceased. These couches were not actually sarcophagus lids but independent *klinai* (*klinē*,

---

152 Toynbee, 74.

153 Marcus Tullius Cicero, *The Republic and the Laws*, trans. Niall Rudd (Oxford: Oxford University Press, 1998), 144.

154 Toynbee, 39.

155 Toynbee, 41.

singular), where the effigies represent the dead reclining on their backs or on their sides propped up by pillows (Figure 8.2).[156]

The poor or homeless of Rome were often taken to what is called a potter's field. Esquiline Hill was where the dead were taken to be disposed of if they were not lucky enough to have a family or private tomb. Grave pits were located on the eastern part of the hill. These were basically refuse pits where the bodies of the poor were placed along with dead animals and trash from the streets. These circumstances were only for the people of Rome who had no one to care for them after their death.[157]

Figure 8.2 Klinē in the British Museum.

[Picture by Kim Woodring.]

During the time of Augustus, when cremation was popular in Rome, the tomb was transformed into a *columbarium*, a place used to house numerous cremation urns. It was affordable for the lower class of Rome. The niches where the urns were to be placed ran in rows horizontally and vertically. The niche was occasionally rectangular but more often half round at the top of the enclosure. The name of the owner was etched above or below the niche. The niche was sometimes constructed large enough to hold more than one urn and was often flanked by columns to give the appearance of a temple.[158]

GRAVE GOODS

The Romans—just like the Celts and most ancient cultures—included items in the burial they believed the deceased would need in the afterlife. They included personal adornments, military equipment, eating utensils, representations of gods, and, especially, gaming pieces in their burials. When the deceased was cremated, an altar would be formed from wood, and the body would be placed there with incense. The grave goods were then placed with the body and were included in the burning process. The ashes were placed in an urn and transported to the *columbarium* for final placement. Although the Romans included grave goods with burials, this aspect of burial did not seem as important to them as the final resting place. Religion and the afterlife were significant in the life of Romans, but it was not until the late empire that they began to realize their actions in the present could have an effect on the afterlife. Religion to the Romans was something that was done out of duty and expected from every citizen. The most important part of death

---

156   Toynbee, 268.

157   Harold W. Johnston, *The Private Life of the Romans* (Chicago: Scott, Foresman and Company, 1903), 316.

158   Johnston, 321.

to the Romans was the remembrance. The living wanted to be remembered after their death, just like their ancestors before them, and the continuance of elaborate tomb building is evidence of this remembrance. The tombs and the festivals were the ways the living remembering their dead. They concentrated on what was done in the present life instead of what would happen after death.

The previous two chapters have given a brief overview—specifically pertaining to religion and burial— of the different cultures of the Romans and Celts before the invasion of Britain by the Romans. Caesar's invasion of Britain was spurred by his campaigns in Gaul in 57 and 56 BC. He discovered the connections between the continental Gauls and those who relocated to the island of Britain. Caesar realized that the island of Britain could provide military aid and a safe harbor for the continental Gauls. Caesar considered the inhabitants of Britain a threat because of their associations with his current conquests. Caesar's invasion attempt in 55 BC was a failure. Scholars have attributed this to the chosen location of the landing (on the Kentish coast near the modern city of Walmer) and the unfortunate delay of his cavalry by weather.[159]

Caesar returned to Gaul and began to plan for another invasion the following year. Caesar's second attempt at invasion was successful enough for him to make it to Trinovantian territory, located in modern-day Essex. Caesar managed to defeat the chief of the Trinovantes, Cassivellaunus. After a short stay in Britain, Caesar returned to the continent due to more uprisings by the Gauls. Caesar's invasion began the implementation of Roman policy, but the success of the policy was not what Rome expected in Britain. Tiberius and Caligula both tried to assert Roman authority, but the Celtic resistance led by Caratacus and Togodumnus made it impossible to rule Britain through diplomacy alone. The resistance of the Celts, coupled with desire for military success, pushed Claudius to invade Britain in AD 43.[160] Officially, the invasion by Claudius marks the beginning of the process of Romanization, but that process started long before Claudius—although minimally—due to Caesar's conquest of Gaul and subsequent tribal trade that occurred between the continent and Britain.

ROMANIZATION HISTORIOGRAPHY

The term Romanization, originally stated as "Romanizing" by Theodore Mommsen, was first analyzed by Francis Haverfield in the 1920s. He believed that Rome tried to nurture what he called "internal civilization," and through this process the "non-Romans were given a new language, material culture, art, urban lifestyle, and religion."[161] Haverfield suggests that after Romanization, distinction between the Roman culture and the culture of the province was smothered, but he adds that it did not occur everywhere and did not destroy all native sentiments. He also proposed that there was class difference in the effect of Romanization, especially in religion.[162]

Haverfield's view of Romanization lasted until the 1930s, when his pupil R. G. Collingwood challenged his mentor's view of Roman Britain. Collingwood looked at the evidence before him and could see not just Roman characteristics but Celtic as well. He did not agree with previous scholarship that asserted that Rome extinguished the native culture, and he wrote that

---

159   John Wacher, *The Coming of Rome* (New York: Charles Scribner's Sons, 1979), 2.
160   Wacher, 51.
161   Jane Webster, "Creolizing the Roman Provinces," *American Journal of Archaeology* 105, no. 2 (April 2001): 211.
162   Webster, 211.

we cannot be content simply to assert that Britain was Romanized. The civilization we have found existing in even the most Romanized parts of Britain is by no means a pure, or even approximately pure, Roman civilization bodily taken over by the conquered race. What we have found is a mixture of Roman and Celtic elements. In a sense it might be said that the civilization of Roman Britain is neither Roman nor British, but Romano-British, a fusion of the two things into a single thing different from either.[163]

Collingwood's idea of Roman Britain existed until the 1970s, when it was challenged by nativists like Vinogradoff and Richard Reece, who suggested that "the slow uptake of Latin, the rapid demise of towns, and an apparent Celtic revival in the later empire" showed that "Romanization was little more than a surface gloss beneath which Celtic lifeways survived unscathed."[164] In the 1990s, a new theory by Martin Millett proposed that Romanization was led by the native Celtic elite. Millett suggests that the native elite who had governing power given to them by the Romans "emulated" the Roman culture to "reinforce their social position."[165] Millett contends the process of Romanization was linked to the native Celts and their active and willing participation. Romanization continues to be a subject of much contention among scholars, but it is my suggestion and intention to provide evidence that Collingwood's theory still offers the most logical answer to the question of Romanization.

In *Britannia: A History of Roman Britain*, Sheppard Frere proposes there are many ways to examine the effects of Romanization, including looking at the development of the towns, language, coinage, art, and religion.[166] Frere contends that these things give a good summary of Romanization, but, just like many of his colleagues, he leaves an important—but controversial—measuring tool untouched in his discussion: burial. During Frere's period of scholarship, burial was very rarely used as a tool to measure changes in culture. Burial was considered to be unreliable as a source to measure cultural change, but the idea has been debated since the late 1800s. Anthropologists such as Alfred Radcliffe-Brown began suggesting that there was a "close correspondence between the manner of burial and the social value of the person buried" in 1922.[167] In 1952, he added that mortuary ritual consisted of two types of acts, one technical and one ritual. The technical component provided for a simple need of the living to dispose of the body, but "ritually, mortuary rites consist of the execution of a number of symbolic acts that may vary in two ways: in the form of the symbols employed, and in the number and kinds of referents given symbolic recognition."[168]

Mortuary practices are directly linked to the culture in which they are performed, and Lewis Binford suggests three things are fundamental for the interpretation of these practices. The first is "culture is man's extra-somatic means of adaption. As such, culture is partitioned into numerous systems composed of energy, matter, and information. Cultural systems have both content and organizational properties, form and structure; the structure of a system conditions the nature and variety of its formal content."[169] For change to

163   R. G. Collingwood, *Roman Britain* (Oxford: Oxford University Press, 1932), 91.
164   Webster, 212.
165   Webster, 213.
166   Sheppard Frere, *Britannia: A History of Roman Britain* (London: Routledge & Kegan Paul, 1978), 344.
167   Lewis R. Binford, "Mortuary Practices: Their Study and Their Potential," *Memoirs of the Society for American Archaeology*, no. 25 (1971): 14.
168   Binford, 16.
169   Binford, 23.

occur in this system, according to Binford, other variables must function to cause the changes. The forces working on this system—for example, another culture—must affect the whole system and change its "organizational properties before this store of knowledge can be drawn upon for developing content elaboration, additions, and changes in the cultural system."[170] Secondly, Binford suggests that human behavior within a culture is divided and distributed among the participants of the culture and is directly related to the complexity of the culture. The sharing of cultural content may result in both cultures evolving as a result of their degree of interaction. Thirdly, he believes that knowledge and ideas are not sufficient enough to cause change in a culture but that "evolutionary processes operating selectively on different segments of human populations result in configurations of variability and change that vary independently of the genetic origins of the populations themselves."[171]

The effects of one culture on another culture, discussed by these anthropologists and archaeologists, are what lie at the core of my thesis. The previous discussion about mortuary practices provides some background anthropological theory for use in support of Collingwood's theory of Romanization and how I intend to support this theory by providing evidence through the examination of mortuary practices and religion in Roman Britain. The first of the two subjects that I wish to examine is that of religion in Roman Britain. There is an extensive amount of evidence on this subject, but the previous chapters have been used to try and narrow down the information presented in this final chapter. It has been stated previously that the religions of the Celts and Romans before the conquest were very similar, which has made it easy for scholars to overlook the differences. But it is not really the differences that we are interested in, either; instead, our interest is in how the population of Britain, mainly made up of indigenous Celts who assumed a Roman identity after the invasion, expressed continuity of their own religion despite the influence of the Romans.

ICONOGRAPHY

There are several ways that the Romano-British religion can be examined by using iconography. Iconography is defined as symbolic representation, especially the conventional meanings attached to an image or images.[172] These symbols can be a multitude of things that show a symbolic representation of a god or any other religious character. Statues are important symbols of religion in Roman Britain. A small number exists, but there are several statues that clearly represent the mixture of the Roman and Celtic religions.

In his outstanding work *Religion in Roman Britain*, Martin Henig presents an example found at King Harry Lane in St. Albans, England, which lies just outside of the Roman settlement of Verulamium. The statue, found in a burial, was a representation of Mercury as the herdsman of the dead. The statue has "two additional attributes which are in marked contrast one to the other and illustrate the influence of both the Mediterranean and Celtic custom in the art and religion of Roman Britain. Mercury is here accompanied by a tortoise, not a native of Northern Europe, and wears a silver neck torque which for the Celts was a symbol of divine authority."[173] The representation of Mercury with Celtic symbolism of divinity such as the torque

---

170 Binford, 24.
171 Binford, 25.
172 "Iconography," *Dictionary.com*, Random House, Inc., accessed February 16, 2013, http://dictionary.reference.com/browse/Iconography.
173 Martin Henig, *Religion in Roman Britain* (New York: St. Martin's Press, 1984), 58.

reveals that the people involved in this burial, and possibly the deceased as well, practiced a religion that was a combination of Celtic and Roman.

JEWELRY

Jewelry is also another type of iconography that can be used to measure Romanization. Jet was a popular material from which to make rings and necklaces in Britain during the Roman period. A jet pendant carved to symbolize Medusa was found in the Eastern Cemetery in London on the Hayden Street site. The pendant (Figure 8.3) has facial features that are common in Celtic art.[174] Several of these amulets have been found in York and are a small but firm reminder that, even in the third century, the production of Celtic-influenced art survived in Roman London. Jewelry was a very personal item and considered to contain the persona of the deceased.

Bracelets and especially brooches are also examined to measure the extent of

Figure 8.3 Medusa amulet in the Museum of London Archaeological Archive.

[Picture by Kim Woodring.]

Romanization. Burial of these items assured the living that the spirit of the deceased continued its journey with the departed to the afterlife.

The final iconography that visibly supports the mixture of the Celtic and Roman religions was found at Bath. It is believed that the hot springs were used by the native population as a place of healing and as a place to worship the god Sul. But when the Romans began to settle the area, they destroyed any previous archaeological evidence through their substantial building projects. Bath was originally named Aquae Sulis by the Romans and served as a popular destination for the healing hot springs and later as a temple to Sulis Minerva.[175] The pediment of the temple, where the inhabitants of Bath and the surrounding area came to worship Sulis Minerva, held an impressive depiction of the deity. Barry Cunliffe, in *Roman Bath Discovered*, describes the sculpture, which "held aloft by two very classical-looking winged Victories, is a circular shield bordered by oak wreaths from the centre of which glowers a Gorgon's head. Although the Gorgon is normally a female in classical mythology, here in Bath he is shown in the guise of a male with the

---

174 Bruno Barber and David Bowsher, *The Eastern Cemetery of Roman London: Excavations 1983–1990* (London: Museum of London Archaeology Service, 2000), 146.
175 Barry Cunliffe, *Roman Bath* (Oxford: Oxford University Press, 1969), 1.

wedge-shaped nose, the lentoid eyes, moustaches and beetling brow of a Celtic god."[176] Cunliffe believes this work is a truly "brilliant merging" of the Roman and Celtic traditions.

The findings at Bath are exceptional because of their very observable presentation of the mixture of the religions practiced at the temple. It is obvious that the people responsible for the building of the temple accepted both religions and found the classical Minerva to be a perfect alliance with the local deity, Sulis. It was this acceptance and realization by the Romans and the Celts that allowed the mixture of their religions to thrive and reduce the effect of Romanization.

INSCRIPTIONS

Inscriptions found on religious altars and tombstones are also a source of examples for the indication of religious syncretization in Britain. A monumental study of the inscriptions was started by Haverfield, continued by Collingwood, and finally published under the title of *The Roman Inscriptions of Britain* in 1965. The compilations of inscriptions are organized alphabetically by the name of the town in which they were discovered. The following inscription, from an altar found in Bath on the Pump Room site located at Stall Street, shows that some of the Roman military also adopted the practice of leaving dedications to local deities: "*Deae Suli pro salute et incolumitate Marci Aufidi Maximi centurionis legionis VI Victricis Aufidius Eu tuches lebertus uotum soluit libens merito.*" Marcus Aufidius Maximus dedicated this altar to the goddess Sulis in gratitude for his and his freedman's safety and welfare. Marcus was a centurion of the Sixth Legion Victrix and was either stationed at or passing through the area of Bath when he commissioned this altar.[177]

A dedication from Colchester suggests that even in the most Romanized settlements, the Celtic religion still survived. The engraving in Latin reads "*Matribus Suleuis Similis Atti filius ciuis Cantius uotum libens soluit.*" Similis, the son of Attus, makes an offering to the Mother Goddesses Suleviae and fulfills his vow. The writing also indicates that Similis was a member of the Cantii tribe, a Celtic tribe that inhabited the southeastern corner of Britain. This is interesting because he clearly states he is a tribal member and is making a vow to the Celtic goddesses, but it is in a Roman style. This shows that Roman Britain religion was very diversified as well as mixed in its practices. Similis obviously wanted to show that he may have been a Celtic tribal member but was also Roman by the fact that he had his vow written in Latin.[178]

The final example I wish to present is that of a more typical inscription. It occurs on a silver votive plate (Figure 8.4) with the words "*Marti Toutati Tiberius Claudius Primus Attii libertus uotum soluit libens merito*" ("Tiberius Claudius Primus, a freedman of Attius, fulfilled his vow, willingly and deservedly leaves this silver plate to Mars Toutatis").

The combination of the Roman god Mars and the Celtic god Toutatis is the most common form in Britain. The name combinations, similar to the one by Tiberius Claudius Primus, are seen all across Britain. In most of the inscriptions, the Roman names typically come first, followed by the Celtic names.

These types of combinations are what Frere and other scholars of Roman Britain refer to as *interpretatio Romana*. The statue or engraving looks classical, but it does have an inscription referring to a conflated

---

176   Barry Cunliffe, *Roman Bath Discovered* (Charleston, SC: Tempus Publishing Inc., 2000), 41.
177   R. G. Collingwood and R. P. Wright, *The Roman Inscriptions of Britain* (Oxford: Oxford University Press, 1965), 45.
178   Collingwood, 63.

deity name, similar to the previous examples. Although these examples are only a small amount of the iconography and *interpretatio Romana* found in Britain, their presence firmly indicates that the Celtic cultural practices were still included by the population of Britain up through the third and fourth centuries.[179]

MORTUARY PRACTICES

The second of the two subjects I wish to discuss in relation to Romanization is mortuary practices. Rituals performed for burials are numerous and vary according to religious beliefs, and some of those

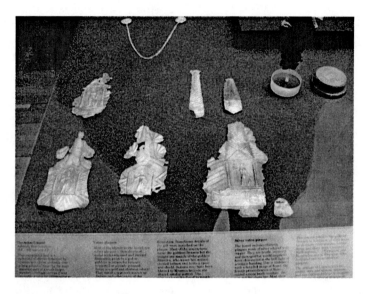

Figure 8.4 Silver dedication plaque in the British Museum.
[Picture by Kim Woodring.]

rituals can be observed in the archaeological record. The continuity or cessation of ritual practice can be followed through time by examining burials. These customs have been discussed previously, but there are two that can be examined particularly for cultural influence. The type and position of the remains are the two customs that can provide the evidence of this change. The type of burial refers to cremation or inhumation. The position of the burial indicates the orientation of the body after interment. The transition seen in burial types for the Celts began with the invisibility due to possible practice of excarnation and secondary burial of the remains to complete inhumation during the late first century BC. The crouched position with the head toward the north was the most common form for Celtic inhumation burial before the invasion of the Romans. The Romans practiced inhumation for the majority of their burial history, except for the period between 400 BC and AD 130, when cremation was the popular type of burial. Extended inhumation with the orientation of west to east was the most common form of Roman burials before the invasion.

There are some regional differences that also can be seen in Britain before and after the invasion. The Arras practice is one of these area differences that are considered to be from an intrusive La Tène cultural group. But this practice was influenced by the local traditions through the addition of the crouched burial. So, the result that is seen in eastern Yorkshire is burials with the characteristic barrow ditches with crouched inhumation, instead of the extended inhumation type found in Europe, where the Arras type originated.[180] This and other regional types of burial are seen throughout Britain but are the minority of burial types. Crouched inhumation can be seen in Roman cemeteries beginning about AD 100. In *Post-Roman Britain to*

---

179   Richard Reece, ed., *Burial in the Roman World* (London: Council for British Archaeology, 1977), 36.
180   Elizabeth O'Brien, *Post-Roman Britain to Anglo-Saxon England: Burial Practices Reviewed* (Oxford, UK: British Archaeological Reports, 1999), 1.

Anglo-Saxon Britain England: Burial Practices Reviewed, Elizabeth O'Brien found that in "early Roman levels at Beckford, four out of eight burials were crouched with heads to the north, and two were flexed, heads south, whereas in the later Roman levels at the same site, only one burial, out of thirteen, was crouched, head north, and was accompanied by hobnails and animal bone."[181] This type and orientation are found in other cemeteries like Poundbury. Sixty-seven burials from the first- and second-century levels reveal crouched inhumation; in the late Roman levels, only twelve of the fourteen hundred burials were in the crouched position. The crouched burial is also characterized by the absence of grave goods, with some rare exceptions. Several sites have produced the same results from the Roman levels that were found in Poundbury. Bath Gate, Cirencester, revealed that thirty-six of the forty-five burials were in the crouched position, and only three of 164 burials at Queenford Farm, Dorchester-on-Thames, were crouched or flexed.

Crouched inhumation continued in areas like Poundbury up to the fourth century. Many scholars, including O'Brien, suggest the reason behind this continuance is the fact that these areas were on the outer limits of the Roman Empire in Britain. If that is the case, then it is possible that Romanization in general occurred in the same fashion. Extended inhumation is thought to have been introduced to Britain by the Romans because of their practice of laying out the dead. It began to be prominent in the Roman world and Britain about the second century AD. The increase of extended inhumation in Britain also brought the change in orientation of the body from north–south alignment to west–east. O'Brien's survey of 2,975 late-Roman extended burials in twenty-one cemeteries in Britain produced a predominance of west–east orientation. Eleven percent had heads to the north; 9 percent to the south; 77 percent to the west; and 2 percent to the east. These results also demonstrate that west–east burial held the majority in the Roman cemeteries, but for the rural, smaller cemeteries, the native north–south alignment persists.[182] Therefore, Romanization occurred far later and with less impact than previously thought by historians and anthropologists.

CONCLUSION

Historians have debated the term "Romanization" and the extent of its effect since Mommsen presented it in the 1920s. The questions of how and what pertained to Rome and the extended reach of the empire are still points of contention with historians today. Through the early part of the twentieth century, historians like R. G. Collingwood produced and deliberated theories about the extent of Romanization in Britain. Collingwood asks how the process of Romanization could be complete when the inscriptional, iconographical, and archaeological evidence reveals the continuous existence of Celtic religious practice. Collingwood also wonders what happened in Britain with the Celtic population and its religious practices that made it so different from any other conquered province of Rome. He answers these questions with the theory of syncretization of religious practices. The local Celtic population never disappeared, and they never stopped practicing their religion. The Romans also never stopped practicing their religion when they came to Britain. Instead, both cultures were accepting of the religious practices that were introduced

---

181   O'Brien, 1.
182   O'Brien, 5.

when Rome came to Britain. In Collingwood's eyes, this acceptance produced a new form of culture: the Romano-British culture.

The Romano-British culture exhibited changes in not only such things as written inscriptions to conflated gods but also in many others, including burial practices. The use of burial evidence was not considered relevant by many anthropologists. The acceptance of burial practices as support for change in cultures only began to be discussed by anthropologists like E. B. Tylor and James Frazer in the late nineteenth century.

But it was Lewis Binford who said "change or variability in mortuary practice is commonly attributed to change or variability in beliefs," and therefore the results from O'Brien's study of the mortuary practices of Roman Britain support the idea of a continuance of the Celtic culture well into the late third century.[183] The continuation of crouched burial with north–south orientation and the near nonexistence of grave goods point to the fact that Romanization did not completely wipe out the native cultural practices. But the implementation of burial evidence as part of cultural determination is still in its infancy, especially in relation to changes like Romanization. I hope these results, coupled with the examination of the iconographic evidence, have demonstrated that Collingwood's theory of Romanization was correct and that the Romans did not completely abolish the Celtic culture. The theory also shows that the coming of Rome did not extinguish the native culture; rather, it propagated the formation of a new Romano-British culture that practiced a combination of Roman and Celtic customs long into the third and fourth centuries AD.

BIBLIOGRAPHY

Adkins, Lesley, and Roy A. Adkins. *Dictionary of Roman Religion*. New York: Facts on File Inc., 1996.
———. *Handbook to Life in Ancient Rome*. New York: Oxford University Press, 1994.
Alcock, J. P. "Classical Religious Belief and Burial Practice in Roman Britain." *Archaeological Journal* 137 (1980): 50–85.
Alcock, Leslie. *Arthur's Britain: History and Archaeology A.D. 367–634*. New York: Allen Lane/Penguin Press, 1971.
Allen, T. G., and, Z. Kamash. *Saved from the Grave: Neolithic to Saxon Discoveries at Spring Road Municipal Cemetery, Abingdon, Oxfordshire 1990–2000*. London: Oxford Archaeology No. 28, 2008.
Arnott, Peter D. *The Romans and Their World*. New York: St. Martin's Press, 1970.
Barber, Bruno, and David Bowsher. *The Eastern Cemetery of Roman London Excavations 1983–1990*. London: Museum of London Archaeology Service, MoLAS Monograph 4, 2000.
Barber, Bruno, David Bowsher, and Ken Whittaker, "Recent Excavations of a Cemetery of Londinium." No. 21 *Britannia* (1990): 1–12.
Barrett, John C. "The Monumentality of Death: The Character of Early Bronze Age Mortuary Mounds in Southern Britain." *World Archaeology* 22, no. 2 (October 1990): 179–189.
Bateman, Thomas. *Ten Years' Diggings in Celtic and Saxon Grave Hill*. London: Moorland Publishing, 1978.
Beard, Mary, John North, and Simon Price. *Religions of Rome, Vols. I and II*. Cambridge: Cambridge University Press, 1998.

---

183   Binford, 13.

Bede. *The Venerable Bede's Ecclesiastical History of England*. 2nd ed. Edited by J. A. Giles. New York: AMS Press Inc., 1971.

Bédoyère, Guy de la. *Defying Rome: The Rebels of Roman Britain*. Gloucestershire, UK: Tempus Publishing Limited, 2003.

———. *Roman Britain: A New History*. New York: Thames & Hudson, 2006.

Bennett, Charles E., *Virgil's Aeneid Books I–VI*. Boston: Allyn and Bacon, 1904.

Betten, Francis S. "The Adoption of the Roman Easter Calculation by the Island Celts." *Catholic Historical Review* 14, no. 4 (Jan. 1929): 485–499.

Bhabha, Homi K. *The Location of Culture*. London: Routledge, 1994.

Binford, Lewis. "Mortuary Practices: Their Study and Their Potential." *Memoirs of the Society for American Archaeology*, no. 25 (1971): 6–29.

Blair, Peter. *Roman Britain and Early England 55 B.C.–A.D. 871*. Edinburgh, UK: Thomas Nelson and Sons Ltd., 1963.

Bober, Phyllis Fray. "Cernunnos: Origin and Transformation of a Celtic Divinity." *American Journal of Archaeology* 55, no. 1 (Jan. 1951): 13–51.

Boylston, A., C. J. Knusel, and C. A. Roberts. "Investigation of a Roman-British Rural Ritual in Bedford England." *Journal of Archaeological Science* 27 (2000): 241–254.

Bray, Warwick, and David Trump. *A Dictionary of Archaeology*. London: Penguin Press, 1970.

Brewster, T. C. M. "The Garton Slack Chariot Burial, East Yorkshire." *Antiquities* 45, no. 180 (1971): 289–292.

Bristow, P. H. W. *Attitudes to Disposal of the Dead in Southern Britain 3500 B.C.–A.D. 43, Vol. 1*. Oxford, UK: British Archaeological Reports 274, 1998.

Catullus, Gaius Valerius. *Catullus*. Edited by Elmer Truesdell Merrill. Boston: Ginn and Company, 1893.

Chadwick, Nora. *The Celts*. Harmondsworth, UK: Penguin Books, 1970.

Chadwick, Nora K. *Ancient Peoples and Places: Celtic Britain*. New York: Frederick A. Praeger, 1963.

Chapman, Robert, Ian Kinnes, and Klavs Randsborg, eds. *The Archaeology of Death*. Cambridge: Cambridge University Press, 1981.

Christ, Karl. *The Romans: An Introduction to Their History and Civilization*. Berkeley, CA: Berkeley, 1984.

Cicero, Marcus Tullius. *De Re Publica, De Legibus*. Translated by Clinton Walker Keyes. New York: G. P. Putnam's Sons, 1928.

———. *The Nature of the Gods*. Translated by Horace C. P. McGregor. Middlesex, UK: Penguin Books Ltd., 1972.

———. *The Republic and The Laws*. Translated by Niall Rudd. Oxford: Oxford University Press, 1998.

Clark, Giles. *The Roman Cemetery at Lankhills*. Oxford, UK: Oxford Clarendon Press, 1979.

Clayton, Peter. *Archaeological Sites of Britain*. London: Weidenfeld & Nicolson, 1976.

Collingwood, R. G. *Roman Britain*. Oxford: Oxford University Press, 1932.

———. "The Roman Frontier." *Antiquity* 1, no. 1 (1927): 15–30.

Collingwood, R. G., and J. N. L. Myres. *Roman Britain and the English Settlements*. Oxford: Oxford University Press, 1937.

Collingwood, R. G., and Ian Richmond. *The Archaeology of Roman Britain*. London: Methuen & Co. Ltd, 1930.

Collingwood, R. G., and R. P. Wright. *The Roman Inscriptions of Britain*. London: Oxford Clarendon Press, 1965.

Cottrell, Leonard. *A Guide to Roman Britain*. Philadelphia: Chilton Books, 1966.

Coulson, William D. E., and Patricia N. Freiert. *Greek and Roman Art, Architecture and Archaeology: An Annotated Bibliography*. 2nd ed. New York: Garland Publishing Inc., 1987.

Crawford, Osbert Guy. "The Snettisham Treasure: Excavations in 1990." *Antiquity* 65 (1991): 447–465.

Crumley, Carole L. *Celtic Social Structure: The Generation of Archaeologically Testable Hypotheses from Literary Evidence*. Ann Arbor: University of Michigan, 1974.

Crummy, Philip, Stephen Benfield, Nina Crummy, Valery Rigby, and Donald Shimmin. *Stanway: An Elite Burial Site at Camulodunum*. London: Society for the Promotion of Roman Studies, Britannia Monograph Series No. 24, 2007.

Cunliffe, Barry. *The Ancient Celts*. London: Penguin Books, 1997.

———. *Cradle of England*. London: British Broadcasting Corporation, 1972.

———. *Danebury: An Iron Age Hillfort in Hampshire*. York: Council for British Archaeology, 1995.

———. *Europe Between the Oceans: Themes and Variations: 9000 B.C.–A.D. 1000*. New Haven, CT: Yale University Press, 2008.

———. *Greeks, Romans and Barbarians: Spheres of Interaction*. New York: Methuen, 1988.

———. *Iron Age Britain*. London: B. T. Batsford, 1995.

———. *Iron Age Communities in Britain*. London: Routledge & Kegan Paul, 1974.

———. "Pits, Preconceptions and Propitiation in the British Iron Age." *Oxford Journal of Archaeology* 11, no. 1 (1992): 69–83.

———. *Roman Bath*. Oxford: Oxford University Press, 1969.

———. *Roman Bath Discovered*. Gloucestershire, UK: Tempus Publishing Ltd., 2000.

———. *Rome and the Barbarians*. London: Bodley Head, 1975.

Davies, Jon. *Death, Burial and Rebirth in the Religions of Antiquity*. London: Routledge, 1999.

Delaney, Frank. *The Celts*. Boston: Little, Brown and Company, 1986.

Dietler, Michael. "'Our Ancestors the Gauls': Archaeology, Ethnic Nationalism, and the Manipulation of Celtic Identity in Modern Europe." *American Anthropologist* 96, no. 3 (Sep. 1994): 584–605.

———. "A Tale of Three Sites: The Monumentalization of Celtic Oppida and the Politics of Collective Memory and Identity." *World Archaeology* 30, no. 1 (Jun.1998): 72–89.

Dillon, Myles, and Nora K. Chadwick. *The Celtic Realms*. New York: New American Library, 1967.

Dobbs, Margaret E. "A Burial Custom of the Iron Age, and a Suggested Explanation." *Journal of the Royal Society of Antiquaries of Ireland* 3, no. 2 (1913): 129–132.

Dobson, Dina P. "Roman Influence in the North." *Greece and Rome* 5, no. 14 (Feb. 1936): 73–89.

Drury, P. J. *Excavations at Little Waltham 1970–71*. Norfolk, UK: Chelmsford Excavation Committee and Council for British Archaeology, 1978.

Dudley, Donald R., and Graham Webster. *The Rebellion of Boudicca*. New York: Barnes & Noble Inc., 1962.

Dupont, Florence. *Daily Life in Ancient Rome*. Oxford, UK: Blackwell Publishing, 1989.

Dyer, James. *Southern England: An Archaeological Guide*. London: Faber & Faber Limited, 1973.

Eckardt, Hella. "The Colchester 'Child's Grave.'" *Britannia* 30 (1999): 57–90.

Evans, Arthur John. "On a Late-Celtic Urn-Field at Aylesford, Kent, and on the Gaulish, Illyro-Italic, and Classical Connexions of the Forms of Pottery and Bronze-Work There Discovered." *Archaeologia* 52, no. 2 (1890): 315–388.

Filip, Jan. *Celtic Civilization and its Heritage*. Prague: New Horizons, 1960.

Foster, Jennifer. *The Lexden Tumulus: A Re-Appraisal of an Iron Age Burial from Colchester, Essex*. Oxford, UK: BAR British Series 156, 1986.

Fowler, W. Warde. *The Religious Experience of the Roman People*. New York: Cooper Square Publishers Inc., 1971.

Fraser, Rebecca. *The Story of Britain: From the Romans to the Present: A Narrative History*. New York: W. W. Norton and Company, 2003.

Freeman, P. W. M. "Romanisation and Roman Material Culture." *Journal of Roman Archaeology* 6 (1993): 438–450.

Frere, Sheppard. *Britannia: A History of Roman Britain*. London: Routledge & Kegan Paul, 1967.

Fry, Plantagenet Somerset. *Roman Britain: History and Sites*. London: David & Charles, 1984.

Fulford, Michael. "Links with the Past: Pervasive 'Ritual' Behavior in Roman Britain." *Britannia* 32 (2001): 199–218.

Garces-Foley, Kathleen, ed. *Death and Religion in a Changing World*. New York: M. E. Sharpe, 2006.

Gildas. *The Ruin of Britain and Other Works*. Edited and translated by Michael Winterbottom. London: Phillimore, 1978.

Gilley, Sheridan, and W. J. Sheils, eds. *A History of Religion in Britain: Practice and Belief from Pre-Roman Times to the Present*. Cambridge, UK: Blackwell Publishers, 1994.

Glover, T. R. *The Conflict of Religions in the Early Roman Empire*. London: Methuen & Co., 1909.

Going, C. J., Miranda Green, Corinne Duhig, and Alison Taylor. "A Roman Child Burial with Animal Figurines and Pottery, from Godmanchester, Cambridgeshire." *Britannia* 28 (1997): 386–393.

Granger, Frank, and W. Warde Fowler. "Roman Burial." *Classical Review* 11, no. 1 (Feb. 1897): 32–35

Grant, Frederick, ed. *Ancient Roman Religion*. New York: Liberal Arts Press, 1957.

Grant, Frederick C., ed. *Hellenistic Religions: The Age of Syncretism*. Indianapolis: Bobbs-Merrill Company Inc., 1953.

Grant, Michael. *The Fall of the Roman Empire: A Reappraisal*. Pennsylvania: Annenberg School Press, 1976.

Green, Miranda. *Celtic Myths*. London: British Museum Press, 1993.

———. *A Corpus of Religious Material from the Civilian Areas of Roman Britain*. Oxford: British Archaeological Reports 24, 1976.

———. *The Gods of the Celts*. Phoenix Mill, UK: Sutton Publishing Ltd., 1986.

———. *The Gods of Roman Britain*. UK: Shire Publication Ltd., 2003.

———. "God in Man's Image: Thoughts on the Genesis and Affiliations of Some Romano-British Cult-Imagery." *Britannia* 29 (1998): 17–30.

Green, Miranda J., ed. *The Celtic World*. London: Routledge, 1995.

Green, Miranda J. *Dictionary of Celtic Myth and Legend*. London: Thames & Hudson, 1992.

———. *The World of the Druids*. London: Thames & Hudson, 1997.

Grenier, Albert. *The Roman Spirit in Religion, Thought, and Art*. New York: Cooper Square Publishers Inc., 1970.

Grimes, W. F. *The Excavation of Roman and Mediaeval London*. New York: Frederick A. Praeger, 1968.

Grinsell, Leslie V. *Barrow, Pyramid and Tomb: Ancient Burial Customs in Egypt, the Mediterranean, and the British Isles*. Boulder, CO: Westview Press, 1975.

Halliday, W. R. "Roman Burial." *Classical Review* 35 no. 7/8 (Nov.-Dec. 1921): 154–155.

Halsall, Paul. "Internet Ancient History Sourcebook." April 1998. Accessed October 11, 2010. http://www.fordham.edu/halsall/ancient/asbook.html.

Harding, D. W. *The Iron Age in Lowland Britain*. London: Routledge & Kegan Paul, 1974.

———. *The Iron Age in Northern Britain: Celts and Romans, Natives and Invaders*. New York: Routledge, 2004.

———. *The Iron Age in the Upper Thames Basin*. Oxford, UK: Clarendon Press, 1972.

Harris, Edward C. "The Stratigraphic Sequence: A Question of Time." *World Archaeology* 7, no. 1 (Jun. 1975): 109–121.

Haverfield, Francis J. *The Romanization of Roman Britain*. London: Oxford University Press, 1923.

Heller, John L. "Burial Customs of the Romans." *Classical Weekly* 25, no. 24 (May 2, 1932): 193–197.

Henig, Martin. *A Corpus of Roman Engraved Gemstones from British Sites: Parts I & II*. Oxford, UK: British Archaeological Reports 8, 1974.

———. *Religion in Roman Britain*. New York: St. Martin's Press, 1984.

Henig, Martin, and Anthony King, eds. *Pagan Gods and Shrines of the Roman Empire*. Oxford: Oxford University Committee for Archaeology, Monograph no. 8, 1986.

Herm, Gerhard. *The Celts: The People Who Came Out of the Darkness*. New York: St. Martin's Press, 1975.

Hill, J. D. "The Pre-Roman Iron Age in Britain and Ireland." *Journal of World Prehistory* 9, no. 1 (Mar. 1995): 47–98.

Hope, Valerie M. *Roman Death: The Dying and the Dead in Ancient Rome*. London: Continuum, 2009.

———. "Words and Pictures: The Interpretation of Romano-British Tombstones." *Britannia* 28 (1997): 245–258.

Hubert, Henri. *The Rise of the Celts*. New York: Biblo & Tannen, 1966.

Hume, David. *The History of England from the Invasion of Julius Caesar to the Abdication of James the Second*. Boston: Phillips, Sampson and Company, 1858.

Hunter, John, and Ian Ralston, eds. *The Archaeology of Britain: An Introduction from Earliest Times to the Twenty-First Century*. 2nd ed. London: Routledge Publishing, 1999.

Hutton, Ronald. *The Pagan Religions of the Ancient British Isles*. Oxford, UK: Blackwell Publishers, 1991.

James, Simon. *The World of the Celts*. London: Thames & Hudson Ltd., 1993.

James, Simon, and Valery Rigby. *Britain and the Celtic Iron Age*. London: British Museum Press, 1997.

Jewitt, Llewellynn. *Grave-Mounds and Their Contents: A Manual of Archaeology as Exemplified in the Burials of the Celtic, the Romano-British, and the Anglo-Saxon Periods*. London: Groombridge and Sons, 1870.

Johns, Catherine. *The Jewellery of Roman Britain: Celtic and Classical Traditions*. Ann Arbor: University of Michigan Press, 1996.

———. "A Roman Burial from Snodland, Kent." *British Museum Quarterly* 3, no. 3/4 (Autumn 1973): 144–150.

Johns, Catherine, and Timothy Potter. *The Thetford Treasure: Roman Jewellery and Silver.* London: British Museum Publications Ltd., 1983.

Johnson, Stephen. *Later Roman Britain.* New York: Charles Scribner's Sons, 1980.

Johnston, Harold Whetstone. *The Private Life of the Romans.* Chicago: Scott, Foresman and Co., 1903.

Jones, Michael. "The Failure of Romanization in Celtic Britain." London: *Proceedings of the Harvard Celtic Colloquium* 7 (1987): 126–145.

Jupp, Peter, and Claire Gittings, eds. *Death in England.* New Brunswick, NJ: Rutgers University Press, 1999.

Karl, Raimund. "Random Coincidences or: The Return of the Celtic to Iron Age Britain." *Proceedings of the Prehistoric Society,* no. 74 (2008): 69–78.

Keegan, Sarah L. *Inhumation Rites in Late Roman Britain: The Treatment of the Engendered Body.* Oxford, UK: British Archaeological Reports 333, 2002.

Kendrick, T. D. *The Druids.* London: Methuen & Co. Ltd., 1927.

Kendrick, T. D., and C. F. C. Hawkes. *Archaeology in England and Wales 1914–1931.* London: Methuen & Co. Ltd., 1932.

Kerenyi, C. *The Religion of the Greeks and Romans.* Westport, CT: Greenwood Press Publishers, 1973.

Kerrigan, Michael. *The History of Death: Burial Customs and Funeral Rites, from the Ancient World to Modern Times.* Connecticut: Lyons Press, 2007.

Kidd, I. G. *Posidonius, Vol. III. The Translation of the Fragments.* UK: Cambridge University Press, 1999.

King, Anthony, and Grahame Soffe. "A Roman-Celtic Temple at Ratham Mill Funtington, West Sussex." *Britannia* 14 (1983): 264–266.

Koch, John T., ed. *Celtic Culture: A Historical Encyclopedia.* 5 vols. Santa Barbara, CA: ABC-CLIO Inc., 2006.

Koester, Helmut. *Introduction to the New Testament, Volume 1: History, Culture and Religion of the Hellenistic Age.* New York: Walter De Gruyter, 1982.

Laing, Gordon J. *Survivals of Roman Religion.* New York: Longmans, Green & Co., 1931.

Laing, Lloyd. *The Archaeology of Celtic Britain and Ireland c. AD 400–1200.* New York: Cambridge University Press, 2006.

Laver Family Collection. Reference Code A12964, Essex County Archives, Essex Records Office. Chelmsford, England.

Leech, Roger, Martin Henig, Frank Jenkins, Margaret Guido, Dorothy Charlesworth, E. M. Besly, S. A. Butcher, R. H. Leech, and R. F. Everton, "The Excavation of a Romano-Celtic Temple and a Later Cemetery on Lamyatt Beacon, Somerset." *Britannia* 17 (1986): 259–328.

Lewis, Naphtali, and Meyer Reinhold. *Roman Civilization Sourcebook I: The Republic.* New York: Harper and Row Publishers, 1951.

Liebeschuetz, J. H. W. G. *Continuity and Change in Roman Religion.* New York: Oxford at the Clarendon Press, 1979.

Lindemans, M. F., ed. "Encyclopedia Mythica." 1995. Accessed December 19, 2012. http://www.pantheon.org.

Lindsay, Jack. *The Romans Were Here: The Roman Period in Britain and Its Place in Our History*. New York: Barnes & Noble Inc., 1969.

Littleton, C. Scott, ed. *Gods, Goddesses, and Mythology*. New York: Marshall Cavendish, 2005.

Liversidge, Joan. *Britain in the Roman Empire*. London: Routledge & Kegan Paul, 1968.

Long, William. *Stonehenge and Its Barrows*. London: H. F. & E. Bull Printers, 1876.

Lucian. *Lucian in Eight Volumes*. Translated by A. M. Harmon. Cambridge, MA: Harvard University Press, 1925.

Macbain, Alexander. *Celtic Mythology and Religion*. New York: Cosimo Inc., 2005.

MacCulloch, J. A. *The Religion of the Ancient Celts*. London: Studio Editions Ltd., 1992.

MacLean, Magnus. *The Literature of the Celts*. New York: Kennikat Press, 1902.

Manning, W. H. "Ironwork Hoards in Iron Age and Roman Britain." *Britannia* 3 (1972): 224–250.

Matthews, C. L. "A Romano-British Inhumation Cemetery at Dunstable." *Bedfordshire Archaeological Journal* 15, 1981.

Matthews, Caitlin. *The Celtic Tradition*. Great Britain: Element Books Ltd., 1995.

Mattingly, D. J., ed. "Dialogues in Roman Imperialism: Power, Discourse, and Discrepant Experience in the Roman Empire." *Journal of Roman Archaeology* 23, 1997.

McWhirr, Alan, Linda Viner, and Calvin Wells. *Romano-British Cemeteries at Cirencester*. Cirencester, UK: Cirencester Excavation Committee, 1982.

Merrill, Elmer Truesdell. "The Attitude of Ancient Rome Toward Religion and Religious Cults." *Classical Journal* 15, no. 4 (Jan. 1920): 196–215.

Metcalf, Peter, and Richard Huntington. *Celebrations of Death: The Anthropology of Mortuary Ritual*. 2nd ed. UK: Cambridge University Press, 1991.

Millett, Martin. "An Early Roman Burial Tradition in Central Southern England." *Oxford Journal of Archaeology* 6, no. 1 (1987): 63–66.

———. *Romanization of Britain: An Essay in Archaeological Interpretation*. Cambridge: Cambridge University Press, 1990.

Mills, Nigel. *Celtic and Roman Artefacts*. Essex, UK: Greenlight Publishing, 2000.

Molleson, Theya. "The Anthropological Evidence for Change Through Romanization of the Poundbury Population." *Natural History Museum, Department of Palaentology* 50, no. 3 (1992): 179–189.

Moore, Frank Gardner. *The Roman's World*. New York: Columbia University Press, 1936.

Morris, Ian. *Burial and Ancient Society*. Cambridge: Cambridge University Press, 1987.

———. *Death-Ritual and Social Structure in Classical Antiquity*. New York: Cambridge University Press, 1992.

Morris, John. *The Age of Arthur: A History of the British Isles from 350 to 650*. New York: Charles Scribner's Sons, 1973.

Morris, Michael. "A Lead-Lined Coffin Burial from Winchester." *Britannia* 17 (1986): 343–346.

Morse, Michael A. *How the Celts Came to Britain: Druids, Ancient Skulls and the Birth of Archaeology*. Gloucestershire, UK: Tempus Publishing Ltd., 2005.

Moscati, Sabatino, Otto Hermann Frey, Venceslas Kruta, Barry Raftery, and Miklós Szabó. *The Celts*. New York: Rizzoli International Publications Inc., 1991.

Muckelroy, K. W. "Enclosed Ambulatories in Romano-Celtic Temples in Britain." *Britannia* 7 (1976): 173–191.

Naso, Publius Ovidus. *Ovid's Fasti.* Translated by Betty Rose Nagle. Indianapolis: Indiana University Press, 1995.

Niblett, Rosalind. *The Excavation of a Ceremonial Site at Folly Lane, Verulamium.* London: Britannia Monograph Series No. 14, 1999.

Nock, Arthur Darby. "Cremation and Burial in the Roman Empire." *Harvard Theological Review* 25, no. 4 (Oct. 1932): 321–359.

North, J. A. *Roman Religion.* Oxford: Oxford University Press, 2000.

O'Brien, Elizabeth. *Post-Roman Britain to Anglo-Saxon England: Burial Practices Reviewed.* Oxford, UK: British Archaeological Reports Series 229, 1999.

O'Driscoll, Robert, ed. *The Celtic Consciousness.* New York: George Braziller Inc., 1982.

Ogilvie, R. M. *The Romans and Their Gods in the Age of Augustus.* London: Chatto & Windus, 1969.

Oman, Charles. *A History of England.* New York: Books for Libraries Press, 1972.

O'Shea, John M. *Mortuary Variability: An Archaeological Investigation.* Orlando, FL: Academic Press, 1984.

Pearce, John, Martin Millett, and Manuela Struck. *Burial, Society and Context in the Roman World.* Oxford, UK: Oxbow Books, 2000.

Pearson, Mike Parker. *The Archaeology of Death and Burial.* College Station: Texas A&M University Press, 1999.

Petts, D. "Burial and Gender in Late and Sub-Roman Britain." *Proceedings of the 7th Annual Theoretical Roman Archaeology Conference* (Apr. 1997): 112–124.

Philpott, Robert. *Burial Practices in Roman Britain: A Survey of Grave Treatment and Furnishings A.D. 43–410.* Oxford, UK: Tempvs Reparatvm, Archaeological and Historical Associates Limited BAR British Series 219, 1991.

Picard, Gilbert. *The Ancient Civilization of Rome.* New York: Cowles Book Company, Inc., 1969.

Piggott, Stuart. *The Druids.* New York: Frederick A. Praeger, 1968.

Pine, Jo, and Steve Preston. *Iron Age and Roman Settlement and Landscape at Totterdown Lane, Horcott near Fairford, Gloucestershire.* Berkshire, UK: Ridgeway Press Ltd., 2004.

Potter, T. W., and Catherine Johns. *Roman Britain.* Berkley: University of California Press, 1992.

Powell, T. G. E. "Celtic Origins: A Stage in the Enquiry." *Journal of the Royal Anthropological Institute of Great Britain and Ireland* 78, no. 1/2 (1948): 71–79.

———. *The Celts.* London: Thames & Hudson, 1983.

Priestly, H. E. *Britain Under the Romans.* London: Frederick Warne & Co. Ltd., 1967.

Rankin, David. *Celts and the Classical World.* London: Routledge, 1987.

Redfern, Rebecca. "New Evidence for Iron Age Secondary Burial Practice and Bone Modification from Gussage All Saints and Maiden Castle (Dorset, England)." *Oxford Journal of Archaeology* 27, no. 3 (2008): 281–301.

Redfern, Rebecca C., and Sharon N. DeWitte. "A New Approach to the Study of Romanization in Britain: A Regional Perspective of Cultural Change in Late Iron Age and Roman Dorset Using the Siler and

Gompertz-Makeham Models of Mortality." *American Journal of Physical Anthropology* 144 (2011): 269–285.

———. "Status and Health in Roman Dorset: The Effect of Status on Risk of Mortality in Post-Conquest Populations." *American Journal of Physical Anthropology* 146 (2011): 197–208.

Reece, Richard, ed. *Burial in the Roman World*. London: Council for British Archaeology, 1977.

Rhys, J. *Early Britain: Celtic Britain*. London: Wyman and Sons, 1884.

Rives, James B. *Religion in the Roman Empire*. Massachusetts: Blackwell Publishing, 2007.

Ross, Anne. "Chain Symbolism in Pagan Celtic Religion." *Speculum* 34, no. 1 (Jan. 1959): 39–59.

———. *Druids: Preachers of Immortality*. Stroud, UK: Tempus Publishing Ltd., 1999.

———. *Everyday Life of the Pagan Celts*. London: B. T. Batsford Ltd., 1970.

———. "The Human Head in Insular Pagan Celtic Religion." *Proceedings of the Society of Antiquities* 1957–58: 10–58.

———. *Pagan Celtic Britain: Studies in Iconography and Tradition*. London: Routledge & Kegan Paul, 1967.

Rostovtzeff, Michael. *Rome*. New York: Oxford University Press, 1960.

Rudsdale, E. J. Diaries. Reference Code 888/9,10,31,11, Essex County Archives, Essex Records Office. Chelmsford, England.

Rüpke, Jörg. *A Companion to Roman Religion*. London: Blackwell Publishing, 2007.

Salway, Peter. *The Oxford Illustrated History of Roman Britain*. Oxford: Oxford University Press, 1993.

———. *Roman Britain*. Oxford, UK: Clarendon Press, 1981.

Scullard, H. H. *Roman Britain: Outpost of the Empire*. London: Thames & Hudson, 1979.

Shaw, Brent D., "Seasons of Death: Aspects of Mortality in Imperial Rome." *Journal of Roman Studies* 86 (1996): 100–138.

Shear, Theodore Leslie. "The Excavation of Roman Chamber Tombs at Corinth in 1931." *American Journal of Archaeology* 35, no. 4 (Oct.-Dec. 1931): 424–441.

Shore, T. W. "Characteristic Survivals of the Celts in Hampshire." *Journal of the Anthropological Institute of Great Britain and Ireland* 20 (1891): 3–20.

Showerman, Grant. *Rome and the Romans: A Survey and Interpretation*. New York: Cooper Square Publishers Inc., 1969.

Siculus, Diodorus. *Diodorus of Sicily Books IV–VII*. Vol. III. Edited by E. H. Warmington. Cambridge, MA: Harvard University Press, 1939.

Sorabella, Jean. "A Roman Sarcophagus and Its Patron." *Metropolitan Museum Journal* 36 (2001): 67–81.

Spence, Lewis. *The Mysteries of Britain: Secret Rites and Traditions of Ancient Britain Restored*. New York: Samuel Weiser Inc., 1970.

Stead, I. M. "A Distinctive Form of La Tène Barrow in Eastern Yorkshire and on the Continent." *Antiquaries Journal* 41, no. 1/2 (1961): 44–62.

———. "The Reconstruction of Iron Age Buckets from Aylesford and Baldock." *British Museum Quarterly* 35, no. 1/4 (Spring 1971): 250–282.

Strabo. *The Geography of Strabo*. Translated by Horace Leonard Jones. London: Harvard University Press, 1923.

Stukeley, William. *Stonehenge: A Temple Restor'd to the British Druids; Abury: A Temple of the British Druids.* New York: Garland Publishing Inc., 1984.

Tacitus. *The Histories.* Edited by E. Capps, T. E. Page, and W. H. D Rouse and translated by Clifford H. Moore. London: William Heinemann, 1925.

Taylor, Alison, Miranda Green, Corinne Duhig, Don Brothwell, Elizabeth Crowfoot, Penelope Walton Rogers, M. L. Ryder, and W. D. Cooke. "A Roman Lead Coffin with Pipeclay Figurines from Arrington, Cambridgeshire." *Britannia* 24 (1993): 191–225.

Thompson, E. A. "Gildas and the History of Britain." *Britannia* 10 (1979): 203–226.

Tierney, J. J. "The Celtic Ethnography of Posidonius." *Proceedings of the Royal Irish Academy* 60 (1959/1960): 189–275.

Todd, Malcolm, ed. *A Companion to Roman Britain.* Massachusetts: Blackwell Publishing, 2004.

Toynbee, J. M. C. *Death and Burial in the Roman World.* New York: Cornell University Press, 1971.

Tylor, Edward B. *Primitive Culture: Researches into the Development of Mythology, Philosophy, Religion, Language, Art and Custom, Vols. I & II.* Boston: Estes & Lauriat, 1874.

Ucko, Peter J. "Ethnography and Archaeological Interpretation of Funerary Remains." *World Archaeology* 1, no. 2 (Oct. 1969): 262–280.

Versnel, H. S., ed. *Faith, Hope and Worship: Aspects of Religious Mentality in the Ancient World.* Netherlands: Leiden/E. J. Brill, 1981.

Wacher, John. *The Coming of Rome.* New York: Charles Scribner's Sons, 1979.

———. *Roman Britain.* London: J. M. Dent and Sons Ltd., 1978.

Wacher, John, ed. *The Roman World.* London: Routledge, 1987.

Wait, G. A. *Ritual and Religion in Iron Age Britain.* Oxford, UK: British Archaeological Series 149, 1985.

Ward, John. *The Roman Era in Britain.* New York: Kennikat Press, 1911.

Webster, Graham. *The British Celts and Their Gods Under Rome.* London: B. T. Batsford Ltd., 1986.

———. *Celtic Religion in Roman Britain.* New Jersey: Barnes & Noble Books, 1986.

———. "Roman Britain: The Trend of Recent Ideas." *Greece and Rome, Second Series 5*, no. 1 (March 1958): 16–31.

Webster, Jane. "Creolizing the Roman Provinces." *American Journal of Archaeology* 105, no. 2 (Apr. 2001): 209–225.

———. "Interpretatio: Roman Word Power and the Celtic Gods." *Britannia* 26 (1995): 153–161.

———. "Necessary Comparisons: A Postcolonial Approach to Religious Syncretism in the Roman Provinces." *World Archaeology* 28, no. 3 (Feb. 1997): 324–338.

Wheeler, Mortimer. *Maiden Castle.* London: Her Majesty's Stationery Office, 1972.

———. *Report on the Excavation of the Prehistoric, Roman, and Post-Roman Site in Lydney Park, Gloucestershire.* London: University Press, 1932.

———. *The Stanwick Fortifications: North Riding of Yorkshire.* Oxford: Society of Antiquaries, 1954.

Whimster, Rowan. *Burial Practices in Iron Age Britain: A Discussion and Gazetteer of the Evidence c. 700 B.C.–A.D. 43 Parts 1 & 2.* Oxford, UK: B.A.R, 1981.

White, Roger. *Roman and Celtic Objects from Anglo-Saxon Graves: A Catalogue and an Interpretation of Their Use.* London: British Archaeological Series, 1988.

Williams, Howard. "Potted Histories—Cremation, Ceramics and Social Memory in Early Roman Britain." *Oxford Journal of Archaeology* 23, no. 4 (2004): 417–427.

Williamson, W. C. *The Bronze Age Tree Trunk Coffin Burial Found at Gristhorpe*. London: S. W. Theakston, 1872.

Wilson, C. E. "Burials Within Settlements in Southern Britain During the Pre-Roman Iron Age." *Bulletin of the Institute of Archaeology* 18 (1981): 127–170.

Wilson, Roger J. A. *Roman Remains in Britain*. London: Constable & Company Ltd., 1975.

Woolf, Greg. "Beyond Romans and Natives." *World Archaeology* 28, no. 3 (Feb. 1997): 339–350.

Wright, G. R. H. "The Correlation of the Roman-Celtic Temples." *Man* 65 (May-June 1965): 67–70.

Yaggy, L. W., and T. L. Haines. *Museum of Antiquity: A Description of Ancient Life*. New York: Standard Publishing House, 1882.

Greek and Roman Religion

OBJECTIVES:

1. Define Greek "piety."
2. Understand the hierarchy of the Greek gods and deified mortals.
3. Identify the religious ideas of each philosopher discussed in the article.
4. Define Demiurge.

Greek and Roman Insights into the Nature of Religion: Socrates, Plato, Aristotle, Cicero, Seneca

By Jude P. Dougherty

The Greek mind had a well-developed sense of "piety," piety in the sense that it disposed one to acknowledge debt, e.g., to one's parents, to one's country, and to the wellsprings of one's being.

Socrates (470–399 B.C.) was charged with impiety and thus corrupting the youth because he did not recognize his debt to the gods accepted by the state. Yet it is well known that Socrates was the enemy of neither morality nor the state, affirming as he did that the wise man is both good and happy. This doctrine has a bearing on the present topic, namely, man's attitude toward the divine. Socrates argued that happiness is integrated selfhood, an inner harmony of the self with itself, or put another way, personal integrity. This integrity is achieved through the formation of the will by insight. Insight itself is attained through "training," that is, through "purposeful thoughtfulness." Required is plain, hard, honest, humble thinking in the context of a triple dialogue with oneself, with others, and with the mysterious ultimate that lures man on. Virtue can be taught because the relevant insights can be communicated. The virtue of religion is a species of piety, the acknowledgment of one's debt to the gods, and it can be taught as any virtue is taught.

In *Euthyphro* Socrates discusses piety, which is that part of justice which concerns attention to the gods; the remaining part of justice concerns the service of men.[1] The virtue

---

1 Plato, *Euthyphro,* 12e. In *Dialogues of Plato,* 2 vols., translated by B. Jowett (New York: Random House, 1920).

of justice binds all other virtues into a harmony and brings unity to the person as a whole. What does attention to the gods mean? The gods are not benefited or brought to a greater degree of perfection by anything that men do. The kind of attention Socrates has in mind involves a certain kind of service, a committing of oneself to a divine service. Prayer and sacrifice are modes of service. Such acts as honor, praise, and gratitude bring salvation to individuals, families, and states.[2]

On the subject of prayer, Xenophon (c. 430–356 B.C.) records that Socrates' ideal was "to pray for that which is good, without further specification, believing that the gods best know what is good."[3] In *Alcibiades II,* Plato (c. 428–348 B.C.) has Socrates approve this old Spartan prayer: "Give us, O king Zeus, what is good, whether we pray for it or not, and avert from us the evil, even if we pray for it."[4] Socrates' ideal of prayer is also shown in a beautiful prayer to Pan, which occurs at the end of the *Phaedrus:* "O beloved Pan, and all ye other gods of this place, grant to me that I be made beautiful in my soul within, and that all external possessions be in harmony with my inner man. May I consider the wise man rich; and may I have such wealth as only the self-restrained man can bear or endure." He then turns to Phaedrus and asks: "Do we need anything more, Phaedrus? For me that prayer is enough."[5]

Aristotle, in his day, will say that the word "father" when applied to Zeus includes the idea of his care for men. But this idea first appears in Greek literature in a passage of Plato's *Apology,* in which Socrates says to his judges that "no evil can come to a good man either in life or after death, and God does not neglect him."[6]

Plato followed Socrates in rejecting what he called the "indecent" fables told about the gods. In Plato's judgment, poets who make up such things are dangerous to the health of society. Plato's conception of the divine and of man's relation to the divine was most lofty. In the *Timaeus,* when Timaeus begins his story of "creation," we learn that the eternal model is the Demiurge himself:

> Let me tell you then why the creator made this world of generation. He was good, and the good can never have any jealousy of anything. And being free from jealousy, he desired that all things should be as like himself as they could be.[7]

According to Plato the eternal being of the Demiurge is orderly. When he takes over discordantly moving primordial matter, he brings it from disorder to order. The eternal being of the Demiurge is also intelligent. Therefore, since intelligence cannot be present anywhere without dynamic soul *(psyche),* the Demiurge fashions intelligence *(nous)* within the soul. We may say that he gives intelligence an in-soul embodiment. The Demiurge is also the symbol of "incarnation," the process of embodiment that bridges the gulf between eternal changeless being and time-and-space changeable becoming. This timeless model is brought down to earth and rendered incarnate in a multiplicity of things.

Clearly the Demiurge is not to be equated with Yahweh of the Hebrews; he is not experienced as utterly transcending his creation but as active within it. The Demiurge is pictured as an artist working with

---

2 Ibid., 14e.
3 Xenophon, *Memorabilia,* 1.3.2.
4 Plato, *Alcibaides II,* 143a.
5 Plato, *Phaedrus,* 279b.
6 Plato, *Apology,* 41b. In *Dialogues of Plato,* 2 vols., translated by B. Jowett (New York: Random House, 1920).
7 Plato, *Timaeus,* 30b.

somewhat resistant materials that he has not made but that he struggles to shape in such a way that they express insofar as possible the goodness and the intelligibility of his model—the essential structure of his own being. The parallel between the Demi-urge and human beings struggling to express in their existence the essentially good, orderly, intelligible structure of their selfhood is obvious.

Plato's philosophical outlook includes personal belief in the providence of higher intelligences with regard to human affairs. According to his pivotal philosophical conceptions, no city-state can attain a high degree of culture unless its rulers pattern it after the Ideal. As a matter of historical fact, Athens and other Greek city-states did reach a high and proud degree of civilization, yet some of their greatly revered leaders had not even heard of the Ideal, let alone received training in the doctrine. How account for their success? They ruled, says Plato, not by knowledge but by true opinions, which unfortunately are undependable and insecure because of the lack of any causal tie. The security and dependability of these opinions in the great Greek leaders required some cause apart from their own thinking, some inspiration from a higher type of intelligence than the merely human:

> And therefore not by any wisdom, and not because they were wise, did Themistocles and those of whom Anytus spoke govern … . But if not by knowledge, the only alternative which remains is that statesmen must have guided states by right opinion, which is in politics what divination is in religion; for diviners and also prophets say many things truly, but they know not what they say … . Yes, and statesmen above all may be said to be divine and illumined, being inspired and possessed of God, in which condition they say many grand things, not knowing what they say.[8]

This notion is also present in a passage of the *Republic,* where Plato states that given the actual condition of human government everywhere, based as it is upon traditionally received notions and not upon philosophical knowledge, the good that is present is due to a higher intervention: "… for I would not have you ignorant that, in the present evil state of governments, whatever is saved and comes to good is saved by the power of God, as we may truly say."[9] Plato believes that men so inspired, though few in number, are always to be found.

In the *Laws* Plato does not hesitate to propose legislation regarding religious observance. One magistrate at least will sacrifice daily to some god or demi-god on behalf of the city and citizens and their possessions.[10] In Book X of the *Laws* Plato lays down his proposals for the punishment of atheism and heresy.

To say that the universe is the product of the motions of corporeal elements, unendowed with intelligence, is atheism. "If you say that nature has bestowed the gifts of earth, you are merely giving a different name to God. For what is nature if not God and divine reason pervading the entire world and its parts? As often as you will you may find some different way to address the author of all that we have. You may call him 'Jupiter,' 'Supremely Good,' 'Supremely Great,' or by some other name."[11]

Plato argues that there must be a source of motion, and that ultimately we must admit a self-moving principle, called soul or mind, which is the ultimate source of cosmic movement. Plato decides that there

---

8   Plato, *Meno,* 99bd.
9   Plato, *Republic,* VI, 492E–493A.
10   Plato, *Laws,* 828b.
11   Ibid., 899d.

must be more than one soul responsible for the universe because there is disorder and irregularity as well as order. There may be more than two. It is heresy to say that the gods are indifferent to men. The gods cannot lack the power to attend to small things. God cannot be too indolent or too fastidious to attend to details; even a human artificer attends to details. Providence does not involve interference with the laws of nature. Divine justice will at any rate be realized in the succession of lives.

According to Plato, a pernicious heresy is the opinion that the gods are venal and that they can be induced by bribes to condone injustice. As to the penalties to be inflicted on those proved guilty of atheism or heresy, Plato prescribes for a morally inoffensive heretic at least five years in a house of correction. A second conviction will be punished with death.

Heretics who exploit the superstition of others for their own profits or who establish immoral cults are to be imprisoned for life. No private shrines or private cults are to be permitted. However, before prosecuting an offender for impiety, the guardians of the law should determine whether the offense has been committed in earnest or from childish levity.[12] Although there is a difference in emphasis between the *Laws* and Plato's earlier works, his overall views are not different from those which he espoused in the much earlier *Republic*.

In the *Republic*, Plato says religion is beyond the sphere of the philosopher and the legislator; tradition is to be followed in these matters.

> To Apollo, the god of Delphi, there remains the ordering of the greatest and noblest and chiefest thing of all. Which are they? he said. The institution of temples and sacrifices, and the entire service of the gods, demigods, and heroes; also the ordering of the repositories of the dead, and the rites which gave to be observed by him who would propitiate the inhabitants of the world below. These are matters of which we are ignorant ourselves, and as founders of a city we should be unwise in trusting them to any interpreter but our ancestral deity.[13]

Unlike Plato, Aristotle (384–22 B.C.) provides no significant texts on the subject of religion, although in one place he offers a psychological explanation of the cause of belief in gods, namely, experience in dreams and the regular order and harmony in the universe. There is no doubt, however, that Aristotle argues to a number of concepts associated with the divine: to an immaterial order, to a first or ultimate cause which draws all things to itself, and to a self-thinking intellect, yet one would look in vain for texts in which he prescribes homage or piety.

Contrary to the lofty and spiritual philosophy of Plato is the analysis of the atomist Epicurus (341–270 B.C.), who taught that religion is a disease of the soul, having its origin in fear of the gods and the hereafter. Religion is not grounded in respect for the eternal law, as Socrates and Plato thought. Quite the opposite. The frightening qualities of nature lead men to search for the sources responsible for them. These sources can hardly be imagined as beneficent. Man has created his gods in part because he is convinced that evildoers will be punished in the hereafter. In this manner, man's evil conscience is at the root of religion.[14] Epicurus

---

12 Ibid., 909d.
13 Plato, *Republic*, IV, 427bc.
14 Cf. *The Philosophy of Epicurus*, translated by George K. Strodach (1963).

subscribed to a mechanistic or purely materialistic or atomistic interpretation of nature, not unlike that of Democritus.

Marcus Tullius Cicero (106–43 B.C.), lawyer, philosopher, statesman, and the greatest of Roman orators, regards social organization as closely related to the divine. In *De legibus* III he considers first the means by which the state should endeavor to win the favor of the gods, and second, the ways by which the state under divine favor should live and function.[15] In the one case, the state acts through religious *De*ceremony and priestly order; in the other, through magistrates and groupings of the chief men and people. He sets forth a code of religious laws, introduced by a preamble in which he urges all citizens of the ideal commonwealth to believe implicitly in the supremacy of the deathless gods. For the gods not only govern the universe, but they also perceive and record the acts and feelings of each individual. Accordingly, if reverence does not of itself inspire adoration, prudence will at least suggest the expediency of worshiping those beings who will be both witnesses against us and judges of our conduct.

Cicero draws up a set of religious prescriptions in legalistic terms. The gods must be approached reverently, in purity of heart, and without costly ceremonial. The manner in which men approach them should be both reverent and fitting. Although the law stresses purity of heart, it does not thereby imply that no importance is to be attached to purity of body. The body of a worshiper should be ceremonially clean. By forbidding costly ceremony, the law opens the rites of religion to all.

The divinities who are to be thus approached do not all possess identical significance. Cicero acknowledges a hierarchy among the gods.[16] In the first place come the gods of heaven; in the second, deified mortals such as Hercules and Aesculapius; next the personified abstractions such as intelligence, virtue, and faith; after these Cicero puts the dead, who are not to be considered as gods. Into this pantheon no new or imported gods will be admitted unless they have been officially accepted by the state. Citizens will not be allowed to worship the personification of any evil abstraction.

Cicero further divides religious observance into urban and rural spheres. Certain practices are at all times forbidden. Women must not participate in nocturnal sacrifices except when duly performed on behalf of the people. No wicked person may offer gifts to the gods in the hope of softening their anger toward him. No one except attendants of the Great Mother of the Gods may collect money for religious purposes, and even they may do so only on the proper days. Cicero is convinced that the custom of taking money consumes property and disseminates superstition. No one may dedicate land that is the sacred possession of all the gods to any special purpose. Vows are to be strictly observed. Violations of the religious law will be punished. From those who are guilty of perjury, two penalties are exacted. Since, on the one hand, perjury is an offense against the gods, the punishment is death; and since, on the other hand, perjury intimately affects human life and interests, death is accompanied by disgrace.

In rural districts, where graves are the religious centers, the simple pieties of ancestral and family worship are to be carefully preserved. Recognizing the importance of religion in the countryside, he decrees

---

15 Marcus Tullius Cicero (106–43 B.C.), *De legibus,* III. Influence of Cicero on Western thought is incalculable. For Aquinas he was the beloved and oft-quoted "Tully"; for the Renaissance, a major source. Cicero's *On the Commonwealth* and *On the Laws* were his first and most substantial attempts to adapt Greek theories of political life to the circumstances of the Roman Republic. Both display an indebtedness to Plato. *On the Commonwealth* and *On the Laws,* translation based on that of K. Ziegler and W. Goerler, edited by James E. G. Zetzel (Cambridge: Cambidge University Press, 1999).
16 Cicero, *De legibus,* II, 9.

days of relaxation, falling at such seasons of the year as naturally coincided with the end of the farmer's labor. In the cities, on the other hand, the gods are to be worshiped in temples, where statues bring them vividly before the eyes and thoughts of men. Among the ceremonial forms accompanying urban observance is that of public games.

Ritual is subject to the guidance of *sacerdotia* or public priests. Priests fall into distinct groups. The first that Cicero mentions are the *pontiff* who preside over all public and private ceremonies and supply information as to the proper form of all ritual. Within their competence also falls the duty of punishing with death any *vestal* who fails to keep her vow of chastity. Certain priests in this group are assigned to the worship of a particular divinity. These Cicero identifies as *flamens*, but their duties are not related.

Another class that Cicero identifies with sacral functions is the *vestals*, groups of women who direct the worship of Vesta. They guard the sacred fire, symbol of the city's domestic life, and may never allow it to become extinguished. Selected as young girls, *vestal* virgins are committed to thirty years of service.

A second group of priests are the *augurs*. They expound the will of Jupiter by the interpretation of signs and auspices. They are to determine, by appropriate ritual, whether the gods favor the state, its crops, and its officials. Their pronouncements, duly delivered after formal observation, are law to magistrates in the city and even to military commanders in the field. Mandates are to be enforced on penalty of death. The chief and pre-eminent power in the commonwealth is that associated with the authority of the *augurs*. Declaring war, concluding peace, or striking a treaty is done with the sanction of religion (the Fetial College). In Roman belief, political power, considered abstractly, flows from the gods. Human agents may properly exert political authority only when that authority is divinely sanctioned.

Seneca (c. 48 B.C.–65 A.D.), Rome's leading philosopher in the mid-first century A.D., in his treatise "On Private Life," raises the question: "What service to God is there in contemplation?" and he responds: "That the greatness of his work be not without witness."[17] Elsewhere he writes:

> It is not by sacrificial victims, however fat and glittering with gold, that the gods are honored, but by uprightness and holiness of will in the worshiper. Good men with no more to offer than groats and meal-paste are devout, while the wicked cannot avoid impiety, however much they stain the altars with blood.[18]

Speaking of the value of prayer, he offers this insight:

> Who ever says (that God does not grant favors) has closed his ears to the sound of prayer, of vows made in all places, in private and in public, with hands raised to heaven. This would not happen, I tell you, it could not be that nearly all mankind would have joined the lunacy of addressing deities that cannot hear and gods that cannot act, unless we had some knowledge of their favors toward us, of favors sometimes brought to us of their own accord, sometimes granted in answer to a prayer, of favors great and timely that free us from mighty threats by their coming.

---

17 Seneca, "On the Private Life," in *Moral and Political Essays,* edited and trans. by John M. Cooper and J. F. Procopé (Cambridge: Cambridge University Press, 1995), 175.

18 Seneca, "On Favours," in ibid., 202.

His titles can be as many as his services to us … . Wherever you turn, you will find him coming to meet you. Nothing is void of him; he fills his own creation. You waste your time, most ungrateful of mortals if you say that you owe yourself not to God but to nature. You cannot have nature without God, nor God without nature. Each is the same as the other, differing only in function … . God confers on us the greatest and most important favors without any thought of return. He has no need for anything to be conferred, nor could we confer anything on him.[19]

---

19   Ibid., 276–80.

African Religion

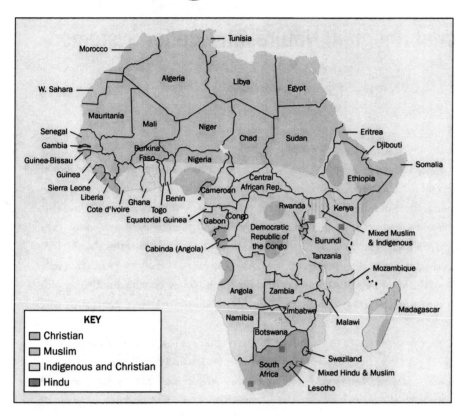

KEY
- Christian
- Muslim
- Indigenous and Christian
- Hindu

OBJECTIVES:

1. Define religion according to African beliefs.
2. Identify characteristic features of African religion.
3. Understand the significance of the wooden mask in African religion.
4. Identify three other sources, besides oral tradition, of African religion.

African Traditional Religion, Nature, and Belief Systems

By Ibigbolade Simon Aderibigbe

INTRODUCTION

Religion is found in all established human societies in the world. It is one of the most important institutional structures that make up the total social system. There is hardly a known race in the world, regardless of how primitive it might be, without a form of religion to which the people try to communicate the divine. This religion becomes inseparable with the total life experience of the people. It thereby permeates into every sphere of the people's lives, encompassing their culture, the social, the political, and the ethical, as well as the individual and societal expectations in their ups and downs. As is the case of nearly every other people in the world, religion is one of the keystones of African culture and is completely entwined in the people's lifestyle. A basic understanding of African religion will provide an awareness of African customs and belief systems.

Perhaps no religion has been so confused in the minds of Western audiences as the African Traditional Religion. The images of this religion have been presented as hopelessly savage and full of ugly superstition. This is solely because the earliest investigators and writers about the religion were mostly European and American anthropologists, some missionaries, and colonial administrators who had no knowledge of the true African spiritual situation. Their works portrayed a distorted image of a religion drawn from half-truths and fertile imaginations. However, an increasing number of African theologians are conducting valuable studies in the African Religion. They have been able to unveil the position that the tenets, spiritual values, and satisfaction which are found in the other world religions—namely, Christianity, Islam, and Buddhism, to mention a few—could also be found in African Traditional Religion. Furthermore, it is imperative to say that these researches have left a positive impact, in the sense that they have helped highlight the general truths, concepts, and trends about the religion, thereby dispelling most of the popular misconceptions about the religion.

The emphasis of this chapter will be on the basic concepts of African Traditional Religion. These are its nature, characteristic features, and its conceptual framework.

THE NATURE OF AFRICAN TRADITIONAL RELIGION

The African Religion is the religion of the Africans and strictly for the Africans. It is not a religion preached to them, but rather a part of their heritage that evolved with them over the years. They were born and not converted into it. It has no founder, but rather a product of the thinking and experiences of their forefathers who formed religious ideas and beliefs. Therefore, its existence cannot be attributed to any individual as in other world religions, such as Christianity, Islam, Confucianism, Buddhism, Hinduism, and so on.

Through the ages, the Africans have worshipped without being preoccupied with finding names for their religions. It was the investigators of religion who first supplied labels such as paganism, idolatry, and fetishism, to mention a few. In order to correct the misconception of such derogatory terms, it became important to designate the religion with a name that describes its true and real nature.

The name African Traditional Religion has been used by scholars to describe the religion. The name was not coined in order to brandish the religion as primitive, local, or unprogressive—rather, it is employed to reflect its location in geographical space and to underscore its evolution from the African personal experience (Aderibigbe, 1995). Furthermore, it is used to distinguish the religion from any other type of religion, since there are other religions in Africa that did not grow out of the African soil but were brought from outside. This shows that the religion is particular to the people, and it would be meaningless and useless to try and transplant this religion to an entirely different society outside of Africa (Mbiti, 1975).

To the African, religion is a hidden treasure secretly given by the Supreme Being solely to the African as a vehicle of communicating and for expressing himself before the sacred entity. In order for a non-African to see and appreciate the wealth of spiritual resources embedded within the religion, he needs to actively participate in order to unveil the nature of the religion, which cannot be understood by mere casual observation. This is why the true nature of the African Religion has been wrongly described and expressed by many, particularly foreign writers and scholars who were outsiders and had no deep knowledge of the experience of the true African spiritual dynamics. These unfortunate misconceptions have been variously demonstrated in derogatory terms for the religion, the denial of African concepts of God (Aderibigbe, 1995), and as ugly superstition that is demon-oriented. It therefore lacks the spiritual fulfillment necessary for the salvation of the soul. Consequently, their works are full of fabrications, exaggerations, half-truths, and biases against the religion and its adherents.

Nevertheless, their works have left a significant impression on most Westerners. Most people remember the African Religion with the image of a missionary in a cannibal's pot about to be cooked and eaten or an evil witch doctor trying to cast a voodoo spell upon a victim. However, with the increase of scholars in the field of African theology such as E. B. Idowu (1962) and Mbiti (1975), there have been some successful attempts to correct some erroneous ideas about African Religion and its belief systems, thought patterns, rituals, and culture generally. The true nature of African Religion cannot be based on erroneous claims of the Europeans concerning the Religion, but rather on what the Africans think and feel about their religion. The true nature of African religion is hinged on the embodiment of the religion in a belief system and functionalism that are actualized in the everyday life of the indigenous African.

A basic understanding of the religion will provide an awareness of African customs, belief systems, concept of God, relationship with the divinities, spirits, ancestors, and the view of death and life beyond death.

CHARACTERISTIC FEATURES

The fact that African Traditional Religion has no sacred scriptures like other world religions does not necessarily mean that it is devoid of organized religious beliefs and practices. The religion is characterized by a belief system which consists of the totality of the African beliefs, thought patterns, and ritual practices.

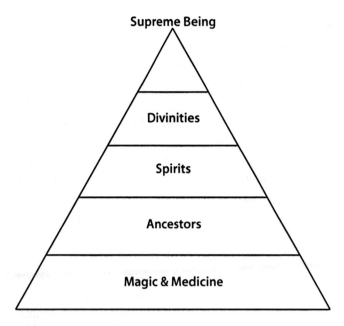

The religious beliefs of African Religion are in two inclusive categories: the major beliefs and the minor beliefs. The major beliefs are in a fivefold classification. The major beliefs in their hierarchical order have significant relevance on the totality of African religious belief systems.

The above diagram represents an overview of the belief system in a hierarchical order.

Belief in the Supreme Being

In the religious belief system, the belief in the Supreme Being is fundamental to all other beliefs and is firmly entrenched in African belief and thought. This is contrary to the Western view that the primitive African is not capable of having any conception of a single Supreme Deity. As Idowu points out:

> Those who take one look at other people's religion and assert glibly that such people have no clear concept of God or no concept of God at all should first look within themselves and face honestly the question, "How clear is the concept of God to me …" (Idowu, 1973).

The Africans believe in the Supreme Being and recognize Him as the ultimate object of worship. He is not an abstract power or entity, neither is He an idle Negro king in a sleep of idleness occupying Himself only with His own happiness (Baudin, 1885). Rather He is actively involved in the day-to-day affairs of the people. The people strongly attest to the fact that He is the creator and author of all things in heaven and on earth. The names and attributes of God clearly connote the people's belief in Him. He is regarded as omnipotent, holy, the creator and source of all other beings that originate from Him and are in turn responsible to Him. The exalted place of the Supreme Being as above other creatures gives rise to His worship in various African societies, either fully as is the case of the Ashanti of Ghana and the Kikuyu tribe of Kenya, or with partial worship as the Ewe and Abomey peoples of Togo do. Among the Yoruba and Igbo of Nigeria, the lack of an organized cult such as temples, shrines, altars, or priests for Him does not in any way diminish His presence and significance. He is believed to be present everywhere. At the same time, this is why He is not limited to a local shrine or represented in images or symbols. God is real to the Africans—His name is constantly on their lips. Each people have a local name which uniquely belongs to Him. The names by which the Deity is called in Africa are descriptive of His character and emphatic of the fact that He is a reality and that He is not an abstract concept (Idowu, 1973). As Westermann (1937) observes:

The figure of God assumes features of a truly personal and purely divine Supreme Being … it cannot be overlooked that he is a reality to the African who will admit that what he knows about God is the purest expression of his religious experience.

The Yoruba people refer to Him as Olodumare—Almighty God; Olorun—owner or Lord of Heaven; Aterere Kari aye—Omnipresent God. The Igbo refer to Him as Chukwu—the Great Source Being or Spirit; Chineke—the Source Being who created all things. The Akan of Ghana refer to Him as Onyame—the Supreme Being, the Deity. The Memde of Sierra Leone refer to Him as Ngewo—the Eternal One who rules from above. These various names and their meanings give us a vivid understanding of the African concept of the Supreme Being. To Africans, God is real, the Giver of Life and the All-Sufficient One.

BELIEF IN DIVINITIES

The belief in divinities form an integral part of the African belief system. The divinities were created for specific functions and do not exist of their volition. The relationship of the divinities to the Supreme Being is born of African sociological patterns. Most African countries have a king or chief as the head of the society, and he is always approached by other chiefs who are lesser in rank to the king. This is due to the belief that the king is sacred and must not be approached directly. The role of the divinities like the lesser chiefs as intermediaries between the Supreme Being and man is that of serving as a conventional channel of communication, through which man believes he should normally approach the Supreme Being. This distinctive role of the divinities led to the erroneous conclusion of the Europeans that the Supreme Being is never approached directly by Africans.

To the African, divinities are real, each with its own definite function in the theocratic government of the universe. The divinities are halfway as a means to an end and can never be ends in themselves. The real and final authority comes from the Supreme Being. This is why after each prayer and supplication before the divinities the Yoruba end the devotions with -ase, meaning "may it be sanctioned by the Supreme Being." The divinities have different names in different African societies. The Yoruba call them Orisa. To the Igbos, they are known as Alusindiminuo. The Akan address them as Abosom. There are numerous divinities in Africa, and their number varies from one community to another or from one locality to another. Their number ranges between 201 and 1,700 in various Yoruba localities. The names of divinities depict their nature or natural phenomenon through which they are manifested. For example, the divinity first associated with the wrath of God among the Yoruba was Jakuta, meaning "he who fights with stones." The same god among the Igbos is known as Amadioha. Among the Nupe the same divinity is called Sokogba—Soxo's ax.

The divinities in African concept can be classified into three categories. First are the primordial divinities. These are believed to have been in existence with the Supreme Being before and during the creation of the world. They are believed to have partaken in the creative works of God. Their origins are not known and are beyond man's probing. One of such divinities is Obatala, a Yoruba divinity believed to have been entrusted with the creation work of the physical part of men. Consequently, he is popularly referred to as Alamorere (the fine molder). He is also called Orisanla and designated as an arch-divinity; he is believed to be the deputy of Olodumare, deriving his attributes from those of the Supreme Being.

The second are the deified ancestors—those who were heroes during their lifetime by living extraordinary and mysterious lives are deified after their death. They are no longer mere ancestors, but absorb the characteristics of an earlier divinity. A vivid example is Sango, the deified Alaafin of Oyo, who assumed the attributes of Jakuta, the erstwhile thunder divinity in Yoruba land.

There are also divinities that found expression in natural phenomena. Such divinities are spirits associated with natural forces such as rivers, lakes, trees, mountains, forests, etc. Their habitations are considered sacred, and there are usually priests who are custodians of such places and through whom the spirit may be consulted. An example of this is the Olokun (water divinity), which is common among the Yoruba and Edo people.

Finally, divinities are believed to be ambidextrous. With this nature, they are capable of being good and bad simultaneously. Positively, they help in solving people's various problems by helping in procreation, fertility, increasing man's prosperity, and so on. On the other hand, when denied veneration, they could inflict misfortunes on a community.

Belief in Spirit

Africans believe in and recognize the existence of spirits referred to as apparitional beings who inhabit material objects as temporary residence. According to African belief, spirits are ubiquitous and can inhabit any area of the earth because they are immaterial and incorporeal beings. Though divinities and ancestors are sometimes classified as spirits, they are, however, different from the kinds of spirits being discussed here, in the sense that they are more positively associated with the people. They are, in fact, described as "domesticated" spirits. While men venerate, respect, and communicate positively with the divinities, he associates with the spirit out of fear and awe. Spirits are normally synonymous with inimical activities detrimental to man's prosperity, so the people try to placate them so that their progress may not be hindered. Spirits inhabit such places as rivers, hills, water, bushes, and trees. Such places are naturally sacred. For instance, among the Yoruba, the Akoko (known by the Igbo as Ogilisi) is reputed to be an abode for spirits.

Spirits have been classified into groups. Among the Yoruba, there are spirits known as Abiku or Ogbange. The Igbo refer to them as born-to-die children. These are considered sadistic spirits that specialize in entering into the womb of women in order to die at a specific period, thereby causing their victims pain and anguish. Such spirits could plague a particular woman several times if treatment is not applied. This is why in Yoruba land pregnant women are not allowed to walk about at noontime, because it is believed that this is the time the spirits roam about and they are capable of ejecting the original fetus of the pregnant woman and implant themselves as substitutes for the ejected fetus.

The second category of spirits is believed to be spirits of the dead whose souls have not been reposed. These are spirits the dead whose bodies have not been buried with due and correct rites. It is believed that their spirits will not be admitted to the abode of the departed. Thus, until they are properly buried, they will continue to wander about. Such spirits could also belong to those who engaged in wicked works while alive and also died wicked. Such spirits could haunt the community, wreaking havoc if not continually appeased.

The spirit of witchcraft belongs to the third category of spirits. It is a human spirit, and it is believed it can be sent out of the body on errands of havoc to other persons or the community in body, mind, or estate. Such spirits may cause diseases, miscarriages in women, insanity, or deformity in human beings.

Finally, Africans recognize spirits in anthropomorphic terms since they are believed to possess the same human characteristics such as tastes, emotions, and passions.

Belief in Ancestors

This belief is based on the concept that the world is dual: it is comprised of the physical world and the spiritual world. The spiritual world is recognized as an extension of the physical, thereby controlling it. Africans have a strong belief in the continued existence of their dead. The communal and family bonds are held to continue even in the next world. They are usually referred to as ancestors or the living dead. They are closely related to this world, but are no longer ordinary mortals. The Africans believe they can come to abide with their folks on earth invisibly to aid or hinder them to promote prosperity or cause adversity. This is why belief in them is not only taken seriously, but is also one of the most important features of the African Religion. The ancestors are factors of cohesion in the African society. This is because of the respect and honor given to them as predecessors who have experienced the life the living are now treading.

However not all the dead are ancestors. There are conditions laid down that must be fulfilled before assuming the exalted status of an ancestor. The first condition is that the dead person must have lived a good and full life. Second, he must have died a good death and not an abominable death caused by accident, suicide, or a violent or unusual death such as from chronic diseases. Finally he must have died in old age and be survived by children and grandchildren. When these conditions are fulfilled, he automatically becomes an ancestor and receives veneration so intense as to be erroneously regarded as worship. Idowu has this to say of the African belief in ancestors:

> To some extent, they are believed to be intermediaries between the Deity or the divinities and their own children; this is a continuation of their earthly function of ensuring domestic peace and the well-being of their community, to distribute favors, to exercise discipline or enforce penalties, to be guardians of community ethics and prevent anything that might cause disruption (Idowu, 1973).

Based on this belief, the Africans bury their dead in the family compound in the hope that they will continue to influence their lives. In the African societies, there are various ways of venerating the ancestors. It may be by pouring a libation of food and drinks and/or by prayers. It may be carried out by individuals or on a communal basis. Furthermore, there are also religious festivals which are usually carried out in the ancestral cult. In Yoruba land, the Oro and Egungun festivals are the symbolical representations of the ancestral cult.

Almost all the tribes in Africa have one form of ancestral cult with festivals associated with it for the veneration of the ancestors. An example is the Ashanti of Ghana, where we have the sacred Golden Stool, which is the ancestral symbol of the Ashanti. Other tribes in Africa with ancestral cults are the Mende of Sierra Leone, the Lugbara of Central Africa, and the Ovambo of Southern Africa.

Belief in Magic and Medicine

Magic and medicine form a significant part of the traditional beliefs of Africans. By definition, magic is an attempt on the part of man to tap and control the supernatural resources of the universe for his own benefit (Idowu, 1973). Through the use of supernatural powers, he tried to achieve his own desires through self-effort. Man's use of this power could either be positive or negative, depending on his conception of the power. Medicine, however, is the science or art of the prevention, treatment, and cure of disease. The art of medicine is important because man recognizes that health can be lost and medicine helps the body return to its normal state.

Basically, the difference between magic and medicine is that in the use of magic, man tries to enforce his will by using supernatural powers at his disposal; while through the use of medicine, man tries to utilize the powers at his disposal to prevent or cure any form of misfortune which might befall his body or estate. This is clearly seen in the words of R. S. Rattray, concerning the Akan belief about medicine:

If God gave you sickness, he also gave you medicine (Rattray, 1923).

This is why medicine men, known as traditional doctors, abound in Africa. They regard their powers as a gift from God through the divinities. They claim they are given the art of medicine by divinities through dreams or through spirit possession. Among the Yoruba, the tutelary divinity of medicine is Osanyin. The divinity is believed to be the custodian of the art of medicine. Though magic is negatively viewed, when it is associated with medicine, the two become so interlinked that it becomes difficult to know where one ends and the other begins. This is because both employ supernatural powers and can be employed for both evil and good, depending upon the individual involved.

Another common trait about magic and medicine highlighted by Awolalu and Dopamu in writing about the religion of West Africa is that some tribes in Africa have a common name for magic and medicine. For example, the Yoruba call oogun, *egbogi*, and *isegun*. The Igbo call them *ogwu*, while the Akans of Ghana call them *suman*.

Finally, it is essential to point out that both magic and medicine constitute a part of the mysteriousness of the African Religion. This is because they derive their supernaturalness, efficacy, taboos, and custodians from the religion. This is why incantations and rituals are common features of magic and medicine in the African Religion.

Other Beliefs in African Religion

There are some other beliefs within the African Religion that are basically derived from the five major beliefs discussed above. They complement the major beliefs, and together they form the totality of the African Religious Belief. They are referred to as minor beliefs.

Belief in the Hereafter

Like all other world religions, the concept of a life after death is firmly entrenched in the people's belief: African Religion also holds the view that life exists beyond this physical world, which is considered the temporary abode of men while heaven is the spiritual and real home of man. Africans believe that man is made up of both body and soul. The soul does not die like the physical body, but rather it returns to the

Supreme Being, who is believed to reside in heaven. The Supreme Being is the final destination of man to whom he belongs and must return. This belief is clearly illustrated in the Yoruba adage *Aye loja orun nile*—that is, the world is a marketplace and heaven is home. No one sleeps in the marketplace. After each day's transactions he or she returns home to rest.

However, not everyone is qualified to enter into heaven. Only those who have engaged in good works while on earth would be granted eternal rest with the Supreme Being, the Supreme Judge of all men. Among the Yoruba there is a saying which encourages man to do good while on earth in order to earn eternal life: *Serere to ri ojo ati sun*—do good so you can earn eternal life. It is believed that those who live an ungodly life on earth will be banished and separated from the Supreme Being.

Belief in Morality

Morality in African Religion is religiously based, since every sphere of the African life is closely associated with being religious. This is why Adewale (1988) asserts that the ethics (morality) of Africans from one to another is religious. Africans have a deep sense of right and wrong, and this moral sense has produced customs, rules, laws, traditions, and taboos which can be observed in each society (Mbiti, 1975).

Morality deals with human conduct, and this conduct has two dimensions, the personal and the social. It guides people in doing what is right and good for both their sake and that of their society. It evolved in order to keep society in harmony, which is achieved through the system of reward and punishment. African morality is centered around some basic beliefs. It is believed that morals are God given and were instituted simultaneously with creation. Therefore, its authority flows from God and must not be challenged. For his part, man is compelled to respond appropriately to these moral demands; failure to comply could incur the wrath of God. This is why certain calamities which may befall a community or person are often interpreted as a punishment from God.

Furthermore, Africans believe that some supernatural beings like the ancestors and the divinities keep watch over people to make sure they observe moral laws. They could punish or reward moral behavior. This further strengthens the authority of the morals. Human beings also play an active role in controlling the morality of the people. The individuals keep a close watch on those with bad moral attitude and often uproot them before they turn the society into an immoral one. This is based on the belief that the welfare and solidarity of the people are closely related to the moral action of individuals. Good deeds are normally encouraged, for these bring harmony, peace, and prosperity. On the other hand, misdeeds could bring calamities of all kinds.

Finally, the importance of morality to Africans cannot be overemphasized. It is evident in their myths, legends, and proverbs, which stress the need to keep the moral demands of human conduct.

Belief in Worship

The act of worship is an integral part of any religion and African Religion is not excluded. It is believed that through worship, one turns to his object of worship in adoration and supplication. Worship in African Religion is directed to the Supreme Being and veneration to the divinities. It is believed that if there is effective worship of both, there will be peace and harmony between the supernatural beings and man.

There are various forms of worship in African Religion. There is the formal and also the informal, the direct and the indirect. In parts of Africa with a direct form of worship, it is characterized by altars, priests, and sacrifices. This is especially so with the worship of the Supreme Being. In the case of indirect worship, there are no temples or priests specially designed for the Supreme Being.

The veneration of divinities could be done regularly on a communal level or individually. This is because they are frequently called upon for one favor or another. On the individual level, the informal type of veneration is carried out privately at the personal shrine normally located in the compound. At the communal level, the formal kind of veneration is carried out at the public shrine, where everyone within the community participates, including family heads, clan heads, priests, priestesses, and traditional rulers.

The main components of worship and veneration are prayers, songs, libations, invocations, and offerings. On the whole, worship or veneration in African Religion is employed to show adoration of and communication with the supernatural beings. It is believed that when these beings are adequately worshipped or venerated, they will bestow upon man the necessary blessings required for successful living on earth.

SOURCES OF INFORMATION ON AFRICAN TRADITIONAL RELIGION

Africans have a rich cultural heritage, which has been handed down from one generation to another. The richness of their heritage reflects in all spheres of their lives, especially in the area of the Traditional Religion. Though the religion does not have a sacred scripture like other world religions, it has means by which its religious beliefs and practices can be known and appreciated. These devices are categorized into oral and non-oral. The oral devices are proverbs, myths, pithy sayings, legends, liturgy, everyday speech, songs, and Theocratic names. The non-oral devices consist of artistic expression.

Oral Traditions

This is regarded as the scriptures of African Traditional Religion. The lack of knowledge in the art of reading and writing caused the African society to employ a means of preserving and transmitting their religious beliefs and practices through oral traditions. They are testimonies of the past, which are transmitted from person to person over the ages. Some of them are records of actual historical events memorized by the people. Others are created by the people's imagination. Consequently, some are regarded to be more reliable than others. For example, proverbs, pithy sayings, and names are believed to be more reliable than legends, myths, daily speeches, and folktales, which are often distorted and cannot be regarded as authentic for grasping the people's beliefs and practices. Here are some forms of oral traditions and their functions:

Myths

In the African traditional society, storytelling at night is the most common recreation in many homes enjoyed by the children and young people. Myths attempt to explain certain things, especially the origin of man and the world. They are vehicles for conveying certain beliefs about man's experience in his encounter with the created order and with regard to man's experiences in the supersensible world. Through myths, man tries to find explanations for certain things. For example, how death came into world; why only women conceive; why they must labor before giving birth to children; why different languages in Africa came into being. Answers to such questions are conveyed in stories which help to preserve them in the memory, making it easier for retention. Myths give us an insight into some of the religious concepts of the Africans who evolve them. Myths are variable sources of information in African Religion because they serve as practical ways of preserving the nonliterate beliefs for possible transmitting without losing their theological themes, since most of these myths are popular stories that draw from beliefs and ideas familiar to the people. Some myths, especially those used during rituals, may enjoy a high degree of authenticity. Such myths could provide the basis for the scriptures of African Religion.

Proverbs

Proverbs are a major source of African wisdom and a valuable part of her heritage. They are a rich deposit of the wisdom of many generations and are held in high esteem. There are hundreds of such proverbs in different African societies which carried with them theological instructions, moral teachings, and metaphysical significance (Jacob, 1977). These proverbs reveal a lot about African religious beliefs, since they are mostly formulated from human experiences and reflections that fit into particular situations of life throughout the ages. It is no gainsaying that among Africans, proverbs are cultivated as an art form and cherished as an index of good oratory. For example, among the Yoruba, proverbs are regarded as "horses for retrieving missing words" that are used for conveying deeper meaning. From some of these proverbs one can learn the various attributes of God as creator, omnipresent, holy, merciful and upright, etc. Thus, we find many proverbs referring to God as an object of religious beliefs, such as the Akan proverb "If you want to tell God anything, tell it to the wind"; "God drives away flies for the cow with no tail" (Yoruba); "God has both the yam and the knife, only those whom he cuts a piece can eat" (Igbo). The importance of proverbs to Africans cannot be overemphasized, and this is clearly expressed in the Igbo adage, "A child who knows how to use proverbs has justified the dowry paid on his mother's head."

Names of People

Names are given immediately upon birth and considered to be very much a part of the personality of the person. In most African countries, the name of the Supreme Being is often made part of the child's name (Mbiti, 1969). This shows that they recognize the Supreme Being. Such names are used as practical demonstration of people's religious feelings, an expression of worship, and the events prevailing at the time of birth. This practically demonstrates how much the people associate the Supreme Being with the continuation of life and the birth of children. There are many names which signify a particular attribute of the Supreme Being. This would mostly depend on the circumstances surrounding the child's birth. Among the Yoruba, we have such names as Oluwatobi (God is great), Oluwaseun (God is victorious). The Burundi name their children Bizimana, meaning "God knows everything." A careful study of various names by researchers of African Traditional Religion could give a deeper insight into the people's religious beliefs, especially their belief in the Supreme Being.

Prayers

Prayers are an essential part of religion. They constitute the act of communicating with the Supreme Being, which is the essence of religion. Like other world religions, prayers are an integral part of African Traditional Religion. Africans pray to the Supreme Being for guidance, blessings in matters of daily life, good health, protection from danger, etc. These prayers are directed to Him, the deities, and the ancestors requesting for one favor or another. The prayers may be made privately by an individual or communally at public meetings and for public needs. When Africans pray, their prayers are always short and straight to the point. They do not "beat about the bush." There are different modes by which the people pray to the supernatural beings. There is the direct form of prayer, where people communicate with the Supreme Being without the help of intermediaries. However, the indirect form of prayer is when people pray on behalf of others. These include priests (both men and women), rainmakers, chiefs, kings, and sometimes medicine men (Mbiti, 1975). Africans pray because they believe the Supreme Being listens to them and accepts and answers their prayers. He is believed to be everywhere simultaneously. Here are a few examples of prayers in African Traditional Religion as illustrations.

For example, in the morning, the Yoruba have prayers like, "God, let us be successful today." Before worshipping, the Yoruba also pray, "Father, accept our offering and supplication to you."

When there is drought, Africans pray, "God, give us rain"; "Help us, O God"; "God, pity us." In times of sickness, African prayers implore the Supreme Being: "God, heal our sickness, let the sick be well again"; "Take this sickness away from our house, our town, our tribe." When a journey or other forms of a project are to be embarked on, Africans pray for God's protection and successful completion of the project. Prayers such as, "May God go with you"; "May God help you," etc., are offered. There are also general prayers of blessings, such as "God preserve you and keep you." Prayers are also offered for long life, such as "May God spare you to see your children's children."

It must be stressed that in all situations, the Africans pray to show their belief in and dependence on the Supreme Being. The prayers also provide information on the African concepts about the Supreme Being. These concepts form the center of the African Traditional Religion.

Non-Oral Sources

Apart from the oral sources, through which valuable information on African traditional religion is secured, there are some non-oral devices which provide valuable information on the beliefs and practices of Africans where their religion is concerned. These non-oral sources are identifiable in three forms: (i) artifacts; (ii) wooden masks; and (iii) the sacred institutions (Abioye, 2001). These three non-oral traditions are essentially artistic expressions that in concrete terms "showcase" the African traditional religion in all its ramifications. Here is a brief discussion of each of them.

Artifacts

All African societies are very rich in artifacts. These artifacts have become concrete reflections of African belief and devotion to the Supreme Being, the divinities, and the ancestors. The artifacts associated with the African Religion are in two categories. There are objects that are products of archeological findings. Artifacts in the second category are made up of the works of contemporary artists. Archeological excavations have, in some cases, led to more information and better understanding of certain African beliefs and practices. An example of this is the discovery of the temples and altars of Onyame, the Ashanti Supreme Deity, by R. S. Rattray. This singular discovery has gone a long way to show the inadequacy of the foreigners' usual claim that Africans had no organized worship of the Supreme Being because they did not have the idea of God. Indeed, the discovery has led to the search and successful discovery of many other different forms of organized worship among various African tribes. In addition, contemporary artifacts comprising of dance staffs, apparatuses for divination, musical instruments, votive figures, and many other forms of ritual objects provide information on African religious beliefs and practices. Many of these objects are found in shrines, while others are part of the general stocks of artistic works of many African artists attempting to recapture the rich African cultures in different forms.

Wooden Masks

These are concrete forms of covering the face in the attempt to hide the identity of the persons putting on the masks. The practice of putting on masks covers the whole of Africa and is regarded as a part of basic rituals, particularly having to do with the ancestral worship and the cult's expressions of the African people. In the first form, people who are regarded as incarnations of the spirits of the ancestors put on masks to conceal the earthly personality behind the mask and give cogency to the belief that the person wearing the mask is an ancestral spirit. In the second form, members of secret societies in Africa put on masks. Examples of mask usage are found among the Ogboni in Yoruba land and the Poro among the Mende of Sierra Leone.

In addition to the masks, there have been stools found in shrines. They are regarded as having religious implications in their artistic expression. The stools become objects of religious expression by the fact that they are not only found in shrines, but also in some other places. For example, among the Akan of Ghana, the stools have become altars upon which the head of the Akan lineage offers food and drink to their ancestors on appropriate occasions, thereby praying for the protection of the lineage. He also prays for good health and long life with an abundance of harvests.

Sacred Institutions

Beliefs of Africans in the Supreme Being and all other aspects of their religion are reflected in the several traditional institutions all over Africa. Traditionally, these institutions are regarded as sacred. An example of such institution is the traditional ruling institution. Among Africans, the traditional rulers are not mere political heads. They indeed represent the Supreme Being. Thus, the authority they have is in trust for the Supreme Being. This is why traditional rulers are not seen as ordinary persons. They are sacred. For example, the Yoruba call an *oba Igbakeji Orisa* (deputy of the Supreme Being). Among the Ashanti, the golden ornaments the king wears symbolize the belief that the Supreme Being is personified by the sun. Thus, when the Ashanti king wears the golden ornaments, he signifies the eternal fire of the sun (Abioye, 2001). In addition, among the Yoruba and the Akan, the cult of thunder has become a kind of sacred institution. In both African societies, the ax has assumed the symbol of the Supreme Being's judgment. The Supreme Being is regarded as the ultimate judge, and he can express his wrath against evildoers. The ax is the tool for this wrath. For the Yoruba, the divinity executing Olodumare's wrath is Sango. Consequently, axes are found in his shrines. Indeed, the original thunder divinity among the Yoruba was Jakuta, which literally means "one who throws stones." The stones are also found in the shrines of Sango, the new divinity of thunder. The Akan of Ghana refer to the ax as *nyame akuma* (God's ax), and the ax is found in the shrines of Onyame as a symbol of his wrath.

BIBLIOGRAPHY AND FURTHER READING

Abioye, S. O. 2001. "African Traditional Religion: An Introduction," in G. Aderibigbe and D. Aiyegboyin, eds. *Religion: Study & Practice*. Ibadan: Olu-Akin Press.

Abraham, W. E. 1982. *The Mind of Africa*. London: Weidenfeld & Nicolson.

Aderibigbe, G. 1995. "African Religious Beliefs," in A. O. K. Noah, ed. *Fundamentals of General Studies*. Ibadan: Rex Charles Publications.

Adewale, S. A. 1988. *The Religion of the Yoruba: A Phenomenological Analysis*. Ibadan: Daystar Press.

Awolalu, J. Omosade. 1979. *Yoruba Beliefs and Sacrificial Rites*. England: Longman.

Awolalu, J. O. and P. A. Dopamu. 1979. *West African Traditional Religion*. Ibadan: Onibonoje Press.

Bascom, William. 1969. *Ifa Divination: Communication Between Gods and Men in West Africa*. Bloomington: University of Indiana.

Courtlander, H. 1973. *Tales of Yoruba Gods and Heroes*. New York: Crown Publishers.

Ekpunobi, E. and S. Ezeaku, eds. 1990. *Socio-Philosophical Perspective of African Traditional Religion*. Enugu: New Age Publishers.

Ellis, A. B. 1894. *The Yoruba-Speaking People of the Slave Coast of West Africa*. London: Chapman & Hall.

Idowu, E. B. 1973. *African Traditional Religion: A Definition*. London: SMC Press.

_____. 1962. *Olodumare: God in Yoruba Belief*. London: SMC Press.

Jacobs, A. B. 1977. *A Textbook on African Traditional Religion*. Ibadan: Aromolaran Press.

Kayode, J. O. 1979. *Understanding African Traditional Religion*. Ile-Ife: University of Ife Press.

Kierman, Jim. 1995b. "African Traditional Religion in South Africa." In Martin Prozesky and John de Gruchy, eds. *Living Faiths in South Africa*. Cape Town: David Philip.

_____. 1993c. "The Impact of White Settlement on African Traditional Religions." In Martin Prozesky and John de Gruchy, eds. *Living Faiths in South Africa*. Cape Town: David Philip.

King, M. O. 1970. *Religions of Africa*. New York: Harper & Row Publishers.

Lucas, J. O. 1948. *Religions in West Africa and Ancient Egypt*. Lagos: CMS Books.

Mazrui, Ali A. 1986. *The Africans: A Triple Heritage*. London: BBC Publications.

MacVeigh, Malcolm J. 1974. *God in Africa: Conception of God in African Traditional Religion and Christianity*. Cape Coast: Claude Stark.

Mbiti, J. S. 1991. *Introduction to African Religion*, 2nd ed. Oxford: Heinemann.

_____. 1982. *African Religion and Philosophy*. London: Heinemann Educational Press.

_____. 1970. *African Concept of God*. London: SMC Press.

Merriam, A. P. 1974. *An African World*. Indiana University Press.

Mesoamerican Religion

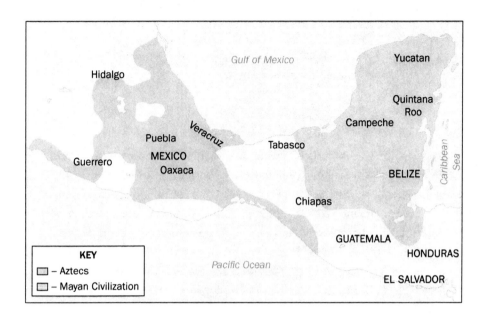

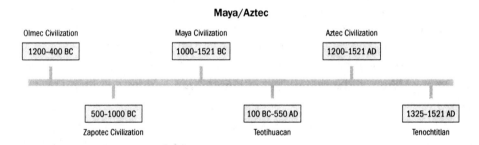

From Teotihuacan to Tenochtitlan: Their Great Temples

By Eduardo Matos Moctezuma, translated By Scott Sessions

ANTECEDENTS

One of the cities whose characteristics have always attracted attention, even after being buried by the sands of time, is, without a doubt, Teotihuacan. We already know of the Aztecs' periodic visits in pre-Hispanic times to revere the ancient urban center, for even though it was covered with earth and vegetation, the general plan of the city, as well as the monumental complexes of the Ciudadela and the great mounds of the Pyramids of the Sun and Moon, had not disappeared. Moreover, if ceramic fragments bearing witness to the site's occupation are found here and there today, in Aztec times they must have been even more abundant and have caught the attention of new groups who saw ancestral traces without knowing with complete certainty who had created them. Thus, what was the work of humans became the work of the gods to later groups who came to know the site. From here to myth there is only one step: the old city becomes imbued with sacrality, and an extraordinary act will take place: the creation of the Fifth Sun brought about by the sacrifice of the gods.

On many occasions, we already have discussed how the quest to know more about the City of the Gods induced the Aztecs to excavate at the site. No less than forty Teotihuacan objects have been found in different offerings at the Templo Mayor of Tenochtitlan (López Luján 1989). Moreover, there is also imitation in the city's plan itself, organized as it is into four major barrios, and the presence of *talud-tablero* buildings and mural painting remind us of those at Teotihuacan. Furthermore, a sculpture of the Old God appeared near the Aztec Templo Mayor in the same position that a representation of Huehueteotl was found at Teotihuacan. To all this we suggest adding something of great importance, which is the purpose of the present study: the location, orientation, and characteristics of the principal buildings that mark or indicate the center of the city itself, the axis mundi, from which the four directions of the universe emanate. We will speak more about this later in the chapter.

After the European Conquest, indigenous buildings were destroyed. Teotihuacan, already buried after a little more than seven centuries of abandonment (except for minor occupations in a few places in the city) was not an object of this destruction, but rather attracted the attention of some sixteenth-century chroniclers who made reference to it. What is interesting about this is that these chroniclers became aware of the myth of the birth of the Fifth Sun in Teotihuacan. Thus, we read in the works of Bernardino de Sahagún (1995), Diego Múñoz Camargo (1995), the *Leyenda de los Soles* (1995), and elsewhere (see Matos, ed. 1995), about the myth that undoubtedly caused the tallest monuments in the city to be named the Pyramids of the Sun and Moon as well as assigned their dedication to these two astral bodies, even though today we are able to find associations to other important elements.

In the seventeenth century, we have an event of great importance for the history of archaeology: Carlos Sigüenza y Góngora, the learned Mexicanist, tried to excavate at the Pyramid of the Sun. Lorenzo Boturini has left us a record of Sigüenza y Góngora's attempt in his *Historia general de la América Septentrional* (1746):

> This ancient hill was perfectly square, whitewashed, and beautiful, and one used to climb to the top by way of some steps, that today cannot be seen, for having been filled in by their own ruins and earth deposited by the winds, upon which trees and thistles have sprouted. Nevertheless, I was on it and out of curiosity measured it, and, if I am not mistaken, it is two hundred *varas* tall. Thus I ordered that it be recorded on a map that I have in my archive, and walking around it I saw that the celebrated Carlos Sigüenza y Góngora had tried to bore his way into it, but had encountered resistance (Boturini 1995: 49).[1]

Along with Boturini's remarks, we must also mention those of another traveler from the end of the century, Giovanni Francesco Gemelli Careri. In his *Giro del mondo*, published in 1700 in Italy, we see how he visited the site and made several assertions that had no relation to reality, though one of them has recently attracted interest. He mentions that some of the caves found in Teotihuacan are artificial, that is, made by human hands. The traveler tells us:

> Indeed it is certain that there where they were was previously a great city, as evidenced by the extensive surrounding ruins, and by caves, artificial as well as natural, and by the quantity of mounds thought to be made in honor of the idols (Gemelli Careri 1995: 47–48).[2]

In subsequent centuries, authors such as Francisco Clavigero (1780–1781, 1995), Alexander von Humboldt (1811, 1995), Frances Calderón de la Barca (1843, 1995), José María García (1860), and Ramón Almaraz (1865, 1995) would mention Teotihuacan in their writings. Almaraz, as part of the Report of the Pachuca Scientific Commission, wrote in 1865 that he had visited the site and made the first map using precision instruments. He also referred to topics such as the orientation and construction of the pyramids and was the first to mention the "rampart" (*muralla*) that surrounds the Pyramid of the Sun. Closer to our times are the works of Désiré Charnay (1885) and Leopoldo Batres (1906, 1995) himself. Along with Batres's discoveries at the end of the nineteenth century, such as the Temple of Agriculture murals on the west side of the so-called Street of the Dead, we must add his work beginning in 1905 to shed light on the Pyramid of the Sun. The investigations initiated by Manuel Gamio in 1917, presented in his monumental *La población del Valle de Teotihuacán* (1922), and considered the first in modern Mexican anthropology, deserve separate mention. From this moment on, many researchers and institutions—foreign as well as Mexican—have carried out work in Teotihuacan, offering valuable contributions to the understanding of the urban center (see Matos, ed. 1995).

Now let us begin our study of the aforementioned topic—"From Teotihuacan to Tenochtitlan: Their Great Temples"—in which we will speak of the buildings that we think had the role of the symbolic "center" in the two cities. Although they are separated by at least six centuries, they will be joined together by a series of characteristics that we already have discussed in previous studies (see Matos 1994, 1995a).

SACRED SPACE

We know from the study of religions how the founding of ancient cities was imbued with a sacred and symbolic character. Historian of religions Mircea Eliade (1979) is clear in this respect. He explains how the place where the new city will be located is always preceded by landmarks or signs that sacralize the place. Sacred space is thus validated and clearly separated from the profane, or other surrounding space, which we prefer to call "space of less sacrality." As Eliade tells us:

> The founding of the new city repeats the creation of the world; in fact, once the place has been ritually validated, a wall is raised in the form of a circle or square interrupted by four gates that correspond to the four cardinal points. . . . The cities, like the cosmos, are divided in four; in other words, they are a copy of the universe (Eliade 1979: 374).[3]

Various archaeological and symbolic indicators allow us to determine how the pre-Hispanic peoples of Central Mexico adopted a series of elements to clearly distinguish what we have called the "center of centers" or the fundamental center of the city—inasmuch as the city itself, in its totality, was conceived of as the center of the universe, inside of which was established this space of greater sacrality which, in turn, was an image of the cosmos. These internal spaces of the city are those that we will proceed to analyze in Teotihuacan and Tenochtitlan, although it is necessary to state that in Teotihuacan we see two centers with more or less similar elements: the Pyramid of the Sun and the Ciudadela. Therefore, we have suggested that, given its greater antiquity, the Pyramid of the Sun was the center of what we call the "old city," which subsequently was moved south to the site occupied by the Ciudadela and the Temple of the Feathered Serpents or of Quetzalcoatl.

We find the following elements present in both cities:

a. A landmark or sign situating and constituting the fundamental, sacred center of the city.

b. A principal building erected on this landmark or sign, which acquires the character of a sacred mountain where the distinct celestial, terrestrial, and underworld levels of the cosmos meet and the four cardinal directions emanate; thus its character as the center of the universe.

c. The same orientation of this building or sacred mountain.

d. The presence of water. Inside this sacred mountain are kept the water and maize kernels that provide sustenance for the community, which we see in its *altepetl* or "mountain of water" character, around which the settlement is organized.

e. The presence of human sacrifice and a place of offering where the principal myths are repeated through ritual performance.

f. A platform surrounding it or the buildings that give it its axis mundi quality. These platforms are elements serving to distinguish the sacred from the profane or less sacred space.

Now, we will examine each of these elements.

THE LANDMARK OR SIGN FOR THE FOUNDATION OF THE CITY

In the case of Teotihuacan, archaeologists have found a cavity underneath the Pyramid of the Sun that is thought to be what motivated the construction of this monument. This cavity—whether natural or artificial, since Federico Mooser (1968) considers it a geological formation while Linda Manzanilla (chapter 2 of this volume) thinks it may be human-made—constitutes the sign indicating the place selected by the gods. Here it does not matter if the cavity is natural, artificial, or even a combination of the two, but rather that humans "discover" and make or adapt the place. What is important is the dual character of caves in the pre-Hispanic world: it was the birthplace of peoples—recalling Chicomoztoc, with which this cave shares certain characteristics (see Heyden 1975, 1995)—and at the time it was conceived as the entrance to the underworld; thus the duality of life and death is present there.

In the case of Tenochtitlan, the landmark or sign is the well-known image of the eagle perched on the cactus, in addition to certain earlier Toltec symbols that, we believe, the Aztecs appropriated to legitimate the sacred space. These include the streams of blue and red water, which is nothing other than the *atltlachinolli* or war symbol, along with the presence of the color white in fish, frogs, serpents, reeds, and cattails, which are the same symbols that the Toltecs saw in the sacred city of Cholula, if we accept what the *Historia toltecachichimeca* (1976) tells us (aspects that we have already mentioned on another occasion).[4]

THE CONSTRUCTION OF THE TEMPLO MAYOR

The location of the Pyramid of the Sun at Teotihuacan in relation to the cavity doubtless means that it was intentional and motivated by the previously stated reasons. Although we do not have written documentation for such early times that would tell us about the character of the "sacred mountain," it has always been suggested that the massive Pyramids of the Sun and Moon imitate mountains in the surrounding landscape. The characteristic shape of the pyramids' four *talud* sections seek this adaptation to the natural surroundings. Concerning the Templo Mayor of Tenochtitlan, we definitely can draw upon a greater amount of information from sixteenth-century narrative accounts and pictographs, such as plate 1 of the *Codex Mendoza* (1992), where the center of the city is the place where the eagle is perched on the nopal cactus, and we know that the Templo Mayor was erected there at that center. We also have accounts of the founding of the city and how the separation of sacred and profane space was achieved by constructing the principal temple in the middle of the sacred precinct. As for its "sacred mountain" character, in this case it is invested in a singularity consisting of two mountains: Coatepec, or the sacred mountain where the battle between Huitzilopochtli and Coyolxauhqui takes place, and Tonacatepetl, or the mountain where maize kernels are guarded by the assistants of Tlaloc, who presides over this part of the temple. In this way, the Templo Mayor resonates two principal Nahua myths, in addition to being the fundamental center of the universe in their cosmovision where the celestial levels and the underworld meet, and from which the four cardinal directions emanate.[5]

ORIENTATION OF THE PRINCIPAL BUILDINGS

The Pyramid of the Sun, the Temple of Quetzalcoatl, and the Templo Mayor of Tenochtitlan are all oriented toward the west. Evidently, the movement of the stars, especially the sun, determined the position of these temples.

THE *ALTEPETL*, OR "MOUNTAIN OF WATER"

Water, as a vital element for the subsistence of these peoples, acquired a transcendent importance that is present in myths and in the importance of the gods associated with it. It was common belief that water was kept inside mountains or hills; therefore it would not be strange that the sacred mountain would be where the liquid giving life to plants and humans would be kept. In the case of the Pyramid of the Sun, it seems, a stream of water ran inside the aforementioned cave and some stone channels have been found in its interior. The most recent archaeological excavations around the Pyramid of the Sun have resulted in the discovery of a canal, 3 meters wide, surrounding the pyramid on all sides. It has been thought that perhaps this could be a street for specific ceremonies, but the avalanche of water that would come down the sides of the pyramid during the rainy season makes us think seriously that it was a canal. The other "center" of the city of Teotihuacan, the Temple of Quetzalcoatl, has undulating serpents surrounded by snails and conch shells depicted on its façade that speak of the importance of the aquatic element. Furthermore, archaeologist Rubén Cabrera says that a looters' tunnel inside the building was discovered running into the center, where an inexplicable degree of humidity was detected, suggesting that a source of flowing water might be found just below it.

In the case of Tenochtitlan, particularly the Templo Mayor, we have already mentioned the streams of water and the maize kernels kept inside.

It would be interesting to analyze the *altepetl* character more deeply, because its relation to the community is important from the symbolic as well as social-organization, kinship, and other points of view.

THE PRESENCE OF SACRIFICE AND OFFERINGS

When Leopoldo Batres excavated the Pyramid of the Sun at the beginning of this century, he found the skeletal remains of children in each of the corners of the four sections that make up the building. This fact is particularly interesting given that we know how children were dedicated, in later times, to the cult of the water god, Tlaloc. It would not be strange that this cult would have come from Teotihuacan, since many aspects present in Tenochtitlan previously existed in the earlier city. As for the Temple of Quetzalcoatl, we have the ceremonial burials found by archaeologists Rubén Cabrera and Saburo Sugiyama in specific places and numbers. One of the characteristics of the individuals deposited there, male (nine in number) and female (in groups of four), was that their hands were tied behind their backs. This has been interpreted as human sacrifice in honor of the temple in association with the calendar and agriculture.

As for the Aztec Templo Mayor, various studies speak of the presence of multiple offerings of decapitated skulls, child burials (forty-two on the Tlaloc side in Offering 38), and ritual sacrifice by heart extraction practiced on the side dedicated to Huitzilopochtli, about which various historical sources have left us information.[6]

THE SURROUNDING PLATFORM

In Teotihuacan we see only two places inside the city with large platforms that enclosed and delineated, in our judgment, the spaces of great sacrality and buildings that were the fundamental center of the city: the Pyramid of the Sun and the Temple of Quetzalcoatl in the Ciudadela. The first of these buildings was excavated in 1993 in the Proyecto Especial Teotihuacán, although a portion of the south side, in the so-called House of the Priests, was partially excavated by Batres several years earlier. Surely it was Batres who destroyed part of the platform near the southwest corner to remove debris from the pyramid and constructed his camp on top of the south side, and its excavation has continued in recent years. Returning to the topic at hand, in the past this platform has been interpreted in several different ways. It was first mentioned in the Report of the Pachuca Scientific Commission (Almaraz 1865) on the map of the center of the city, which referred to it as a "rampart" (*muralla*). Later on, it was Batres who said that its function was to provide stability to the great mass of the Pyramid of the Sun, something that evidently did not correspond to reality. Other studies such as Gamio (1922, 1995) and Marquina (1951: 69–76; 1995) only mentioned it, without attributing to it a specific function, while Rémy Bastien (1995), who conducted a study of the Pyramid of the Sun for his 1947 thesis in the School of Anthropology, referred to three functions: 1) mechanical, seeing its absence at the Pyramid of the Moon and "its importance at the Ciudadela"; 2) aesthetic, related to the visual appearance of the complex, and 3) military, or defense. Concerning what he says about the absence of this and other elements we have mentioned from the Pyramid of the Moon, they were omitted so that the Pyramid of the Sun would be considered the "center" of the city.

As for Tenochtitlan, we have various pictographs in which we see the great platform framing the principal plaza with, according to Sahagún (1989), its seventy-eight buildings, inside. Archaeologically, sections of the platform from a later stage of the Templo Mayor have been found with walls that alternate with stairways. The same arrangement is seen at Tlatelolco, where one can examine a large section, including the inside southeast corner. In the case of Tenochtitlan, the rampart or walled-platform is clearly a delimiter of sacred space from which the great causeways running north, west, and south emanated.

In summary, we think that this platform divided two types of space: the interior, consisting of a great plaza imbued with enormous sacrality, and the exterior, profane, or less sacred space.

CONCLUSIONS

In the case of Central Mexico, all these elements had to be present to identify a building as the principal temple, as an axis mundi, with all its implications. In Teotihuacan, evidently, two fundamental centers were established: the Pyramid of the Sun and the Temple of Quetzalcoatl in the Ciudadela. There is also another important fact in relation to this second building: the excavations of Rubén Cabrera allow us to see that this second "center," in turn, was desacralized. There is evidence of a looters' tunnel penetrating the southeast corner that terminates at the center of the building. Subsequently, the building, at least its principal façade, was covered by another building stage less rich in elements than the one preceding it. Other tunnels made by Teotihuacanos themselves were found in the La Ventilla excavations carried out in the Proyecto Especial Teotihuacán. This leads us to think about the city's development, because this clearly did not occur during a time of internal peace, but rather there were many moments (at least three) in which disturbances in Teotihuacan society must have occurred. These three moments are: 1) when the "center" of the city passed from the Pyramid of the Sun to the Ciudadela, which must have been an enormous transformation with important religious and social implications; 2) when the Temple of Quetzalcoatl was covered and desacralized to such a degree that it was looted; and 3) when we see in later phases (Tlamimilopa-Xolalpan) that looters' tunnels were made in different places in the ceremonial area. All of this occured before Teotihuacan's final devastation around 700 C.E., when its preeminence ended and it passed into a form of the myth in which later peoples would transform the city into the place where the gods were born.

NOTES

1. "Era este cerro de la antiguedad perfectamente cuadrado, encalado, y hermoso, y se subía a su cumbre por unas gradas, que hoy no se descubren, por haberse llenado de sus proprias ruinas, y de la tierra que arrojan los vientos, sobre la cual han nacido árboles, y abrojos. No obstante estuve yo en él, y le hice por curiosidad medir, y, si no me engaño, es de docientos varas de alto. Ansimismo mandé sacarlo en mapa, que tengo en mi archivo, y rodeándole vi, que el célebre don Carlos de Singüenza y Góngora había intentado taladrarle, pero halló resistencia" (Boturini 1995: 49).

2. "Sí es cosa cierta que allí donde ellas están hubo anteriormente una gran ciudad, como se advierte por las extensas ruinas alrededor, y por las grutas, tanto naturales como artificiales, y por la cantidad de montecillos que se cree que fueron hechos en honor de los ídolos" (Gemelli Careri 1995: 47-48).

3. "La fundación de la nueva ciudad repite la creación del mundo; en efecto, una vez que el lugar ha sido validado ritualmente, se eleva una cerca en forma de círculo o de cuadrado interrumpida por cuatro puertas que corresponden a los cuatro puntos cardinales. . . . Las ciudades, a semejanza del cosmos, están divididas en cuatro; dicho de otra manera, son una copia del universo" (Eliade 1979: 374).

4. The Toltec elements present in the founding of Tenochtitlan are discussed in the official guide-book of the Templo Mayor (Matos 1993).

5. For more about these characteristics of the Templo Mayor, see Matos (1986, 1995b).

6. See Juan Alberto Román Berrelleza (1990), as well as Diego Durán (1867–1880,1994) and Bernardino de Sahagún (1989).

REFERENCES

Almaraz, Ramón

1865. *Memoria de los trabajos ejecutados por la Comisión Científica de Pachuca en el año de 1864, dirigida por el ingeniero Ramón Almaraz.* Mexico: J. M. Andrade y F. Escalante.

1995. "Apuntes sobre las pirámides de San Juan Teotihuacan [1865]." In E. Matos Moctezuma, ed., *La pirámide del Sol, Teotihuacán: Antología.* Mexico: Artes de México/Instituto Cultural Domecq, pp. 65–75.

Bastien, Rémy

1995. "La pirámide del Sol en Teotihuacan [1947]." In E. Matos Moctezuma, ed., *La pirámide del Sol, Teotihuacán: Antología.* Mexico: Artes de México/Instituto Cultural Domecq, pp. 209–258.

Batres, Leopoldo

1906. *Teotihuacán: Memoria que presenta Leopoldo Batres . . . año de 1906.* Mexico: Imprenta de F. S. Soria.

1995. "Pirámide del Sol [1906]." In E. Matos Moctezuma, ed., *La pirámide del Sol, Teotihuacán: Antología.* Mexico: Artes de México/Instituto Cultural Domecq, pp. 100–117.

Boturini Benaducci, Lorenzo

1746. *Idea de una nueva historia general de la América Septentrional.* Madrid: Imprenta de Juan de Zúñiga.

1995. "Idea de una nueva historia general de la América Septentrional [1746]" (excerpt). In E. Matos Moctezuma, ed., *La pirámide del Sol, Teotihuacán: Antología.* Mexico: Artes de México/Instituto Cultural Domecq, pp. 49–50.

Calderón de la Barca, Frances E. I.

1843. *Life in Mexico, During a Residence of Two Years in That Country.* Boston: C. C. Little and J. Brown.

1995. "Carta XVI [1840]." In E. Matos Moctezuma, ed., *La pirámide del Sol, Teotihuacán: Antología.* Mexico: Artes de México/Instituto Cultural Domecq, pp. 59–64.

Charnay, Désiré

1885. *Les anciennes villes du Nouveau Monde. Voyages d'explorations au Mexique et dans l'Amérique Centrale, par Désiré Charnay, 1857–1882.* Paris: Hachette.

Clavigero, Francisco Javier

1780-1781. *Storia antica del Messico.* Cesena, Italy: G. Biasini.

1995. "Apoteosis del Sol y la Luna [1780]." In E. Matos Moctezuma, ed., *La pirámide del Sol, Teotihuacán: Antología.* Mexico: Artes de México/Instituto Cultural Domecq, pp. 51–53.

Codex Mendoza

1992. Edited by F. F. Berdan and P. R. Anawalt. Berkeley: University of California Press.

Durán, Fray Diego

1867–1880. *Historia de las Indias de Nueva España y islas de Tierra Firme.* Mexico: J. M. Andrade y F. Escalante.

1994. *The History of the Indies of New Spain.* Translated, annotated, and with an introduction by D. Heyden. Norman: University of Oklahoma Press.

Eliade, Mircea

1979. *Tratado de historia de las religiones.* Trans. T. Segovia. Mexico: Ediciones Era.

Gamio, Manuel

1922. *La población del Valle de Teotihuacán representativa de las que habitan las regiones rurales del Distrito Federal y de los Estados de Hidalgo, Puebla, México y Tlaxcala.* Mexico: Dirección de Talleres Gráficos.

1995. "En cuatro grupos [1922]." In E. Matos Moctezuma, ed., *La pirámide del Sol, Teotihuacán: Antología.* Mexico: Artes de México/Instituto Cultural Domecq, pp. 126–127.

García, José María

1860. "Las pirámides de San Juan Teotihuacán." *Boletín de la Sociedad Mexicana de Geografía y Estadística* 8: 198-200.

Gemelli Careri, Giovanni Francesco

1700. *Giro del mondo.* Napoli: G. Roselli.

1995. "De los cúes o pirámides de San Juan Teotihuacan [1700]." In E. Matos Moctezuma, ed., *La pirámide del Sol, Teotihuacán: Antología*. Mexico: Artes de México/Instituto Cultural Domecq, pp. 46–48.

Heyden, Doris

1975. "An Interpretation of the Cave Underneath the Pyramid of the Sun in Teotihuacan, Mexico." *American Antiquity 40*, no. 2 (April): 131–147.

1995. "Una interpretación en torno a la cueva que se encuentra bajo la pirámide del Sol en Teotihuacan [1975]." In E. Matos Moctezuma, ed., *La pirámide del Sol, Teotihuacán: Antología*. Mexico: Artes de México/Instituto Cultural Domecq, pp. 286–311.

Historia tolteca-chichimeca

1976. Edited by P. Kirchhoff, L. Odena Güemes, and L. Reyes García. Mexico: INAHCIS/SEP.

Humboldt, Alexander von

1811. *Essai politique sur le royaume de la Nouvelle-Espagne*. Paris: F. Schoell.

1995. "Los antiguos monumentos de Teotihuacan [1807–1811]." In E. Matos Moctezuma, ed., *La pirámide del Sol, Teotihuacán: Antología*. Mexico: Artes de México/Instituto Cultural Domecq, pp. 56–58.

Leyenda de los soles

1995. "Leyenda de los soles [1558]" (excerpt). In E. Matos Moctezuma, ed., *La pirámide del Sol, Teotihuacán: Antología*. Mexico: Artes de México/Instituto Cultural Domecq, pp. 27–28.

López Luján, Leonardo

1989. *La recuperación mexica del pasado teotihuacano*. Mexico: INAH/Proyecto Templo Mayor/GV Editores/Asociación de Amigos del Templo Mayor.

Marquina, Ignacio

1951. *Arquitectura prehispánica*. Mexico: INAH.

1995. "Descripción de los edificios [1951]." In E. Matos Moctezuma, ed., *La pirámide del Sol, Teotihuacán: antología*. Mexico: Artes de México/Instituto Cultural Domecq, pp. 259–267.

Matos Moctezuma, Eduardo

1986. *Vida y muerte en el Templo Mayor*. Mexico: Ediciones Océano.

1993. *Templo Mayor: Guía oficial*. Mexico: INAH/Salvat.

1994. "Teotihuacán." *Arqueología Mexicana 2*, no. 10 (October-November): 75–79.

1995a. "La pirámide de Sol y el primer *coatepantli* conocido del centro de México." In M. H. Ruz and J. Arechiga V., eds., *Antropología e interdisciplina: Homenage a Pedro Carrasco. XXIII Mesa Redonda, Villahermosa, Tabasco, 1994*. Mexico: SMA.

1995b. *Life and Death in the Templo Mayor*. Trans. B. R. Ortiz de Montellano and T. Ortiz de Montellano. Niwot: University Press of Colorado.

Matos Moctezuma, Eduardo, ed.

1995. *La pirámide del Sol, Teotihuacán: Antología*. Mexico: Artes de México/Instituto Cultural Domecq.

Millon, René

1973. The Teotihuacan Map. Austin: University of Texas Press.

Mooser, Federico

1968. "Geología, naturaleza y desarrollo del Valle de Teotihuacán." In J. L. Lorenzo, ed., *Materiales para la arqueología de Teotihuacán*. Mexico: INAH, pp. 29–37.

Muñoz Camargo, Diego

1995. "Tenían ansimiso este engaño [siglo XIV]." In E. Matos Moctezuma, ed., *La pirámide del Sol, Teotihuacán: Antología*. Mexico: Artes de México/Instituto Cultural Domecq, p. 39.

Román Berrelleza, Juan Alberto.

1990. *Sacrificio de niños en el Templo Mayor*. Mexico: INAH/GV Editores/Asociación de Amigos del Templo Mayor.

Sahagún, Fray Bernardino de

1989. *Historia general de las cosas de Nueva España*. Eds. A. López Austin and J. García Quintana. 2 vols. Mexico: CNCA/Alianza Editorial Mexicana.

1995. "Historia general de las cosas de Nueva España [1565–1577]" (excerpt). In E. Matos Moctezuma, ed., *La pirámide del Sol, Teotihuacán: Antología*. Mexico: Artes de México/Instituto Cultural Domecq, pp. 29–32.

Section IV

Rise of Universal Religions: Christianity and Islam

The following chapters include articles that discuss some of the most enduring religions in the world, including Islam and Christianity. In Chapter 12, "The Classical Backgrounds of Mediaeval Christianity" supplies information about which classical religions influenced Christianity. In Chapter 13, "The Rise and Expansion of Islam" discusses Muhammad's prophecies and the effects of trade on the spread of Islam. In Chapter 14, "The Return of Greek Science: The First Byzantine Humanism" presents information on the relationship between science, philosophy, and religion in Byzantium and the importance of Constantine's influence on the rise of Christianity.

Medieval Europe: Rise of Christianity

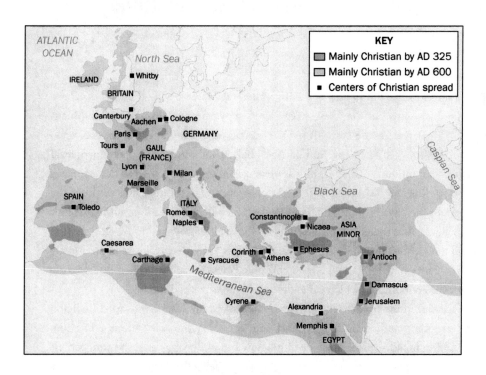

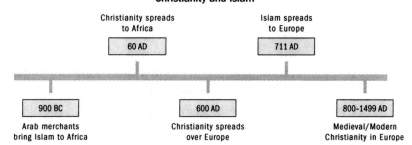

Christianity and Islam

Christianity spreads to Africa — **60 AD**

Islam spreads to Europe — **711 AD**

900 BC — Arab merchants bring Islam to Africa

600 AD — Christianity spreads over Europe

800–1499 AD — Medieval/Modern Christianity in Europe

OBJECTIVES:

1. Identify ways in which Greek and Roman civilization influenced medieval culture.
2. Understand the transition of beliefs from polytheism to monotheism, particularly Christianity.
3. Understand the impact of philosophy on Christianity.
4. Identify which philosopher had the greatest influence on Christianity.

The Classical Backgrounds of Mediaeval Christianity

By Frederick B. Artz

Sociologists usually begin with the Flood and the Fijis; writers of history, with the Greeks. These "spoiled darlings of the historians," as they have been called, may often be allowed too dominant a place in world history, but their role in the story of mediaeval culture is fundamental. Indeed, present views not only tie modern times closer to the Middle Ages, but, at the other end, make mediaeval civilization a long chapter of later antiquity. There is, in this view, something of a return to the estimates of mediaeval men who, long before the Renaissance, thought of themselves as part of the world of the ancients. From Philo the Jew, in the days of Jesus and Saint Paul, to Pico della Mirandola in the fifteenth century it was commonly believed that the Greek philosophers—above all Plato—had imbibed their first inspiration from Moses and the Hebrew prophets. Mediaeval men, thus, were deeply aware of an organic relation among the various currents of history, though their chronology was usually muddled, and, like the wife of Disraeli, they never could remember "which came first, the Greeks or the Romans."

The civilizations of Greece and Rome influenced mediaeval culture in a multitude of ways, in religion and philosophy, in law, government, and social usage, in art and technology, in science and education, in language and literature, and in music. It is on the side of religion and philosophy that the connections between antiquity and the Middle Ages are deepest and the debt of mediaeval thinkers to their Greek and Roman ancestors is most profound. Interest here centers in the long story of the growth of asceticism, mysticism, and monotheism in the religious and philosophical experience of antiquity. So, like mediaeval men, who used from the riches of classical culture those parts that seemed germane, the author has, at this point, selected from the whole Graeco-Roman heritage only that part that influenced mediaeval religion and philosophy. Later on, he will have frequent occasions to discuss many other Greek and Roman influences in mediaeval civilization. The men of the mediaeval centuries were the inheritors of a long evolution of Greek and Roman culture, a culture that in spite of many common elements changed greatly in the eleven centuries between Homer and St. Augustine. In the fields of religion and philosophy, as in nearly every other branch of culture, the history of Roman civilization after about 300 B.C. began to merge with that of Greek culture; hence there is much justification for treating the story of Graeco-Roman civilization as a single development.

TRADITIONAL RELIGION IN THE GRAECO-ROMAN WORLD

Greek and Roman religion started independently with simple interpretations of the forces of nature which included methods of trying to make these forces work for man's good. The thought of primitive men everywhere lacks a sense of natural causation. There are no laws of nature, there are only unpredictable forces. These forces are in trees and springs and stones and animals; they are everywhere, and these forces are like men. If a primitive man hits his head against a tree in the dark, he says: "that tree meant to do me harm. It must be propitiated." So by prayers and ritual forms, the performance of certain acts, like a libation of milk or wine or burning a cake or an animal, and by taboos (the avoidance of other acts) the spirits that dwell in all things may be made to work for man and not against him. Here, close together, are the beginnings of religion, art, and music. These attitudes and experiences of primitive man are older than logic, and, even in highly civilized men, often remain stronger than logic.

Among all primitive peoples, a vast polytheism of many gods is built up, so numerous the ancients often said there were more gods than men. In the course of time these forces of nature were given personalities, and stories about them grew. Still later, some gods became more important than others and a hierarchy of divine forces was developed with Zeus or Jupiter as the chief of the great gods of Olympus. Be sides the family gods of the fireside and the fields, and the gods of the city-state, there was added by Alexander the Great the worship of the ruler, and this cult was continued in the Hellenistic states and still later in the Roman Empire. Both these high gods and the innumerable lesser spirits are superior to men, not in spiritual or moral qualities, but only in outward gifts, strength, beauty, or immortality. There was no inward and spiritual relation of the individual with a moral force as in later religions and philosophies; it was a sort of contractual relation, to every god and spirit its due. Such a religion, common among all primitive peoples, knew little of the dark by-ways of mysticism. If men acquitted themselves of their obligations to these deities of the hearth, the field, and the marketplace, they would enjoy divine favor, or, at least, be unmolested.

The fight of Christianity was less against the great gods who dwelt on Olympus or, among the early Germans, in Walhalla, less against Zeus and Apollo, Odin and Thor, than against this vast multitude of lesser deities, a fight that the church lost. For the early Christian missionaries soon found the belief of the people in these spirits that would help in specific situations so deeply rooted that they early developed the cult of the saints and the cult of relics to take its place. "Remember," said Pope Gregory the Great, "you must not interfere with any traditional belief or religious observance that can be harmonized with Christianity." The theologians of the church never gave these saints any role except that of mediators between man and his God, but the masses made no such fine distinctions; they took the heroes of the new faith to their hearts, embraced them, and worshipped them as deities.[1]

The view of life of the average man of classical antiquity was confined to this world. It accepted this world and was largely indifferent to the promise of a future life. The growth of conscience, a sense of sin and shortcoming, and any great longing for a future life were of slow development. The traditional religion of the family and the state had no founder, no prophets, no inspired leader, no sacred books, no fixed theology or rules of orthodoxy, no religious caste. It did not produce a comprehensive code of ethics nor did it place emphasis on the need of right living. It was largely concerned with forms and outward acts of devotion. The need of peace with the gods produced a sort of religious legalism. Only in

1   G. L. Laing, *Survivals of roman religion* (New York, 1931) esp. pp. 8–15 for lists of saints and special curative function of each, one for toothache, one for child-birth, and the rest, and their relation to gods of the ancient world: also cf. V. D. Macchioro, *From Orpheus to St. Paul* (New York, 1930), pp. 23–5.

minor religious currents connected with the cults of Dionysus, of Orpheus, and of Demeter was there any indication of a mystical desire for moral purity and for union with the god. The for mal and legal side of religion is what is meant by paganism. The old traditional religion of the family and the state lived on, at least among the masses, for centuries; it even survived the fall of the Roman Empire in the fifth century A.D. When St. Benedict in the sixth century climbed the hill at Monte Cassino to found what was to become the mother house of his great monastic order, he discovered the inhabitants of the village all turned out for a feast of Apollo, and his eyes fell on a scene similar to the one Keats saw on the Grecian urn. The persistence of the ancient cults was due to the natural conservatism of all men in matters of religion and to the great inertia which any long-established usages possess. The old cults recalled the glories of the past, the ritual was attractive, and the state worship was the mother of art, literature, and music, and was all tied up with them.

In the course of centuries these traditional religious ideas and practices were modified by the poets, artists, and philosophers, and by a steady growth of mystery cults. The writers and the artists, for example, created the concept of Zeus as the creator and sustainer of a moral order in the universe and connected the gods with ethical ideals. As a result of these currents of art and literature, and of philosophy and the mystery religions, the old traditional paganism was overlaid, but it never disappeared. The old cults failed to satisfy certain classes who reached out toward a monotheistic view of religion; they were inadequate in that they paid little attention to matters of morality; they showed little concern for the problems of an after life and they failed to touch the hearts of many individuals or to satisfy their minds. Religious thinking came to exist on a number of levels at once, and the story of Greek and later Roman religion, from about 600 B.C. on, must be considered as proceeding in a sort of polyphonic manner. The new comes in alongside the old, but the old does not disappear.

THE IMPACT OF PHILOSOPHY

The legacy of Greek philosophy to the Middle Ages was enormous, and in the long centuries when Greek science, art, and literature were as good as forgotten throughout much of the West, the work of the Greek philosophers and of their Roman commentators formed the basis of Christian theology and the learning of all mediaeval schools.

Greek and Roman philosophy, like the rest of classical culture, went through a long evolution; its story from Thales of Miletus and Pythagoras to St. Augustine and Boethius is the greatest single chapter in the history of man's adventurous mind. Philosophy and science among the Greeks began together about 600 B.C., over two centuries later than Homer. They began together as an approach other than religion to explain the nature of things. Thales of Miletus was the first of a series of thinkers who were interested in astronomy, physics, and mathematics, and who tried to explain man and the universe on purely mechanical and rational lines. Thales believed "all came from water and to water all returns," The universe is explained chiefly on the basis of the processes of the weather. Ignoring old ideas, these thinkers were indifferent rather than hostile to religion. They explained the universe in the processes familiar to the farmer, the smith, and the sailor. They were eminently practical; Thales, for example, was later (falsely) reputed to have foretold an eclipse, and to have introduced from Egypt the methods of land measurements and founded geometry. Anaximander probably invented the sun-dial. Practical as they were, they were also the first thinkers who raised the basic questions of philosophy: What, in the final analysis, is real? What is the character of being?

This school of Miletus founded not only Western philosophy in general but, more specifically, a current of that philosophy that has remained more or less mechanistic in outlook. This mechanistic current came to its first adequate presentation in the philosophy of Democritus, an older contemporary of Plato, who reduced all reality to atoms and a void. In him we have the first clear statement of philosophic materialism in its modern meaning. His reduction of all reality to quantitative difference ultimately made possible that application of mathematics to the treatment of phenomena which is essential to the modern notion of scientific law. These theories of Democritus were later taken over by the Epicurean school and formed the basis of the magnificent philosophic poem of Lucretius, the *De Rerum Natura* of 55 B.C. This mechanistic current in ancient philosophy, important as it was, had no great influence on thought until the sixteenth century.

Contemporary with the work of Thales and his followers was that of Pythagoras, who is the founder of the great current of ethical and religious philosophy out of which ultimately came the Jewish, Christian, and Mohammedan philosophy of the Middle Ages. Ernest Barker once remarked: "The Middle Ages begin with Plato"; he might better have said: "The Middle Ages begin with Pythagoras." Pythagoras grew up in Ionia from whence had come the philosophy of Thales and his followers, and he was thoroughly trained in the best science of the period, in mathematics, physics, astronomy, music, and medicine. From these studies he conceived of a great world order, apart from man, perfect and harmonious in form and embodying principles of order and justice. It was the work of the Greek idealist philosophers to find a way of life for man that accorded with this world order. The early success of the Greeks in mathematics, physics, and astronomy is the determinant element in the growth of Greek idealism from Pythagoras to Plotinus.

Besides the influence of Ionian science, Pythagoras was also early influenced by Orphism, an ascetic and mystical Greek religious movement. Orphism held that the soul (the life-breath) was imprisoned in the body, that "the body is the tomb of the soul," and that this life is a preparation for life hereafter. The aim of life is redemption from the wheel of rebirth by a system of purifications. The soul can escape and rejoin the original divine essence only by death. It is possible, however, to anticipate this reunion by virtue of a religious mystery or ceremony that temporarily delivers the soul from its bodily prison and brings it into communion with the divine essence. What men call life is really death. The soul is divine and immortal, but through the sins of his ancestors, the Titans, man has fallen from his earlier high estate and must be released through a series of reincarnations. The mystic union with the hero Orpheus, including the eating of an animal which embodied his spirit, was one of the means of purification and of an eventual return to a higher level of existence. The initiate enjoyed the privilege of knowing divine things. Wicked souls live after death in men or in darkness under the earth; good souls, after many reincarnations, go to a blessed land. Here is the idea of the war of the soul on the body, a sense of weakness, sin, and shortcoming, and the idea of winning immortality partly through the moral effort of the individual, as, for example, abstaining from eating meat, and partly by a mystic identification with a divine savior. Here was a religion that could satisfy both the head and the heart. Orphism, in its various forms, not only inspired Pythagoras but it had a deep influence on Plato, and through him on Stoicism, Neo-Platonism, and early Christian theology—systems in which knowledge is no longer a desire for power over nature, but a means of virtuous living identified with the well-being of the soul.

Pythagoras combined the science of his time with elements of the various religious currents he knew and created something that he was the first to call philosophy, literally "the love of wisdom." He founded a religious order in southern Italy and for it laid down elaborate rules for the study of science and music, for a life of stern renunciation on the one hand, and on the other, a contemplation of the divine order of the world in which all was law, proportion, order, and harmony. Pythagoras' aim was to find a way of life by which the soul could es cape from the body and return to its maker. With all the Greek philosophers before Plato, including Pythagoras, we cannot be certain that we have anything they themselves wrote, and we must reconstruct their thought from fragments they are supposed to have written and from descriptions of their ideas in the writings of Plato, Aristotle, and later Greek philosophers. From such sources we can see that Pythagoras had an elaborate philosophic system that included a metaphysics and a system of ethics. He was the first to discover, by experimenting with a vibrating cord, that the intervals of the scale which seem to the ear concordant are associated with definite proportions of one string to another. He had a strange theory that everything could be explained in a system of numbers that corresponded to the tones in a musical scale, which in turn corresponded with a pre-existing harmony in the universe. This number symbolism had a great appeal to mediaeval men and was much used for centuries as a means of attempting to solve ethical and scientific problems. In Pythagoras we see the beginning of an idealistic, mystical, and ascetic philosophy that was later developed by Plato, the Stoics, and the Neo-Platonists, and from them entered Jewish and Christian thought.

The intervening generations between Thales of Miletus (d. *ca.* 546 B.C.) and Pythagoras (d. *ca.* 497 B.C.) and Socrates and Plato (d. 347 B.C.), a period of about a century and a half, saw a brilliant series of Greek thinkers concerned with trying to adjust the rival claims of science and ethics, of popular religious ideas, and purely mechanical ex planations. Philosophy now became the center of education, where it remained through all the later phases of Greek and Roman antiquity and during the Middle Ages. The idea of a single force—the *logos* Heraclitus called it, Parmenides named it the *One,* and Anaxagoras *nous* or mind—that created and sustained the universe, and the idea of an ordered cosmos were the chief contributions of the thinkers be tween Pythagoras and Socrates. As Xenophanes wrote: "One God there is, midst God and men the greatest; in form not like to mortals; he without toil rules all things; ever unmoved in one place he abideth."

The political and social upheaval caused by the Persian wars, soon followed by a bitter internal strife between Athens and Sparta, caused a sort of moral anarchy in Greek thought in the fifth century B.C. Ideas of all types poured into Athens. The old and the new were in conflict, and the result was often skepticism, cynicism, and defeatism. Many of the intellectual classes rejected all attempts to explain the world; orthodox religious ideas were declining, and old notions of right and wrong were called into question. In this world, travelling teachers, the Sophists, taught young men the arts of rhetoric and oratory, one of the chief roads to success in the democratic cities of the time. We know the Sophists chiefly through Plato, who disliked them. Most of them seem to have placed the emphasis of their teaching not on fundamental problems of science or philosophy or ethics but on the art of getting on and the ability to argue for any point of view irrespective of its truth. Aristophanes makes a Sophist say, in effect, that nothing is either good or bad, but thinking makes it so, or as Protagoras put it, "man is the measure of all things"; everything is relative. There are no values, no standards of right and wrong, no objective truth or morality can exist; all is relative, all is flux. In some ways the Sophists stood for emancipation and freedom. Most of the Sophists did not pretend to be philosophers and they probably reflected rather than created a certain elegant contemptuousness toward conventional religion and morality, but they deeply exasperated the noblest soul of their age, Socrates (d. 399 B.C.), and were the first cause of his life-work.

"Saint Socrates, pray for us," wrote Erasmus in the sixteenth century, and that may stand as the judgment of history on this extraordinary teacher and spiritual leader. No one in the history of philosophy so changed its course simply by what he was. In the midst of confusion, disintegration, and cynicism, this humble stone-cutter's son set out on an earnest quest for a knowledge of the good life. Personally he was ugly of countenance and shabby of dress, but he possessed enormous physical and intellectual vigor and a warm temperament. He was a stimulating talker, full of irony and earnestness. Those who knew him adored him. He seems to have begun as a Sophist, but soon broke with them; like the Sophists, he rejected many of the commonly held ideas of his time, and he questioned all the common concepts of the good and the true. But he rejected the facile cynicism of the Sophists. Among conflicting opinions he tried to find a solid core of truth, particularly in matters of ethics. His method was that of close questioning of those about him, insisting all the while on a consistent and exact use of words, and on clarification of all concepts used. All of Plato's abstracts were developed from Socrates' basic definitions. Man's first need is to take care of his soul, which he defined as the whole intellectual and moral personality, the responsible agent in all man's actions. After Socrates, his conception of the soul and his conviction that the development of the soul is the most significant thing in life become central in philosophy. Socrates' teaching on the soul stands for one of the great changes in the history of thought and is the most significant development in Greek philosophy in preparing the way for Christianity.

Along with his interest in the growth of the soul, Socrates taught that the universe is ruled by intelligent and moral forces. Something of this good world order can be known by the soul, though the chief guidance for the soul is knowledge of sound principles of ethical action. Virtue lies in knowledge, by which he seemingly meant full comprehension, of the good. To act rightly one must first know the right; all wickedness is due to ignorance. Socrates, though he left no writings, accomplished a revolution in Greek thought. He turned away from scientific to ethical and metaphysical problems. Before his time, philosophy had been chiefly concerned with the origins of all things. Socrates turned philosophy around and bade it look to the end for which the world existed; he turned from facts to values. The result of his teaching was that the later systems of Greek philosophy looked for the nature of things no longer in simple materials but in some final perfection toward which all things aspire. The effect on science was, in the long run, disastrous. The world of fact began to recede into the background, and, in the end, the Greek mind became too entranced with its own creations.

Socrates' moral doctrine is self-contained; it is the old Greek "know thyself"; it requires no support from older religious beliefs. His distinction between good and evil must be known directly; no supernatural sanction is needed. Socrates is said to have met an East Indian to whom he declared that he sought to understand human life, and the Hindu replied that man cannot know himself without knowing God. This story may show that some of Socrates' successors were aware that the recognition of right and wrong demanded by the master could not be separated from the recognition of an ultimate force who made and sustains the universe and a great moral order.

Aristotle states positively that Socrates was chiefly a teacher of ethics, who did not "occupy himself with the general nature of things" and that Plato was responsible for his own metaphysics. In any case, Plato as Socrates' leading disciple is our chief source for the master's ideas. Plato (d. 347 B.C.) himself is the first philosopher whom we can know well through his surviving works. He came of a well-to-do Athenian family, received an excellent education, and early fell deeply under the influence of Socrates. He was twenty-eight years old when Socrates was put to death; at the age of forty, Plato established a school, "The Academy," which lasted from 387 B.C. to A.D. 529, a longer time than any university has endured.

Plato's mind ranged widely, and he worked over the ideas of the earlier Greek philosophers. From Thales and the School of Miletus he drew his interest in mathematics, physics, and astronomy; from Heraclitus he got his belief in the transitoriness of all sensible things; from Parmenides came his vision of eternal being; from Anaxagoras came the idea that the moving cause of all things is mind. From the Pythagoreans he drew his ideas of the nature and destiny of the soul, his belief in order in the universe and in an eternal reality transcending our senses, and some of his asceticism and mysticism. All of these conceptions inherited from his predecessors were transformed and reordered in the light of the teaching of Socrates.

Plato outlined the great problems of philosophy, including a metaphysics, and, based on this, a psychology, an ethics, a theory of education, a system of aesthetics, and a philosophy of politics. He left gaps in his system; it is often difficult to find his final solution of some of the great metaphysical problems he raises, and he frequently contradicts himself. Nevertheless, his philosophy is the first elaboration of a theistic philosophy of a divinely made and directed universe. Plato's basic doctrine holds that there exists a world of eternal realities, of Forms or Ideas, entirely separate from the world our senses perceive. These Forms make up an organic and harmonious structure, the world of real being. Above all these separate Forms is the highest Form of the Good, the first principle of reality. This Form of the Good is not God in the Hebrew-Christian sense, for the Form of the Good does not include all the other Forms. Plato, thus, approached the monotheistic conception of the Old Testament but he never reached it. In the *Timaeus* he shows the Divine Force in three aspects, a sort of Trinity: first, the Divine Craftsman, then the Forms or Ideas, and finally the World Spirit, a deputy or agent of the Divine Craftsman. Christian theologians were at a later period to find this useful.[2]

The notions men have of the eternal Forms, which lie behind all the things we can see and know, are but feeble copies of these spiritual realities. But that men are able to know these Forms at all is due to the fact that the soul knew the Forms before it entered the body and is reminded of them by perceiving, through the senses, those things in this world that participate in them. The world of the senses is a world of flux; it is but half real. Things and events are but symbols of the great realities that lie behind and beyond this world. He who is willing to undergo the appropriate discipline can come to conceive Justice itself and Beauty itself, realities that are real as nothing in this world is real. It is only of these wholly immaterial and unchanging realities that man may have knowledge; all the rest is mere sensation and opinion. The purpose of man's life is to bring into the state and the life of man, the microcosm, something of the moral order and purpose

---

2 "The shortest cut to the study of the philosophy of the Middle Ages is to commit the 'Timaeus' to memory," P. Shorey, *Platonism, ancient and modern* (Berkeley, 1938), p. 105.

that exists in the universe, the macrocosm. Man's highest faculty is reason, which should be fully trained, but the life of reason is insufficient: it is only a ladder up to a religious experience in which man surveys all time and all existence.[3]

Plato's fundamental position is bottomed on an act of religious faith in a divinely directed universe. It is, as we have seen, a conception of all existence that approaches monotheism. It is a view of life that is mystical in that Plato wishes to help men identify themselves with the divine forces. A philosophy or a religion is not mystical when it is inspired merely by reverence and loyalty and even love for a divine being or force. It becomes mystical when, in addition to these sentiments, there is an inner sense of insufficiency and a desire for a union and fusion with the divine.[4] Plato's view of life is super-rational in that it aims at achieving a knowledge that is beyond perception and reason. His system of education shows how a man may aim at mystical heights by toiling up a long hard road of physical and intellectual discipline. Plato's is also a view of life that is somewhat ascetic. The joys of this world are evanescent and delusive. He protests that men confuse a round of pleasures or the pursuit of power and wealth with true happiness. Philosophy can deliver men from false and shallow judgments, and it can teach men to avoid an inner division in the soul by showing them that the goods of fortune are worth little; goods of the body are worth more, but goods of the soul are worth most. The way of the fullest life is also a way of renunciation. Finally, Plato's view of life is no longer the man-centered view that we commonly associate with the classical Greeks. It is a view of life that is centered, if not in God, at least in an immaterial and spiritual world, and the measure of time and

---

3   Interesting modern examples of the Platonic theory of reality are the following:
   a. from a sonnet of Michelangelo:

> Heaven-born, the soul a heavenly course must hold;
> Beyond the visible world she soars to seek
> (For what delights the sense is false and weak)
> Ideal form, the universal mould.
> The wise man, I affirm, can find no rest
> In that which perishes; nor will he lend
> His heart to aught that doth on time depend.

—R. W. Livingstone, ed., *The legacy of Greece*
(Oxford, 1921), p. 27.

   b. from Shelley's *Adonais*, stanza 52:

> The one remains, the many change and pass;
> Heaven's light forever shines, earth shadows fly;
> Life like a dome of many colored glass,
> Stains the white radiance of eternity,
> Until death tramples it to fragments.

   c. and finally from Proust:

There are two worlds, one the world of time, where necessity, illusion, suffering, change, decay, and death are the law; the other the world of eternity, where there is freedom, beauty, and peace. Normal experience is in the world of time, but glimpses of the other world may be given in moments of contemplation or through accidents of memory. It is the function of art to develop these insights and to use them for the illumination of life in the world of time.

—Cited in H. March, *The two worlds of Marcel Proust*
(Philadelphia, 1948), p. 1.

4   For an excellent brief definition of the mystic's attitude cf. E. R. Good. enough, *An introduction to Philo Judaeus* (New Haven, 1940), pp. 27–8.

space is not man or this world but eternity. For Plato life is only secondarily a series of events in this world; for him life has become primarily an adventure in eternity.

The weaknesses of Plato's philosophy were the weaknesses of much of Greek philosophy. He does not distinguish between illustrations and brilliant analogies and real argument. He indulges frequently in mere abstraction detached from either concrete observation or precise definition. Plato, like many Christian theologians later, seems, at times, to think that the greater the abstraction the more profound the truth. The Greeks made remarkable progress in mathematics, especially in geometry, and they wrongly supposed that a system of thought explaining the universe and man could be built as easily. So they were always hunting for unchanging reality, the elements, the truth, the moral law, and the absolute. Hence, Plato's system did not deal adequately with the finite world and had no method of expanding factual information about man and the world. Finally, his philosophic system is not only incomplete and often vague but over subtle, and these defects became exaggerated in the work of his successors, the Neo-Platonists and the Church Fathers.

But Plato's greatness has transcended many of these limitations. His superb literary style, which is the greatest of all the philosophers', gives his work, as Milton would say, "a life beyond life." And his great system has a superlative sweep, offering an explanation of man's destiny matched only by some of the greatest Jewish prophets and by Jesus of Nazareth. His enormous influence was on the side of a super-rational, though not an anti-rational, mysticism, and on the side of monotheism and of a reasonable asceticism. Men were particularly interested in his conception of human life as a pilgrimage to our true home. This last current, which came chiefly from Pythagoras, was passed on by the Stoics and the Neo-Platonists from which sources it entered Christianity.

The measure of Plato's influence on the whole history of Western thought is shown in Whitehead's statement: "The safest general characterization of the whole Western philosophical tradition is that it consists in a series of footnotes to Plato."[5] Only the "Timaeus," the most obscure of Plato's dialogues, was available in Latin translation during the Middle Ages; yet, through his influence on Cicero and on the Church Fathers, the system of Plato dominated the whole theology of the Christian Church from the first century through the twelfth, when the influence of Aristotle came in alongside that of Plato. Beyond this, the ideas of Plato were so diverse and so protean and they have so penetrated all Western thought that, on many subjects, to think at all means to think in terms of Plato. Emerson once loaned a Vermont farmer a copy of *The Republic*; later the farmer told Emerson: "that book has a great number of my ideas."

The philosophy of Plato was deeply modified, though not replaced, by that of Aristotle (d. 322 B.C.). Aristotle's father was the physician of Philip of Macedon, and later Aristotle became the tutor of Alexander the Great, though this relation seems to have had little influence on either teacher or pupil. The earliest influence on Aristotle was that of Ionian scientific thought. He began his intellectual career as a biologist; it is important to remember that he had a different beginning from that of Plato. At eighteen, he became a pupil of Plato, who was then sixty years old, and he remained a member of Plato's Academy until Plato's death twenty years later.[6] Jaeger has shown that Aristotle's thought went through a long development. His earlier works were critical of Plato; then he tried to combine his ideas with those of Plato, and from this he

---

5   A. O. Lovejoy, *The great chain of being* (Cambridge, Mass., 1936) p. 24.

6   Plato was twenty-eight years old when Socrates was executed, and sixty years old when he first met Aristotle. Aristotle was in close relations with Plato for twenty years.

finally constituted his own philosophy, which is basically a reconstructed Platonism. He is known for a long series of treatises on metaphysics (called by Aristotle "first philosophy"), on logic, on physics (in which he was very reactionary), on anatomy and physiology (in which he was forward-looking), on politics, ethics, rhetoric, and poetics. No other man made such important contributions to so many branches of knowledge. Nothing, it seems, was too great or too small to arouse his curiosity. The enormous range of his interests, his passion for classification, his orderliness, and, finally, his inspired common sense, which made him able to see both sides of most questions, give his philosophy a range possessed by no other in history.

Aristotle, being of a definitely scientific turn of mind, was greatly interested in what had been found out and what might be discovered by careful and objective investigation. In this he possessed a temperament fundamentally different from that of Plato. He accepted many of the ideas of Plato, but he objected to Plato's radical separation of the eternal Forms from the actual things of experience. Aristotle believed in Plato's Forms, only he maintained that they exist in this world and are in things and have no independent existence apart from them. Matter and Form are relative terms; only God has any real existence apart from matter. It is only the mind that separates them, and Form is grasped only after a prolonged study of individuals. The purposefulness of things is bound up with them, though this purposefulness is directed toward a transcendent end.

At the bottom of the great chain of being which constitutes the universe, stands pure matter, though, as one finds matter, it is always in some rudimentary form. The first stage upward from pure matter, in which matter has already taken on form, is to be found in the four elements: earth, air, fire, and water. Unfortunately for the future of science, Aristotle rejected the contemporary theory of matter of Democritus. From these four elements, we pass upward, through level after level of inorganic life, to organic life. In organisms, we advance from the vegetable life of the simplest plants to the animal soul, which is capable of sensation and motion, and from the animal soul to man, the rational being, each step being governed by an upward impulse which constitutes the goal toward which it is striving. At the top of the great chain of being is the first cause, God, who is pure form with out matter. Unmoved himself, he is the first mover of the universe. God is the ideal toward which the whole of creation moves as by an inner necessity. Each ascending existence or reality in this great chain, made up of its own form and matter, becomes, in turn, the matter of a higher form: a brick is form given to clay, the brick in turn becomes matter for the form of the wall, the wall becomes matter for the form of the temple. In Plato's universe there was just one world of forms sharply set off from one world of matter, and Plato gives no adequate explanation of the relation of these two worlds. In Aristotle's world there is an interlocking hierarchy of forms from lowest to highest.

The Aristotelian idea of a great chain of being dominated the thought of the West down into the seventeenth century. It is extremely important for the theology, philosophy, and science of the Middle Ages. What was to be the common mediaeval conception of this hierarchy of being is summed up by the Neo-Platonist Macrobius. Writing in the fourth century A.D., he says: "Since from the supreme God, mind arises, and from mind, soul, and since this, in turn, creates all subsequent things and fills them all with life, and since this single radiance illumines all and is reflected in each as a single face might be reflected in many mirrors placed in a series; and, since all things follow in continuous succession, degenerating in sequence to the very bottom of the series, the attentive observer will discover a succession of parts from the supreme God down to the last dregs of things, mutually linked, and without a break."[7]

In ethics, Aristotle took the position that emotions like anger, envy, love, and hatred, and actions like eating and drinking are, in themselves, neither good nor bad. Any emotion or action in excess will throw a man's soul off its balance. It is measure that a man needs, not mere suppression. Act always midway between two extremes; follow the "golden mean"; "nothing in excess."

In each part of Aristotle's philosophy there is a closely co-ordinated and organic structure of scientific fact, common sense, and this-world activity. His metaphysics is much more tightly knit than Plato's, and this world and the world of ideas are more integrated. For example, Plato regarded the soul as an entity separated from the body; he compares the soul to a rider controlling the horse on which he is mounted; with Aristotle the soul and body are united; the soul is the form by which the substance of the body is actualized and without the body the soul would have no existence. Both Plato and Aristotle believed the soul immortal though Aristotle rejected Plato's belief in a personal immortality and his idea of successive reincarnations.

Aristotle had a system of philosophy; Plato had created only the out lines of a philosophy. With Aristotle, however, there are some gaps. All seems closely knit; then, suddenly, we find that the structure has towered out of this worldly atmosphere and we are in a world of pure spiritual being, with forms that are divine, eternal, and transcendent. Aristotle was for twenty years in the closest contact with Plato. Though he usually seems determined to avoid the transcendental, the influence of the older teacher is always there. This is shown by the fact that when he comes to the farthest point to which his own system will take him, he then takes refuge in metaphors of a mystical character for which the reader is not prepared; this is especially true when he is dealing with the soul and with the First Mover. At heart, Aristotle always remained a good deal of a Platonist in spite of himself. He is, however, far less mystical and less ascetic in outlook than Plato, though he is more clearly monotheistic in his centering of all creation in God.

Plato's philosophy is set forth in a style that charms and sometimes bewilders the reader as does a great poem. Plato's writing casts a spell. Aristotle's philosophy, in the form in which we have it, is written in jottings, rather like telegrams, sometimes giving the barest bones of his thoughts, sometimes in epigrams and brilliant turns, occasionally in repetition or in mere confusion. Cicero, who knew some of Aristotle's original dialogues, speaks of his "golden stream of speech." But the extant writings of Aristotle seem to be skeleton memoranda prepared for his students.

Aristotle, in 335 B.C., founded a school, the "Lyceum," which ran parallel with Plato's Academy until A.D. 529. Plato's influence on later antiquity and on the Middle Ages down into the twelfth century was greater than that of Aristotle. During much of this long period, out of all of his works only two of Aristotle's logical treatises, the *Categories* or classes of propositions, and the *De Interpretation* on parts and kinds of sentences, both elementary treatises, were available in Latin translations of Boethius. But in the twelfth and thirteenth centuries the rest of Aristotle's writings were translated into Latin; his philosophy captured the schools, and he became, for many besides Averroes and Dante, the "master of those who know."

The Jewish, Christian, and Mohammedan theologians who used Aristotle found three great stumbling blocks in their way. Aristotle's system denied the idea of divine providence and the possibility of God's

---

7 Lovejoy, *op. cit.,* p. 63.

sudden intervention in an ordered universe; no miracles were possible for Aristotle's unmoved First Mover. Aristotle, also, did not believe in a special creation of the universe as described in Genesis; with him matter is eternal. And, finally, Aristotle denied personal immortality. But the Jews, the Christians, and the Mohammedans used his system, and for the orthodox he is still the basis of their theology. In artistic, literary, and musical criticism many of Aristotle's concepts like that of form and matter have remained the stock in trade. Many of the ideas of the great trinity of Greek philosophy, Socrates, Plato, and Aristotle, reached the early Christian Fathers and the writers of the Middle Ages through later schools of Greek philosophy, especially through Stoicism and Neo-Platonism, and through Latin Works of popularization, above all those of Cicero and Seneca.

After 350 B.C. Alexander the Great destroyed the free self-governing Greek city-states and set up a dictatorship. At the same time, his conquests and the trade developments that followed him went far to wipe away the old differences between Greeks and barbarians and to spread the language and culture of the Greeks through the whole of the Near East. Old national groups and old distinctions between classes of society were blurred or wiped out. But Alexander, having swept away the old order, did not live long enough to establish a new one. For the next three centuries—from about 300 B.C. to the time of the founding of the Roman Empire by Augustus, just before the beginning of the Christian Era—there were nearly incessant wars and insurrections through the Graeco-Roman world. These constant upheavals through out the whole Mediterranean area swept away the old landmarks; nowhere was there any longer a stable society where men knew and respected one another and where the details of life were controlled by the opinion of a compact body of citizens. The civilized world for much of the time in the three centuries before Augustus and Jesus was a vast scramble where millions of men, each on his own, struggled for themselves. In such a world, a man would often rise to great power and riches and then suddenly be flung into the mire. There seemed to be no reason or sense or principle of order any longer. The individual often found himself uprooted, isolated, and alone. Men were hurled along like sticks in a torrent.

The old Greek city-state had had its weaknesses; it offered its marvellous opportunities to only a few; the states had much internal strife, and they often fought one another. But to Plato and Aristotle the old Greek city-state was not merely a government; it was also a training school for youth and a place in which the citizen could in his own work and in service in the army, the navy, the courts, and the assembly realize the highest possibilities of his being. The state was a moral and spiritual corporation; it had an ethical function. It was not merely an institution that collected taxes, built roads, and furnished police protection. It was a great spiritual bond for the perfecting of its members. An individual citizen could only realize himself in and through the state. The old Greek city-state was, then, something like the mediaeval church and like the state in the philosophy of Hegel; there was little idea of a conflict between the interests of the individual and the interests of the state.

The destruction of freedom in the Greek city-states, the gradual loss of faith in the old gods, and the long succession of wars and disorders raised the whole question of self-perfection apart from the group. How could one achieve fullfilment and peace and the good life out side the state? The state was now considered evil; it was widely regarded as a great killing machine, an engine of might without right, in which unprincipled adventurers and tyrants scrambled for rich prizes. Likewise, to many men life itself seemed bad. Everything depended on whim and chance. Men came to fear life. Every interest a man had was like a filament going out from his heart and attaching itself to some object. If this object was unstable, he was pulled miserably this way and that after it. The way of freedom and peace was to reduce the field of interest, to cut all these strands going out in all directions and attaching one to family, property, honors, riches, and the state. Confidence was shaken; aspirations were lowered; there was a withdrawal from high endeavor. Men were turning to philosophies and religions of renunciation and consolation. There was a gradual "failure of nerve."[8]

All these changes in the ways of life led to a search for new philosophies and religions. Some sought to revive old Greek mystery cults; others in both the eastern and the western ends of the Mediterranean turned to mystery religions from Egypt, Asia Minor, Syria, Persia, and finally Palestine. Others revived Pythagoreanism and Platonism or turned to new philosophies. Everywhere men were no longer at home in this world; they felt themselves wayfarers seeking peace.

To Plato and Aristotle the origin of philosophic inquiry had been a desire to forge ahead to know more about man and the universe. To the Stoic Epictetus the source of philosophy is "a consciousness of one's own weakness and inadequacy"; to Cicero "philosophy is the healing of the soul"; to Plutarch it is "the only medicine for spiritual diseases." The philosopher is no longer the bright star going before the earnest seekers after truth; he has become a stretcher-bearer following in the wake of the struggle for existence and picking up the wounded. The philosopher has become the physician of the soul.

New religions and philosophies now offered schemes of personal development and personal salvation entirely independent of the fate of any earthly state, independent even of the fate of the great Roman Empire. All were highly cosmopolitan; they were for all men everywhere, for the whole of humanity, and were not confined to any nation or any class of society. The community is redefined, and it becomes world-wide. At the same time that the new philosophies and religions became cosmopolitan, they also became highly individualistic, appealing directly to the mind and heart of the believer.

One of the most attractive of these philosophies was that of Epicurus (d. 270 B.C.). The Cyrenaics, a group that stemmed from Socrates, had earlier developed a philosophy that showed men how to avoid distress by forgetting the gods and the soul and thereby finding a key to inner peace. Epicurus developed these ideas into a doctrine and founded a school called the "Garden." The Epicureans were largely indifferent to learning; they took up the materialism of Democritus to rid them selves of any belief in the soul, in immortality, and in God. The gods exist, but they live a life apart from this world. Don't bother about them. Most of the evils men fear can be avoided; if they come, they can be endured. It is anticipation of pain that

---

8   This "failure of nerve" is a long story.

Anyone who turns from the great writers of classical Athens, say Sophocles or Aristotle, to those of the Christian Era must be conscious of a great difference in tone. The new quality is not especially Christian; it is just as marked in the Gnostics and Mithra worshippers as in the Gospels, in Plotinus as in Jerome. It is a rise of asceticism, of mysticism, of pessimism, a loss of self confidence, of hope in this life and of faith in normal human effort; a despair of patient inquiry, a cry for infallible revelation; an indifference to the welfare of the state. It is an atmosphere in which the aim of the good man is not so much to live justly, to help the society to which he belongs; but rather, by means of a burning faith, by contempt for the world and its standards, by ecstasy, suffering and martyrdom, to be granted pardon for his unspeakable unworthiness, his innumerable sins. There is an intensifying of certain spiritual emotions; an increase of sensitiveness, a failure of nerve.

—G. Murray, *Five stages of Greek religion*
(2nd ed., Oxford, 1925), p. 155.

makes men wretched and saps their courage. Death is like sleep, an unconscious forgetful ness. Reject the world and its prizes. Be unambitious.

> *There is nothing to fear in God*
> *There is nothing to feel in death;*
> *What is good is easily procured*
> *What is bad is easily endured.*[9]

Epicurus, desirous of removing every disturbance from without, advised men not to take part in public life, to avoid marriage, to withdraw from the world and live a hidden life. Pleasure, as he defined it, is mainly negative, avoiding the world so as to gain a peaceful state of mind. Like Heine's Englishman, Epicurus seems to have "taken his pleasures sadly." There is an essential distrust of life, an escapism, about this faith that warns one not to attract the world's attention and then the world will not hurt one. Its essential hedonism and its materialism made Epicureanism, after 200 B.C., popular among intellectuals and the well-to-do of the Graeco-Roman world. It inspired the greatest philosophic poem of antiquity, the *De Rerum Natura* (55 B.C.) of Lucretius, but its materialism and atheism had no attraction for the early Christians or for the men of the Middle Ages. It came back into vogue in the sixteenth century and later, and appealed deeply to thinkers like Montaigne, Thomas Hobbes, and Holbach.

Much more influential than Epicureanism, both in later antiquity and in the Middle Ages, was Stoicism, which derives from another group of Socrates' followers, the Cynics. Poor men who were never organized in a school, the Cynics were at war with established ideas and institutions. They used ridicule and witty abuse, and, foreswearing all the comforts of civilization, they travelled from place to place, making public harangues and giving moral advice to individuals. The Cynic and later the Stoic teachers moved about like missionaries ministering to men. They were consulted for advice on moral problems; a Stoic teacher was often attached to a Greek or Roman family as a sort of chaplain. The discourses he delivered were like the sermons of the Christian church of a later time. The cardinal point of the teaching of the Cynics was the supreme value of virtue and the utter insignificance and worthlessness of all else. Desire and the world must be set aside. Possess nothing; fear nothing except evil; desire nothing but virtue. They allowed no distinctions between men except on the basis of virtue alone; Greek and barbarian, rich and poor were words that meant nothing to the Cynics. It was a strongly ascetic creed; one Cynic said: "Look at me, I am without house or city, property or slave. I sleep on the ground. I have no wife, no children. What do I lack ? Am I not without distress or fear ? Am I not free ?"[10] It all sounds like St. Jerome or one of the early Christian ascetics. The life of virtue they loved to compare with the life of an athlete, a figure of speech often used by Seneca and St. Paul.

The activity of the Cynics forms the background for Stoicism, whose founder, Zeno (d. 263 B.C.), opened a school, the "Stoa" or "Porch," in Athens some years before Epicurus founded his school. Zeno's doctrine is severe. He accepted Socrates' idea that knowledge is virtue, and the general theory of Plato about the

---

9   Found scratched on a wall in Herculaneum. W. W. Hyde, *Paganism to Christianity in the Roman Empire* (Philadelphia, 1946), p. 30 note.

10   *Cambridge ancient history*, XI, pp. 690–6.

universe. The universe is not a place where senseless atoms swirl chaotically about. It is a great moral order created by God and governed by "natural law."

This "natural law" is independent of popular conventions and of human legislation; it is the rule of reason and justice that lies at the heart of the universe. Men and institutions should strive to follow it. Reason is man's highest faculty and he must use his reason to suppress his emotions and to attain temperance, courage, and peace. Man may then come to live in harmony with God's ordered universe.

The strongest forces in Stoicism that influenced later thought were, first, its emphasis on duty, duty to family, to friends, and to all obligations; second, its belief that a man must listen to his conscience, his inner light; third, its injunction to join with men of good will everywhere to extend justice among mankind; and, finally, its great doctrine of "natural law." Maintain your soul as a fortress. You have to fight alone. Listen to your conscience, follow your duty not your desires, attune your spirit to a great world order, be just to your fellow-men, and live a life of inner strength, of stern self-sufficiency, inaccessible to grief and undisturbed though the heavens fall. As with other schools of Greek philosophy, there is no reliance on a loving God or on a personal savior.

Few early Stoic writings survive, and the chief sources are Roman writers after 100 B.C., Cicero, Epictetus, Seneca, and Marcus Aurelius. The earlier Stoics were interested in metaphysical problems, but the surviving Stoic writings are chiefly concerned with ethics. Stoicism, like Epicureanism, is more significant in history as a way of life than as a philosophy. The spirit of Stoicism is deeply religious. "Have courage to look up to God," wrote Epictetus, "and say, 'deal with me as thou wilt. I am thine. I flinch from nothing so long as thou thinkest it good. Wouldst thou have me hold office or eschew it, be rich or poor? For all this I will defend thee before men.'"[11] Cicero wrote, regarding the brotherhood of man: "and there shall no longer be one law at Athens, and another at Rome, one law today another tomorrow, but the same law, everlasting and unchangeable, shall bind all nations, and there shall be one ruler of all, even God, the creator of this law, and he who will not obey it shall be an exile from himself."[12] Seneca compared the world of the spirit and the world of material things to two cities; one is the everyday world of transitoriness and discord, the other, the real and spiritual world: "each of us owns two fatherlands, one the country in which we happen to be born, the other an empire on which the sun never sets." This concept evidently became common centuries before Augustine wrote his *City of God*.

The Stoics first denounced the myths about heroes and gods, but in time, though they were monotheistic in outlook, they took over the whole classical polytheism, and they began the use of allegory in explaining myths. For example, Homer's story of how Hera was fettered by Hephaistos and liberated is said to show that the order of the universe depends upon the balance of the elements; when Zeus hangs Hera suspended in the air, this points to the origin and succession of the elements. Everything in mythology could be given a physical or moral meaning. This method was passed on to the Jews and the Christians and played an enormous role in the interpreting of the Scriptures. The Stoics also accepted many superstitions about astrology and a whole system of astral religion that came to flourish in the Greek and Roman world after 200 B.C.

---

11   E. Bevan, ed., *Later Greek religion* (London, 1927), p. 111.
12   S. H. Mellone, *Western Christian thought in the Middle Ages* (London, 1935), p. 20.

They taught submission to authority in politics. In general, doing one's duty meant submission to anything that comes to you. Stoicism made a strong appeal to many of the statesmen, judges, lawyers, administrators, and businessmen who held together the Roman Empire. It profoundly influenced the Roman law both in legislation and in legal interpretation in the courts, pushing law always in the direction of the ideal of justice embodied in the concept of "natural law." It improved the treatment of women and slaves and helped to bring justice to the peoples Rome conquered. The most famous figure in Latin literature, Virgil's Aeneas, is a Stoic who follows the stern road of duty. Stoicism influenced St. Paul and some of the early Christian writers. So close was the spirit of Stoicism to Christianity that Seneca was considered almost a Church Father by the Middle Ages, and a curious legend arose that he had a long correspondence with his contemporary, St. Paul.[13]

Marcus Aurelius said, "our days are a pilgrimage and a sojourning," but the journey, unlike Christianity, had no clear goal. Stoicism throve because it was a philosophy of suffering; it fell because it was a philosophy of despair. For Stoicism held out no hope for the future of mankind. In this dead air of later antiquity one of the many things Christianity brought was a hope for the future of both the individual and society. Often the Stoic made a desert in his heart and called it peace; the price is excessive. But Stoicism still remains as the nearest approach to an acceptable system of ethics for those who cannot accept revelation but still keep some faith that there is a purpose in things. Finally it should be observed that in Epicureanism, and still more in Stoicism, we see the ancient world slowly turning from the "nothing in excess" of the famous inscription of Delphi and the golden mean of Aristotle's ethics to an ascetic view of life. Passions and desires, which were in themselves neither good nor bad except in the manner of their use, are now declared evil. For the earlier classical ideas of temperance there is gradually substituted a doctrine of renunciation.

Faith in reason had in one phase or another characterized Greek philosophy through all its changes from Thales of Miletus down, though from the time of Pythagoras on, reason was often subordinated to ethical ideals and values, and, at the same time, was related to some sort of a vast spiritual world order. This second current of moral philosophy steadily got the upper hand, and the older Greek interest in scientific problems gradually declined. The last great works of Greek science, Ptolemy on astronomy and Galen on medicine, appeared about A.D. 160. A decline in Greek science parallels the growing interest in ascetic and other-worldly philosophies and religions that offer ways of self-perfection or even of self-annihilation outside the state and beyond the bounds of men.

The first three centuries of the Christian Era saw many rival schools of philosophy and many religions flourishing side by side. The old philosophic schools—the Platonists, the Aristotelians, the Cynics, the Skeptics, the Cyrenaics, the Stoics, and the Epicureans—were still active. Alongside them grew up new schools of Neo-Pythagoreanism and Neo-Platonism, and, in addition, philosophic sects of astral theology, of Gnosticism, and of Hermes Trismegistus, strange mixtures of philosophy, traditional religion, science and pseudo-science, mystery religions, and plain superstition. These philosophies and religions borrowed extensively from each other's ideas and rites. Eclecticism and syncretism became so extended that all of the

---

13   Seneca said: "The mind unless it is pure and holy comprehends not God." St. Matthew says: "Blessed are the pure in heart for they shall see God." Seneca wrote: "Let us give as we wish to receive"; St. Matthew says: "Whatsoever ye would that men do unto you do ye even so unto them." Many of the Stoic ideas, especially the doctrine of the inner light and the idea of the brother-hood of man were independently reproduced in Quakerism.

philosophies and religions shared many ascetic and mystical ideas, and their differences frequently lay in the emphasis placed on one philosophic theory or on one religious rite as against another.

Most interesting and significant of these currents for later history is the Neo-Platonic school. The philosophy of this famous school is one of the last creations of the Greek philosophic spirit, the other being early Christian theology. No schools of Greek philosophy carried abstraction further. Both were characterized by an extreme subtlety and an abuse of analysis which ended in mazes of innumerable distinctions, but all the analyses were heated by a deep emotional fervor and exaltation. Alexandria was the greatest commercial and cultural center of the eastern Mediterranean world, and it was there the Neo-Platonic school was founded by a Christian, Ammonius Saccas, who had deserted the faith. Among his pupils were the philosopher Plotinus, Longinus, and Origen, the greatest of the Greek Fathers of the church. The presence of the young Plotinus and the young Origen in the same school inevitably reminds one of a later day when John Calvin and St. Ignatius Loyola were both students together in the University of Paris. Plotinus (d. A.D. 270), after studying in Alexandria, stayed for a time in Persia, and finally settled in Rome, where he founded a school. From his youth, he seems to have been filled with a conscious ness of sin and a need for achieving peace. He was an extreme ascetic and mystic; tradition has it that he was ashamed he had a body and that he could never remember the names of his parents or the date of his own birthday.

At the center of Plotinus' system is a transcendent force, the One God. All flows out of the One by a series of emanations and to him everything returns. Though everything flows out of the One, he is never diminished. The One is apart from the world, is all powerful but is essentially indefinable, for to define the One is to limit him. The God-head, to Plotinus, is a trinity. From the One, the first emanation is universal Mind, the world of ideas, containing the archetypes of all things in the phenomenal world. From Mind comes the next emanation, Soul, which manifests itself in individual souls and gives existence to all things in the world of phenomena. By study, by prayer, and by ascetic practices we may attain to some knowledge of the One. The world of phenomena is due to a falling away from the One, but there persists in every human soul a longing to return to it. Man may rid himself of some of the restrictions of matter, and, rising above the world of the finite, penetrate to the universal. Evil is an illusion, as in modern Christian Science; evil is a matter of misguided mortal man.

On the heights of a mystic experience, the distinct conceptions of the intellect fade into the haze of an immediate identity with the One. So the philosopher—the faith is for the few, not for the many—rises first above the life of the senses, then above the life of the intellect to a sort of cosmic consciousness, "the flight of the alone to the alone." Plotinus is super-rational but not anti-rational. He does not despise the intellect, for man's intellect is nearest of all exalted things to the One. The cultivation of an intellectual insight into the structure and purpose of the universe and into the values of all types of existence is an essential preliminary task on the road to the good life of contemplation. On this road the philosopher hopes for an occasional ecstasy in which personality and consciousness are left behind and in which he feels a fusion with the divine, a union in which there can be no shade of separation. Plotinus had an ascending ladder of virtues in which the highest form of existence possible to man is a life of pure contemplation. His biographer tells us that he was himself warmed by the divine presence three or four times in a long lifetime. (This ecstasy with Plotinus is of a corroborative character, and is not, as with some of his followers, a substitute for philosophic inquiry.) We already begin to breathe the atmosphere of the catacombs and the cloister.

Plotinus' great work, the *Enneads,* presents a very subtle and complicated metaphysics warmed by a pulsating religious faith. He is everywhere absorbed with the problem of how the soul can pierce the curtain about it and escape from this charnel house of the flesh and the world. It is a philosophy of the intellect enraptured, a system of thought based on Plato and on Aristotle's chain of being, but much more other-worldly. Matter becomes almost an illusion. His system, unlike that of Plato, provided a vast hierarchy of intermediate beings or existences who bridged the distance from God to this world. There were also some evil spirits, powers of darkness, scheming man's misery. All these concepts squared with popular notions of good and evil spirits active in the world. In his elaborate and detailed descriptions of spirits in his hierarchy of the emanations from God, Plotinus and his followers contributed mightily to the vogue of angelology, demonology, magic, and astrology of all the later Christian centuries.

Neo-Platonism profoundly influenced Christian theology and philosophy. Origen in the East and Augustine in the West were both immersed in Neo-Platonism. Augustine's conversion to Neo-Platonism was the last step of a long spiritual Aeneid before his final conversion to Christianity. He finally renounced Neo-Platonism because it was too cold and impersonal, could not reach the masses of mankind, and above all because it lacked a religious leader like Jesus.[14] Writing in the eleventh century, Psellus, the Byzantine scholar, defined God in purely Neo-Platonic terms: "God is not the sky, nor the sun, nor anything that can be perceived, nor the best possible mind, nor a Platonic form apart from matter. God is of an unfathomable nature."[15] Western Christian thought got a second great infusion of Neo-Platonism through the writings of John Scotus Erigena in the ninth century and a third infusion through the works of Ficino and Pico della Mirandola in the fifteenth century.

The Christian thinkers all recognized that both Plato and the Neo-Platonists had a great conception of the Divine, but by the time of Plotinus, Christianity was two centuries old. By the third century, both inside and outside Christianity the goal of life was salvation in another world, a world far beyond the power of mortal mind to comprehend or mortal effort to attain. Only a sublime and supernatural strength coming down from God could assure weak mortals of attaining their goal. These assurances came to men, through philosophy or through religion or through both, as a "gift of the spirit," "a radiant vision," or "an illumination." Union, with the divine came only through experience of Him. The soul, in its essential nature, is capable of coming into contact with the One, for it is akin thereto, but is hindered by its connection with the corporeal. The soul must train itself to wait in holy stillness in which all sense-perceptions are set aside; the soul must be taught to turn in upon itself and reject all consciousness, even self-consciousness. Then in the soul's depths there is a union with the One. This union with the One must be experienced; it cannot be described. This union is an illumination which gives assurance of the existence of the One but not full knowledge of its nature. By this union man becomes divine. Knowledge is no longer obtained by mental effort alone but by revelation.

The weaker sides of Plotinus were carried further by some of his followers. Porphyry was a great popularizer; he edited the *Enneads* and prepared them for publication. In his own writings he introduced a lavish amount of allegorizing and laid great emphasis on ascetic practices. His best known work, *An Introduction to*

---

14 The great passage in Augustine's *Confessions* (IX, 10) which tells of his farewell to his mother, Saint Monica, is based on Plotinus' *Enneads,* V, i, 2; beyond this Augustine's whole outlook is deeply penetrated with Neo-Platonism.

15 J. Hussey, *Church and learning in the Byzantine Empire 867–1185* (Oxford, 1937), p. 79.

the Categories of Aristotle, was translated into Latin by Boethius in the sixth century and became of enormous importance for mediaeval philosophy. Another Neo-Platonist was Iamblichus the Sublime, whose works are a tedious collection of remarks on all sorts of subjects with masses of quotations from every kind of writer, at once diffuse, commonplace, and confused. He admitted all the pagan deities to his system, allegorized them, mixed magic, superstition, and bits from the philosophers of the past to make a sort of united front against the Christians. Julian the Apostate made Iamblichus' synthesis of religion, philosophy, and magic the official doctrine of the empire for a time in the fourth century. With Iamblichus one is groping in a murky atmosphere of theosophical fantasies. Iamblichus believed that the divine powers that emanate from the One can animate that which has no soul and set in motion that which cannot move—pebbles, bits of wood, and the like. The wheel has come full circle and we are back where we started with a belief in the forces that lie in all things in nature. Old seeds that had long lain dormant put forth new shoots. The philosopher now yearns for magic and sorcery and is credulous on principle. In this mystic atmosphere of late antiquity strange ideas shot up like weeds in a hot house. Iamblichus' life, as told by his Neo-Platonic biographer, is as full of miracles as the contemporary life of St. Anthony by Athanasius. The common superstitions of the masses had now wound themselves into the systems of thought of the highest philosophers.[16]

The last of the Pagan Neo-Platonists was Proclus (d. A.D. 485), who tried to systematize the whole body of Neo-Platonic writing and joined it with the cults of paganism. His work is a sort of metaphysical museum with all the stages of being catalogued and laid out on their proper shelves. He was so eclectic that he is said to have practiced the ceremonial abstinences prescribed for the sacred days of all religions. Proclus' works are very well organized and systematic and he was much studied by the Greek Fathers of the church. The whole system of Dionysius the Areopagite was built on that of Proclus, and, through Dionysius, Proclus deeply influenced the thought of both the Greek East and the Latin West throughout the whole mediaeval period. When in A.D. 529 Justinian closed the schools of ancient philosophy (because they were not Christian), they were all deeply under the influence of Neo-Platonism.

THE MYSTERY RELIGIONS

The popular mystery religions did much more to modify the traditional religious ideas of the Greeks and Romans than did art, literature, or philosophy. As the intellectuals lost faith in the old gods and as the worship of the ruler seemed but an empty rite, they often turned to philosophy. When this loss of faith affected the masses they usually looked to the mystery religions. Back of these mystery religions was a long evolution about which little is known. The only persons who could have left us information about these cults were the initiates themselves and they were pledged to secrecy. So historians have had to depend on scattered literary references, on archeological finds, and on the descriptions of the mystery religions in the early Christian writers who regarded these religions with a somewhat jaundiced eye. Each cult seems to have begun as a

---

16 Bidez in *Cambridge ancient history*, Vol. XII, p. 653, calls Iamblicus a "nincompoop"; T. Whittaker, *The Neo-Platonists* (2nd ed., Cambridge, 1918), pp. 124–5, defends him. Gibbon called the whole Neo-Platonic school "the second childhood of human reason." This charge may, perhaps, be applied to Iamblicus, but it hardly fits the commentators and systematizers, Porphyry and Proclus, and it is absurd if applied to Plotinus, who was one of the world's important religious philosophers and the greatest philosophical mind between Aristotle and Aquinas.

nature rite connected with the change of the seasons, but, in the course of time, the old myths had been reinterpreted and the rites reorganized to turn on the birth, death, and resurrection of man.

The oldest cults in the Graeco-Roman world were those in Greece that were connected with the worship of Dionysus, of Orpheus, and of Demeter. With these very interesting cults there were myths that explained that man had a twofold nature; he was part divine and part earthly. In the beginning the rites connected with the cult of Dionysus were of a barbaric nature, characterized by ecstatic transports and erotic excesses, processions with torch bearers at night, shrieks and howls, tearing to pieces of animals, and the eating of their still palpitating flesh. Thus the initiate might have the feeling that he shared in a larger life and shared too in the spirit of the god embodied in the animal eaten. He became "enthusiastic," literally the state in which "God is in man." As early as the sixth century B.C. there was connected with the cult of Orpheus (a spiritualized Dionysian cult) the idea that ritual purity was not enough. Through some ascetic practices a moral purity must also be striven for, and the lower world, where dwelt the spirits of men after death, was transformed into a place of punishment.

Much the most is known about the rites of Demeter, first celebrated at Eleusis in Attica and spreading from there to other centers. The ceremonies there included a dramatic passion play and a communion service in which the initiate shared the sorrow of Demeter in giving her daughter to the king of the underworld each autumn, and her joy in her daughter's return in the spring. The old cult rites had been given a higher spiritual meaning at least as early as 500 B.C. The initiate felt his soul lifted from the body in which it had been imprisoned, and he gained an inner assurance of salvation. Besides the ceremonies, the initiate had to perform various ascetic acts such as abstaining from certain foods. Here we can see, as in other mystery religions, an old act of ritualistic purification being transformed into an act of moral purification.

The Greek mystery cults, which undoubtedly influenced deeply the philosophies of Pythagoras and Plato and their followers, were never much extended either in Greece or outside Greece. The great changes in popular religion after 300 B.C. were due to the spread of mystery religions originating in the Near and Middle East of which the most important were those of Magna Mater from Asia Minor, of Isis from Egypt, and of Mithra from Persia. The story of the spread of these and similar cults lies chiefly between 300 B.C. and A.D. 300. In the Greek and Roman world before 300 B.C. one finds currents of Orphism and cults like that of Eleusis and of some foreign mystery religions and the philosophic schools of the Pythagoreans and the Platonists. At the other extremity, in A.D. 300, Christianity is about to become the official religion of the Roman Empire. To find these cults accepted among large numbers of people, and to find a wholesale borrowing of gods, of rites, and of religious ideas until syncretism had made practically one religion in the vast Roman world, one would have to come down to A.D. 100. The two centuries between A.D. 100 and 300 constitute the period of most rapid change, and they form the most fascinating chapter in the history of the West. Everywhere men were saying: "Here on earth we are under tension and trial; how deep is the pain, of what worth is the act; what must I do to be saved?"

One of the oldest of the non-Greek cults was that of Magna Mater, which spread from Asia Minor through the Greek world from the sixth century B.C. on, and reached Rome in 204 B.C. According to her myth, the Great Mother, the source of all life, was infuriated at the unfaithfulness of Attis, her lover. She drove him mad so that he emasculated himself beneath a pine tree into which his spirit passed; at the same time his blood was transformed into violets. The Great Mother mourned over her dead lover and brought him back to life. It is a nature myth: Attis, the god of vegetation, is loved by Mother Earth, but vegetation fades. The mother mourns in autumn and winter, but in the spring she is able to restore Attis (vegetation) to life. In the rites of the cult, the annual festival was celebrated in March. After preliminary ceremonies, a pine tree was felled on the 21st of March and taken, wrapped like a corpse in woolen bands and garlands of violets, to the temple of the goddess. After some days of mourning, the pine was buried amid highly emotional ceremonies in which the priests made shrill cries, clashed cymbals, played piercing notes on flutes, and flagellated themselves. Those who intended to join the priesthood in the height of the ceremonies emasculated themselves with stones, repeating the experience of Attis, and, at the same time, giving the goddess all their fertility. Then followed a vigil during which the worshipper was supposed to be united with the goddess. On the 25th of March there was a wild jubilation, the pine was dug up, Attis had come to life. The ceremonies ended on the 27th of March with a procession through the streets of the town.

Connected with the rites of Magna Mater was a baptismal ceremony, the *taurobolium*. Widely spaced planks, or an iron grill, were placed over a ditch in which stood the candidates for baptism. A bull was then slain, the blood ran down like red rain onto the naked initiates; this act was supposed to wash away human sin and weakness and to give initiates a second birth. The pit probably signified the kingdom of the dead; the initiate who entered the pit is thought to die; the bull is Attis, and the blood that rains down is his life principle. When the initiate leaves the pit he is said to be born again, and to symbolize this regeneration, he is, as a newborn infant, given milk to drink. After twenty years the ceremony was repeated. There was also a sacred meal at which the initiates ate bread, sacred to Attis and embodying his spirit. The bread and other food eaten were served from a drum and a cymbal, instruments sacred to Magna Mater. The rites of Magna Mater were crude, though a highly spiritual interpretation came to be given to them, and the rites became vehicles for a deep religious experience.

The cult of Isis from Egypt seems to have been more refined. It too involved a supreme female deity and her lover, Osiris, who gave the arts and laws to men. Osiris is killed and is reborn by the efforts of Isis. As one text says (the words refer to an initiate of the cult): "As truly as Osiris lives, he also shall live, as truly as Osiris is not dead shall he not die."[17] Isis, like Demeter and Magna Mater, was a mother goddess personifying the force of life in nature and the human hope for a final triumph of life over death. The ceremonies of the cult were elaborate and to the worshipper deeply impressive; the cult of Isis had a great attraction for women in the Greek and Roman world. The public services included a daily liturgy in the morning and a benediction in the afternoon; these were accompanied by chanting, the ringing of bells, the sprinkling of holy water, and the burning of candles and incense. As with the official cults and the other mystery religions, the shrines were left open, and the faithful could come at any hour to meditate and pray. "Indeed," says Frazer, "the stately ritual with its shaven and tonsured priests, its matins and vespers, its tinkling music, its baptisms as aspersions of holy water, its solemn processions, its jewelled images of the mother of god, presented many points of similarity to the pomp and ceremonies of Catholicism."[18]

The keenest competitor of Christianity and the most moral of all the mystery religions—and several have been omitted from this account—was Mithraism from Persia. Here was a form of old Zoroastrianism, a dualistic system in which the powers of light and darkness were con tending for mastery over the universe and over the soul of man. Mithra was an agent of light, the upholder of truth and virtue, and the implacable

---

17   F. Cumont, *Oriental religions in Roman paganism* (Chicago, 1911), p. 100.
18   J. Frazer, *Adonis, Attis, and Osiris* (2nd ed., London, 1922), p. 347.

enemy of evil. His legend represents him as a mighty hunter who slays the bull. To a nation of herdsmen, the wild bull stood for the idea of unrestrained power, needing to be brought under control for the service of man. Mithra is represented as chasing the wild bull and finally mounting his back and slaying him. The birthday of Mithra was celebrated on the 25th of December, and his sacred day was the first day of the week. Mithra was an unfailing help to mortals in their struggle for a life of virtue. He strengthened his followers against the spirit of evil and the temptations of the flesh. For those who merited it, he assured a happy immortality. Sacred rites and ceremonies, including a baptismal rite with water and later the *taurobolium* (borrowed from the cult of Magna Mater) and the eating of a sacred repast of bread and wine identified the worshipper with a hero-savior. Moral living deepened this identification. Mithraism seems to have had no woman devotees, and its great appeal was to soldiers; from one end of the Roman Empire to the other, from Scotland and the Rhineland to the sands of Africa and the borders of Persia, often in the most out-of-the-way army posts as well as in the big cities, shrines of Mithra have been dug up. As in the other mystery religions the worshippers were gathered into organized companies bound by ties of secrecy, brotherhood, and mutual help.

The Church Fathers denounced the mystery religions as inventions of the devil to trick the unwary. Modern scholarship is not in agreement on the subject of how much Christianity drew from the mystery religions. At one extreme scholars hold that the borrowing of the Christians was extensive; at the other extreme, the critics believe that what influence on Christianity was exerted by the mystery religions was indirect, through the general atmosphere diffused by them. On one aspect of the subject there is widespread unanimity: the mystery religions, through their teachings, their ceremonies, and the moods they invoked, helped to prepare the masses and smooth the way for the acceptance of Christianity.

The range of the mystery religions was as great as that which lies between Greek Orthodoxy or Roman Catholicism and Quakerism or Unitarianism in modern times. And in any given religious cult there was evidently a great interval between the highest and lowest manifestations, a long gamut in the spiritual life. But in spite of all such differences and contrasts, all the mystery religions and Christianity had much in common. All embodied an imaginative and emotional appeal that the old traditional paganism of Greece and Rome lacked. Like the later schools of Greek philosophy, but in much simpler terms, they offered full explanations of the meaning of life. All appealed, at once, to both the head and the heart. All borrowed freely from each other and each, except Christianity, identified its deities with those of another, so that the Phrygians recognized their Great Mother in the Syrian goddess, the Greeks and Romans saw Dionysus or Bacchus in the person of Osiris and Hercules in the Hebrew Samson; in the Persian sun god, the Greek and Roman saw Apollo, and in Magna Mater and in Isis they recognized Demeter or Ceres. So the varied religions became translatable one in terms of another. This syncretism is shown in the frequent assertion in mystery documents that a given deity rep resented the totality of the divine nature. Rites, formulae, and ritual passed freely from one religion to another. All, except Christianity, were tolerant, and a person could belong to several mystery cults at once. They all taught, however, that without initiation into a mystery, there was no hope of immortality for the individual. All were supported by volunteer brotherhoods recruited mostly, though not entirely, from the lower classes. Unlike the official religion, they received no state support.

Each of these cults had a long and venerable tradition as old as that of classical paganism or older, and each had a set of sacred writings, stories, ideas, and ritual practices that were capable of a lofty and spiritual interpretation. The oriental mysteries and Christianity had each a professional priesthood which ministered to the needs of the individual and usually conducted missionary work. Only the priest could administer the sacred rites. All were, at the same time, both monotheistic and polytheistic; one deity made the world and sustains it, but other divine forces are at work—saviors, heroes, spirits, or saints.

All of these religions were God-centered, not man-centered in outlook; all were other-worldly and regarded life as an adventure in eternity. All were filled with a sense of the weakness and shortcoming of man, but all believed there was a divine element in man which could be released. All were indifferent to or belittled reason. Man could not save himself; only some force outside this world could start man up ward. All satisfied a demand for a future life and regarded this life as a preparation for a more real existence beyond the grave. Man's rebirth and salvation was the result of a quasi-magical and quasi-spiritual operation. All, except Mithraism and Christianity, were primarily religions of faith rather than of works; the divine was released by correct ritual, and correct knowledge (*gnosis*), and communion with the divine was secured by emotional rather than by ethical means. Most were colored by some ascetic ideals and practices. All were supernatural and rose above reason, above man and above the world. Each had a place for a savior-mediator between the individual and the supreme divine force. The individual achieved a mystic union with the savior by prayer, by ascetic practices, by the eating of some symbol of his being, by the passionate contemplation of the spectacle of his suffering death and his resurrection, and, finally, in certain religions, by living a more moral life. All had impressive rites and ceremonies with candles, flowers, holy-water, chanting, bells, and incense. All were international, for all peoples and all classes, and all were highly individual, speaking directly to the heart of the worshipper, and all laid emphasis on the dignity and value of the individual.

By A.D. 300 this variety of religions in the Roman Empire had become so impregnated by Stoicism, Neo-Platonism, astrological myths, and Oriental mysteries that there seemed to be only a single religion whose doctrines were the following: adoration of the elements, the rule of one god with many spiritual attendants, assurance of salvation by sacred rites, punishment for the evil ones, and an eternal life for the saved. The temples of the old gods still stood open and the official priests, supported by the state, still performed the ancient rites. The traditional routine of ceremonial worship was still performed, but crowds no longer thronged these temples. The day of the old gods was passing. "Let us suppose," says Cumont, "that in modern Europe the faithful had largely deserted the Christian churches to worship Allah or Brahma, to follow the precepts of Confucius or Buddha; let us imagine a great confusion of all the races of the world in which Arabian mullahs, Chinese scholars, Tibetan lamas, and Hindu pundits should all be preaching fatalism and predestination, ancestor-worship and devotion to a deified sovereign, pessimism and deliverance—a confusion in which all those priests should erect temples of exotic architecture in our cities and celebrate their disparate rites therein. Such a dream would offer a pretty accurate picture of the religious chaos in which the ancient world was struggling before the age of Constantine."[19]

Slowly the classic world had turned, during a millennium, from animism and a simple type of nature religion through rationalism to monotheism, asceticism, and mysticism. Steadily the ancient world was turning mediaeval long before it became Christian. Slowly ancient culture had swung from the primitive religious animism of early ages through clear channels of logical thought to a sense of world worthlessness and from belief in man as man to an emotional immolation to the supersensuous and the super-rational. It had changed from the love of the beauty of the human body and of this world to flight from this world and condemnation of all that was corporeal. The Greek word for athlete, "asketés," has become the word for ascetic. So the old wisdom had become foolishness and the old foolishness wisdom. The world of Homer had become, at long last, after nearly twelve centuries, the world of Constantine. Here, if anywhere in man's long history, was a re-evaluation of all values.

---

19 Cumont, *op. cit.,* pp. vii–viii.

Islamic Religion

13

The spread of Islam, 622–750 CE

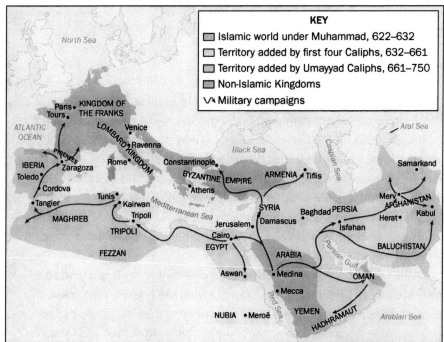

KEY
- Islamic world under Muhammad, 622–632
- Territory added by first four Caliphs, 632–661
- Territory added by Umayyad Caliphs, 661–750
- Non-Islamic Kingdoms
- Military campaigns

OBJECTIVES:

1. Identify the two empires that ruled the Middle East at the rise of Islam.
2. Identify the two phases of Muhammad's prophethood.
3. Understand the link between trade and the spread of Islam.

The Rise and Expansion of Islam

By William L. Cleveland and Martin Bunton

O n the eve of the rise of Islam, the settled lands of the Middle East were ruled by two competing imperial states, the Roman-Byzantine Empire in the west and the Sasanian Empire of Iran in the east. The Byzantine emperors were successors to the Caesars and presided over an imposing edifice of high cultural and political traditions that blended Greek learning, Roman administration, and Greek Orthodox Christianity. In the early seventh century, the emperor's territorial possessions stretched from the Italian peninsula across southern Europe to the magnificent capital city of Constantinople. The empire's Middle Eastern provinces included Egypt, Palestine, and Syria, as well as parts of Iraq and Anatolia. Supported by a standing professional army, a highly developed bureaucracy, and the priesthood of the Orthodox church, the rulers of Byzantium appeared to be powerful and secure.

In the late sixth and early seventh centuries, however, Byzantium was weakened by challenges to its military, religious, and administrative authority. Beginning in 540, the imperial rivalry between the Byzantines and Sasanians broke out into open warfare that continued almost uninterrupted until 629. Campaign and counter-campaign exhausted the military forces of both empires, depleted their treasuries, and inflicted extensive damage to the lands and cities lying between the Nile and the Euphrates. To meet the financial demands of constant warfare, the Byzantine emperors periodically raised taxes, a measure that alienated their subjects, who had already suffered economic hardships from the passage of warring armies back and forth across their lands.

Religious divisions created additional tensions between the Byzantine state and its subjects. Once the Byzantine Empire adopted Greek Orthodox Christianity as the state religion in the late fourth century, the emperors and the church attempted to enforce popular acceptance of this officially approved version of the faith. But peoples within the empire continued to adhere to other forms of Christianity, and to Judaism, and to use their own vernacular languages for scripture and ritual. Unwilling to tolerate these challenges to official orthodoxy, the state branded them as heretical and undertook to suppress them. The persecution of Jews and of Christians outside the Greek Orthodox community caused great disaffection within the empire and explains in part why many Byzantine subjects welcomed the arrival of the more religiously tolerant Muslim rulers.

The Sasanian Empire of Iran, with its capital at Ctesiphon on the Tigris River, contested Byzantium for control of the territories between Iraq and Egypt. Heir to the 1,200-year-old Acheminid tradition of universal Iranian empire, the Sasanian state was based on the principle of absolute monarchy. The emperor was the king of kings (*shahanshah*), a distant and all-powerful ruler living in palatial splendor and surrounded by elaborate ceremonial trappings. Over the centuries, Iranian bureaucratic practices had become refined, and the Sasanian Empire was administered by a large and experienced scribal class. Like their Byzantine counterparts, the Sasanian emperors had at their disposal an effective standing professional army, which was noted for its heavily armed and armored cavalry.

Yet the Sasanian Empire's apparent strength was, like Byzantium's, diluted by popular discontent, much of which stemmed from religious diversity. By the late sixth century, the official Sasanian state religion of Zoroastrianism had become more significant as a ceremonial faith for the ruling elite than as the religion of the population at large. In the western portion of the empire in particular, people were more attracted to various strains of Christianity and Judaism than to the religion of the imperial court. In the absence of a unifying religious affiliation with their ruler, many subjects of the Sasanian Empire lacked feelings of loyalty toward the state.

Although the Byzantine and Sasanian empires were in a period of transition when Islam first extended into them, it is important to recognize their impact on the development of Islamic governing practices and religious doctrine. Formative Islam would be influenced by the Greek legacy of Byzantium, by the bureaucratic tradition of Iran, and by the concepts of emperor that had developed in the courts of Constantinople and Ctesiphon. Islam must be understood as a product of the societies into which it spread as well as of the society in which it originated.

PRE-ISLAMIC ARABIA

With the exception of Yemen in the south and a few scattered oasis settlements elsewhere, the Arabian Peninsula is a vast desert. It is the home of the Arabs, an ancient Semitic people whose origins cannot be traced with certainty. In contrast to the rigorously administered domains of the Byzantine and Sasanian empires, the Arabian Peninsula of the early seventh century lacked any central organizing authority. It had no state structure, no common legal system, no administrative center. Tribes were the largest units of social and political organization to which an individual's loyalties were given. Each tribe was an entity unto itself bound by ties of kinship based on a belief in common descent from a founding ancestor. The majority of Arabia's inhabitants were pastoral nomads engaged in raising camels, sheep, or goats. The scarcity of pasture-lands in the harsh environment of Arabia required constant movement from one grazing ground to another. Competition for the scarce resources of the land created rivalries among the tribes, and warfare became ingrained as a way of life. All males were expected to be warriors, and accounts of the exploits of the most daring among them became enshrined in tribal culture. The widespread experience of the Arabs in warfare was to be a significant factor in the early expansion of Islam.

Notwithstanding the divisions inherent in the tribal structure of pre-Islamic Arabia, forces of cultural unity were present. The Bedouin ethos of bravery and honor was celebrated in a special style of Arabic poetry known as a *qasidah*. The existence of this poetry, which was recited at market fairs and tribal gatherings, has convinced historians that the Arabs of the seventh century possessed a common poetic language that could be understood in different regions of the peninsula. This was of the utmost significance for the spread of Islam because it meant that the Prophet Muhammad's religious message could be communicated to Arabic speakers across a broad expanse of territory.

Isolated though it was, the Arabian Peninsula was not completely cut off from the forces that shaped Middle Eastern civilization. On the eve of the rise of Islam, two Arab tribal confederations guarded the northern Arabian frontiers as client states of Byzantium and the Sasanians, respectively. Both of these Arab confederations were Christian, providing evidence of the spread of the concept of monotheism among the Arabs before the time of Muhammad.

At the southwestern tip of Arabia, Yemen was another source for the entry of external influences into the peninsula. Unlike the rest of Arabia, Yemen was a fertile and well-watered region able to support a settled agricultural society. By the fourth and fifth centuries AD, several Arab communities in southern Arabia had adopted Christianity, and the ruler of Yemen's last pre-Islamic dynasty converted to Judaism. Yet despite the fermentation of religious doctrines in the settled regions of northern and southern Arabia, most of the tribes of the interior continued to practice various forms of animism, worshipping local idols or deities.

During the two centuries before Islam, Arabia acquired increasing importance as a commercial transit route between the Middle Eastern empires and Yemen. The wars between Byzantium and the Sasanians disrupted the east–west overland routes and gave rise to a brisk north–south caravan trade through the Hijaz, Arabia's coastal plain adjacent to the Red Sea. The main Arabian beneficiary of this commercial network was the city of Mecca, which developed into the most important commercial center of the peninsula. By the early seventh century, Meccan merchants had accumulated sufficient capital to organize their own caravans and to provide payments to an extensive network of tribes in exchange for pledges to allow the caravans to pass in peace.

In addition to its role as a commercial center, Mecca was a religious site of major significance. The city's shrine, the Ka'ba, became the center of an animistic cult that attracted worshipers throughout western Arabia. By the time of Muhammad's birth, the Ka'ba had become the site of an annual pilgrimage during which warfare was suspended, and Mecca's sanctuary became a kind of neutral ground where tribal disputes could be resolved. The city derived considerable income from its religious role, and its leading families recognized the importance of the sanctuary as a source of wealth and influence.

The leading clans of Mecca were all members of the Quraysh tribe that settled the city, established its religious role, and dominated its political and commercial life. Although formal municipal organizations did not exist, the affairs of the city were loosely regulated by a council of prominent Quraysh merchants. Historians have suggested that Mecca was in a state of transition between the vanishing tribal ways and a nascent urbanism spawned by merchant capitalism. The customary tribal values were being displaced, but no fully developed set of communal values suitable for an urban setting had yet emerged.

MUHAMMAD AND THE FOUNDATIONS OF ISLAM

Muhammad ibn Abdullah, the future Prophet of Islam, was born in Mecca around 570. His early life gave little indication of the compelling prophet and skillful statesman he would later become. He was born into the clan of Hashim, a subtribe of the Quraysh. Orphaned at the age of two, Muhammad was raised and sheltered by his uncle, Abu Talib. As a young man, he engaged in the caravan trade and may have journeyed to Damascus. His financial position was secured when, in his early twenties, he married a wealthy widow, Khadijah. Khadijah holds an honored place in the history of Islam; she was the first convert to the new faith after Muhammad himself, and she supported him during the difficult early years of his prophethood when he was scorned by most of Mecca's population.

Although Muhammad was widely respected as a decent and trustworthy individual, he lived an otherwise ordinary life as merchant, husband, and father to the four daughters born to Khadijah. But as Muhammad neared his fortieth year, his behavior gradually began to change. He often left Mecca, sometimes for days at a time, to meditate in solitude in the mountains outside the city. Some scholars have conjectured that Muhammad was reflecting on what he saw as the problems that afflicted Meccan society and was seeking ways to resolve them. It was during one of his solitary vigils on Mount Hira that Muhammad was summoned to his prophetic mission, an event known in Islam as the Night of Power. The summons came as a command from God, transmitted through the angel Gabriel, for Muhammad to recite to his fellow Meccans the divine messages that he had been chosen to receive. The Night of Power marked the beginning of a movement that would transform Arab life and lead to the emergence of a universal monotheistic religion.

For the remaining twenty-two years of his life, Muhammad continued to receive revelations, which his companions recorded, memorized, and later collected into a single book, the Quran (Recitation), which constitutes the core of the Islamic faith. The Quran is a sacred work in both form and content. Not only does it contain God's commands, it also represents the direct word of God; its language is therefore divine and unchangeable. Throughout the centuries since the Night of Power, non-Muslims, especially the Christian and Jewish monotheists for whom Islam represented the most direct challenge, have found it difficult to accept the idea that the Quran contains God's words, not Muhammad's. The point here is not to debate the contesting claims to religious truth but to insist on the depth of Muhammad's experience and the utterly convincing language in which that experience was conveyed. The verses of the Quran, especially those from the Meccan period, reveal an individual possessed of a compelling sense of urgency and inspired by a commitment that transcended his previous existence and pushed him into the role for which he believed he had been chosen—as the Prophet of God.

Muhammad's prophethood can be divided into two phases, the period at Mecca (610–622) and the years in Medina (622–632). The difference in the Prophet's circumstances during these two periods of his life is reflected in the style and content of the revelations. The Quran was revealed in a series of chapters (suras) and is organized according to the length of the chapters, with the longest first and the shortest at the end. The shorter chapters are from the Meccan years, when Muhammad concentrated on establishing the theological foundations of the faith. The central element of the Meccan period was an uncompromising monotheism. As an early Meccan revelation insisted,

> Say: He is God, One, God, the Everlasting Refuge,
> who has not begotten, and has not been begotten,
> and equal to Him is not anyone.
> (Sura 112)[1]

The Arabic word for one supreme God, *Allah*, refers to the monotheistic deities of Judaism and Christianity as well as Islam. It is thus incorrect to employ the term *Allah* in an exclusively Islamic context. The term translates as *God*, and that is how it should be employed and understood.

---

1   A. J. Arberry, *The Koran Interpreted* (New York, 1955). All subsequent Quranic quotations are from this translation.

What did the omnipotent deity of the Quran want from his human creations? In the Meccan revelations, he demanded that they practice prescribed patterns of worship and behavior. They were to submit to his will and show their gratitude toward him as the provider of the bounties of the earth. Islam means submission, and the followers of the faith, Muslims, are those who have submitted to the will of God. In addition to matters of ritual, God set forth commandments on how human beings should relate to one another in their daily social intercourse. He warned the people of Mecca to pay more attention to the less fortunate in society and to moderate their search for wealth. The following bluntly critical passage demonstrates God's displeasure at practices in the Mecca of Muhammad's day:

> No indeed; but you honour not the orphan,
> and you urge not the feeding of the needy,
> and you devour the inheritance greedily,
> and you love wealth with an ardent love.
> (Sura 89)

The Quran chastised those who were uncharitable and warned those who felt that their wealth had made them immune from punishment that God would be the final judge of their afterlife. The concept of the Day of Judgment was a central element of the faith. The revelations warned the people of Mecca that their deeds, their attitudes, and even their innermost thoughts would be assessed by the Almighty on Judgment Day. The theology of the Quran was thus basic and straightforward. Humans were instructed to obey the revealed will of an omnipotent God of judgment: Those who accepted him and followed all of his commands would be rewarded with paradise; those who rejected God and deviated from his commands would be condemned to the fires of Gehenna.

Muhammad's preaching attracted few converts and aroused considerable opposition during the Meccan period of his mission. After all, he posed a challenge to the social, economic, and religious structure of the city. Not only did he criticize the attitudes of the wealthy Quraysh merchants, he also condemned the religious practices that made Mecca a prosperous pilgrimage center. As the years passed and the Meccan opposition turned from scorn to threats of physical harm, Muhammad and his followers began to search for a more hospitable location. When an invitation came to them to settle in the city of Yathrib (later Medina), Muhammad accepted it.

Located some 200 miles (322 km) north of Mecca, Medina was a fertile oasis city suffering from the ravages of an extended blood feud among its several tribes. Muhammad was invited as a mediator and was promised by Medinan representatives that any Muslims who accompanied him would receive protection. In 622 the small community of Muslims gradually migrated from Mecca to Medina. The event, known as the *hijrah* (emigration), marks a turning point in the development of Islam: 622 is the first year of the Muslim calendar.

During his ten years in Medina, Muhammad's status rose dramatically. From a scorned prophet with few followers, he became the head of a small state and the dominant figure throughout Arabia. This transformation was achieved through a combination of warfare, negotiation, and preaching, the success of which seemed to confirm Muhammad's right not only to prophethood but to political leadership as well. Muhammad consolidated his authority in Medina by convincing influential personalities in the city to embrace Islam and accept his leadership. Once he established his power base, he was able to take measures against the groups that continued to deny his prophetic and political authority. Among the latter were several Jewish tribes whose members would not accept the legitimacy of Muhammad's claim as the Prophet. Muhammad eventually expelled them from Medina and ordered their property confiscated and distributed among the Muslim emigrants.

Even as he was consolidating his position in Medina, Muhammad made plans to bring Mecca into the expanding Islamic community. His strategy was to disrupt the caravan trade on which Mecca's prosperity depended. Within a year of his arrival in Medina, he ordered the first of what would become an ongoing series of raids on Meccan caravans. The initial raid occurred during one of the sacred pilgrimage months, when, according to established custom, hostilities were to be suspended. This was disturbing to the many Muslims of Medina who continued to respect existing traditions. However, a divine revelation sanctified warfare against unbelievers and designated all Muslims who engaged in spreading Islam through force of arms as deserving of special merit.

In retaliation for Muhammad's attacks on their caravans, the Meccans launched several campaigns against the Muslims in Medina, but each time, the outnumbered Muslim forces managed to hold their own and even to gain limited victories. Muhammad emerged during these encounters as an innovative military tactician, and his success in thwarting the Meccans enhanced his prestige among the neighboring tribes. Many swore their allegiance to him not because they fully understood or accepted the religious message of Islam but because association with Muhammad's endeavor appeared to guarantee victory, and with victory came the spoils of war. The increasing size of the Prophet's forces and his effective alliances with the tribes enabled him to stifle the trade of Mecca to the point where the city's prosperity was seriously threatened. In 630 Muhammad led a force of 10,000 men to the outskirts of Mecca; demonstrating his qualities as a states- man, he promised the inhabitants that their lives would be spared and their property would remain secure if they surrendered the city and accepted Islam. The Quraysh leadership agreed to the terms, and the Prophet made a victorious entry into the city from which he had fled just eight years earlier. According to accounts of the occasion, Muhammad went to the Ka'ba and had the idols destroyed, proclaiming the shrine sacred to God. Mecca would remain a pilgrimage center, and the Ka'ba would become the focal point of the new faith.

In the years between the *hijrah* and the surrender of Mecca, Muhammad's leadership role became more complex. Medina developed into a small city-state with a treasury, a military, and an ever-increasing num- ber of converts. The content of the Quran reflected the changing circumstances by offering instructions on how the expanded functions of the state were to be organized and how human beings should conduct their relations with one another. In these commandments, the all-embracing nature of Islam was established. For example, contracting a debt agreement as the Quran required—in writing before a witness—was a reli- gious duty, and failure to follow the prescription was a sin. In this way, the details of marriage, inheritance, divorce, diet, and economic practice were made part of the religious experience of Muslims. Muhammad created a community (*ummah*) in which the laws of human behavior in daily life were prescribed by God.

It would be an exaggeration to call Arabia a cohesive, unified state after the surrender of Mecca. Nevertheless, the transformation created by the Prophet had been substantial. He had implanted the core concept of a community of believers united in their recognition of a single Supreme Deity and in their acceptance of that deity's authority in their daily lives; he had conveyed notions of social morality that forbade alcohol and the blood feud and that recognized the legal status of women and demanded protection for the less fortunate in society. Muhammad combined in his person the roles of prophet, state builder, and social reformer. Today there is much emphasis on the martial elements of Islam, but to comprehend fully Muhammad's mission, we need to consider the importance of Quranic passages like this one:

> Be kind to parents, and the near kinsman,
> and to orphans, and to the needy,
> and to the neighbour who is of kin,
> and to the neighbour who is a stranger,
> and to the companion at your side,
> and to the traveller.
> (Sura 4)

THE ARAB CONQUESTS AND THE FIRST EMPIRE

When Muhammad died in 632, it would not have contradicted historical patterns if Arabia had rejected the Prophet's summons and taken up the old ways again. Instead, Muslim factions in Mecca and Medina resolved to continue the development of the new religious community and competed with one another to assert their control over it. Because Muhammad had no sons and because the Quran contained no clear instructions on how a successor should be chosen, the question of the leadership of the community was open to different interpretations. The early converts to Islam who had suffered with Muhammad in Mecca and participated in the *hijrah* to Medina preempted all other claimants by naming one of their own, Abu Bakr, as the new head of the community. The other factions accepted Abu Bakr's leadership, but the dispute over the first succession sowed seeds of conflict that have affected Islam throughout its history.

Abu Bakr (632–634) was simply called the successor—*khalif*—anglicized as caliph. Eventually the term *caliph* came to designate the religious and political leader of the Islamic community, and the office became known as the caliphate. Abu Bakr and his three successors, Umar (634–644), Uthman (644–656), and Ali (656– 661), are known in Islamic history as the Rashidun (rightly guided) caliphs in recognition of their personal closeness to the Prophet and their presumed adherence to Quranic regulations. Although two of them were assassinated and their reigns were filled with political and social turmoil, Muslims of later and even more troubled times looked back with nostalgia on the era when the four companions of the Prophet launched the movement that thrust the Arabs out of the peninsula and into world history.

The second caliph, Umar, recognized the need to direct the raiding instincts of the tribes away from intercommunal conflict and authorized attacks against the southern flanks of Byzantium and Sasanian Iran. Thus began the epoch of the Arab conquests and the building of an Islamic empire.

The speed and extent of the Arab conquests were remarkable. In 637 the Arab forces defeated the imperial Sasanian army at the battle of Qadisiyya, an encounter that was quickly followed by the capture of Ctesiphon and the beginning of the difficult Arab campaign across the Iranian plateau toward the Indian subcontinent. Success against Byzantium was equally swift. The Arabs captured Damascus in 635, and in 641 they occupied parts of the rich agricultural province of Egypt. By 670 the western campaign against Byzantine and Berber resistance had reached present-day Tunisia, and in 680 the daring Arab commander

Uqba ibn Nafi led a small force from Tunisia through Algeria and Morocco to the Atlantic Ocean. The westward expansion of the Arabs culminated in the conquest of Spain in the first half of the eighth century. Within 100 years of the Prophet's death, Arab forces had reached the Indian subcontinent in the east, and in the west they had occupied Spain and crossed the Pyrenees into France before they were finally halted by the forces of Charles Martel at the battle of Poitiers in 732. In this first wave of conquests, the Sasanian Empire was completely destroyed and its territory absorbed within an Arab-Muslim administration. Byzantium, although it suffered the loss of its core Middle Eastern and North African provinces, retained control of Anatolia and the Balkans and presented a formidable barrier to Muslim expansion until it was overcome by the Ottomans in the fourteenth and fifteenth centuries.

Even more stunning than the speed and extent of the conquests was their durability: With the exception of Spain, which retained an Arab-Islamic presence until the fifteenth century, the areas occupied during the first century of expansion have remained Islamic, if not Arabic, to the present day. In North Africa, as in Egypt and the eastern Mediterranean—the heartlands of Hellenism and early Christianity—and in the long-settled region of Iraq, the Arabic language and the Islamic faith became dominant. Persian language and culture eventually reasserted themselves in Iran, but they were expressed in an Islamic idiom.

The conquests would not have been so swift or so durable without the existence of a combination of social, economic, and religious factors that facilitated the local population's acceptance of the new Arab rulers. First, as we discussed earlier, monotheistic religions were widely practiced among the peoples in the conquered territories, and the Islamic assertion of monotheism placed it within the existing religious traditions. Second, Islam manifested considerable tolerance toward non-Muslims. The Quran commanded Muslims to protect "people of the Book"—that is, Jews and Christians who possessed a revealed scripture. In practice, this toleration was extended to the Zoroastrians of Iran and the Hindus of the Indian subcontinent. Forced conversions played only a small part in the Arab conquests, and for at least two centuries the majority of the inhabitants of the Islamic empire were non-Muslims. They were known as *dhimmi*s, a term meaning followers of the religions tolerated by law. *Dhimmi*s were allowed the freedom to practice their religion and to manage their internal affairs through their own religious officials. However, *dhimmi*s were not regarded as the equals of Muslims and were required to pay a special poll tax (*jizyah*); they were prohibited from serving in the military and from wearing certain colors, and their residences and places of worship could not be as large as those of Muslims. Although these and other restrictions constituted a form of discrimination, they represented an unusually tolerant attitude for the era and stood in marked contrast to the practices of the Byzantine Empire.

The taxes imposed by the Arab-Islamic state were less burdensome than those levied by the Byzantine and Sasanian empires. Moreover, the Arab rulers tended to leave existing administrative practices undisturbed and did not interfere with local customs. Although some of the conquered peoples adopted Islam, the Arabs did not encourage conversions during the first century of their rule. This was partly because the *jizyah* constituted an important source of state revenue and partly because the Arabs, at this early stage in the development of Islam, regarded it as an exclusively Arab religion.

THE FIRST CIVIL WAR AND THE END OF THE RASHIDUN CALIPHATE

The question of the succession to the caliphate had been largely ignored in the rush of the early conquests. But when the caliph Uthman was murdered by mutinous Arab tribesmen in 656, the succession issue reemerged. It was resolved only after a civil war that left an enduring schism within the Islamic *ummah*. Ali was chosen to succeed the murdered Uthman. Next to the Prophet himself, Ali is the most revered of the founders of Islam: He was the Prophet's cousin, the husband of the Prophet's daughter Fatima, and one of the most dedicated of the early converts to Islam. Indeed, in some quarters of the *ummah*, the belief existed that Muhammad had intended for Ali to be his immediate successor. By the time he was finally selected as caliph, Ali represented a broad coalition of interests calling for greater equality among all Muslims, both Arab and non-Arab, and for the restoration of the leadership of the community to the house of Muhammad. But Ali's right to the caliphate was contested by Mu'awiyah, the powerful governor of Muslim Syria.

The forces of the two claimants to the leadership met at the battle of Siffin in 657. The results of the encounter were inconclusive, leaving both Ali and Mu awiyah in the same positions they had held before the fighting began. In the aftermath of the battle, a substantial portion of Ali's forces withdrew their support, allowing Mu awiyah to expand his power in Syria and Egypt and preventing Ali from establishing his uncontested right to the caliphate. Though Ali set up a capital in Kufa, one of the Arab garrison cities in lower Iraq, his position continued to deteriorate, and he was murdered in 661. Ali's caliphate was short and divisive but far from inconsequential. It came to represent the validity of the legitimist position of authority within the Islamic *ummah* and, as we will see in later chapters, stood as an enduring symbol of the desire of a substantial minority of Muslims to embrace a communal leader directly descended from the family of the Prophet. Indeed, attachment to the memory of Ali and his family and the tragedy associated with them was infused with such great passion and vitality that it gave rise to a permanent schism within the Islamic community.

FROM ARAB EXCLUSIVISM TO ISLAMIC UNIVERSALISM: THE UMAYYAD AND ABBASID EMPIRES

Ali's passing marked the end of the first phase in the development of the Islamic community and the beginning of a new period of imperial expansion and consolidation. Mu awiyah was recognized as caliph throughout the empire and became the founder of the Umayyad dynasty (661–750). He was a pragmatic ruler whose principal concerns were continued expansion of Islam, management of the state's resources, and consolidation of his dynasty. During his caliphate, the political center of the empire was transferred from Mecca, the small caravan city of its origins, to the ancient city of Damascus, with all its Byzantine associations. Mu awiyah adopted certain Byzantine administrative practices and employed former Byzantine officials and craftsmen, initiating the transformation of the Arab empire into a Byzantine successor state and surrounding the caliphate with the trappings of monarchy.

Although the conquests continued to bring material wealth to Damascus under Mu'awiyah's successors, the Umayyad Empire was troubled by internal dissension. Part of the dissent was caused by the policy of Arab exclusivism adopted by the Umayyad ruling elite. They continued to equate Islam with Arab descent and to administer the empire's fiscal and social affairs in such a way as to favor the Arabs and to discriminate against the growing number of non-Arab converts to Islam. The discontent culminated in a revolution that overthrew the Umayyad house in 750 and brought to power a new dynasty, that of the Abbasids.

The office of the caliphate remained with the Abbasids from 750 to 1258. Under the Abbasids, the heroic age of the conquests gave way to the development of administrative institutions, commercial enterprises, and a legal system. The bureaucrat, the urban merchant, and the learned judge replaced the Arab warrior as the favored element in society. The consolidation of the conquests in the geographical center of a centuries-old admixture of cultural and religious traditions resulted in a complex interaction between the existing cultures and religions of the Middle East and the dynamic infusion of energy from Arabia. The new and vibrant Islamic civilization that arose found its first, but by no means its last, expression in the period of the high caliphate (750–945) of the Abbasid Empire.

The first 150 years of the Abbasid Empire, represented by such caliphs as al-Mansur (754–775), Harun al-Rashid (786–809), and al-Ma'mun (813–833), were a period of relative political stability, immense economic prosperity, and increasing universalism within the central Islamic domains. These conditions, in turn, created the possibilities for the flowering of a rich and diverse civilization. The Abbasids abandoned the Arab exclusiveness that had generated so much discontent under the Umayyads. In its place, they adopted a universalist policy accepting the equality of all Muslims, regardless of their ethnic origins. This attitude, coupled with the revitalization of urban life and the expansion of commercial activity, led to a growing cosmopolitanism within the empire as converts from among the conquered peoples participated fully in the economic and political life of the state.

The universalism of the Abbasids was symbolized by yet another transfer of the imperial capital, this time from the predominantly Arab city of Damascus eastward to a newly created city, Baghdad, which the caliph al-Mansur established on the west bank of the Tigris. The change of location brought the Islamic political center into more direct contact with Iranian imperial traditions, with their emphasis on royal absolutism and bureaucratic specialization, and added yet another layer of influences to the Arab and Byzantine experiences of the Islamic state. Abbasid administration was modeled on Sasanian government and employed large numbers of converted Iranians in its increasingly elaborate bureaucratic structure. Sasanian practices also had an impact on the office of the caliphate. During the era of the Rashidun, the caliphs functioned as first among equals and lived modestly on the model established by Muhammad. This emphasis on simplicity changed under the later Umayyads, who distanced themselves from the population, took pleasure from the riches that flowed into the treasury at Damascus, and became less consultative and more authoritarian. The Abbasid rulers, with their more direct exposure to the Iranian idea of an absolute king of kings, carried the evolution of the caliphate to absolutist monarchy further than any of their predecessors. The Abbasid caliphs lived in luxurious palaces, isolated from all but their most trusted inner circle of courtiers and advisers. They came to identify themselves not simply as successors to the Prophet but as "shadows of God on earth," and they exercised vast powers over their subjects. Thus the Abbasid solution to the problem of political authority was to centralize it and to place it in the hands of an absolute monarch who exercised the powers of both secular king and spiritual head of the Islamic *ummah*. For nearly two centuries following the revolution of 750, this Abbasid formula worked reasonably well and brought to the empire unprecedented prosperity, dazzling intellectual achievement, and general political stability based on the widespread acceptance of the benefits of caliphal absolutism.

But no monarch could maintain absolute control of an empire that stretched from Morocco to India. In the late eighth century, North Africa slipped away from Baghdad's authority and became a region of autonomous Islamic states. During the ninth century, independent and often short-lived dynasties rose and fell in various parts of Iran. Yet despite the emergence of new centers of power, the Abbasid caliphs remained the dominant rulers of the Middle East until the tenth century, and the imperial court at Baghdad set a style of royal behavior that was imitated in provincial capitals and breakaway dynasties throughout the vast territories in which Islam had become established.

CONCLUSION

In the historically short span of time from the Prophet Muhammad's death in 632 to the transfer of the imperial capital from Damascus to Baghdad in the 750s, the Islamic *ummah* had expanded from its Arab origins to embrace a universal world empire. The epoch of the Arab conquests constitutes a decisive period in world history, one that transformed a nomadic desert population organized along tribal lines into the ruling elite of an imperial structure concentrated in the heartlands of classical antiquity. Arabic replaced Greek, Persian, Aramaic, and other established literary traditions as the language of administration and high culture; Islam replaced, though it did not eliminate, Judaism, Christianity, Zoroastrianism, and paganism as the dominant religion in the Middle East. This process of replacement raises important questions. In its interaction with the existing literary, religious, and administrative traditions of Byzantium and Iran, how could the Islam of the revelations, the Islam of the Prophet's caravan city of Mecca, survive as a guide to administrative, economic, and social practices? How could the peoples living within the territories of the extensive Arab conquests, with their long-established traditions, be organized to obey the commands on proper human behavior that God revealed to a Meccan merchant in seventh-century Arabia? In developing answers to these questions, or simply in developing certain patterns of living and worship, Muslims affirmed their belief in the validity of Muhammad's mission by creating a civilization centered on the revelations contained in the Quran.

Byzantine Empire and Religion

14

II The Byzantine Empire and the Ottoman Turks in 1355.

Fig. 14.0: William R. Shepherd, "Byzantine Empire," https://commons.wikimedia.org/wiki/ File:Byzantine_empire_1355.jpg. Copyright in the Public Domain.

OBJECTIVES:

1. Identify the largest influence on religion in Byzantium.
2. Understand the relationship between philosophy and religion.
3. Understand the relationship between science and religion.
4. Understand the importance of Constantine in the rise of Christianity.

The Return of Greek Science:
The First Byzantine Humanism

By Efthymios Nicolaidis and Susan Emanuel

S cience and religion in Byzantium entered a new phase in the ninth century, characterized by a revival of Greek science. Two of the most visible faces of this revival were John the Grammarian and Leo the Mathematician. John was born sometime during the last quarter of the eighth century. A brilliant student, he became a professor, hence the nickname Grammatikos (grammarian). He then entered a monastic order and became *hēgoumenos* or abbot of the monastery of Sergios and Bakchos in Constantinople. At the start of the iconoclast Leo V's reign (813–20), he took the side of the enemies of the icons, and in 814 the emperor charged him with looking among the manuscripts of Constantinople for a copy of the acts of the iconoclast council of 754, because the original had been destroyed by the iconodules. Mission accomplished, John was considered a man of great erudition, who had the ability to persuade his opponents with well-chosen arguments. John's knowledgeable command of the manuscripts was a new factor at the end of the iconoclast period. One of the signs of this change was that two of the rare scientific codices we have date from this era: the *Vat. gr.* 1291, an illustrated manuscript that includes Ptolemy's *Handy Tables* and other astronomical and astrological texts; and the *Leidensis BPG* 78, which also includes Ptolemy's *Tables*.

Tutor of the future emperor Theophilus (r. 829–42), John became Patriarch John VII under his reign, but he was dethroned in 843 by iconodule regents, specifically the widow of Theophilus, Theodora (mother of Emperor Michael III, who was then age four), and Theoktistos, an influential eunuch (and effective ruler until his execution in 855). What is of interest to us is his visit as Theophilus's ambassador to the court of Caliph al-Ma'mūn in Baghdad, at a time when interest in Greek science was very lively there. Among the most notable developments was the creation of a library where Arabic translations of Greek science texts were kept. Coming back to Constantinople, John persuaded the emperor to reconstruct his palace in Vrya (in Bithynia) in the manner of al-Ma'mūn's and to add a number of automatons, which he helped fabricate.

Although the Byzantines seem to have abandoned the Greek tradition of making scientific instruments, they inherited the technology of automatons, developed by Heron of Alexandria (first century BCE), including the technique of gears, developed in a magnificent way by the first century BCE in devices such as the famous planetary called the "Antikythera mechanism." In spite of the fact that we have no mention that such mechanisms existed in the Byzantine era, devices like those constructed at Vrya to impress visitors are evidence of the perpetuation of a tradition of working with gears.[1]

---

1   For the Antikythera mechanism, see www.antikythera-mechanism.gr/.

After John the Grammarian's death, the iconodule patriarchs who succeeded him accused John of magic and had his remains disinterred and burned. His enemy and immediate successor, the patriarch Methodios, said of him that "he envied the lives of Pythagoras, Saturn, and Apollo," and the Byzantine chronicles described him as indulging in sordid practices in his dark laboratory.

Why were such accusations leveled against Patriarch John? Could it be related to his close involvement in science and technology? We know that astrology and alchemy belonged to the sciences in the eighth century, and any savant such as John who loved the sciences would be interested in them. If we add the crafting of automatons, this was sufficient evidence for his enemies to formulate accusations of magic at a time when the sciences were just beginning to be reestablished within the Byzantine Empire.[2]

At the end of the iconoclast era, interest in the sciences was resuscitating. We saw in the preceding chapter that one of the reasons for this renaissance was the renewal of interest in Aristotelian logic because it could furnish arguments to both parties, iconoclast and iconodule. Study of logic led inexorably to rereading philosophical texts and, hence, to natural philosophy. But whatever the root cause, very soon there was a veritable revival of the arts and sciences. This revival was called by the French Byzantinist Paul Lemerle (1903–89) the "first Byzantine humanism" because of the vivid interest shown by scholars of this period in ancient Greek literature.[3] Although the iconodule party was more open to secular knowledge, the two first figures contributing to this renaissance were the iconoclast patriarch John the Grammarian and his young cousin and protégé of an iconoclast emperor, Leo the Mathematician.

Leo was born around the turn of the ninth century. Son of an aristocratic family, he found that in the iconoclastic context the teaching of sciences in Constantinople left something to be desired; he could find a teacher for the *trivium* but not for science (the *quadrivium*). In the absence of not only educational structures but also a tradition of education, he sought a master with whom he could deepen his knowledge, eventually finding one on the island of Andros (near Athens, a week by ship from Constantinople). There he studied rhetoric, philosophy, and arithmetic. However, discovering that this teacher's knowledge was also limited, Leo ransacked the libraries of the monasteries of Andros for old manuscripts about science, finding a forgotten knowledge, still preciously guarded in the dark libraries of scattered monasteries. After years of research and reading, Leo recovered a whole domain that had been forgotten for more than a "dark" century during the debate over icons.[4]

The story handed down about the life of Leo claims that he followed a path of study that was characteristic of the Western Middle Ages: first find a teacher to acquire the basic knowledge and then dig into the monastic archives for manuscripts that were either hidden or forgotten. In Byzantium, this practice became a literary *topos* found in many "lives of saints," whose intent was to glorify the hero: by claiming that the knowledge of his teachers was not sufficient, the student went looking for—and found by himself— knowledge that did live up to his aspirations. But it is possible that during the restructuring following the iconoclast period, the renaissance of science did go through a period of "rediscovery" that exceeded the

---

2   Gianna Katsiampoura, "John Grammatikos, Scientist and/or Magus?" [in Greek], in K. Skordoulis et al., eds., Ζητήματα επιστήμης: ιστορία, φιλοσοφία και διδακτική [Questions of science: History, philosophy and didactics] (Athens: Nissos, 2008), pp. 29–36.

3   Paul Lemerle, *Le premier humanisme byzantin* (Paris: PUF 1971).

4   Ibid., pp. 149–50.

teaching by acknowledged masters and thus required research into neglected manuscripts. Leo symbolized this quest and became the very image of scientific renewal.

The rest of Leo's story is mixed with legend. Returning to Constantinople, he gave courses in philosophy, specifically the *quadrivium*. One of his students, secretary of a general, was taken hostage by the Arabs, who sent him to Baghdad as a slave. There, at the court of al-Ma'mūn, Leo's student distinguished himself for his expertise and impressed the caliph's surveyors by showing himself more able than they in demonstrating the theorems of Euclid. When the courtiers asked him if Byzantium had many savants like him, he responded in the affirmative, saying that he considered himself only a student and that his master lived in poverty in Constantinople. And so al-Ma'mūn liberated the young man and sent him to Constantinople with a letter of invitation to Leo, to whom he promised enormous riches if he agreed to come. Leo wisely showed the letter to the emperor (Theophilus), who finally recognized his talent and granted him a salary to give courses in public at the Church of the Forty Martyrs. Meanwhile al-Ma'mūn insisted he come to Baghdad and even offered him a large quantity of gold, plus a treaty of eternal peace to the emperor if he would let him leave. But Theophilus refused, not wanting to reveal to his enemies the knowledge that was the glory of the Greeks. To console Leo, he asked John the Grammarian, then patriarch of Constantinople, to name him metropolitan of Thessalonica. So—and this part of the story historians can verify—we find Leo as metropolitan of Thessalonica from 840 to 843. But in line with the fate of his iconoclast protector, he was soon dismissed by the iconodule regents.[5]

During the reign of Theophilus, Leo conceived the famous optical telegraph to transmit signals from the eastern frontiers of the empire to the capital. The novelty of this system was that it was based on two synchronized clocks, one on the frontier and the other in the capital. The clocks were divided into twelve intervals of time, and every two hours corresponded to a precise message. A message sent at midday signified "invasion"; at two o'clock, "war"; and so on. The signals were supposed to arrive within an hour.[6]

The involvement of Leo with the iconoclast emperor and patriarch did not have a negative impact on his career as a scholar. His continued service, combined with the fact that the emperor gave him a salary and privileges, shows that the prestige of science had indeed risen around the middle of the ninth century. Leo's legend (containing an element of truth) is quite different from the legend that claims that a century earlier an emperor had burned the university and its professors. In the story of Leo and al-Ma'mūn, the sciences are exalted and considered to be a great treasure for Byzantium.

The change in the attitude of secular power (which generally went hand in hand with that of the patriarch, who was appointed by the emperor) toward science is also attested by the palace's interest in higher education at the start of the reign of young Michael III (842–57). Bardas, the brother of the queen mother Theodora, was regent between 856 and 866 and uncontested master before being assassinated. He was one of the rare Byzantines to bear the title of kaiser without being brother to an emperor. This important personage showed great favor toward secular knowledge. Probably inspired by Arab policy to foster the sciences (the legend concerning Leo the Mathematician can be read in this way), he founded a school where science, especially mathematics, was taught. The School of Magnaura in Constantinople was founded

5   Ibid., pp. 150–52.
6   On the telegraph, see Milton Anastos, Ἱστορία του Ἑλληνικοῦ Ἔθνους [History of the Greek nation], vol. 8 (Athens: Ekdotiki Athinon, 1979), p. 268.

around 855, after the royal palace of the same name. Leo the Mathematician was placed at the head of the philosophy department (which showed it was considered the most important subject), and his student Theodore at the head of the geometry department; Theodegios led astronomy, and Komitas led grammar. The professors were paid by the state, and tuition was free.[7]

The public education given at the Church of Forty Martyrs undoubtedly inspired the new school. From its curriculum, it seems evident that it was specifically a scientific school in which theology was completely absent. The school became an important institution that outlived both Bardas (assassinated in 866) and Leo (who probably died during the 870s) and would constitute the principal scientific institution in Byzantium for two centuries. During the reign of Constantine VII Porphyrogenitus (913–59), the school remained divided into four departments, with philosophy still at the top, and at its head the *protospatharios* Constantine. At this time, a *protospatharios* was equivalent to a member of the Senate, which no longer had any power. Constantine would later be appointed *eparch*, which means prefect of Constantinople. For the first time in Byzantine history, a high government official was serving as professor of philosophy, an occurrence that would become common later as the aristocracy mingled with the scholarly caste.

During the reign of Constantine Porphyrogenitus, state power took an additional step toward the institutionalization of nonreligious education when a school administrator was appointed for each town. The panegyric addressed to an emperor by a chronicler in the eleventh century signifies this change in attitude toward science: "He restored the sciences, arithmetic, music, astronomy, geometry, solid geometry, and all of philosophy, which had been neglected and lost for a long time because of the ignorance of powerful men, and he sought and found the best teachers in each domain."[8]

Religious support for literature and science had actually made its appearance earlier. The ninth century witnessed the first patriarchate of Photius (858–67), one of the most erudite scholars of the Byzantine world, author of a famous library catalog, in which he summarized the 279 books he had read (158 religious books and 121 secular ones). This is a fabulous and precious work, since almost half of the books he covered are lost today. A scholarly patriarch, lover of Greek literature, Photius observed with a benevolent (if not enthusiastic) eye the scientific renaissance that was taking place.[9]

It seems that Byzantine power, both political and religious, was ready to accept the cultural change brought about by humanism. Note that the patriarch was a political figure, often appointed by the emperor, not by the synod, and sometimes he had little relation with the clergy. Photius came from an aristocratic family and was a layman who held the offices of *protospatharios* and *protoasikritis* (the latter being equivalent to head of the imperial secretariat). In order for the synod to be able to name him patriarch, his protector Bardas arranged for him to enter holy orders and rise through the ecclesiastical grades—in only six days! Photius was criticized by clerics, who saw him as a mere layperson. Bishop Nikitas David depicted him as a true scholar but one interested only in secular knowledge. His vast expertise led him to be arrogant; instead

7 Christine Nomikou and Gianna Katsiampoura, "The School of Magnavra. Sciences in Byzantium" [in Greek], in Skordoulis et al., Ζητήματα επιστήμης, pp. 37–43.
8 Georgios Kedrenos, Σύνοψις Ιστοριών [Summary of histories], ed. I. Bekker (Bonnae, 1838–39), vol. II, p. 326. It is a compilation of the history of mankind since the Creation to the emperor Isaac Komnenos (r. 1057–59).
9 On Photius's library, see Warren T. Treatgold, *The Nature of the Bibliotheca of Photius*, Dumbartron Oaks Studies 18 (Washington, D.C.: Dumbarton Oaks Center for Byzantine Studies, 1980), and A. Markopoulos, "Νέα στοιχεία για τη χρονολόγηση της βιβλιοθήκης του Φώτιου" [New evidence for the dating of Photius's Library], *Byzantina Symmeikta* 7 (1987): 183–91.

of being a humble servant of God, he built on the rotten foundations of profane science.[10] Among society as a whole and the lower clergy, a legend existed that Photius in his youth had sold his soul to a Jewish magician.[11] It is true that there would never be a condemnation of Photius in the way the other "magus," the iconoclast John the Grammarian, had been condemned, but the sciences were still viewed with some distrust by Byzantine society.

A statement written by Constantine the Sicilian, a former student of Leo's, sheds additional light on attitudes toward his master. In a mock obituary, Constantine placed an anathema on Leo, who taught all the profane wisdom of which the ancients were proud but lost his soul in that sea of impiety. According to Constantine, Christ punished Leo as a renegade who venerated Zeus and then sent him down to Hades to join Chrysippos, Socrates, Proclus, Plato, Aristotle, and Epicurus, as well as Leo's favorites, Euclid and Ptolemy. Educated Byzantines were scandalized to see such ingratitude from a student to his master, but Constantine escaped punishment.[12]

Historians of science have often stressed the role of ninth-century Byzantium in safeguarding Greek scientific literature. In effect, the most ancient copies of most of the Greek scientific works that have come down to us do date from this era, as attested by the study of their offshoots found in later manuscripts. This was happening three centuries before the Latin West rediscovered the basic texts of ancient science and finally became interested in scientific knowledge. However, tension between Eastern and Western churches, together with the ignorance in the Latin West of Greek, the language of ancient science, prevented the spread of the scientific knowledge that had been safeguarded by the Byzantines to the network of the monasteries in Western medieval Europe. In contrast, the Arabs, who were already exploiting ancient Greek science, showed a vivid interest in Greek scientific literature as preserved and edited by Byzantine scholars. But while the Arabs tried to develop ancient Greek science by correcting Ptolemy and contributing to mathematics, the Byzantines treated Greek scientific texts in the same manner as the texts of the fathers of the church. They copied them, taught them, but rarely developed them.

As part of their revival of interest in the sciences, Byzantines copied ancient manuscripts, even when there were no specialists to exploit them fully. The case of astronomy is clear: the only new contributions that are extant are a table of thirty bright stars dated to 854, an updating of Ptolemy's table using the precession value of the great Alexandrian astronomer (one degree every one hundred years, which means that the stars ought to have moved seven degrees since Ptolemy), and some elementary commentaries on his *Tables*.[13] What a contrast there is between this lack of expertise and the magnificent astronomical manuscripts, composed in uncials (despite the appearance of cursive writing) and sometimes illuminated, that have survived from this century. It is significant that four manuscripts of the *Handy Tables* are extant, the two mentioned at the start of this chapter, copied under the reign of Leo V (813–20), plus two others copied under the reign of Leo VI the Wise (886–912). The choice is not by chance, for the *Handy Tables* are (as their name indicates) a simplified version of Ptolemy's *Almagest*, laying out the practical side of his astronomy; because the tables were used to determine the position of stars at a given moment, they were highly prized by astrologers.

---

10 Patrologia Graeca, 105, col. 509.
11 Basil Tatakis, *La philosophie byzantine* (Paris: Presses Universitaires de France, 1949), p. 131.
12 Lemerle, *Le premier humanisme byzantin*, pp. 172–75.
13 Anne Tihon, "L'astronomie byzantine (du Ve au XVe siècle)," *Byzantion* 51 (1981): 609.

The contribution of Leo the Mathematician and his entourage (especially his students) to safeguarding science manuscripts was crucial in the ninth century. This group recopied all the extant works of Euclid, Archimedes, Ptolemy, and Proclus.[14] Around the middle of the century, Byzantines collected the works of Aristotle, followed by those of Plato.[15] Leo had not only rediscovered and taught Greek scientific texts but had copied them himself and had recruited copyists. Leo and his students considered themselves the heirs of Greek science and applied themselves to the task of saving dilapidated manuscripts before the sources of this knowledge disappeared forever. This represented a major change from the spirit that had prevailed only a few decades earlier, when the Byzantines judged ancient Greek knowledge to be pagan, useless, and dangerous for the health of Orthodox minds.

HELLENISM AND ORTHODOXY: THE CASES OF PSELLOS AND JOHN THE ITALIAN

I have stressed the prime role played by the Byzantine emperors in relations between science and Orthodoxy. When an emperor was favorably disposed to secular knowledge, then teaching was encouraged and subsidized by the state, which gave science an important status that the clergy and society could not ignore. The history of Byzantine science is marked as much by the personalities of emperors as by those of scholars. Leo VI the Wise was himself a scholar who had studied under Photius. His successor, Constantine VII Porphyrogenitus, also strongly supported science. In contrast, Basil II the Bulgaroctonos (r. 976–1025), as his name Bulgarslayer indicates, was more concerned with killing Bulgars than with cultivating knowledge. Under this emperor, the institutions of higher education were once again abandoned. Two decades later, Constantine IX Monomachos (1042–55) took an interest in sciences and education and was assisted by his adviser Michael Psellos.

Michael Psellos (1018–78 or 1096) is the Byzantine scholar best known in western Europe. His name at birth was Constantine. Son of a civil servant, he studied in Constantinople and Athens and followed a political career. He took part in several intrigues that made or unmade emperors, which led to his being called the *paradynasteuon* (prime counselor of the emperor). In 1045, under the reign of Constantine Monomachos, as *protoasikritis* he also became *hypatos* (consul) of philosophers, the equivalent of rector of the University of Constantinople. Psellos seems to have been the principal instigator in reforms undertaken by Constantine to improve studies in Constantinople. In effect, in 1047 the emperor founded the faculty of law and named Psellos director of the philosophy faculty. It is not clear if Constantine founded a new institution or simply revamped what already existed by creating the post of *hypatos* of philosophers.

But in 1054 Psellos left the university in disgrace (for unknown reasons) and became a monk under the name Michael. He returned to Constantinople two years later when Empress Theodora Porphyrogenitus during her short reign (1055–56) recalled him to the capital. He again took an active part in court intrigues that shifted power until the accession of Michael VII Doukas (1071–78). Although Michael had been one of

---

14 Lemerle, *Le premier humanisme byzantin*, pp. 169–72. We know also that Leo possessed works by Kyrinos and Markellos, Apollonius, Theon of Alexandria, Proclus, Ptolemy Archimedes, Euclid, as well as a number of astrological texts.

15 Ibid., p. 220.

his students, he did not give Psellos a post as elevated as he desired. He was ~~probably exiled~~ to a monastery under Nikephoros III (1078–81).

Psellos's involvement in politics and his aspiration to the highest posts conferred on him an authority in science that went beyond that of a simple savant. Called the "universal man," he was also one of the most prolific writers of Byzantium; his writings deal with history, philosophy, theology, and science. His renown went beyond the borders of the empire, and he claimed that among his students were Celts, Arabs, Persians, Egyptians, and Ethiopians. Although he was not modest by nature, this assertion seems true.[16]

Psellos illustrates the complicated and ambiguous relations of the Orthodox world of his day with the sciences. On the one hand, he affirmed himself as an Orthodox believer who found in faith the answers to his spiritual questions. On the other hand, his curiosity and erudition in the secular knowledge of ancient Greece remained unquenched, and he went on to practice astrology, alchemy, and even magic. A Platonist, he knew and commented on Aristotle and admired the ancient Egyptians and Chaldeans. He boasted of his interest in five different civilizations: Chaldean, Egyptian, Greek, Hebraic, and Christian.[17]

Such pride at knowing the literature of non-Christian civilizations, as well as Psellos's practice of sciences condemned by the church (astrology and magic), gave his many enemies ample opportunity to attack him. An astute politician, he managed several times to survive these attacks by periodically making an act of loyalty to Orthodoxy, and he wrote a confession of faith during the reign of Constantine Monomachos. When he was accused of being under the decisive influence of Plato, he defended himself by maintaining that many elements of secular science were useful, citing Saint Basil and Gregory of Nanzianzus as corroboration.

To defend himself from accusations that he practiced astrology, he wrote a short declaration inspired by the church fathers that asserted that astrology is in contradiction with providence and free will.[18] And as for magic, he took cover behind his various acts of faith. But he was rather compromised, even publicly, when he wrote: "I will not reveal to you how to fabricate amulets that chase away sickness, for it is possible you will not imitate me correctly."[19]

If Psellos's acts of faith appear to be merely the maneuvers of a politician, there is in fact a text in which he seems to give an explanation from the bottom of his heart for his intellectual contradictions. In the funeral oration he gave for his mother, after saying that Christian faith cannot give an answer to every question, he affirmed that "because one cannot think that the life that was granted me suffices in itself, but that it is at the service of others and is going to be absorbed as from an overflowing vessel, for this reason I concern myself with idolatrous culture, not only in its theoretical aspect but also in its history and poetry."[20]

---

16 On Psellos, see Christian Zervos, *Un philosophe néoplatonicien du XIe siècle: Michel Psellos, sa vie, son oeuvre, ses luttes philosophiques, son influence*, preface by François Picavet (Paris, 1920; New York: B. Franklin, 1973); Anitra Gadolin, *A Theory of History and Society with Special Reference to the Chronographia of Michael Psellus: 11th Century Byzantium and a Related Section on Islamic Ethics* (Amsterdam: A. M. Hakkert, 1987).

17 On Psellos's alchemy, see Gianna Katsiampoura, "Transmutation of Matter in Byzantium: The Case of Michael Psellos, the Alchemist," *Science and Education* 17 (2008): 663–68.

18 Mstislav Antonini Sangin, *Codices Rossicos (Catalogus Codicum Astrologorum Graecorum)*, XII (Brussels: H. Lamertin 1936), p. 167.

19 E. Kurtz and F. Drexl, *Michaellis Pselli: Scripta minora*, vol. I (Milan: Societa editrice Vita e Pensiero', 1936), p. 447.

20 K. Sathas, *Annuaire de l'association pour l'encouragement des etudes grecques dans la France*, 5 (Paris, [1881]), p. 58.

Psellos was concerned with the knowledge of "idolaters" in order to communicate it; hence, this knowledge was worth being known and studied.

Psellos was a child of Byzantine humanism but at the same time a scholar in the Middle Ages. His love of the apocryphal sciences, to seek knowledge in supposed hidden meanings in texts and various symbols, led him to investigate Egyptian science, which, according to him, was the source of later science, including that of the Greeks. The discussion that bears on the roots of Hellenic sciences and especially the role of Egypt was not new, dating from at least the era of the historian Herodotus. Ancient Egypt had fascinated the Greeks and continued to fascinate Byzantine scholars. Psellos claimed that Pythagoras was the first to introduce Egyptian civilization into Greece and that Plato was wrong to believe that the Greeks had improved on the ideas of foreign peoples—on the contrary, the Greeks were lazy about searching for the truth, notably concerning God. Psellos even thought that Diophantus had been influenced by Egyptian methods of calculation.[21]

With respect to nonapocryphal sciences, Psellos's contributions were to mathematics, astronomy, and the philosophy of nature.[22] His best-known didactic work is *General Education*, which presents notions of natural philosophy.[23] However, his unequaled renown in the sciences caused a number of scientific texts to be misattributed to him, such as the oldest Byzantine *quadrivium* that has come down to us, entitled *Synoptic Treatise in Four Lessons*, which was written in 1008 (before his birth), as well as *On Natural Things*, actually by Simeon Seth.

Psellos comes across as an independent spirit who dared on several occasions to flout the commandments of the Orthodox Church in the interests of his curiosity, which ran from the traditional secular sciences to any sort of apocryphal science. If he was not reprimanded by the church, it was because he knew how to maneuver and, during the Doukas dynasty, had powerful support.

Nevertheless, Psellos's work was by no means subversive. Byzantines would positively remember his commentaries on the philosophy of nature and his texts of a practical nature, such as the calculation of the date of Easter or the catalog of minerals and their characteristics.[24] His name became a reference for Byzantine science in the following centuries, and his didactic texts on natural philosophy would be replaced only by those of Nicephorus Blemmydes two centuries later.

Psellos may not have had major difficulties with the church, but the same was not true for his student and successor in the post of *hypatos* of the philosophers, John Italos (c. 1025–90). As his name suggests, John was born in the south of Italy; his father was a Norman mercenary. Protected by the Doukas family, he settled in Constantinople around 1049, where he followed Psellos's courses, but he was soon arguing with him. Under the reign of Michael Doukas, he was accused of impiety for the first time, but the affair did not have any repercussions. John's most heretical ideas related to the incorruptibility of the world and to challenging the Neoplatonic thesis of the creation of the world. He argued that science alone could approach the

---

21 See Kurtz and Drexl, *Michaellis Pselli*, p. 441, and J. Boissonade, *Michael Psellus: De operatione daemonum* (Nuremberg, 1838), pp. 153–54.

22 On the *quadrivium* of 1008, see chapter 3.

23 Διδασκαλία παντοδαπή, in *Michael Psellus de omnifaria doctrina*, ed. L. G. Westerink, with a critical text and introduction (Utrecht: J. L. Beijers, 1948).

24 The titles of these two texts are in Greek: Ποίημα του μακαριωτάτου Ψελλού περί της κινήσεως του χρόνου, των κύκλων του ηλίου και της σελήνης, της εκλείψεως αυτών και της του Πάσχα ευρέσεως and Περί λίθων δυνάμεως.

truth, that ideas (like matter) were eternal, that miracles must have a physical explanation, and that there had been no creation *ex nihilo*—in short, things that would enrage even the most moderate theologians.

Around 1076, John was indicted by theologians for his impious theses about the creation of the world, but the case did not go to trial. A few years later, Alexius I Komnenos became emperor (r. 1081–1118). Though interested in science, Alexius was also a pious man who sought to re-Christianize higher education by introducing the study of Holy Scripture at the highest levels. Thus, for the first time, the patriarch was granted the right to supervise the content of higher education. It was not the most propitious moment for John Italos, who had neither the breadth of knowledge nor the diplomatic capabilities of Psellos. He lost the emperor's favor, was again accused of impiety, in 1082, and this time went on trial. The court condemned him as a heretic and a pagan for his philosophical ideas, such as his denial of the creation *ex nihilo*, which came into flagrant contradiction with dogma. The court sentenced him to perpetual reclusion in a monastery—but only after a sequence of eleven anathemas were pronounced against him.[25]

The condemnation of John Italos provided an opportunity for the Orthodox Church to condemn secular study more generally. Taking advantage of the occasion, the synod added to the Sunday service the following reading: "Upon those who indulge in Hellenic studies and do not study them solely for education but follow their futile opinions—anathema." This official condemnation of some ideas associated with Hellenic science (e.g., the eternity of the world) has been read in Orthodox churches up until the present day. Note that it does not forbid the study of Hellenic sciences—provided that they are considered not as true but only as part of a general education, as exercises of the mind.

AN ELEVENTH-CENTURY MANUAL OF NATURAL PHILOSOPHY: SETH'S PHYSICS

The reforms by Alexius I did not signify the abandonment of secular science, which very probably continued to be taught at the same level as before, but henceforth theology would crown these studies.[26] Ironically, the very Christian Alexius, according to the testimony of his daughter, kept at his court four astrologers, two of whom were Egyptians, one an Athenian, and the other Simeon Seth.[27]

Simeon Seth, a contemporary of Psellos's, was an astrologer and doctor who at one time probably withdrew to a monastery in Bithynia, a common practice for Byzantine dignitaries who had fallen into disgrace. Later he appeared in Egypt (1057–59) and at the courts of Michael Doukas and Alexius I Komnenos, where he must have ended his days.[28] Emperor Alexius's daughter, Anna, described him as an able astrologer who predicted the date of the death of Robert Guiscard, a Norman warrior well known to the Byzantines because

---

25   L. Clucas, *The Trial of John Italos and the Crisis of Intellectual Values in Byzantium in the Eleventh Century* (Munich: Institut für Byzantinistik der Universität München 1981).

26   On the roles of church and state in education at this time, see Robert Browning, *Church, State and Learning in the Twelfth Century Byzantium* (London: Dr Williams's Trust, 1981).

27   The daughter of Alexius, Anna Komnena (1083–1153), recounted the history of her father in her *Alexiad*, an important medieval source. The text had many editions, for example *The Alexiad of Anna Comnena*, ed. and trans. E. R. A. Sewter (Harmonds worth: Penguin, 1969).

28   According to one observation of an eclipse that he mentioned, which may well have taken place in 1086 and not in 1058. Seth's dates are subject to discussion.

he had contributed to the Norman conquest of Italy. Seth knew Arabic so well that he had translated some animal fables from Arabic. His best-known works were *On Natural Things*, a treatise in five books; *On the Properties of Foods*, in which he described 228 sorts of plants and animals and advocated Oriental medications rather than those of Galen; and *On Beer*.[29] *On Natural Things* circulated widely in the Byzantine and post-Byzantine world. No fewer than twenty manuscripts of it have come down to us, dating from the thirteenth to the eighteenth century. It was even translated into modern Greek at the start of the eighteenth century. This treatise, dedicated to the emperor Michael Doukas, presented the philosophy of nature as popular science. Seth showed that the earth is spherical by using traditional arguments, such as the difference in the local time of observations of eclipses, the visibility of parts of the sky that depend on latitude, and the appearance of mountaintops before low-lying land when ships approach a coast. He explained the division of latitudes of the northern hemisphere into seven climates and gave the size of the *oikoumenē* (the inhabited earth that extended from China to the Canary Islands) as twelve hours, which was equivalent to half the earth's circumference. He attributed phenomena such as rain, hail, snow, thunder, lightning, and earthquakes to natural forces. Indeed, Seth maintained that everything in the sublunary world had a physical explanation and could be explained by the characteristics of the four elements interacting with the heat or light from the sun. God never intervenes.

Seth invoked God only in discussing the plurality of worlds, where he mentioned that certain philosophers believed in the existence of multiple worlds, each with its own human beings and animals. He repudiated the notion, held by certain Greeks, that the heavenly spheres had souls; for him, all celestial movements were purely natural. Concerning the important theological question of the incorruptibility of the world, he presented Aristotle's belief that the world is uncreated and that heaven is incorruptible and Plato's claim that it is created and incorruptible, and then he advanced its own thesis that all bodies have a limited force that is renewed by diurnal movement. The world is made of order and disorder; things here below are irregular and without order, in the sky irregular and ordered, and in the beyond regular and ordered. Seth defended the Platonists against the thesis of the Aristotelian fifth element by borrowing his arguments from Philoponus. He also followed Ptolemy's cosmology based on epicycles and not Aristotle's concentric world system. But he referred to Aristotle in declaring that a void cannot exist either in the created world or outside it; for the void is a place without bodies that can receive a body, and in the outside heaven there is no "place" at all but instead the spiritual world. Thus, except for a few passing references, one could scarcely distinguish between Seth's text and a work of pagan Greek philosophy. Nevertheless, the church left him undisturbed. No doubt his astrological abilities led Alexius I to pardon his deviations from Orthodox teaching.[30]

---

29   The Greek titles are: *Σύνοψις φυσικής, περί χρείας των ουρανίων σωμάτων; Σύνταγμα κατά στοιχείον περί τροφών δυνάμεων;* and *Περί φουκάς.* On astrology and Seth, see Paul Magdalino "The Byzantine Reception of Classical Astrology," in Catherine Holmes and Judith Waring, eds., *Literacy, Education and Manuscript Transmission in Byzantium and Beyond* (Leiden: Brill, 2002), pp. 33–57.

30   Edition of *On Natural Things* (or *Synopsis of Physical Problems*) in Patrologia Graeca, 122, cols. 783– 819. In the Patrologia Graeca, this work by Seth appears under the name Psellos; also edited by A. Delatte, *Anecdota Atheniensia et alia II: textes relatifs à l'histoire des sciences* (Paris: E. Droz, 1939), pp. 1–89. See also Manolis Kartsonakis, "Η σύνοψις των Φυσικών του Συμεών Σηθ" [On natural things of Symeon Seth], in George Vlahakis and Eft hymios Nicolaidis, eds., *Βυζάντιο-Βενετία-Νεώτερος ελληνισμός* [Byzantium-Venice-Modern Hellenism] (Athens: NHRF, 2004), pp. 129–37.

Astrology flourished during the Komnenos dynasty (1081–1185). The emperor Manuel I (1143–80) himself practiced astrology so much that the court grammarian, Michael Glykas, dared to attack the imperial ruler, using arguments dating back to the church fathers. Manuel defended himself against Glykas's accusations by addressing a letter to an anonymous monk. Glykas, far from submitting, replied with a book that explained the difference between astronomy and astrology to demonstrate the utility of the former and the impiety of the latter.[31] Glykas was somewhat exceptional in his opposition to astrology. His contemporary John Kamateros, the best-known astronomer of his day, took a great interest in the practice. He dedicated two astrological poems to Manuel and wrote a treatise on the astrolabe, the primary instrument used by astrologers. It is notable that the arguments advanced by enemies of astrology remained the same as those of the church fathers. Nine centuries after Basil the issue returned, and this time it was the Christian emperors, not the pagan philosophers, who were proving to be "impious."[32]

Despite the varying attitudes of emperors, the sciences in the twelfth century were well anchored in both higher education and the mentalities of Byzantine savants. New schools of higher education appeared, and the one in Thessalonica achieved sufficient importance to attract students from the capital. The Orthodox Church became reconciled to the fact that secular science should be part of the curriculum of educated people; extreme reactions against scientific education (as in the case of John Italos) occurred only if someone flagrantly contradicted what had been taught by fathers such as Basil or Gregory of Nyssa.

We can get an idea of what constituted secular science for an educated Byzantine around the second quarter of the twelfth century from a letter that Michael Italikos addressed to the empress Irene Doukas: "I know these sciences [geometry, arithmetic, and agriculture] and do not deny them, and I have checked Aristotle and Plato and verified the periods of stars and their many constellations, and I swear on the sacred head that I do not overlook what Hipparchus and the very scholarly Ptolemy have said about astronomy or what the very mathematical Aristarchus has written."[33] Basic science education no doubt consisted of the *quadrivium* plus the Aristotelian philosophy of nature. Those seeking more advanced knowledge would have to study Euclid, Diophantus, and Archimedes in mathematics; Theon and Ptolemy in astronomy; and Galen and Hippocrates in medicine.

---

31 Glykas's reply: Μιχαήλ του Γλυκά, Ανταπολογητικόν προς την εγχειρισθείσαν αυτώ γραφήν του κραταιού και αγίου ημών βασιλέως κυρού Μανουήλ του Κομνηνού [Michael Glykas's reply to the given to him letter from our saint and omnipotent king Manuel Komnenos], in F. Cumont, ed., *Catalogus Codicum astrologorum graecorum*, vol. V, part 1 (Brussels: H. Lamertin, 1904), pp. 125–40. The work of Glykas: Ει χρη μαθηματικήν επιστήμην αποτρόπαιον ηγήσθαι παντάπασιν, ibid., pp. 140ff. See Fl. Evaggelatou-Notara, "Οποίον εστί μέρος της αστρολογίας κακιζόμενόν τε και αποτρόπαιον (Αστρολογία-Αστρονομία και οι σχετικές αντιλήψεις κατά τον ΙΒ΄αιώνα)" [What part of astrology is nasty and horrible (Astrology-astronomy and related concepts during the 12th c.)], in Nikos Oikonomides, ed., *Το Βυζάντιο κατά τον 12ο αιώνα. Κανονικό Δίκαιο, κράτος και κοινωνία* [Byzantium during the 12th c.: Canonical law, state and society] (Athens: Etaireia Vyzantinon kai Metavyzantinon Meleton, 1991), pp. 447–463.

32 The titles of Kamateros's poems are Περί του ζωδιακού κύκλου και των άλλων απάντων των εν ουρανώ [On the zodiacal circle and on all the stars in the sky], and Εισαγωγή αστρονομίας [Introduction to astronomy]. On Kamateros's treatise of the astrolabe, see Anne Tihon, "Traités byzantins sur l'astrolabe," *Physis* 32 (1995): 323–57. For discussion of the validity of astrology in Byzantium, see Paul Magdalino, *L'orthodoxie des astrologues: La science entre le dogme et la divination à Byzance (VIIe–XIVe siècle)*, Réalités byzantines 12 (Paris: Lethielleux, 2006).

33 See P. Gautier, ed., *Michel Italikos, Lettres et discours* (Michael Italikos, letters and discourses), Archives de L'Orient Chrétien 14 (Paris: Institut Français d'Études Byzantines, 1972), p. 95.

We have said little about medicine so far, but the Byzantines excelled in this area. Building on a long-standing tradition of charitable enterprises, they began in the fourth century to develop hospitals, not only to provide food and shelter for the sick but also to treat their illnesses. Apparently for the first time in history, the Orthodox staffed their institutions with physicians, pharmacists, and medical assistants. They also used these hospitals to train medical workers. Today the best known of these hospitals is the Pantocrator Xenon, created in 1136 by Emperor John II Komnenos as part of a monastery in Constantinople. According to the hospital's surviving rule book (the *Typikon* of the monastery), there were fifty beds divided into five sections or wards: for patients suffering from wounds or fractures, for those with diseases of the eyes or intestines, for women, and two for men. Each section was attended by two physicians, three ordained medical assistants, two additional assistants, and two servants. Female physicians and staff ministered to the women patients. In addition, the hospital employed five pharmacists and operated a separate infirmary for the monks and an outpatient clinic. It stood in the community as a monument to Christ the healer.[34]

The institutionalization of scientific study, the privileges given to professors, and the involvement of the emperor and the patriarchate all gave status to science, which became part of the Byzantine culture of the eleventh and twelfth centuries. By the end of the twelfth century, the Patriarchal School in Constantinople seems to have become much more important than the one financed by the emperor; apart from theology, students learned rhetoric, medicine, philosophy, and mathematics. The school created a new chair, *maistor* (master) of philosophers, second in prestige only to the *hypatos* of philosophers, named by the emperor. But the centralized system of Byzantium, together with the importance of the town of Constantinople compared to the other towns of the empire, prevented the development of the high schools newly created in other cities. The school of Thessalonica, the second most important city of the empire, was an exception, but it soon declined. During the same period, in the Latin West the newborn universities multiplied. These universities, unlike Constantinople's high schools, had a certain autonomy, at least in the appointment of professors. In centralized Byzantium, the emperor and the patriarch nominated their protégés as heads of the university and the Patriarchal School. Thus, the status and the protection provided to science by the heads of the empire carried the seeds of stagnation. Although scientific teaching progressed, there were no vigorous discussions of scientific matters, and Byzantine contributions to science remained marginal.

---

34 Timothy S. Miller, *The Birth of the Hospital in the Byzantine Empire* (Baltimore: Johns Hopkins University Press), 1985.

CPSIA information can be obtained
at www.ICGtesting.com
Printed in the USA
LVOW09s2010190118

563229LV00007B/15/P

9 781516 500611